Transforming State-Society Relations in Mexico

U.S.-Mexico Contemporary Perspectives Series, 6
Center for U.S.-Mexican Studies
University of California, San Diego

Contributors

JOHN BAILEY

VIVIENNE BENNETT

JENNIFER BOONE

FERNANDO CÉLIS CALLEJAS

OSCAR F. CONTRERAS

WAYNE A. CORNELIUS

ANN L. CRAIG

DENISE DRESSER

JONATHAN FOX

ALEC IAN GERSHBERG

ENRIQUE GONZÁLEZ TIBURCIO

CAROL GRAHAM

PAUL HABER

LUIS HERNÁNDEZ NAVARRO

ALAN KNIGHT

NORA LUSTIG

JULIO MOGUEL

JUAN MOLINAR HORCASITAS

PETER M. WARD

JEFFREY A. WELDON

Transforming
State-Society Relations
in Mexico

The National Solidarity Strategy

Edited by
Wayne A. Cornelius
Ann L. Craig
and
Jonathan Fox

Center for U.S.-Mexican Studies
University of California, San Diego

771202

c

Printed in the United States of America by
the Center for U.S.-Mexican Studies
University of California, San Diego

1994

ISBN 1-878367-14-5

Contents

PART V: COMPARATIVE PERSPECTIVES

Tables

Figures

Preface

This volume is the product of a two-year project based in the Center for U.S.-Mexican Studies at the University of California, San Diego, but involving researchers at twelve different institutions in Mexico, the United States, and the United Kingdom. The project grew out of our collective fascination with the implications, both short- and long-term, of the National Solidarity Program (PRONASOL) for Mexico's political, social, and economic development. We were also motivated by our frustration with the methodological and conceptual difficulties of studying such a huge, complex, constantly evolving public program. We sought a road map through what some of our project members quickly dubbed "the jungle" of PRONASOL.

The National Solidarity Program, in addition to being the principal initiative of the Carlos Salinas administration in the area of social policy, has been the object of endless speculation and heated controversy concerning its *political* motivations and consequences. Much less attention has been devoted, by both scholars and nonacademic commentators, to Solidarity's efficacy in alleviating poverty and more generally for cushioning the dislocations of economic restructuring and North American economic integration.

In mapping out our project and the publication to result from it, we opted to address the Solidarity program in all its dimensions and complexity. This called for a multidisciplinary approach that could shed new light on the operations of Solidarity at both macro and micro levels. As befits such a heterogeneous program, a wide variety of research methodologies—from conventional historical techniques to sample surveys, ethnographic research, and quantitative analysis of aggregate data sets—have been used by our project members to study it.

In assembling the research team, the Center for U.S.-Mexican Studies cast the net as widely as possible, involving academic analysts as well as "practitioners" from government and NGOs who have had direct experience with PRONASOL; Mexicans as well as analysts of other nationalities; prominent critics as well as defenders of the program, and researchers who had not participated in public debates concerning it.

While the introduction to this volume identifies certain major points of agreement among the contributors, the editors have made no effort to force a "consensus" within this highly diverse group on the overall merits or prospects of Solidarity. The reader will therefore encounter a wide range of findings and interpretations, some of which are difficult if not impossible to reconcile. Nevertheless, any attempt to resolve the apparent contradictions and provide a definitive evaluation of the program at this historical juncture would be quite premature, particularly given the continuing limitations on micro-level data sources available to scholars for research on this topic.

This book emphasizes fieldwork-based research on Solidarity, which has been undertaken by most of the contributors during the past two years. While all of us are dependent to some extent on official statistics generated by the National Solidarity Program and the recently created Ministry of Social Development (SEDESOL) of which it is now a part, we have done our best to test hypotheses suggested by these statistics against our observations in specific rural communities, urban neighborhoods, cities, regions, and states. Accordingly, five of the chapters of this book take the form of case studies based on information pertaining to particular states or localities, and several other, thematic chapters (for example, John Bailey's analysis of PRONASOL and political centralism) are grounded in field data from one or two specific states. We consider the case study approach to be especially valuable at this stage of the research enterprise, because inputs, outputs, and outcomes can be analyzed with greater clarity in the context of how specific Solidarity programs operate in particular states or municipalities. We hasten to add that primary data collection on the functioning and impacts of Solidarity is still in its infancy. We hope that this first, book-length, scholarly study of Solidarity will stimulate interest in pursuing the wealth of opportunities for future fieldwork-based research.[1]

We must underscore the preliminary and incomplete nature of the findings presented here. Our contributors have captured the National Solidarity Program at one point in time—roughly, the 1989–1992 period. From its launching in the first days of the Salinas administration, Solidarity has been a rapidly evolving program, with new subprograms being added continually. Even as this book goes to press, the emphasis of Solidarity investments is beginning to shift from small-scale infrastructure and human service provision to support for productive enterprises and other permanent job-creating activities. As President Salinas characterized this latest, still uncharted phase of Solidarity, "The pro-

---

[1] The most detailed previous examination of Solidarity can be found in a special issue of *El Cotidiano* (Universidad Autónoma Metropolitana-Azcapotzalco) 49 (July–August 1992), which is devoted entirely to evaluative articles on Solidarity. The Mexican government has published several books on the program: see SEDESOL 1993; C. Rojas et al. 1991; PRONASOL 1991b.

gram was originally created to lay a basic foundation for meeting the social needs of all Mexicans. Now an additional floor is also being built to deal with production and employment and to provide economic development options" (Salinas de Gortari 1993: 66–67). We can expect further modifications in the program's structure and functions as the post-Salinas *sexenio* unfolds.

The Center for U.S.-Mexican Studies research project on Solidarity and the publication of this book were financed entirely with the Center's own unrestricted funds. The principal sources of these funds have been a core grant to the Center from the William and Flora Hewlett Foundation, and sales of the Center's own previously released publications. No funds from any government were utilized for the project. Paper contributors and editors of this volume worked without financial compensation and found their own sources of funding for their field research. All proceeds from the sale of this book will be reinvested in the publications program of the Center for U.S.-Mexican Studies.

The first drafts of the papers appearing in this volume were presented at a Research Workshop held at the Center for U.S.-Mexican Studies on February 25, 1992. The workshop discussions were greatly enriched by the participation of several commentators, including Cassio Luiselli (former national coordinator of the Sistema Alimentario Mexicano), Kevin Middlebrook (Center for U.S.-Mexican Studies), Maria Cook (Cornell University), Gabriel Székely (Center for U.S.-Mexican Studies and El Colegio de México), and Jorge de la Rosa (Instituto Mexicano del Seguro Social). We also benefited from the comments and criticisms of more than eighty scholars who attended a Center-organized panel session on Solidarity at the 1992 International Congress of the Latin American Studies Association, where second drafts of several of the papers included in this volume were presented.

The Center and the editors wish to extend special thanks to Jorge de la Rosa, co-coordinator of the Semana Nacional de la Solidaridad in 1991, for helping to convince us that a preliminary assessment of the National Solidarity Program was feasible; to Sandra del Castillo, for her characteristically superb editorial work on the contributors' final drafts; to Aníbal Yáñez (California State University-San Marcos), for exceptionally fluid translations delivered in the most timely manner; and to John Bailey (Georgetown University), for active and thoughtful engagement in the project both during and after his stay as a Visiting Research Fellow at the Center, and for his painstaking work in compiling the Appendix to this volume.

Wayne A. Cornelius
Director, Center for U.S.-Mexican Studies

La Jolla, California
December 31, 1993

I

Introduction

1

Mexico's National Solidarity Program: An Overview

Wayne A. Cornelius, Ann L. Craig, and Jonathan Fox

From its inception, the Salinas administration's National Solidarity Program (PRONASOL) has had two basic foci: material (social services/ infrastructure provision; poverty alleviation) and institutional (the rearrangement of state-society relations, and of the coalition supporting the ruling Partido Revolucionario Institucional, PRI). These two basic emphases were pursued simultaneously, through a bewildering array of subprograms broadly categorized as "Social Welfare," "Production," "Regional Development," and "Special" programs (see González Tiburcio and Appendix, this volume). Some of the specific material needs addressed by this seemingly all-encompassing program include the building and refurbishing of public schools, community electrification, street paving and feeder road construction, potable water, health care, nutrition, housing, legal aid, regularization of land titles in both urban and rural areas, agricultural infrastructure, preservation of natural resources, and, most recently, small business development. The inevitable result of such broad scope and multiple objectives has been considerable confusion and skepticism about the true objectives of the program.

As it plunged ahead with a much more sweeping and accelerated economic liberalization and restructuring project than had been attempted by the preceding de la Madrid administration, the Salinas government relied on PRONASOL to repair the tattered social safety net that it had inherited from the economic crisis and austerity measures of the 1982–1988 period. As such, Solidarity was intended to remind the Mexican people, as well as the outside world of governments, multilateral funding institutions, and potential private investors, that the technocrats presiding over Mexico's so-called neoliberal economic revolution were not insensitive and unresponsive to the social costs of the market-oriented policies that they espoused. While it could not be expected to eliminate the massive social deficit that had accumulated in Mexico during the "lost decade" of the 1980s, a program like Solidarity could at least attempt to ameliorate the hardships still being experienced by most Mexicans and keep alive their hopes for future economic improvement.

In explaining and promoting the program, the Salinas administration emphasized the social welfare, antipoverty thrust of Solidarity, as well as its potential contributions to modernizing, pluralizing, and democratizing state-society relations. To this would later be added an ideological thrust: Solidarity would serve as the most visible, concrete expression of Carlos Salinas's newly articulated doctrine of "social liberalism"—a mode of governance that ostensibly seeks to avoid the worst excesses of both unfettered, free market capitalism and heavy-handed state interventionism, by steering a careful middle course between these "failed" extremes.[1]

However, the opposition parties and many independent observers quickly surmised that the key rationale for the program was partisan-political (see, e.g., Dresser 1991). PRONASOL, in their view, was a barely veiled project to create a *political* safety net for the PRI-government apparatus, to help it recover from the electoral debacle of 1988 and fortify it for the midterm elections of August 1991, in which the PRI might lose control of the Congress. A loss of legislative control at the national level would have been a serious blow to presidential power.

Some analysts went further, interpreting Solidarity as a Machiavellian scheme to reestablish personalist, authoritarian presidentialism as the guiding principle of the political system (see, e.g., Meyer 1993, and the official response to Meyer's argument, C. Rojas 1993). Such a restoration seemed much needed in the aftermath of a *sexenio* in which the traditional, metaconstitutional powers of the Mexican presidency had been seriously eroded by what was widely perceived as ineffectual leadership by outgoing President de la Madrid, and by a national election in which the PRI's presidential candidate, Carlos Salinas, showed unprecedented weakness at the polls.

Solidarity has also become Mexico's principal entry in the global sweepstakes to create new institutional arrangements and structures to sustain the open, market-oriented economic development strategies to which most developing countries in the Third World as well as former Soviet bloc nations have committed themselves. The program's success

---

[1] The "social liberalism" doctrine was defined by President Salinas in his second State of the Nation address, on November 1, 1989. For a full elaboration, see Villarreal 1993. President Salinas discussed the National Solidarity Program as a "concrete application of the doctrine" at an international academic seminar held in June 1993 (see Salinas de Gortari 1993b).

has been touted by President Salinas as one of the sources of Mexico's new prestige and influence in international organizations (see, e.g., Salinas de Gotari 1993a: 69). Of course, the exportability of the "Solidarity model" to other developing countries struggling to satisfy the political requisites of economic liberalization remains to be demonstrated.

What, then, are we dealing with in this book? A conventional social welfare/compensatory relief program? A new type of demand-based, carefully targeted, poverty reduction program? An effort to buffer social class conflicts? A strategy for relegitimating the regime? A reassertion of centralized, authoritarian presidential rule? A cosmetically improved form of populism or clientelism? An infusion of U.S.-style, constituency-sensitive pork barrel politics? The "new mass politics" of a highly urbanized, modernized Mexico? A "new grassroots movement" which empowers citizens through "an experience of direct democracy" (Salinas de Gotari 1993a: 69) and gives preexisting, local-level popular movements new leverage in their dealings with the state?

All of these labels, and many more, have been applied to Solidarity by its promoters and critics. The simple reality is that this sprawling, multidimensional public program defies easy categorization. Moreover, it is extremely difficult to generalize about the operation and effects of Solidarity because they can vary significantly by territorial unit (state, region, *municipio*, village, neighborhood), the social characteristics and traditions of those areas (e.g., whether a community is predominantly Indian or mestizo; the presence or absence of a tradition of collective organization), the type of program activity (e.g., PRONASOL's component programs permit quite different levels of grassroots participation), and time period (because of Solidarity's constant evolution, the analyst is always dealing with a moving target). The case studies presented in this book demonstrate the importance of analytically deconstructing Solidarity, given the myriad activities grouped under its umbrella and the manifestly different state and local political economies through which the program passes and is transformed. Multiple, conflicting "subnational regimes" can—and do—coexist in Mexico, ranging from democratic Chihuahua State in the north to oligarchical, violence-prone Chiapas in the south. The disposition of officials within these subnational regimes to cooperate with the Solidarity program and implement its prescribed norms of conduct can vary greatly (see Fox, this volume; Rubin 1990; Knight 1990a).

Each of the contributors to this volume has adopted his or her own preferred characterization of Solidarity and has marshalled the best available evidence in support of it. As editors, it is not our function to anoint any one of these divergent interpretations as the most empirically accurate or theoretically powerful. Rather, in this introductory chapter we seek to clarify the broader political and economic context in which

Solidarity has developed, to define as sharply as possible the debates that continue to swirl around the program, and to highlight preliminary findings reported in this volume that can serve as valuable building blocks for future evaluation research.

ORIGINS, BASIC PRINCIPLES, AND PROGRAM DEVELOPMENT

The chief intellectual architect of the National Solidarity Program was none other than Carlos Salinas de Gortari. The program's conceptual underpinnings can be found in his doctoral dissertation, which was based on field research conducted in several rural communities in the states of Puebla and Tlaxcala during the 1970s (Salinas de Gortari 1978, published as Salinas de Gortari 1980, 1982). Based on his direct observations and interviews, Salinas concluded that the traditional forms of federal government spending in rural communities were not yielding sufficient popular support for the system, and that the poor quality of relationships between government agencies and beneficiaries was largely to blame. His findings also sensitized Salinas to the deficiencies of local political leadership in rural Mexico, and led him to recommend a concerted effort by the PRI-government apparatus to promote the emergence of a new generation of leaders at the community level who could serve as more effective interlocutors between citizens and the state. A decade later, both types of deficiencies noted by Salinas during his sojourns in the Sierra de Puebla would be addressed in the design for the National Solidarity Program.

During the 1988 presidential campaign, Salinas proclaimed his commitment to a national reform project in three parts: economic, political, and social modernization. The last of these three proposed reforms, "social modernization," was first and most extensively developed in a campaign speech delivered in Chalco, an irregular settlement of about one million impoverished people on the periphery of the Mexico City metropolitan area. Candidate Salinas promised to create a new "social floor" for Mexico's modernization, raising social well-being to the level necessary to carry his country into the twenty-first century. In Salinas's speech, "social" modernization clearly referred to improvements in the standard of living and the reduction of absolute poverty in Mexican society. But his administration's subsequent references to "social modernization" have also been used to suggest greater state support for popular participation and organization in obtaining collective benefits.[2] In sum, Salinas-style "social modernization" also proposes changing the relationship between state and society in ways that would allow

[2]It is important to differentiate here between state tolerance for greater activism by villages, neighborhoods, and "autonomous" popular movements, on the one hand, and the endorsement of increased citizen participation channeled through *political parties*, on the other. The Salinas government's position on partisan political activity has been much more ambiguous.

greater initiative and independence, as well as responsibility, on the part of citizens. The most prominent mechanism for advancing this type of social modernization became the Programa Nacional de Solidaridad (PRONASOL), known simply as Solidarity.

Salinas's first official act as president, on December 2, 1988, was to announce the formal objectives and general design of Solidarity. The program, the president explained, was designed to reach the 48 percent of the Mexican population that lived below the official poverty line, and especially the 19 percent (nearly fifteen million people in 1989) who were classified by the government as living in "extreme poverty" (see Córdoba 1994: 273). Solidarity would also bring about a new pattern of interaction between the state and civil society, based on four fundamental principles (see, e.g., PRONASOL 1991a: 5–6; Salinas de Gortari 1990: 48–49):

• Respect for community initiatives—i.e., community-generated statements of need, and community-based organizing efforts.

• Full and effective participation by community members in all actions related to the Solidarity program.

• Joint responsibility for activities—i.e., a shared obligation by the state and beneficiaries to finance and implement the projects chosen for a given community or neighborhood.

• "Transparent," honest, and efficient management of resources committed to Solidarity projects.

President Salinas explicitly linked these four principles to what he has described as Solidarity's overarching goal of promoting justice, pluralism, and democracy in everyday life. The strict application of Solidarity's basic principles should, he argued,

> eliminate all vestiges of paternalism, populism, clientelism, or political conditionality in the improvement of the welfare of the population in poverty. . . . The activities carried out under the National Solidarity Program represent an investment in physical and social welfare infrastructure that *by their very nature* promote justice and democracy.[3]

Solidarity staffers at the national level have gone even further, asserting that "the program has become a space for the exercise of freedom and democracy. . . . It encourages criticism and dialogue and

---

[3]President Carlos Salinas de Gortari, remarks at the conclusion of the Segunda Semana de Solidaridad, as reported in *Unomasuno*, September 15, 1991; and Salinas de Gortari 1990: 49–50. In his fifth State of the Nation Report (1993a: 69) Salinas described the Solidarity program as "an experience in direct democracy."

contributes to the development of [democratic] political culture in our country" (for further elaboration of this argument, see SEDESOL 1993, especially pp. 19–23).

Over the 1989–1993 period, Solidarity developed into one of the most important signature projects of the Salinas administration. President Salinas himself became the program's most visible and tireless advocate, spending nearly every weekend visiting urban neighborhoods and rural communities where Solidarity projects were under way. Solidarity's budget rose impressively, from the equivalent of U.S. $680 million in 1989 to $950 million in 1990, $1.7 billion in 1992, and over $2.5 billion in 1993, with real increases averaging 36 percent annually. Total federal and state government investment in the Solidarity program during its first five years of operation reached about U.S. $12 billion (Córdoba 1994: 269). In each year of the Salinas *sexenio*, spending on Solidarity has risen more rapidly than total federal government investment, by an increasingly large margin (for exact statistics, see SEDESOL 1993: 25, 234).

By November 1993, President Salinas could report that more than 150,000 local Solidarity Committees had been established throughout Mexico, and that Solidarity projects had been undertaken in more than 95 percent of the country's 2,378 municipalities (Salinas de Gortari 1993a: 66). While the actual degree and quality of citizen participation in many of these projects could certainly be questioned, it would be difficult to identify another government program in the postrevolutionary period whose penetration of Mexican society had been so rapid and extensive.

Not surprisingly, Solidarity has become a lightning rod for critics of the Salinas administration's overall political and economic management. The program's defenders point not only to its observable short-term, material accomplishments but also to its potential for fostering basic social and political change in the long term.

THE MACROECONOMIC AND POLITICAL CONTEXT OF SOLIDARITY

In the aftermath of the PRI's 1988 electoral reverses, there was deep dissatisfaction with existing political structures among the technocratic "modernizers" who had gained the upper hand over members of the traditional political class, concentrated in the PRI and those government ministries devoted to political management. Some technocrats wanted to jettison completely the ruling party's ossified "sectoral" organizations (which nominally represented the PRI's supporters in the countryside and among organized labor) and all other trappings of the entrenched corporatist system. Not only had the PRI's "sectors" clearly lost electoral control over their own members; since 1968 they had been challenged increasingly in low-income urban and rural communities by leftist-inspired, independent popular movements. The independent movements attacked presidentialism, corporatism, clientelism, and excessive centralism in Mexican politics (see Moguel, this volume).

Other political modernizers were more cautious, no doubt troubled by the absence of any readily available substitute for the old PRI-affiliated structures and their local-level agents (caciques). But the ruling technocrats, including President Salinas and his handpicked PRI chief, Luis Donaldo Colosio, were agreed on the necessity of creating new and broader bases of popular support, not only for the PRI (to replace the millions of votes that the old-line sectoral organizations could no longer reliably deliver in national elections) but also for the radical economic restructuring project to which the incoming administration was strongly committed. As Carlos Salinas analyzed the situation, six weeks after taking office:

> In previous decades, the PRI could count on cam-
> pesinos who had received land from agrarian reform,
> and unionized workers who were the product of im-
> port-substituting industrialization. Now the country is
> experiencing a formidable process of transformation.
> We must seek new bases of support for the party. We
> must build alliances with new groups, some of which
> are unorganized now; others are organized for various
> purposes, but don't want to participate in political
> parties. We must convince them to participate (in Cor-
> nelius, Gentleman, and Smith 1989a: 27–28).

One of the key questions raised here is whether its commitment to drastically restructuring the economy "forced" the Salinas government to develop a program like Solidarity, which could compensate politically and materially for the high social costs of adjustment. In other words, was Solidarity a functional requisite of the Salinista economic project, needed as much to forestall a social explosion as to rebuild support for the ruling party and the presidency?

As John Bailey reminds us in his contribution to this volume, structural adjustment of the magnitude attempted by the Salinas government inevitably means "large groups of losers in the short term"—a situation that can extend into the medium term if adjustment is not followed immediately by a period of sustained, robust economic growth. In the case of the Salinas administration, economic recovery has been held back by a global recession and, until November 1993, by investor uncertainty over the fate of the North American Free Trade Agreement. The need for a well-targeted relief program to compensate the numerous losers from Salinas's policies of state-shrinking (privatization), deregulation, deficit reduction, and unilateral trade liberalization only increased as the *sexenio* progressed. Solidarity programs benefited many of these direct "losers," as well as large numbers of other Mexicans who had not been directly affected by structural adjustment.

Until the early 1980s, the Mexican government had, in general, pursued an actively interventionist economic development. In its interventionism the state did not seek to eliminate poverty, nor did it attempt to prevent the emergence of increasingly sharp inequalities in the distribution of personal income, goods, and services (see Sheahan 1991; Lustig 1992; Maxfield 1990). It certainly did not become a generous welfare state, even by the standards of Latin American and Caribbean countries (see Ward, this volume). But federal legislation did nominally regulate ownership (of land, public services, etc.) and impose certain conditions on direct foreign investment. The government heavily subsidized infrastructure development for both large-scale agriculture and industrial production. Numerous goods and services of mass consumption were also subsidized.

It was widely believed that, up to the 1982 debt crisis, much of the Mexican regime's legitimacy was attributable to economic performance (measured by high aggregate rates of growth) and the delivery of symbolic and material benefits to key constituencies. A significant fraction of the pre-crisis society was incorporated in some way into the clientelistic system, and got something out of it. The discourse of public officials linked government subsidies, regulation of the private sector and foreign investment, and public investment in development to the gradual achievement of social justice.

Numerous analysts have argued that the protracted economic crisis of the 1980s and the dramatic policy shift toward economic liberalization after 1985 contributed (along with the mismanagement of the presidential succession of 1987–1988) to the legitimacy crisis shared by the ruling party and the Salinas team as the latter assumed power. In their analysis, Solidarity has provided a response to the legitimacy crisis while protecting the new economic strategy. Denise Dresser, in this volume, suggests that Solidarity "has provided state elites with the political conditions necessary to sustain the neoliberal model." The program achieves this objective, she argues, by expanding the regime's constituencies to include the lower middle class and the urban informal sector (groups not otherwise included in the social coalition benefiting from market-oriented economic policies), and by making the political elite more representative by incorporating social reformers from the political left who might otherwise defect to the Cardenista opposition.

Whether or not it sustains the new economic model, Solidarity clearly does not undermine it. Unlike some "big-ticket" government social programs of the past (e.g., the CONASUPO retailing system), Solidarity projects do not generate competition for the private sector. It does not replace the subsidies to basic foods and services consumed by the poor that have been cut from the government budget. By requiring community contributions of labor and/or money to projects conducted under Solidarity's auspices, it emphasizes the role of self-help in solving the problems of the poor. None of this threatens the private sector or interferes with "the market." In fact, private businesses can benefit from the purchase of inputs for Solidarity projects (cement, copper pipes, street pavement materials, paint, roof tiles, metal window grates, etc.). Indeed, the only major inconsistency between Solidarity and the new economic model is an ideological one: i.e., Solidarity projects by definition emphasize collective, solidary action, through which individuals may benefit by cooperative effort. This is a marked departure from the individualized agency that pervades the free market model.

Some commentators have speculated that privatization and the reduction of state intervention in the economy have made Solidarity *possible*, rather than necessary. During the first year of the program, President Salinas indicated that revenues from privatization would be used to finance social improvements such as electrification. Subsequently, Solidarity officials stated even more explicitly that the government's macroeconomic and tax reforms (including a vigorous crackdown on corporate and individual tax evasion) were generating the resources being used to finance the program. Enrique González Tiburcio reports in this volume that "resources have come mainly from tax revenues (approximately 97 percent in 1992) and from savings achieved through various elements of Mexico's macroeconomic strategy: privatization of state enterprises, selective use of the contingency fund,[4] and fiscal reform."

In 1993, the financing of Solidarity was extended to the United States, where the Mexican Foreign Relations Ministry entered into an agreement with Mexican citizens residing in Los Angeles. Beginning with those coming from the state of Zacatecas, every dollar contributed by the immigrants toward Solidarity projects in their home state will be matched by the Solidarity program and the state government, on a 1:2 basis. This program is to be extended to migrants from other Mexican states in the near future. Given the billions of dollars remitted each year by Mexicans working in the United States to their communities of origin, this pool of savings could prove to be a significant new source of financing for Solidarity-related development projects in areas of high out-migration.[5]

---

[4]The Salinas administration's multi-billion-dollar "contingency fund," created with proceeds from the sale of state enterprises, has been used primarily to reduce government indebtedness.

[5]Using the best available data sources and measurement techniques, Fernando Lozano has estimated that Mexican migrants in the United States transferred to Mexico, through both formal and informal channels, approximately U.S. $3.2 billion in 1990. Remittances of this magnitude equal or exceed the earnings of several key sectors of the Mexican economy and have strong regional impacts in areas of concentrated out-migration (see Lozano Ascencio 1993).

THE POLITICAL CONSEQUENCES OF SOLIDARITY

By far the most intense debates provoked by the National Solidarity Program have focused on its alleged consequences for electoral politics and for the institution of the presidency. Particularly in the early years of the Salinas *sexenio*, Solidarity funds, state and local Solidarity program representatives, and community-level Solidarity Committees were used by the president and his political team to challenge the PRI to reform its practices and to strengthen the president's authority over the party's machinery as well as state governments, two-thirds of which were led by PRIísta governors who did not owe their appointments to Salinas.

In many parts of the country, through Solidarity, Salinas managed a deft end run around a sclerotic PRI and government bureaucracy as well as rigid power brokers in state and local politics. When he encountered particularly uncooperative PRIísta state governors or other officials, Salinas did not hesitate to use the Solidarity program to create an alternative power base. For example, in the case of Durango, discussed in this volume by Paul Haber, Salinas's delivery of Solidarity funds to the CDP (Comité de Defensa Popular) movement, over strong opposition from local PRI and government officials, contributed significantly to the CDP's victory in the 1992 municipal election. Similarly, the leftist COCEI movement, which now controls the *municipio* of Juchitán in Oaxaca State, has benefited considerably from federal government funding channeled through the Solidarity program (see Rubin n.d.; Fox and Moguel n.d.).

The Salinas administration also set out to use Solidarity as its principal instrument for increasing the *responsiveness* of the political system—but not necessarily its accountability at the national level—to low-income groups. At the outset of the *sexenio*, the declining effectiveness of entrenched corporatist structures in meeting the needs of the poor was matched by that of the federal administrative bureaucracy, which managed the lion's share of public investments and expenditures in Mexico's thirty-two states and federal territories.[6] Mexico City-based officials were slow to respond to even well-organized demand making, and the federal agencies' investments in low-income communities were usually uncoordinated and inefficient. Bureaucracies siphoned limited resources for public services through corruption and high administra-

---

[6]In Mexico the federal government traditionally has controlled about 85 percent of public revenues, the state governments less than 12 percent, and the municipalities about 3 percent. The *municipios'* share of public spending has risen to about 5–7 percent since the mid-1980s. Municipal governments typically depend on the federal government for about 80 percent of their budget, raising the balance from local sources (property and real estate sales taxes, charges for services such as water and sewerage connections, etc.). Since the economic crisis of the 1980s dried up many of these local sources of income, federal revenue sharing has become a particularly important source of income for states and municipalities. These entities share in federal tax revenues according to formulas dependent in part on how much of the aggregate tax revenues the state or municipality itself collects. See Bailey, this volume, for further details.

tive overhead costs. Ministries declined to consult and cooperate with each other. These problems were compounded when the *state*-level agencies replicated the federal pattern, and when they became engaged in conflicts with the federal government over appropriate responses to community demands. There were few mechanisms for promoting accountability within the executive branch, even in the face of growing demands from opposition parties (especially the National Action Party, PAN) for greater transparency in the management of public funds. PANista charges of corruption were matched by demands from the leftist opposition for the elimination of clientelist criteria in allocating public investments and social services.

Thus, the National Solidarity Program was introduced by the new president into a political system already suffering from diminished capacity to represent mass political constituencies, control political opposition and resistance, and respond quickly and decisively to demands for public goods and services. Much of the controversy surrounding Solidarity today derives from differing assessments of how the program has responded to these challenges, and whether it has done so *at the expense* of political parties (especially the opposition parties, but even of the ruling party itself), legislatures, and the broader process of democratization in Mexico.

Among our contributors and other observers, there is considerable agreement that since 1989 the National Solidarity Program has *contributed* to changing the electoral and governing environment in Mexico. Our emphasis here is important: Solidarity has contributed to rearranging the political landscape, but to some unmeasurable degree and *in conjunction* with improvements in national economic performance (especially the dramatic reduction in inflation, from triple-digit to single-digit levels by 1993), economic restructuring policies, changes internal to the political left in Mexico, and the administration's strategies of political negotiation. The contributors to this book do not attempt to allocate a precise share of the credit or blame for political change in Mexico to Solidarity; rather, they suggest that it has played a key role in the process of change.

The difficulty of isolating Solidarity's relative contribution to such phenomena as the PRI's impressive recovery at the polls in the 1991 midterm elections and the declining fortunes of the opposition parties (particularly the PRD, the left-of-center Cardenista party) can be illustrated by reference to the political significance of the Salinas government's successful inflation reduction effort since 1989. In an economy where most people's incomes were not indexed, high inflation was at least as regressive in its effects on income distribution as the painful government budget cuts of the 1980s. The analytic challenge of disentangling the political benefits accruing to the regime from Solidarity programs and those resulting from inflation reduction is formidable

indeed. It is impossible to come to a definitive conclusion about whether
regime legitimacy during the Salinas *sexenio* was boosted more by the
government's overall economic program (inflation reduction plus at least
the hope of an economic recovery) or by the social buffering effects of
Solidarity, but the latter clearly helped.

Has Solidarity fortified the presidency as an institution and its
incumbent during the 1988–1994 *sexenio*? The answer appears to be,
clearly, "yes": The program has strengthened the hand of the executive
branch by greatly enhancing the president's personal popularity and
giving him greater control over the distribution of discretionary funds.
Denise Dresser, in this volume, contends that the greatest beneficiary of
Solidarity has been President Salinas himself, as measured by the sharp
increase in his public approval ratings since taking office (in public
opinion polls taken since 1989, Salinas's personal popularity consistently has exceeded that of the party he leads, sometimes by as many as
20 percentage points) and by the concentration of discretionary spending authority in the Office of the Presidency.

But how much of this effect on presidential power can be attributed
to the Solidarity program per se, and how much to Carlos Salinas's
personal activism and skill in advocating and managing it? Salinas put
his own stamp on Solidarity not only by introducing it as many of his
predecessors had also done in launching their own "signature" programs,[7] but by explicitly and with great public fanfare associating
himself and his political future with the program and its beneficiaries.
He traveled incessantly to isolated communities to inaugurate Solidarity
projects and to directly receive petitions. In doing so he created an
image of great accessibility, second only to that of President Lázaro
Cárdenas in the 1930s. Close presidential attention to the program's
implementation was implied by physical location of key planners: Solidarity's director general, Carlos Rojas, and his staff had their offices in
Los Pinos (the Mexican "White House"). For several years, the president's older brother, Raúl Salinas, was in charge of Solidarity's Technical
Committee for Program Evaluation, and most accounts suggest that the
program's expenditures were approved by a small circle that included
the president. It is for these reasons that Solidarity has become known as
a "presidentialist" program *par excellence*.

The high degree of centralization in spending authority that is
reflected in PRONASOL's management structure, together with the
president's presumed capacity to use these funds to override state and
local officials and PRI functionaries, has itself been a major source of
controversy. Much of the criticism of Solidarity emphasizes executive—
especially presidential—discretion in determining program content,

[7]Compare, for example, the handling of the Sistema Alimentario Mexicano, a vast new
agricultural subsidy and rural development program, by President José López Portillo in
the early 1980s. See Fox 1993.

overall spending priorities, and the allocation of funds. It must be noted, however, that in the absence of a strong legislature, the federal executive in Mexico has had great discretion in spending since the early 1930s, checked only partially by bureaucratic and party machinery. Moreover, only when state governors and municipal leaders had some independent power base of their own were they positioned to "compel" the president to negotiate with them. What seemed to distinguish Solidarity during the first half of the Salinas administration was that even these internal checks did not appear to generally shape Solidarity expenditures. This centralization might nonetheless have some reformist consequences if it challenged entrenched bureaucratic interests and procedures, as it appeared to do during Solidarity's first three years of operation. By forcing additional consultation and planning, and providing a model for more rapid response from federal agencies (such as CFE, the Federal Electrification Commission), the Solidarity program generated pressure for administrative reform from the ground up.

Solidarity may be a politically and bureaucratically efficient mechanism for delivering public goods and services in quick, targeted responses to a seriously backlogged *demanda social.*" But John Bailey, in this volume, develops the argument that Solidarity *deconcentrates* without *decentralizing* administration, thus reinforcing executive dominance. The distinction is an important one, since decisions to "deconcentrate" can easily be revoked from above, while true "decentralization" involves a redistribution of power—with a potential loss of political control—that is much more difficult to reverse. Given the way in which budget allocations and revenue sharing are negotiated through concertation between municipal and state governments, and between state governors and the federal executive, it could be argued that, on balance, state governors, municipal presidents, and the president of the republic benefit from these arrangements, potentially at the expense of legislatures and political parties.

One of Solidarity's most frequently stated goals has been that of strengthening municipalities as service providers. Traditionally the federal government has shared with state governments the responsibility for public investment in social welfare (health, education, and pensions, for example).[8] *Municipios* have been charged with financing local government positions, community policing, garbage collection, some share of the cost of providing potable water and sewerage, local road maintenance, public lighting, and maintaining public places such as plazas and markets. In practice, in most municipalities budgets have been too small to allow for more than keeping administrative accounts,

---

[8]In recent years, public education has become an exclusively state-level responsibility—the most important element of Salinas's administrative decentralization effort. See Rodríguez n.d.

with a slight margin for investment in urban infrastructure and no involvement in productive activities.

Solidarity has moved to increase municipal discretion in spending, particularly through the creation of the Fondos Municipales de Solidaridad.[9] The World Bank loaned Solidarity U.S. $350 million between 1989 and 1993 to improve rural service provision and support regional development in four of Mexico's poorest states: Oaxaca, Guerrero, Chiapas, and Hidalgo. Of these funds, over $100 million went into Fondos Municipales. The funds have been used to support basic infrastructure projects (e.g., small-scale irrigation, corn mills, animal husbandry), social infrastructure (street paving, sidewalk construction, school expansion, potable water and sewage systems, sports facilities), and basic infrastructure (roads, electrification).

Solidarity's administrative reforms bring with them added financial and staffing burdens upon municipal governments, which often are not funded to acquire the staff and equipment needed to conduct technical studies and implement new programs. This may mean that only the larger *municipios* possessing significant numbers of trained personnel, or those that are well connected to political party bureaucracies capable of providing this type of assistance, will be able to take maximum advantage of the Fondos Municipales.[10]

As noted above, numerous observers have contended that PRONASOL has been used not only to strengthen the presidency and Carlos Salinas personally, but also in a partisan manner, to rebuild electoral support for the ruling PRI. This suspicion is rooted in the presumption that the Solidarity program works in traditional clientelist fashion, binding voters to the party in power in return for the provision of material benefits. Most criticism has focused on the alleged politicization of the process by which levels of PRONASOL funding are determined (per state, locality, etc.) in such a way that the program's funds are targeted to areas of demonstrated opposition party strength.

In this volume, Molinar and Weldon find that, based on their analysis of state-level expenditure data, electoral considerations *are* important predictors of where and how much Solidarity funds were spent during the run-up to the 1991 midterm elections. Their analysis

---

[9]Under Solidarity, municipal governments have been given particular responsibility for the Escuela Digna program, Niños en Solidaridad, Fondos de Solidaridad para la Producción, basic "urban" improvements, and legalization of urban property titles. See Monahan 1993.

[10]In her analysis of PRONASOL and its potential contributions to true decentralization in the Mexican political system, Victoria Rodríguez expresses similar concerns, but she does not rule out the possibility that the program could prove to be an effective mechanism for enhancing the autonomy of municipal governments. By granting money directly to *municipios*, rather than making allocations to them via their state governments, "Solidarity may be able to grant municipalities the autonomy they have been unable to achieve thus far" (Rodríguez 1993: 142).

suggests that in states that held gubernatorial and congressional elections in 1991 and in which the PRI faced significant opposition, electoral criteria are better predictors of Solidarity spending levels than are indices of poverty (i.e., expenditures scaled to material needs). This finding, if it can be replicated for subsequent elections and with spending data disaggregated to the congressional district level, could lead us to conclude that the Solidarity program is, in fact, employed strategically by the PRI-government apparatus as an asset in the electoral arena. However, as Molinar and Weldon argue, this finding does not necessarily support the opposition parties' view of Solidarity as traditional clientelism. Rather, in their view such a pattern of resource allocation reveals the Mexican government's new *electoral responsiveness*: "Despite its decades-long history of noncompetitive elections, the regime is demonstrating that it is [now] willing to compete for votes" by resorting to the pork barrel common to all electoral democracies. Moreover, in those cases where the program's norms of community participation and co-responsibility are strictly adhered to, the result is a much less paternalistic form of government assistance to the poor and a sense of citizen involvement and empowerment. In other words, "the political efficacy of PRONASOL does not necessarily equate with the strengthening of authoritarianism."

In the second quantitative study included in this volume, Gershberg's study of allocations under Solidarity's Escuela Digna program, the results indicate that voting for the Cardenista opposition in the 1988 election seemed to hurt a *municipio's* chances of receiving Solidarity funds in 1990. Thus, there is some evidence that PRD strongholds may be "punished" in the allocation of Solidarity funds but no statistical support for the proposition that such funds have been used to "buy back" states that supported the Cardenista presidential candidate in 1988. Anecdotally, however, the scale of Solidarity spending in recent years in states having strong opposition parties (such as Michoacán, Chihuahua, and the Estado de México) makes it clear that some members of the PRI-government elite regard the program as a powerful weapon in the ruling party's electoral arsenal.[11]

During the Salinas *sexenio*, Solidarity may, indeed, have helped to "deactivate" the Cardenista opposition, as evidenced by its weak performance in the 1991 midterm elections and various state and local elections held since then. But Julio Moguel's chapter, outlining the complex strategic and ideological debates within the Mexican left since 1968, suggests that there are elements of the "social left" that have found

---

[11] The right-of-center National Action Party (PAN) has complained about the utilization of Solidarity funds to boost PRI candidates in some of its state and local strongholds. However, the PAN's 1994 electoral platform calls for PRONASOL to be retained, albeit with some significant administrative modifications, if a PANista government were to take power at the national level.

resonance in and support for their objectives within the Solidarity program. As Molinar and Weldon point out in this volume, Solidarity has an ideological component (the goal of transforming state-society relations) that makes it attractive to many grassroots activists of the left. Moguel notes that, rather than simply being co-opted by the program, some activists who have chosen to cooperate with or participate in Solidarity programs "firmly and honestly believe that they are carrying forward a cause that transcends Salinas's six-year presidential term, and that Salinismo may be for the twenty-first century what Cardenismo [that of the father] was for the twentieth."

Haber's chapter in this volume describes the case of an independent urban popular movement, the Comité de Defensa Popular in Durango. CDP leaders found themselves with the opportunity to do business with a president whom they had not supported in the 1988 campaign and against whom Cardenista opposition leaders still railed, but who was willing to respond through Solidarity to some of the CDP's long-standing demands. According to Haber's account, the CDP leadership made a strategic calculation to negotiate with Salinas, a decision which they felt strengthened their organization and legitimated it as the prime local interlocutor for low-income people, bypassing the PRI and its affiliated corporatist organizations. In Haber's words, the CDP became "convinced that the Salinas administration represents an opportunity for concessions [from the state] and movement empowerment." Such moves by previously "autonomous" social movements may, indeed, have inhibited the institutionalization of the PRD, which remains Mexico's principal opposition party on the left. Solidarity has "sometimes prevented social sectors or movements that 'naturally' might have sympathized with the PRD from joining forces with it" (Méndez, Romero, and Bolívar 1992: 66).

But if the Solidarity program has weakened the opposition to the PRI in various ways, it has also created problems for some elements of the ruling party itself. Solidarity's early development coincided in time with an important attempt to reform the PRI's structure and internal governance, which ended in failure. While the party has always had a dual structure, both sectoral and territorial, the former has clearly predominated. Upon entering office, the Salinas team saw an urgent need to rebuild the PRI as "a party of individual citizens, in their homes," as newly installed PRI president Luis Donaldo Colosio put it in January 1989. This would involve

> changing the basic terms of the relationship between the PRI and its mass base. Workers' votes are influenced more by the problems in their immediate environment; by their lives outside the work place. The lack of water, sewerage, and other services; crime; deficient schools—

that's what concerns them. The votes for the PRI are not
in the [sectoral] organizations, but in the homes of the
workers" (in Cornelius, Gentleman, and Smith 1989a:
28).

Nevertheless, an effort by Salinista reformers at the PRI's 14th
National Assembly in September 1990 to shift the emphasis toward
territorially based organization was strongly—and successfully—resisted by entrenched leaders of the *sectores*. Attempts to reorganize the
so-called popular sector of the party (a catchall sector ostensibly representing the urban poor, small merchants, and middle-class professionals) bogged down when a territorially based movement, a citizens
and organizations front, a young people's parliament, and a women's
congress—innovations tolerated at the PRI's 1990 National Assembly—
were summarily rolled back by another party congress in 1993.

Under these circumstances, the Solidarity program emerged as a
kind of parallel structure, absorbing some of the most energetic, young
leaders who might otherwise have sought to build their political careers
within the PRI. Some PRI cadres have received important organizing
experience through work with local Solidarity Committees. Government technocrats with political ambitions have gained practical experience and firsthand knowledge of community problems. There are
indications that some PRI candidates for elective office in recent years
earned their nominations through service with Solidarity. In cities like
Durango, as described by Haber in this volume, PRONASOL became
the Salinas administration's "undisputed lead effort" to reach out and
respond to the needs of the urban poor, to the chagrin of PRI apparat-
chiks.

During the first half of the Salinas *sexenio* there was widespread
speculation that local Solidarity Committees might become the framework for a new party or a reformed PRI. However, it gradually became
clear that the Solidarity Committee structure could not sustain a new
party. President Salinas's proposal, made in 1991, to scale up local
Solidarity organizations into national-level *"coordinadoras"* (confederations) was quietly dropped. Nor were reformists able to induce the PRI
to dissolve its sectoral structure and reorganize the party along territorial lines.

On the other hand, it is not at all clear that a closer linkage between
Solidarity and the PRI would serve the stated objectives of the Solidarity
program. Solidarity officials have pointed out that the most formidable
obstacles to program implementation are typically (1) the PRI sectoral
organizations, and (2) local interests (such as caciques) linked to the PRI.
When local PRI activists or PRIísta state governors have tried to use
Solidarity Committees for electoral mobilization, or have insisted that
Solidarity Committees be based on the PRI's sectional (block-level)

committees, citizen participation has been low, group solidarity has been undermined, Solidarity Committees have lacked autonomy in the selection and planning of projects for their communities, and the general public has reacted negatively to utilization of the Solidarity program for electoral purposes. In one northern state, duly constituted Solidarity Committees were not "recognized" by the governor, who reportedly proceeded to form new committees headed by state employees to act on the promises that had been made by the governor in various places during his electoral campaign. Such clientelistic manipulation is totally antithetical to Solidarity's stated norms of conduct. In sum, the program seems to work best, in terms of its own basic principles and criteria of success, when it is able to keep its distance from partisan political competition, and especially from the local PRI machinery (see Contreras and Bennett, this volume).

The nonpartisan leftist activists who had worked with autonomous social movements and who became involved in designing Solidarity had several specific goals. They envisioned a program that would empower independent community organizations and, through them, help to strengthen and extend solidaristic communal traditions and political culture. They hoped to use Solidarity Committees to promote active citizen participation in setting local resource allocation priorities, making local government more responsive, reducing corruption, and increasing financial accountability.

However, as many of the contributors to this volume observe, the Solidarity Committees created thus far have varied considerably in their capacity to mobilize broad citizen participation, create a sense of community empowerment, and maintain autonomy from political parties and other organizations with different agendas. Depending on local conditions (e.g., leadership, party structure, the presence or absence of solidaristic traditions), the formation of Solidarity Committees and the allocation of Solidarity funds have led to a reinforcement of authoritarian clientelism, a shift toward semi-clientelist arrangements, or a more genuinely competitive, pluralist pattern of local governance (see Fox, this volume).

By official count, the National Solidarity Program has generated an extraordinary number of community-based committees—some 71,000 in the first three years of the program, rising to 150,000 by November 1, 1993, according to President Salinas. A high-ranking architect of Solidarity's community organizing strategy estimated that about one-third of these committees, on a national basis, were fully functional, had real "presence" in their communities, and were capable of making some demands upon government (interviews with J. Fox, June 1993). While this may seem a low percentage, the absolute number of functioning Solidarity Committees is still quite large.

Most committees have been involved only with a single project, but others have extended their organizational activity into new, follow-on projects under the Solidarity program's auspices. According to the official rules for the program, the Solidarity Committee leaders should be democratically elected, in publicly convened, open meetings. Each committee bears responsibility for proposing projects for its community or neighborhood in response to residents' expressed preferences, and overseeing project implementation. There is, of course, an important distinction between grassroots participation in project selection and implementation, on the one hand, and involvement in the design of Solidarity programs and the setting of state- or national-level funding priorities, on the other. Thus far, there seems to have been a great deal of the former and virtually none of the latter. Moreover, program manuals make it clear that SEDESOL officials have the last word on any big decision taken at the Solidarity Committee level.

Prior to the Salinas *sexenio*, the political left in Mexico had emphasized popular struggle over civic struggle, the defense of class interests more than citizenship rights, and universal causes over particularistic local demands (see Moguel, this volume). The shift to a discourse of citizenship rights and local community participation, encouraged by Solidarity, has required adaptation by the left as well as the PRI-government apparatus. As Dresser points out in this volume, Solidarity's effort to redefine Mexicans as consumers, residents of specific territorial units, urban squatters in search of land titles, and so forth can be viewed as a fundamentally conservative strategy, aimed at minimizing social class conflicts. Within the left, as well as in the government, debates have flourished over whether the state can (or should) promote the establishment of an independently organized and empowered society, and whether existing popular organizations should pursue concertation (or what Alan Knight, this volume, calls a "consensual" relationship) with the state.

It is too early to gauge how deeply the organizational model and formal operating principles of the National Solidarity Program have penetrated local communities and popular movements, and thus possibly contributed to the emergence of a new political culture in Mexico. The available data, however fragmentary and limited to a particular stage in the evolution of Solidarity, offer grounds for skepticism on this point. In their survey of residents of three northern border cities, Contreras and Bennett (this volume) found little understanding of the organizational and participatory ideology of the Solidarity program. Moreover, the character of citizen participation in Solidarity Committees varied widely, from the purely instrumental (participation aimed at increasing one's capacity to extract material benefits from the political system) to the "political-societal" (where participation transcends the instrumental plane and creates conditions necessary for a fundamental transformation of the state-society relationship). However, their survey data suggest that, thus far, only about a tenth of the population benefiting from Solidarity programs have been personally engaged in these programs in a potentially "transformative" way.

SOLIDARITY AS AN INSTRUMENT OF POVERTY ALLEVIATION

Whatever the political motivations of its architects or its potential consequences for the evolution of the political system, can PRONASOL be an effective, efficient instrument of poverty alleviation in Mexico? Most of the contributors to this volume who address this question conclude that Solidarity is best described as a targeted, compensatory relief program whose capacity for reducing extreme poverty and social inequality is limited. Given the magnitude of Mexico's accumulated problems of poverty, unemployment and underemployment, and deficits in basic human services, which increased significantly under the structural adjustment policies adopted after the 1982 debt crisis,[12] Solidarity alone cannot reasonably be expected to "solve" these problems. However, in specific communities and among selected segments of the population, Solidarity can alleviate some of the worst symptoms of the country's uneven development.

The essays in this book suggest the range of difficulties faced by scholars seeking to evaluate whether Solidarity has led, thus far, to changes in social welfare in Mexico. The Solidarity program accounts for a significant portion of the increase in social spending by the federal government that has occurred under Salinas, albeit from a very low base (the last of President Miguel de la Madrid's austerity budgets). In his fifth State of the Nation address, President Salinas reported that overall social spending grew by almost 85 percent in real terms during the 1989–1993 period, with increases of almost 90 percent in education spending, 79 percent in health care expenditures, and 65 percent in spending for environmental protection, drinking water, and other urban improvements. In 1993, social spending accounted for more than half (54 percent) of the federal government's programmable outlays (equivalent to 10 percent of GNP), compared with only one-third of federal spending at the outset of the *sexenio*. Salinas claimed that "never before has this proportion of social spending been achieved" in Mexico (Salinas de Gortari 1993a: 29, 34; cf. Ward, this volume).

But who has benefited from these expenditures and others associated with Solidarity? The available evidence does not support the conclusion that the poorest segments of Mexican society (*"los que menos tienen"*) are consistently the foremost beneficiaries of Solidarity expenditures. For example, independent analysis of publicly available govern-

---

[12]For an overview of the social costs of the economic crisis and adjustment measures of the 1980s, see González de la Rocha and Escobar Latapí 1991; Sheahan 1991; Lustig 1992.

ment data shows that, on a per capita basis, Mexico's poorest states were not privileged in the allocation of PRONASOL funds between 1990 and 1992; rather, it was the middle tier of states, in terms of indices of poverty and underdevelopment, that benefited most. This pattern is consistent with the findings of several of the contributors to the present volume (see, for example, Molinar and Weldon). It is possible, however, that a more disaggregated analysis would show that, *within* states, Solidarity programs have successfully targeted extreme poverty at the individual and local community levels.

The largest share of Solidarity expenditures has gone to projects in the "Social Welfare" category. President Salinas's chief of staff, economist José Córdoba, has claimed that Solidarity spending in this area, together with a gradual economic recovery, has had a measurable impact on poverty defined in "structural" rather than personal or family income terms. Thus, a summary index constructed from such indicators as quality of housing construction materials, the number of persons per room, access to basic services such as water, electricity, and sewerage, children's school enrollment, and the relationship between family size and the number of income earners shows only slight improvement between 1984 and 1989 (an annual average of 1.3 percent) but significantly greater progress during the 1989–1992 period (3.8 percent per annum).[13]

Such improvements in household standards of living should not be too casually dismissed by critics seeking more fundamental reductions in poverty. Projects like street paving, installation of potable water and sewage lines, electrification, and even the painting of house facades often respond to deeply felt needs in the low-income population. Such changes can improve household health conditions, ease women's work in the home, increase personal safety for women and children, contribute to a sense of human dignity in poor communities, and even create modest employment opportunities. For example, residents of Chalco, on the outskirts of Mexico City, noted that a PRONASOL electrification project made it possible to establish small repair shops, in a place where

---

[13]Córdoba 1994: 270–71. It must be noted, however, that this improvement in household living standards has not been matched by a decline in income inequality (Córdoba acknowledges that the Gini coefficient, the standard index for measuring equality in income distribution, remained constant between 1989 and 1992), nor in a major reduction in the number of Mexicans living in "extreme poverty," as measured by their capacity to purchase a minimum "market basket" of basic foodstuffs. According to a controversial sample survey conducted jointly by INEGI (the Mexican government's statistics and census agency) and CEPAL (the United Nations Economic Commission for Latin America), that number fell from 14.9 million people (18.8 percent of total population) in 1989 to 13.6 million (16.1 percent of the population) in 1992. However, the absolute number of Mexicans living in extreme poverty, according to the official statistics, was still *higher* in 1992 than in 1984, when the figure was 11.0 million people (15.4 percent of the population). At that point in time, Mexico was two full years into the economic crisis of the 1980s.

local employment opportunities had been nonexistent (interviews by A. Craig, 1992).

In the absence of more detailed information about the recipients of PRONASOL funds, one way of addressing the "who benefits?" question is to focus on the types of projects being funded. Based on the predominance of expenditures for "urbanization" projects—water supply, sewerage, electrification, and roads—Nora Lustig (this volume) expresses skepticism that the country's extremely poor households, nearly 70 percent of which are concentrated in rural areas, can be Solidarity's real targets. However, we do not know which neighborhoods or towns received these services, and in any event, 30 percent of the extremely poor households in Mexico live in *urban* areas. To further complicate the analysis, rural communities (defined officially as localities having fewer than 2,500 inhabitants) often request these "urban" improvements. While it seems doubtful that the poorest households and the poorest states in Mexico consistently receive a disproportionate share of Solidarity's total resources, it may be that some very poor states (e.g., Oaxaca, Guerrero) and population segments (Indian communities) benefit more from certain types of programs (e.g., those conducted under the joint auspices of the Instituto Nacional Indigenista and Solidaridad, as described in Fox's chapter).

Carol Graham, in her contribution to this volume, points out that none of the poverty alleviation programs that she has studied in Latin America, Africa, and Eastern Europe was particularly successful in targeting the poorest members of the population. Indeed, she found that benefiting the poorest was more difficult in open political systems, and that, ironically, Chile under military rule was the most successful case of such "targeting" among the antipoverty programs that she examined. Graham argues that for Solidarity to have a greater impact on absolute poverty and income inequality in Mexico, it would have to complement sectoral policies designed to create permanent employment opportunities. Lustig (this volume) adds that a successful effort to reduce extreme poverty will require some government intervention to *redistribute* income, which, she argues, could be achieved without excessive costs in terms of efficiency or foregone national income by reducing the rate of personal income growth among the wealthiest segment of the population. In the absence of such policies, Solidarity can improve the living standards of the poor, but not significantly diminish their absolute nor relative poverty in terms of income.

There are indications that the Mexican government recognizes this basic limitation and is beginning to shift the emphasis of Solidarity to reduce poverty through programs that directly increase incomes and employment opportunities. In establishing PRONASOL, the Salinas administration was quite clear that it did not wish to replicate the traps that it saw imbedded in the U.S. experience with "welfarist" programs (interviews by A. Craig, 1992). With the exception of Niños en Solidaridad (see Appendix, this volume), transfer payment programs have been avoided. As Nora Lustig points out in her chapter, most Solidarity expenditures have been for nonresellable assets. Therefore, current income and consumption problems have not been addressed, save for the short-term local employment effects of infrastructure-building projects.

The Salinas administration's new emphasis on production-related, permanent job-creating projects under the Solidarity banner is being implemented primarily through the National Fund for Solidarity Enterprises (created in December 1991) and Solidarity Funds for Production. However, the investments thus far in each project or individual beneficiary have been small. Revolving fund loans to individual farmers are limited to about U.S. $100 per year. In the production program most amply described in this book (see chapter by Hernández Navarro and Célis Callejas), the government has allocated funds to coffee producers that represent about one-ninth of the total credit needed by them. Coffee growers funded through the Solidaridad para la Producción program did not receive support adequate to offset the structural obstacles to investment, savings, and growth that they encounter in the coffee sector. For example, autonomous social organizations are willing and able to take on the tasks of storing and marketing coffee, but they lack adequate resources.

The total number of new permanent jobs resulting from Solidarity's production-related programs is still quite small. President Salinas reported in November 1993 that the establishment of 9,210 Solidarity companies had created some 42,000 jobs (Salinas de Gortari 1993a: 68). The contributors to this volume who address the relationship between Solidarity and poverty alleviation conclude that significant poverty reduction can be achieved only by sound macroeconomic policies that promote robust growth and generate sufficient employment for the rapidly expanding labor force. During most of the 1990s, more than 900,000 new jobs will be needed *each year* just to accommodate the new entrants to the country's labor force.[14] Programs like Solidarity can be a useful complement but not a substitute for such policies. Hernández and Célis argue that, to maximize Solidarity's contribution to employment creation, less emphasis should be placed on the local Solidarity Committees that emerged under the Salinas administration and greater support should be provided to regional and national organizations of small producers.

---

[14]Employment opportunities must also be created to absorb those workers who are displaced by industrial restructuring (which has eliminated an estimated half million jobs in Mexico since 1989) and by North American free trade, which is a direct threat to the survival of noncompetitive small and medium-sized businesses in Mexico.

LOOKING AHEAD

As President Salinas moved into the second half of his term, he took steps to institutionalize the Solidarity program within the newly established Ministry of Social Development (SEDESOL). Some observers fear that this change could weaken the capacity of Solidarity officials to force responsiveness from lethargic state and federal bureaucracies. No longer just a coordinator among government agencies, Solidarity, by being subsumed within a cabinet ministry, has become one actor among rival agencies. After President Salinas's selection of Luis Donaldo Colosio (who moved from the PRI to become the first head of SEDESOL) as the PRI's 1994 presidential candidate, Solidarity inevitably will be seen as a prime resource in the hands of one of the future contenders for presidential power.

Moreover, part of the efficiency of the program from the outset derived from its capacity to deliver funds, directly and quickly, into the hands of community-level beneficiaries. Less money was consumed by bureaucratic overhead and lost through corruption along the way. Standardizing rules for distributing funds may reduce personalism and the influence of partisan-political criteria in allocating Solidarity funds, but it may also mean that the program loses some of its flexibility and efficiency.

If this scenario proves accurate, it may set up the sternest test yet of Solidarity's contributions to the emergence of a new conception of citizenship in Mexico and to the empowerment of local communities and autonomous social movements. As Carol Graham notes in this volume, demand-based poverty alleviation programs like PRONASOL can make revolutionary changes at the local institutional level, by stimulating the participation of previously marginalized groups and providing more effective channels for demand making. Developed under the tutelage of the world's longest-surviving one-party-dominant regime, Solidarity may have to take on a life of its own if its components are to continue to serve as effective interlocutors between state and society.

II

Social Welfare Policy in Mexico

2

Solidarity: Historical Continuities and Contemporary Implications

Alan Knight

Digging up the historical roots of Solidarity is no easy task. The phenomenon itself is not yet five years old; its character is still being formed; it is not therefore clear what aspects of Solidarity would repay retrospective analysis. Nor are matters helped by the tendency of Solidarity participants—both givers and receivers—to stress the novelty of the program even in contexts where, it is clear, forms of government patronage and local self-help are far from new.[1] Perhaps one of Solidarity's successes—in the realm of political public relations—has been its capacity to cover its trail, to deny its political paternity, thus to capitalize on the "reverential cult of 'the new' which now characterizes Mexican politics" (Cordera Campos 1991b: 142). Once again, therefore, a historian of Mexico is wheeled out to proclaim there is nothing new under the sun, that we've seen it all before. Of course, there are many novel elements to Solidarity which should not be denied (albeit the novelty is perhaps more striking if we take a short time frame, such as the 1980s, the years of the "crisis"); and I hope that, in this analysis, I do not underestimate these novelties. But as a historian, it is both my personal inclination and, perhaps, my public obligation to look for precedents in the past. Such an exercise can be justified with the usual argument: That without some historical perspective, "immediatist" enthusiasms may take over; we may be taken in by the journalistic hype and forget the wise words of Ernest

---

[1]This, and a number of other impressions, were acquired during a brief trip made in order to meet Solidaridad officials and see Solidaridad activities, chiefly in México State and Michoacán, in January 1992. I will cite these as "personal impressions, January 1992." For additional assertions of novelty, see PRONASOL 1991b: 18, 42, 48.

Gruening: "continuity is the marrow of Mexican history beneath changing surface events."[2]

The practical difficulties are very apparent. Solidarity embraces a host of activities. To chase up the origins of each would be an impossible task in a brief paper. Solidarity involves collective labor; should we go back to the colonial—even pre-Conquest—*tequio*?[3] It helps build roads; should we follow the roads of the revolutionary regime back to the *camino real* of the colony? It encourages children to attend school; should we wade through the weighty historiography of Mexican education, from Revolution through Porfiriato, to Restored Republic and, ultimately, back to the colony? Even if we decide to focus—as I shall—on the postrevolutionary period, the problem of selection remains acute. Furthermore, while some antecedent themes (such as education) have been well studied, others (such as poverty) have not.[4] In contrast to European social history, that of Mexico has given little attention to the poor qua poor. (The Mexican poor have figured, of course, as Indians, rebels, and rioters, especially in the historiography of the last twenty years; but there have been very few studies of the poor as a distinct social group, or of the measures taken—from above or below—to alleviate their poverty.)

All this is by way of preamble and preemptive excuse. The analysis that follows will be selective and partial. It will focus on aspects of Solidarity that reveal some historical antecedents and it will try to tease out of these antecedents possible clues about Solidarity's likely impact and future. However, the whole exercise is tentative, less a definitive genealogical statement than an invitation to further discussion and research.

As other scholars have demonstrated, Solidarity fits neatly within the current project of the Salinas administration; it is the jewel in the crown of "social liberalism."[5] As the state becomes slimmer and trimmer—or, perhaps, meaner and leaner—so the allegedly indiscriminate subsidies of the past must give way to targeted programs, designed to help those most in need (and, perhaps, those who by virtue of collective self-help are most deserving) (Salinas, quoted in *La Jornada*, February 15, 1992). That this should spring from the fertile brain of President Salinas is not surprising, in light of his earlier lucubrations and writings on the

---

[2]Gruening 1928: x. Against which we may set the not so wise words of Manuel Villa: "cada vez parecen ser menos atractivas y dignas de atención las consideraciones de orden histórico en relación a los procesos políticos y sociales" (Villa 1991: 213).

[3]*Tequio* obligations have survived in some Indian regions, such as Zapotec Oaxaca, down to the twentieth century (see Whitecotton 1984: 231). More recently (and relevantly), the practice is cited as a precedent for Solidarity by Carlos Rojas himself (1991b: 25).

[4]González Navarro 1985 is a rare exception; it contains abundant information but less systematic analysis.

[5]As President Salinas stressed during his recent address at the Royal Institute of International Affairs, Chatham House, London (see *Proceso*, July 27, 1992, p. 11). Dresser 1991 is the best general study—and critique—of Solidarity, on which I have relied considerably for this paper.

subject (Salinas de Gortari 1980). Thus, even as the state divests itself of public enterprises and across-the-board subsidies, it now takes upon itself the role of *concertación* (Aguilar Villanueva 1991: 132–33), coordinating programs of self-help, "empowering" citizens, and channeling limited resources to particular and urgent problems. Supporters of the program therefore stress psychological as well as material rewards and invoke "the new sentiment of self-dignity and self-esteem of the Mexicans."[6] The "fit" with current policies of privatization is highlighted by Salinas's declaration that the resources raised by the sale of Mexicana de Aviación would go to provide electrification for half a million of Mexico's poor.[7] The program is timely and appropriate in another sense, in that it appeals to popular distrust of traditional political parties, the paternalist state, and its corporate institutions—a distrust discerned by several students of the "new social movements" of recent years.[8] It is now almost de riguer for supporters of Solidarity to disparage and deny the legacy of populism (C. Rojas 1991b: 31; Cordera Campos 1991b: 141–42, Morales 1991: 209; Villa 1991: 213).

This is not to say that the ideology of Solidarity is flawless and free of contradictions (Fernández Santillán 1991: 155). There is a certain irony in that a program stressing the values of collective effort and communal solidarity (the very name conjures up visions of an insurgent civil society and a "solidary" working people) should be yoked to a neoliberal project which lauds efficiency, free enterprise, and market production. To take but one minor example: the Niños en Solidaridad (Children in Solidarity) program appears to encourage collective cooperation for the common good.[9] Will this ethos prepare children for the competitive jungle that lies beyond the school gates?

Although the example is a minor one, it relates to a broad—and obvious—problem which should be addressed at the outset. In replacing the state intervention of yesteryear with the Solidarity program of today, the state has effectively reduced its commitment to economic and social interventionism (that may be good, or bad, according to taste, but surely it cannot be disputed). Since the early 1980s, the Mexican government has sold off some nine hundred state and parastatal companies, reduced the government's share of GDP from around 25 percent to 17 percent, cut the government deficit from 17 percent to around 2 percent, and, by eliminating a range of state subsidies, contributed to significant

---

[6]On the supposed transition from the *Estado obeso* or *Estado propietario* to the *Estado solidario*, see C. Rojas 1991b: 22, 37.

[7]On the relationship between Solidarity and privatization, see Dresser 1991; Barry 1992: 99–100.

[8]"Nuestro comité es apolítico" was the constant refrain heard by researchers who investigated social movements in Guadalajara in the 1980s; see Regalado Santillán 1986: 139).

[9]Impression based on a swift review of Solidaridad literature, Mexico, January 1992.

increases in most basic necessities.[10] Expenditure on Solidarity programs has not compensated for this retrenchment. Of course, it is difficult to calculate Solidarity expenditure.[11] Many existing programs (e.g., road building) have simply received the imprimatur of Solidarity. Other programs are genuinely new, but their budgets—insofar as they can be calculated—do not appear to compensate for the swinging cuts in social expenditure that have taken place since the early 1980s; according to one informed critic, "PRONASOL is little more than a short-term, compensatory program with partial and selective economic impact."[12] In part, of course, that is what it is meant to be: partial, selective, and compensatory; as for "short-term," more of that in a moment.

Meanwhile, the general course of the Mexican economy in these years has implied a massive transfer of wealth out of the country and a massive redistribution of wealth within, as per capital real income fell by 15 percent and real wages by perhaps 50 percent. Since 1988, it is true, the economy has revived briskly, the prospects are now much better (in the eyes of pundits and public opinion alike), and by Latin American standards—which is no longer to damn with faint praise—Mexico looks to be in reasonable economic shape.[13] Nevertheless, the legacy of "the crisis" remains: severely eroded real wages—which in turn constrain the national market; a labor surplus, derived partly from the high birth rates of the 1960s and 1970s, partly from the more capital-intensive industrialization of recent years, which in turn keeps wages low; a vulnerability to external vicissitudes, such as interest rate or oil price fluctuations; and a large balance of payments deficit, which requires a constant inflow of foreign capital. To this must be added the future effects of NAFTA and the reform of the ejido. Within such a scenario—improving, but far from enviable—Solidarity can be no more than a socioeconomic palliative (and, perhaps, a means to raise consciousness and disseminate information).[14] By its very definition, it cannot interfere substantially with the logic of the market. "Fondos de Solidaridad para la Producción (Solidarity for Production)" is in this respect one of the most important but also one of the most problematic components of the program (C. Hernández 1991: 92–93; Martínez Nateras 1991: 200). After all, the state is not trying to "pick winners"; nor is it, according to its own lights,

---

[10]Barry 1992: 90–99; Eckstein (1988: 222–23) notes a prior fall in social expenditure (as a percentage of total government spending) between the early 1970s and the early 1980s.

[11]Peter Ward (1992) puts total Solidarity spending at nearly $1 billion in 1990 and (projected) $1.7 billion in 1991; A. Craig (1992a) offers a detailed breakdown of Solidarity activities and expenditures, 1989–91.

[12]Dresser 1991: 11. Likewise Ward (1992): "fundamental reforms that would seek to go beyond 'papering over the cracks' have not been embarked upon."

[13]On recent (favorable) public opinion: *Nexos* 42 (December 1991): 69–70; see also "Latin America Cheers Up," *The Economist*, April 18–24, 1992, pp. 11–12.

[14]On the latter role (neglected in some analyses): *Proceso*, August 3, 1992, pp. 24–27.

seeking to featherbed existing production or to encourage new production that lacks market viability. That would be to return to irrational economic interventionism. Indeed, from a strict neoclassical point of view, the state should play little or no role in bolstering production: the provision of materials, credit, markets, etc., should follow the genius of the market (a genius which the current administration reveres in most areas of economic activity). At best, therefore, and assuming that Solidarity remains true to its broad remit, it cannot play a major role in aiding, say, small producers; the future of the privatized ejido lies in association with private capital (the Vaquerías/Gamesa association being the locus classicus); artisan producers must look to the market, not to Solidarity and the state, for their livelihood. That does not prevent Solidarity from playing an occasionally useful role, but it is a role which must, if its rationale is to remain intact, be limited and ancillary to the market.

Thus, for better or worse, Solidarity cannot affect the broad pattern of economic change. It does not propose a substantial hike in the minimum wage, the benchmark of well-being cited by the man in the street. If, with the (probable) advent of the North American Free Trade Agreement, Mexican corn farmers go to the wall, Solidarity cannot rescue them. It lacks both the resources and the rationale. Without some drastic change in character, it won't become a Mexican Common Agricultural Policy. Equally, if real wages continue in the doldrums, Solidarity will not revive them. It is more a band-aid than a crutch. Conversely, the major economic changes will be dictated by market forces, fine-tuned by a government of trained economists and *técnicos*. Improvements in popular living standards will depend on the tender mercies of "trickle-down," as has historically been the case in post-1940 Mexico.[15]

If, in the economic realm, Solidarity is by its very nature of limited significance, its sociopolitical role is something else. Most observers, even those disposed to be critical, have been impressed by its growth and the positive reception it seems to have received. Opposition spokes-people—such as Jorge Castañeda and Luis Javier Garrido—pay the program backhanded compliments when they carp at its capacity to get out an increased vote for the PRI.[16] (Note that the criticism comes from the left. In this, as in much else, political lines seem to be drawn between the PRI and its neo-Cardenista opponents; the PAN—and the Church—

---

[15]James Wilkie (1973: 259–61, 280–83) offers a rather rosy image of this process.

[16]Jorge Castañeda, for example, queries the validity of recent PRI gains in Guadalajara, noting that "no hay mucho Pronasol en la capital tapatía" (*Proceso*, September 9, 1991, p. 34); Luis Javier Garrido indicts the use of government funds for party political purposes; for him, PRONASOL "es políticamente populista, patrimonialista y clientelar" (*La Jornada*, August 9, 1991, p. 8). One Cardenista of my acquaintance referred to the program as "fascism."

appear less overtly hostile, perhaps in part because Solidarity smacks of Catholic "solidarism" and good old-fashioned Christian charity [Fernández Santillán 1991: 155–56].) The figures, too, are impressive: 150,000 public works over three years, benefiting "millions of Mexicans";[17] perhaps 70,000 Solidarity Committees established; 400,000 children in receipt of Solidarity scholarships; 500 communities provided with electric power (Dresser 1991). In Michoacán alone, we are told, there are now 10,000 Solidarity Committees, embracing 80 percent of the state's population.[18] The impacts of these programs, we may hypothesize, are out of proportion to their cost, since they come in the wake of some seven lean years, during which government expenditure fell and official concern for the poor ebbed.[19] Thus, we might say, the sociopolitical multiplier effect is enhanced; after a long drought, even a gentle drizzle is welcome. This seems to be borne out by the impressionistic evidence culled from localities. The smallest *municipio* in Michoacán (Aporo, population 4,500) boasts over fifty Solidarity Committees.[20] Juchitán is buried in an "avalanche" of committees (Sánchez 1991: 111). Even prisons have their Solidarity Committees and converts (Hernández Alvarez 1991: 55–58). In the bleak *colonias* of Chalco, Solidarity activists display a convincing enthusiasm for and commitment to the program, and similar reactions have been discerned by other Solidarity-watchers who have done a good deal more watching than I.[21] Of course, these committees are wedded to the program and, to some extent, they are self-selecting. Meetings with Solidarity Committees—conducted with Solidarity officials present—are hardly what Habermas would call "ideal speech situations."[22] Thus it would be rash for a foreigner, engaged on a fleeting visit, to draw overly firm conclusions. However, even if the committees are spinning a line, it is significant that they exist, in considerable numbers, spinning their line with some consistency and apparent enthusiasm.

Indeed, there is a sense in which it is not only impossible, but also unnecessary, to probe the inner motive of either *políticos* or people. Historians now debate the agrarian reform of the postrevolutionary years in similar terms: Was it dictated from above? Were the ardent *agraristas* an unrepresentative minority? Did the state seek to impart

[17] According to Carlos Rojas, director of the program, Puebla (quoted in *Unomasuno*, February 12, 1992, p. 9).

[18] *Proceso*, July 13, 1992, p. 14. Needless to say, Michoacán is the last redoubt of neo-Cardenismo.

[19] However, Ward (1992) argues that, despite this *relative* fall in social expenditure, the "social" budget, in *absolute* terms, roughly doubled between 1970 and 1988 (reflecting, thereby, the huge increase in total government spending).

[20] Personal impressions, Aporo, January 1992.

[21] Jeffrey Bortz, personal communication.

[22] On the applicability of Habermas's "ideal speech situation," see Scott 1991: 38, 115.

reform or enhance its own power? Did the reform promote clientelism as much as social justice? These questions, though undeniably important, are both difficult to answer and, in some senses, secondary to the obvious point: that the agrarian reform built a powerful constituency, linking elements of the state and civil society in a fashion that was crucial for the political economy of modern Mexico. I do not say that Solidarity will do the same (more of that later); but I believe the relationships being forged by Solidarity are politically significant, irrespective of whether the motives of the state (and its "clients") are transparent or murky.

An additional consideration follows. Solidarity can be plausibly seen as the latest in a long line of projects designed to place government and governed in some sort of consensual relationship. At the risk of seeming absurdly antiquarian, let us consider the colony. Under the Hapsburgs, the Catholic church — the friars, later the parochial clergy — mediated between state and society (several of the Bourbons' problems derived from the rupture of that loose social pact).[23] During the nineteenth century, durable forms of mediation failed; the result was hollow constitutions, widespread *caciquismo,* and endemic instability (Guerra 1985: 176–83). One of the great achievements of the Revolution was its manufacture of new forms of mediation, which were entrusted to new intermediaries: caciques, bosses, "link-men," call them what you will (see Joseph and Nugent n.d.). They stood at the crossroads where the claims of an ambitious central state met the concerns of the local community (a community whose political resources and expectations had often been heightened by the experience of the armed revolution). It was their job to integrate "the people," but also, of necessity, to bring certain limited benefits to the people, since without such benefits (land, schools, roads, irrigation) integration would falter. State patronage was essential to the process of "forging a fatherland."

More recently — roughly since the 1960s — the typical reforms of the Revolution have given way to more "modern" programs aimed to alleviate a recalcitrant and entrenched poverty (poverty which the market not only seemed unable to eliminate, but even tended to exacerbate). These recent programs avoided structural reform — such as land distribution — and focused instead on infrastructure, food production, and distribution. They reflected, in part, the rural population's need for inputs other than land per se, and hence the growing campesino concern for better prices, markets, and extension services. Hence the successive programs of the 1960s and 1970s (CONASUPO, PIDER, COPLAMAR, SAM), which are the direct precursors of Solidarity, at least in terms of their goal (the alleviation of poverty), their provisions (education, health services, roads, electricity, fertilizer, credit), and

---

[23] As David Brading neatly put it: the Hapsburgs governed with priests, the Bourbons with soldiers.

even, to a degree, their emphasis on decentralization and cooperative labor.[24] Familiar claims were made: "according to López Portillo, the removal of [social] injustices had nothing to do with paternalism or populism"; COPLAMAR was "a program of social solidarity through communal cooperation which undertook to uproot paternalism by means of communal work for collective benefit" (González Navarro 1985: 309, 315). Familiar criticisms were also voiced: PIDER dispersed its resources, offering "something for everyone"; antipoverty programs did not always benefit the most needy (Grindle 1986: 168; Eckstein 1988: 241–42). I am not competent to measure the comparative scale of these programs in economic terms; but they were ambitious and not, I suspect, radically disproportionate to Solidarity.[25] Thus, as the latter's chief architect observed over ten years ago, "Mexico is no stranger to attempts at development programs in the rural sector" (Salinas de Gortari 1980: 79). It is therefore possible to see Solidarity as another attempt, in a long series, to knit state and civil society together in a consensual and nationalist union, with the revolutionary state deploying patronage—initially land, later ancillary benefits—in order to bolster its legitimacy, avert protest, and conform, at least partially, to its public transcript of patriotism and public responsibility.[26]

Certain considerations flow from this perspective. The most obvious is that the success (or failure) of Solidarity may vary greatly from place to place. Previous federal programs have tended to encounter quite mixed receptions. (Indeed, we could again press the comparison further and consider "national" "programs" of such diversity and antiquity as Franciscan proselytization, Bourbon reformism, and Juarista liberalism.) During the 1920s and 1930s, both agrarian reform and federal education made major inroads in the countryside: some communities—or some groups within some communities—eagerly espoused these new causes; some were recalcitrant and resistant (Knight 1990b). More immediately relevant, recent (pre-Solidarity) antipoverty programs encountered mixed receptions (Salinas de Gortari 1980: chap. 4). And it is not always clear what factors induce participation as against indifference—or hostility. Partisan political programs may be somewhat predictable: some communities possess "radical" traditions which have tended to make them receptive to, first, liberalism, later revolutionary reformism: Juchitán (now an important site of Solidarity activities) would be a classic case. Contrasting communities are known for their Catholicism

---

[24]See González Navarro 1985: 305–41; Grindle 1986: 164–74; Ward 1992. Note also Carlos Rojas's citation of these precedents (1991b: 26), and the extensive list of food programs—some associated with PRONASOL, some not—in *Proceso*, August 3, 1992, p. 27.

[25]Dresser 1991 and A. Craig 1992a offer the fullest discussion of the resources devoted to Solidarity. On the scale of such previous programs, see, for example, González Navarro 1985: 310–12.

[26]I touch on these themes in Knight 1992.

and conservatism (e.g., San José de Gracia). Close neighbors—even individual barrios—may diverge according to these rough criteria. Solidarity, however, strives for political bipartisanship; it seeks to distance itself from the PRI, and it claims to offer benefits neutrally, to *municipios* of every political hue.[27] However, it is likely that solid oppositionist communities (PANista, PDMista, and especially, PRDista) will display a degree of suspicion, which can only be overcome by practical demonstration, by deeds rather than words.[28]

A second obvious criterion of differentiation is the urban/rural divide. Whereas several of the government programs mentioned previously (PIDER, SAM, COPLAMAR) were essentially rural programs, Solidarity straddles city and countryside. It takes upon itself public patronage responsibilities which, in the past, may have been separate. Here some interesting questions arise. On the one hand, top-down mobilization, mediated through "modern" forms of government patronage, have traditionally been more effective in the city than in the countryside. The first mass organization "captured," in clientelist fashion, by the emergent revolutionary state was urban labor (the Battalions, the CROM). Revolutionary ideology encountered a warmer welcome in the cities than the countryside, even though the countryside was the seat of popular insurrection. More recently, the cities have been seen as the source of opposition, and the countryside—especially the most backward regions of rural Mexico—remained the electoral bastion of the PRI.[29] It is necessary, however, to disaggregate these grand generalities. Urban middle class opposition to the ruling party has been historically strong: witness Vasconcelos's challenge in 1929, Almazán's in 1940. The origins of the PANista middle class run deep and antedate the foundation of the PAN itself. More relevant for our purposes is urban *popular* opposition. This would seem to be a more recent phenomenon. As late as the 1970s, the urban poor of Mexico City were well disposed toward the PRI (and the PAN was certainly not an attractive alternative); channels of patronage were well lubricated; and Mexico City received a disproportionate share of government resources (e.g., through the media of the IMSS, ISSSTE, and INFONAVIT).[30] The

[27]Spokesmen, top and bottom, are adamant about this. Solidarity resources "no distinguen el origen político de las autoridades municipales" (Salinas, quoted in *La Jornada*, February 15, 1992, p. 4). See also "Niega Rojas que Pronasol sea un instrumento político, *El Universal*, September 5, 1991. Compare Dresser 1991: 15, to the effect that "the main difference between previous [social] programs and PRONASOL is the latter's explicit [sic] goal of capturing support for the PRI in a context of increased party competitiveness." My chief query concerns the adjective "explicit." With respect to the political targeting of Solidarity resources, see note 40 below.

[28]Personal impressions, Maravatio, Michoacán, January 1992. See also PRONASOL 1991b: 60, 64, 81, 118; Martínez Nateras 1991: 196.

[29]See Guillén López 1989, and, for an excellent general study of electoral trends, Molinar Horcasitas 1991.

[30]Ward 1990: 26, 156–63. On the politics of the migrant poor, see Cornelius 1975, a study which heavily influenced Salinas's own research and writings.

1980s witnessed a substantial erosion of this popular support, brought on by obvious factors: sharply declining real income, a deteriorating environment, the 1985 earthquakes and their aftermath.[31] The collapse of the PRI's support in the Federal District became evident in the rise of (apolitical or oppositionist) social movements and, even more dramatically, in the electoral drubbing Salinas received from Cuauhtémoc Cárdenas in 1988 (Martínez Nateras 1991: 194). Given the historic oppositionism of the urban middle class, especially in Mexico City, this was an alarming phenomenon (for the PRI). Solidarity, we may presume, is a crucial weapon in the PRI's battle to restore its credibility, to retake "the high ground" of Mexico City.[32] In particular, Solidarity seeks to win back those urban popular sectors who voted PRI in the 1970s and who deserted en masse in the 1980s. The president, we know, has an unusual expertise in this area; Solidarity, in a sense, was born in Chalco, where recent presidential interventions have been striking and, it would seem, successful.[33]

Outside the Federal District, however, Solidarity's urban strategy is less apparent.[34] Furthermore, some experts have raised doubts concerning the urban feasibility of a strategy that stresses communal self-help and local activism, qualities which are presumed to be more evident in smaller rural communities than in large metropolises populated by migrants.[35] This raises familiar—but knotty—sociological problems for which I lack any real expertise. However, I am skeptical about theories that postulate the pervasive anomie of the city of the *gemeinschaftlich* solidarity of the village; and I am impressed by evidence of self-help and activism among the urban poor, even recent migrants. True, self-help programs may, in the urban context, face particular problems: the prolonged absence of men, for example,[36] or the need to promote cooperation among migrants of diverse backgrounds. While Solidarity may therefore find it easier to operate in smaller, rural communities, possessing traditions of self-help and collective work ("la tradición

---

[31] The social and political effect of the 1985 Mexico City earthquakes probably afforded an important stimulus to the birth of Solidarity (Eckstein 1988: 267–69; C. Hernández 1991: 91).

[32] Ward 1989. However, the regent of the Federal District, Manuel Camacho Solís, engaged in a separate campaign to refurbish the PRI—and to advance his own presidential aspirations—does not appear to be the most ardent admirer of Solidarity; see note 44 below.

[33] Personal impressions, Chalco, January 1992.

[34] There is an element of tautology here, of course: greater Mexico City houses something like a third of Mexico's urban population. Dresser (1991: 17) argues that certain PRONASOL activities, such as the *tortivale* program, have been "directed mainly toward urban areas—particularly the Federal District."

[35] Jeffrey Bortz, personal communication. Aguilar Villanueva (1991: 128–29) offers a thoroughly Durkheimian analysis (and rather mixes up Marx); Martínez Nateras (1991: 193), in what is otherwise a cogent essay, asserts that "los pueblos indios . . . simplemente practican la solidaridad como hábito y modo de ser."

[36] Personal impression, Chalco, January 1992.

histórica de realizar faena"),[37] it seems quite capable of functioning effectively in the teeming metropolis too. It was in Mexico City, after all, that the campaign of the *damnificados* proved so politically effective (Eckstein 1988: 225, 233, 265).

I now turn to the macropolitical effects of the program. An important question, to which answers are scant, concerns the personnel of the program. Who runs Solidarity? No Rod Camp or Peter Smith has (to my knowledge) attempted a prosopography of PRONASOL. My subjective impressions are as follows. First, the program is seen as emanating from the presidency and from the (now defunct) Ministry of Budget and Planning (SPP), the ministry which Salinas headed prior to his election as president. Hence the allegations (to which I will turn in a moment) that Solidarity is an instrument of presidential power. As regards the officials charged with running the program, they do not appear to be party hacks. On the basis of a brief acquaintance, I saw little that was—in Enrique Krause's inelegant phrase—Prinosaurian about them. They seemed to be young, enthusiastic, and of diverse backgrounds. Some, it appears, had emerged from quite heterodox political backgrounds: they had links to the "new social movements" of the 1980s; they had held "apolitical" posts in the parastatal and government bureaucracies; they were even associated with radical political groups. They attest to President Salinas's apparent desire and ability to collaborate with (critics might say co-opt) popular groups and leaders who are beyond the pale of the PRI: independent labor and peasant leaders, for example.[38] Again, this would seem to reflect long-term cogitation, as well as short-term calculation (Salinas de Gortari 1980). At the grassroots, meanwhile, Solidarity implies the growth of new leadership, particularly in recently formed communities that have sprung up with the headlong urbanization of recent decades. Hence the *comités de vecinos* in places like Chalco present themselves as new creations, the direct offspring of the Solidarity program, and the first challenge not only to material squalor, but also to the social anomie of such infant *colonias*. Here, furthermore, women play a major role and, judging by subjective impressions, are the chief grassroots protagonists of the program (Cardosa 1991: 45; C. Rojas 1991b: 52–53). In contrast, the *comités de vecinos* of more established rural communities (e.g., Aporo, Michoacán) have a more "traditional" appearance. It may be, therefore, that the Chalco-style Solidarity has more in common with the "new social movements" of the 1980s (characterized by the involvement of political neophytes, especially women, while the Aporo-style Solidarity follows older traditions of municipal organization (in which men and municipal officials figure more prominently).

---

[37] Words of the *alcaldesa* of Honey, Puebla, quoted in *La Jornada*, February 15, 1992, p. 4.

[38] On Salinas's readiness to establish a dialogue with independent trade union leaders, see Barry 1992: 188.

Either way, the question arises of the durability of the phenomenon. Analysts of Mexico repeatedly point to the co-option of grassroots movements by the state and PRI. Some historical examples suggest, if not an iron law of oligarchy, at least a plastic tendency toward *caciquismo*, whereby the fresh, spontaneous popular movement of today becomes the institutionalized machine of tomorrow.[39] In other words, the Mexican political system has shown a remarkable capacity to absorb, co-opt, and control popular challenges to the status quo. Perhaps Solidarity represents no challenge to the status quo, in which case the claims of its boosters ring somewhat hollow. Perhaps it does offer a genuine means to alleviate poverty, empower the people, and circumvent the arthritic structures of power, in which case it will challenge certain vested interests and run the risk of collision and/or co-option.

This raises an important related question, which may be phrased simply as: Cui bono? Who benefits? Obviously, local communities, children, women, small producers, and other needy groups benefit, to the extent that the program meets its stated goals. But who gets the political credit? The criticisms of the opposition—especially the left—indicate that the program has a political payoff. The electoral role of Solidarity has been highlighted, particularly in contentious states such as Durango, Zacatecas, and, above all, Michoacán.[40] But it would be wrong to see the program as a simple device to boost the fortunes of the PRI: first, because the PRI itself displays a certain ambivalence toward Solidarity; and second, because the very process of "buying off" the opposition can have the perverse effect of rewarding dissent. At best, a politically successful Solidarity will indirectly benefit the PRI by legitimizing the system as a whole, including both the official party and the "presidentialist" executive that goes with it. But it seems likely that it is the president—and therefore "presidentialism"—that gain most credit from Solidarity. The program is (rightly) seen as Salinas's brainchild,[41] an impression which

[39] Proof of the onset of academic middle age, I am now quoting myself: Knight 1990a: 100.

[40] For leftist critiques, see note 16 above. For allegations of PRONASOL politicking, see *Proceso*, July 13, 1992, p. 14 (Michoacán); August 10, 1992, p. 14 (Durango); August 31, 1992, pp. 30, 32 (Michoacán, Zacatecas). By the same token, of course, it is clear that known opposition regions (such as Michoacán) and communities (such as Juchitán) have received ample PRONASOL resources; and opposition movements, such as COCEI, have been prepared to collaborate with Solidarity (see *Cuadernos de Nexos* 48 [June 1992]: xiv). If the "political" role of Solidarity was confined to rewarding PRIístas and denying their opponents, the partisanship would be blatant. As it is, the chief complaint seems to be that PRONASOL targets centers of dissidence, seeking to co-opt or defuse them. Hence the partisanship is more subtle, and the ambivalence of certain PRI elements toward Solidarity more comprehensible.

[41] The *Wall Street Journal*, August 6, 1991, quoted in *La Jornada*, August 7, 1991, calls Solidarity "el rasgo más característico de la política interna del Presidente de México." Compare Ward (1992) who cites Gustavo Verduzco to the effect that Solidarity's "genesis was not national but was required by the IMF to accompany the restructuring process," a view which, though intriguing, seems to credit the IMF with too much sensitivity and Salinas with too little ingenuity.

the president's lavish commitment of time and attention emphasizes. To critics, Solidarity is yet another manifestation of arbitrary presidential power: when he is not arresting labor leaders or deposing elected governors, the president is distributing patronage to the people according to the old principles of revolutionary populism.[42] And the critics are not solely among the opposition. As a prominent PRIísta put it, in an unusual (and unwitting) declaration: with his espousal of Solidarity, the president "has engaged in disloyal competition with political parties" (Jorge Alberto Lozoya, quoted in *Proceso*, September 9, 1991, p. 28).

How widespread are such sentiments? We know that the PRI, for all its outward displays of discipline, is a heterogeneous organization, embodying numerous different "currents," stances, and generations (the *político/técnico* dichotomy being one of the most obvious). Indeed, the PRI's varied makeup and national representativity form the basis of its claim to rule. By the same token, however, the PRI has to accommodate a range of political actors, including some still-powerful provincial elites who are historically leery of centralized power, and who are reluctant to relinquish power at the behest of a reformist "center." That ancient tradition—whereby the refractory provinces obstruct centralized reform— was recently evident in the failure of de la Madrid's electoral *apertura*. Yet more recently, concessions made to the opposition—in Yucatán or Guanajuato—have alienated local PRIístas.[43] How do the latter react to Solidarity—a program which on the one hand promises grassroots mobilization (a risky business), and on the other emanates from Mexico City and the presidency? How, for example, do state governors regard this powerful engine of patronage? Some are singled out for particular praise as enthusiastic collaborators with Solidarity—Governor Ignacio Pichardo Pagaza of the state of México, for example. By implication, some other governors—Heladio Ramírez of Oaxaca, for example—are less than enthusiastic (a fact which is hinted at, but which, to my very limited knowledge, is not much discussed).[44] Certainly it would fit the historical pattern if local and state power holders, while obliged to collaborate with the center to some degree, also took steps to appropriate federal programs where they might prove politically advantageous, or to stymie them where they might prove politically threatening. Such was the history of labor organization, agrarian reform, and *indigenismo* through the 1920s and 1930s; and while the federal programs may have changed, the rationale underlying this center-provincial dialectic has not. During the 1980s, when "decentralization" entered the political agenda, state governors proved able to hijack resources supposedly destined to the *munici-*

---

[42]Dresser 1991; and note the words of Garrido, note 16 above.

[43]On Guanajuato, see *Proceso*, August 10, 1992, p. 17.

[44]Dresser 1991. On Oaxaca, see *Cuadernos de Nexos* 48 (June 1992): xi. It may be worth noting, too, that in the long interview given by Manuel Camacho in *Proceso* 31 (August 1992): 6–13, there is not a single mention of PRONASOL.

pios (Ward 1990: 27). From another perspective, employment as well as power is at stake. If Solidarity creates a new network of political agents—and, by fulfilling its promises of popular empowerment, renders existing agents superfluous—there will be bureaucratic resentment too. Thus, given that the PRI is, according to its leaders, already undergoing a process of internal reform, designed to cope with and accelerate the erosion of traditional corporate structures, there is scope for considerable friction within the party and the system as a whole. "In a corrupted age," as Lord Halifax put it, "the putting the world in order would breed confusion" (Kenyon 1969: 231).

The same interrogative, cui bono?, also raises an important question concerning the durability of Solidarity. We have noted that there were important precursors of Solidarity—PIDER, COPLAMAR, CONASUPO, SAM, the Plan Puebla (to name but the most recent and most closely related ancestors). Some remain, some have disappeared from the scene. Certainly their periods of florescence have been quite brief, and linked to the inexorable cycle of presidential politics. Solidarity is clearly here—a commanding presence—for the rest of this *sexenio*, but its future thereafter must remain uncertain (and, to some extent, at the mercy of the succession). To the extent that it is Salinas's brainchild and project, will it retain its vitality beyond 1994? (Fidel Velázquez and others may declare President Salinas worthy of re-election, but I work on the assumption that this, as they say, is a null hypothesis.[45]) Would a new president be willing and able to promote Solidarity? Can we imagine Pedro Aspe touring the countryside and pressing peasant flesh with the apparent success and enthusiasm of Carlos Salinas de Gortari? (True, Salinas was seen as a desiccated *técnico* prior to 1988; but in light of what he researched and wrote in the late 1970s and what he has done since the late 1980s, we can now see that this was a flawed judgment, an example of the office—SPP—appearing to make the man.) Recall that Cárdenas's peripatetic presidential style was not copied by his successors. Thus, given the close identification of Salinas with the program—and the tendency for programs of this kind to experience cyclical booms and slumps—it may be rash to assume that Solidarity is here to stay, especially if it is, in essence, an "emergency" program, designed to cope with a passing crisis (Sabines 1991: 12). Furthermore, if it does endure, under the ample umbrella of the new Ministry of Social Development (SEDESOL), we may expect the risks of ossification and

---

[45]*Proceso*, August 31, 1992, pp. 16, 17. I also discount, rightly or wrongly, the rumors—current in 1991 and still occasionally heard—that Salinas may encourage the formation of a new "Partido de Solidaridad," designed to replace, or even contend with, the PRI in the 1994 presidential election. The PRI may have its saurian qualities, but it is still a useful workhorse. Furthermore, it is hard to conceive of any paterfamilias of the "revolutionary family," however bold and iconoclastic, risking the stability of decades by pursuing such a risky strategy. No doubt the PRI will, one day, fall from power, but it seems less likely that it will jump than that it will be pushed.

bureaucratization to grow with time. In the past, bold programs of reform have often given way to hollow rhetoric and dull routinization: compare the agrarian reform of the 1930s with that of the post-Second World War; the radical CTM of the 1930s with the emasculated post-*charrazo* confederation of the 1950s. Perhaps the best guarantee of continued vitality is genuine popular engagement. It is not coincidence that, in areas where the agrarian reform responded to strong local mobilizations (e.g., the Laguna) (Martínez Saldaña 1980), the movement and the reform endured, even through hard times. And even where *caciquismo* flourished, some of the caciques enjoyed a genuine popular base. Thus, ossification and bureaucratization were periodically countered by renewed mobilization, of which the state had to take note.

Can Solidarity lay down such enduring popular foundations? Can Solidarity programs and committees achieve a vitality that transcends sexenial cycles and sustains the ethos of self-help, empowerment, and mobilization—perhaps in the teeth of official neglect, even hostility? This would seem to be doubtful. First, because Solidarity, for all its philosophy of empowerment and *concertación*, is clearly a central government initiative. A major shift in central government policy could prove fatal. Second, because in the main, Solidarity involves the distribution of patronage, not the structural reform of society, in which respect it emulates the moderate antipoverty programs of the 1960s and 1970s, such as CONASUPO and PIDER.[46] Here a comparison with the revolutionary agrarian reform is perhaps pertinent. The agrarian reform responded to powerful popular demands (I shall pass over the revisionist argument that posits a top-down, manipulative reform); it was, to some degree, forced upon a reluctant (Carrancista/Sonora) regime by popular efforts; and its triumph involved structural change— the breakup of the hacienda, the creation of the ejido. Those who had struggled felt vindicated; and the ejido—for all its faults—represented the triumph of their struggle. Leaders who had espoused the cause— presidents like Cárdenas, governors like Cedillo, Tejeda, or Carrillo Puerto—acquired cachet and legitimacy (among the *agrarista* constituency, of course; plenty of landlords—and others—execrated these reformers; however, one advantage of the reform was that it substantially weakened these hostile groups, while "empowering" its supporters). Above all, the agrarian reform was the result of prolonged and collective struggle; borrowing a phrase from the Guatemalan lexicon, it was, we might say, the "most precious fruit of the revolution."[47]

---

[46] Jonathan Fox and Gustavo Gordillo (1989: 141, note 27) note that CONASUPO, PIDER, and such reforms "did not produce systematic or rapid changes in the rural balance of power." Grindle (1986: 173) concurs that PIDER and similar programs "did not entail touchy questions such as the structure of landownership or the distribution of water resources." The Cardenista reforms of the 1930s were very different in this respect.

[47] Handy (1988) quoting Jacobo Arbenz (1953).

It is not clear that Solidarity can achieve that same mythic status. The distribution of material rewards per se should not be disdained: roads, drains, warehouses, and clinics are positive benefits which tend to translate into political support (though recall Salinas's own caveat in this context) (Salinas de Gortari 1980). Pursuing the historical analogy, we can see that material patronage helped cement the popularity of presidents like Cárdenas. Presidential *giras*—whether in the 1930s or the 1990s—are also effective devices to forge legitimacy. Ironically, therefore, Salinas appears to have taken several stratagems from the Cardenista playbook (hence, perhaps, the ire of some neo-Cardenista critics): accounts of Salinas, his bodyguards banished from sight, walking arm-in-arm with appreciative campesinos down unpaved streets, are uncannily reminiscent of stories concerning Lázaro Cárdenas's celebrated itineraries.[48] But the Cardenista reforms also involved a good deal of struggle, contestation, and structural change. Peasants fought landlords (and other peasants); workers battled bosses, including foreign bosses. This was the stuff that myths are made of: it was a collective struggle, complete with victories and defeats, heroes, villains, and martyrs. Renan's famous definition of the roots of nationalism—*avoir fait de grandes choses ensemble, vouloir en faire encore* ("having done great things together, and wanting to do them again")—could equally well apply to the formation of political as of national allegiances. Enduring allegiances of both kinds are, perhaps, the product of hard-won battles, rather than the easy pickings of patronage. Public works may win votes in the short term, but they may not lay down the foundations of an enduring legitimacy.

What is more, the structural reforms of the 1930s left an enduring legacy. The ejido, and often the rural school, were monuments to Cardenismo. With Cárdenas's departure from (presidential) office, the closest link was broken; but Cárdenas, by virtue of his continued, though not uncritical, support for the regime, ensured that the credit he had accumulated could be drawn on by the PRI and by subsequent presidents—even by those who set out to reverse much of Cárdenas's work. By analogy, we may hypothesize that Solidarity will certainly rally support in some regions and communities, especially where the program can tap genuine popular commitment and, by overcoming daunting obstacles, engender a sense of accomplishment and—yes—solidarity.[49] It may thus acquire sufficient momentum to carry it through the next *sexenio*, when a new president may well choose to give a lower priority to his predecessor's pet program, in order to better boost his own. (Here, of course, we enter the treacherous terrain of the presidential succession; we may at least speculate that a President Colosio would be more keen to promote Solidarity than, perhaps, a President Aspe, or even a President

---

[48]Personal anecdotes, Michoacán, January 1992. See also Martínez Nateras 1991: 199; Juárez Quezada 1991: 204–05.

Camacho.) Either way, in the absence of struggle, polarization, and victory, it is hard to see Solidarity achieving the mythic status of the agrarian reform.[50] It will likely go down in history as the latest in a long line of projects—some grand, some modest—that sought to alleviate the plight of the poor, to burnish the regime's tainted image, and to strengthen the fraying bonds that tie rulers to ruled, state to civil society.[51] The periodic repair of those bonds has been one of the great tasks and accomplishments of the regime born of the Mexican Revolution. Thus—to change the metaphor—as "revolutionary" regimes elsewhere in the world have foundered, Mexico's has remained afloat, buffeted by storms but still apparently seaworthy. Solidarity, for all its genuine (and rhetorical) novelty, draws upon old traditions. It does not presage a radical new departure, a taking to the boats, a desertion of the sinking PRIísta/presidential system. Rather, in its many forms, it represents a new set of outriggers, designed to stabilize the ship, and to see it through the squally waters of economic liberalization into the safety of a still distant harbor.

---

[49]This may be particularly true when and where Solidarity—and Salinas—facilitate the ratification of contested land titles, thus associating themselves with the reinforcement of community livelihood and identity. In the predominantly urban Mexico of today, this process may be the closest to the ejidal grants of more "revolutionary" days. Indeed, the administration may now be gambling that it can forfeit the support of a dwindling ejidal sector—even to the extent of winding up the ejido—so long as it can build countervailing constituencies in the burgeoning cities.

[50]It is also my (very subjective) impression that, following the hype and publicity of 1990–91, Solidarity has been pushed off the front page (where it has been replaced by NAFTA, textbooks, and the presidential succession). That may be entirely healthy so far as basic social programs are concerned, but it also suggests that, especially now that it is integrated within a new ministry, PRONASOL is going the way of previously acclaimed national projects—toward greater anonymity and routinization.

[51]"Solidaridad como programa, visto a casi tres años de su constitución, ha servido como útil y eficiente medio para facilitar la gobernabilidad" (Martínez Nateras 1991: 202). Ward (1992) similarly sees PRONASOL as a "key element in statecraft and of 'papering over the cracks' of social inequality."

3

Social Welfare Policy and Political Opening in Mexico

Peter M. Ward

SOCIAL WELFARE AND POLITICAL CHANGE

In this chapter I wish to provide an overview of the changing priorities that successive Mexican governments have accorded the social development sector since the administration of President Echeverría (1970–76). This will be set against a backcloth of political reform and an opening of the political space in which non-PRI parties have been allowed to function, albeit under certain constraints. In addition I will examine important changes that have been undertaken both in the nature of social policies themselves and in the patterns and efficiency with which public agencies have delivered this particular social good. I argue that in Mexico, as in many advanced capitalist countries since Bismarck's Prussia during the late nineteenth century, social welfare provision is an important element in the understanding of political management and "statecraft" (Midgley 1984; Malloy 1985; Bailey 1988). As well as providing a temporary palliative to offset some of the negative outcomes of rapid urbanization and accumulation regimes predicated on low incomes and/or slow growth, social policy provides an arena through which scarce societal resources may be negotiated. As I will describe, those patterns of negotiation change for a variety of reasons: as power relations shift; as economies reflate or turn into recession; as the level of state intervention and control intensifies or slackens; as our diagnosis of

The comments from the following colleagues on an earlier version of this chapter are warmly acknowledged: Drs. Agustín Escobar-Latapí, Peter Cleaves, Henry Selby, and Victoria Rodríguez. Of course, they are not responsible for the views or any errors that remain. The findings of this chapter were first presented to the Sociedad Urbana Encuentro Internacional in Monterrey, Mexico, May 1992.

specific problems and the policy instruments we develop become more sophisticated and sensitive to local needs; and last but not least in the context of Mexico, as changes arise from human agency as different presidents take executive office.

Analyzing social policy is a complex business. If one examines different patterns of social welfare expenditure throughout Central and South America, no obvious conclusions can be drawn (Ward 1986). According to World Bank statistics, during the early 1980s formerly repressive regimes such as Uruguay and Chile appeared to spend an equally high proportion on social welfare as did liberal democracies such as Costa Rica (around 60 percent of total central government expenditure). Relatively poor nations and richer ones often expended similar proportions on social welfare (e.g., Bolivia compared with Venezuela, both allocating to social expenditure around one-third of total central investment in the early 1980s) (see Ward 1986; Mesa-Lago 1992). However, it does appear that economic recession leads to cuts being made in social welfare expenditure, and that this occurs, therefore, precisely when needs of the poorer groups are likely to rise.[1] Nine of the twelve Latin American countries for which comparative data are available for 1981–86 experienced a relative decline in social welfare expenditure— and sometimes show a very sharp fall. Measured in per capita terms, real public expenditure on social programs declined in eight of the nine countries included in a recent United Nations Economic Commission for Latin America study (CEPAL 1992: table IV-7). But these data tell us little about the nature of provision in each country, and it is necessary to delve below the surface in order to examine the exact nature of these expenditures. To interpret as welfare investments road construction which links military establishments or those that facilitate fast response and access to volatile neighborhoods is perverse, to say the least, but such expenditures would often be included under "social development" appropriations (Ball 1984).

Moreover, many of these countries have experienced an unprecedented political opening (*apertura política*) during the 1980s. Social welfare is no longer a poverty alleviation program designed to offset the effects of neoliberal economic policies, nor those of so-called bureaucratic authoritarian regimes. Rather it is an arena of competition between political parties vying for power within a genuinely pluralistic system. Mexico, too, has experienced a major political opening since the 1970s. The evolution of that broad process and its rationale are well known and widely documented and will not be repeated here (see Molinar Horcasitas 1991; Alvarado Mendoza 1987; Cornelius et al. 1989a). In short, we observe during the 1970s an easing of restrictions on opposition parties

---

[1]Tamburi 1985 correctly argues that there seems little chance that Latin American countries will move toward income support programs for those out of work or for the very needy. It would impose too heavy a burden on the treasury departments.

that were allowed to exist (particularly those of the left) and their participation within Congress on a partial proportional representation basis. This accompanied a period of growing state intervention in all areas of economic, social, and political activity, but the rationale for creating greater pluralism within the Mexican political system was primarily one of legitimizing and sustaining the continued dominance of the PRI if not its total hegemony and monopoly (Ward 1986; Molinar Horcasitas 1991).

Later, during the early/mid-1980s there was a quickening in support for the political right, resulting in a number of important victories (largely but not exclusively for the PAN) in municipal elections. This occurred after the boom-to-bust period of petroleum-led expansion of President López Portillo. This expansion based on petroleum income failed so badly that it left the country virtually bankrupt in 1982, about to enter a deep recession, and with its banks nationalized in a last-ditch measure by the executive to control capital flight and save face (Whitehead 1980; Teichman 1988). Finally, as a result of President de la Madrid's austerity program, which was sustained throughout the *sexenio*, the PRI began to lose support from among its traditional working-class following, hard hit by sharply declining real wages and by slow or negative growth rates (Lustig 1992). Internal divisions within the PRI, together with concern over the candidacy for the presidential succession in 1988, led to the breakaway of several senior and experienced PRIístas who mounted a severe challenge to President Salinas in the 1988 elections. Since 1988 genuine interparty competition has emerged between the PRI and the National Action Party (PAN), and the newly created Party of the Democratic Revolution (PRD). These two opposition parties have begun to seriously contest the hegemony of the PRI—although it is probably fair to note that the opposition parties (particularly those on the left) have not mounted the challenge that many people expected after 1988. Since that time the PRI has been reasonably successful in winning back much of the electoral high ground, most notably from the PRD.[2] The PAN, on the other hand, has been successful in winning two state governorships outright (Baja California Norte in 1989 and Chihuahua in 1992), and it also governs Guanajuato through an "interim" governor (Rodríguez and Ward 1992).

But when in 1988 President Salinas announced the end of the one-party system in Mexico, he was not simply referring to its political structure but to the whole governmental *system*. Resources for social welfare provision, social policies, and programs are now beginning to

---

[2]There are many possible (and interconnected) reasons for the PRI's success in the 1991 midterm elections which emphasize the internal reform and restructuring undertaken by the party itself: the admiration and respect Salinas has won both at home and abroad; the disorganization within and among the opposition parties; and, of most concern for this paper, effective targeting of social welfare benefits and resources.

form part of the party-political agenda, and not just that of executive policy. Under conditions of *apertura política*, the central question that emerges is, what sort of *rationality* will govern the construction of those programs and the disbursement of those resources? How far will both be subject to partisan political criteria as different parties use—or abuse— social welfare provision as a mechanism to "win votes and influence people," if I may borrow from Dale Carnegie's classic text?[3]

DEFINITIONS AND FUNCTIONS OF SOCIAL WELFARE PROVISION

The term social welfare, or social development sector as it is usually called, embraces a wide range of activities: education, health, work, housing, human settlements, public works, etc. (see table 3.1). According to O'Connor (1973), state expenditure must seek to satisfy the functions of both accumulation and legitimation. He identifies what he calls social capital expenditures that raise the rate of profit (e.g., investments that raise labor productivity, provide sources of energy, improve infrastructure, etc.), together with social consumption expenditures that are indirectly beneficial to capital accumulation insofar as they help to reduce the costs of reproduction of the labor force—i.e., the provision of "social interest" housing, adopting self-help policies that cheapen the costs of housing within society, providing some health care in order to minimize labor force "wastage" through premature death or illness, etc. Much social welfare provision comes under this guise, but Mexico is not particularly different in this respect to most other societies.

There is another set of state functions, also identified by O'Connor, that are concerned with legitimation—what he terms social expense expenditures, and which are not even indirectly "productive." These might include campaigns aimed at tree planting, vaccinations, and delousing; the regularization of "clouded" land titles; community cleanup campaigns; community cultural events (such as the "*carpas*" in Mexico); or sending the water lorry, or *pipa*, to provide poor households with water, etc. These are lightweight and superficial activities ("bread-and-festivals") the state promotes in order to sustain its legitimation functions, pacify the work force, and obscure ideological bases for class or cultural solidarity. However, the point here is not to debate which of these types of expenditure most represent the Mexican case at different points in time. Rather, my purpose in referring to O'Connor's early work is to demonstrate that this is a legitimate function, in which all states

---

[3]Entitled *How to Win Friends and Influence People*. Partisan political rationality takes account of who (individual or group) is trying to influence an outcome rather than basing that judgment on the technical merits of the case according to criteria that are laid down and expected to guide public administration. See Gilbert and Ward (1985: 149) for a more detailed discussion of political versus technical rationalities in public administration in Mexico. Also, see Rodríguez and Ward 1993 for an analysis of partisanship under PANista municipal governments during the 1980s.

TABLE 3.1

FEDERAL PUBLIC SPENDING IN SELECTED SECTORS,
INCLUDING "SOCIAL DEVELOPMENT," 1972–88

Year	GNP in Constant 1980 Pesos (billions)	Debt Service	Adminis- tration[a]	Social Develop- ment[b]	Energy	Industry	% of GNP for "Social Develop- ment"
1972	2,637	—	20	23	28	6	6
1974	3,034	—	19	23	24	9	7
1976	3,232	—	24	25	23	7	9
1978	3,617	30	6	19	18	4	8
1980	4,276	26	5	17	19	5	7
1982	4,592	41	3	15	14	4	8
1984	4,509	40	4	12	9	7	6
1986	4,460	53	3	11	11	5	6
1988[c]	—	55	3	10	10	5	—

[a]After 1978, the public debt was no longer included under the heading of "Administration."
[b]Between 1972 and 1976, social development included education, health, social security, and employee benefits. From 1976 to 1984, employee benefits were excluded, but human settlements and public works were included.
[c]Amount designated in the budget.

Sources: GNP figures calculated by the author from IMF, *International Financial Statistics*, various volumes; José López Portillo, *VI Informe, anexo I* (1982), for 1972; Miguel de la Madrid, *Segundo Informe de Gobierno, anexo política económica* (1984) and *Sexto Informe de Gobierno, anexo política económica* (1988), for 1974 through 1988.

appear to engage, and that the arena of social welfare provision is the dominant dimension through which most people in Mexico today experience Harold Lasswell's classic definition of politics as "Who gets what, when, how."[4] Social development, therefore, forms part and parcel of the cannon fodder of politics and political mediation.

SOCIAL WELFARE PROVISION: A DECLINING PRIORITY?

But are we talking about a political commitment to social *development* in Mexican society, or are we talking about the state indulging in *palliatives*? To anticipate my conclusion we are talking about both. During the past two decades in Mexico, the political commitment toward social welfare has intensified, not because of any altruistic desire on the part of successive governments, but because it has been politically expedient to

[4]Lasswell's (1958) analysis focuses on the allocation of resources that are scarce, not in the sense that these are in short absolute supply, but that such resources are not "unlimited," and once allocated there is no guarantee that they will be renewed or replaced.

do so. Fundamental reforms that would seek to go beyond "papering over the cracks" have not been embarked upon—neither in times of expansion (1972–74, 1978–81, 1990–93) nor during periods of austerity and recession (1976–77, 1982–89). Thus, the commitment has intensified only insofar as it has sought to achieve more effective policies, more efficient implementation, and wider coverage; i.e., to get "more bang for the buck." As we shall observe shortly, there are two ways in which more "bang" may be achieved, but first we need to analyze the changing priority accorded social welfare provision since 1970 as measured by its relative level of funding.

In terms of the social development sector's relative importance within total federal expenditure, there has been a major decline between the early 1970s to the mid-1980s (from 23 percent in 1974 to around one-half of that figure; see table 3.1). Preliminary figures that I obtained for 1988, which suggest a further decline in social expenditure, are corroborated by the work of other authors (see, for example, Cortés and Rubalcava 1992).[5] Data from CEPAL suggest a 30 percent fall in real per capita expenditure on social programs for 1986–88 over the 1971–81 base levels (CEPAL 1992). But there is a strong suggestion that President Salinas is restoring the commitment to social welfare expenditure (see note 5); perhaps more accurately stated, while he is "rolling back" state involvement in other sectors, he is sustaining (and therefore increasing relatively) the commitment to social development. To summarize my argument, the social development sector lost ground systematically during the late 1970s and throughout the 1980s, although its importance may have been restored somewhat since 1990. In part, of course, this decline was due to the sharply rising proportion of expenditure on the debt (see table 3.1) which drew resources away from all sectors.

THE IMPROVING EFFICACY OF SOCIAL WELFARE PROVISION

The first way in which social welfare provision actually managed to improve during this period is through a real increase in resources. It is not axiomatic that this declining share meant a decline in resources; far

---

[5] I should point out that some statistics indicate a sharply rising curve in which social development occupied the following proportion of total spending: 14.9, 17.9, 21.8, and 26.5 percent, respectively, during each of the years from 1988 to 1991 (Dresser 1991: 6; see also Mesa-Lago 1992). The differences between Dresser's and my data (see 1988, for example) arise because in the presidential *informes* from 1987 onward, debt repayments were no longer included within the total expenditure. Calculations for sectoral expenditures, therefore, appeared to rise dramatically—in the case of *desarrollo social*, for example, an apparent doubling. My data in table 3.1 *include* debt repayment expenditure; this was done to sustain the comparative analysis back through the 1970s. The same discrepancy occurs in Lustig's analysis (1992: 79), where she notes a recovery in social welfare provision from 1985 onward and a sharp upturn in 1989 and 1990, which, she argues, is coupled to Salinas's commitment to improve social conditions. Certainly whatever base level one uses, there does appear to have been a rise in the share accorded social development (including, as it does, PRONASOL) since 1989.

from it. In real terms (i.e., constant pesos), total federal expenditure increased fivefold between 1970 and 1982. Although its share of the total diminished, expenditure on social development *tripled* in real terms during the same period. Thus very substantial (and rising) resources continued to be allocated to social welfare. Despite President de la Madrid's insistence that social expenditure remained an important priority within his *"programa de emergencia"* (in order to offset some of the social costs of austerity), the facts suggest the opposite: it continued to lose ground. Even so, in real terms the sector enjoyed double the funding level in 1988 compared with 1970. Graphs by Cortés and Rubalcava (1992: 8) show the real per capita federal expenditure for social development 1980–89, and indicate a rise in 1980–82, a sharp decline in 1983, and a low, rather "flat" profile until 1989, when their data end. Corresponding curves for the public debt show a massive upward trend throughout the period, with the exception of 1982–85, when payments were being rescheduled. All "other" expenditures have declined steadily since 1981 (with the exception of 1988). I conclude that during the 1980s social development was to an important extent "protected" from decisions to reduce public-sector expenditure, and certainly it did not suffer the same level of cuts imposed on other sectors. But this is not indicative of political commitment to develop the sector; rather it reflects a *residual* approach to maintain the functions of the sector in order to provide a palliative to austerity measures and to restructuring.

A second way in which I would describe an improvement in social welfare provision is in the effectiveness of delivery of individual programs, together with improvements in the nature of the policies themselves. In the past decade many agencies and departments with responsibilities for a wide variety of dimensions of social welfare provision have improved their administration of policies and programs. The level of "loss" of scarce resources through corruption, administrative ineptitude, political or personal nepotism, and appointment of non-workers (so called *"aviadores"* who "fly-in" every fortnight to collect their paychecks), and so on have been substantially reduced, especially since 1983.[6] Space does not permit a discussion or an exemplification of this streamlining of administrative and governmental authority, but important initiatives include López Portillo's Administrative Reform (1977) and de la Madrid's anticorruption and antinepotism campaign, his reform of Article 115 giving greater administrative power and autonomy to the *municipio*, and his attempts at decentralizing certain areas of public administration (especially health care). Moreover, the rising influence and presence of *técnicos* within public administration have raised the

---

[6]It is also proving to be a principal mechanism whereby non-PRI governments at the state and municipal levels are managing to do "more with less" (see Rodríguez and Ward 1992).

capacity of agencies to respond to people's needs, and to do so in ways that are more systematic and less partisan in their application (points to which I return below). Although there are important exceptions, blatant overlaps within public administration have been reduced, and agencies have been made more accountable. Thus they have proven better equipped to deliver programs more efficiently.[7]

However, these improvements notwithstanding, much more could be done. There remains considerable scope for the integration of parastatals, statewide agencies, and government ministries, many of which relate to particular spatial or social constituencies in Mexican society and whose operation often accentuates existing patterns of social stratification (see Ward 1990). To offer just a single example, responsibility for health care is split between three principal public agencies—the Mexican Social Security Institute (IMSS), the Social Security Institute for State Employees (ISSSTE), and the Public Health Sector (SS)—and, of course, through the private sector. Each of these has its own "tier" of *derechohabientes* (or clients), and users will benefit according to the level of resources enjoyed *by the organization that serves them*. Over the past two decades there have been several half-hearted attempts to reduce this multiconstituency basis for health care in Mexico, but agencies have tended to resist any erosion of differentials between their own and other institutions. Even where the IMSS has been charged to embrace a new constituency of the population (as under IMSS-COPLAMAR, for example), those newly integrated came in with inferior levels of coverage than existing or original *derechohabientes* (Ward 1986). The effect was to extend coverage to some rural and marginal populations, but also to multiply tiers of differentiated constituency affiliation.

In terms of the policies, too, there have been important improvements. Specifically, programs in the 1980s have proven more effective than those of the previous decade. They were better targeted to populations in need (e.g., toward marginal urban settlements and rural areas); they were more in tune with people's needs rather than with planners' or administrators' perception of what people needed; they were "low-tech" and lower cost; they were applied more widely; they embraced community participation and indigenous practices; and their impacts were less likely to be regressive socially and financially. One is able to observe this "improvement" in a large number of fields. López Acuña (1980: 182) as early as 1980 noted the important shift that had already occurred in the nature of curative health facilities that had moved away from high-tech, large-scale, high-cost public medical centers—which he disparagingly described as white elephants and which "vorazmente consumían los escasos recursos asignados a la salubridad de México"—toward hospi-

---

[7]See Ward 1986, 1990, for various examples in the field of health care, housing, land regularization, planning, and the provision of basic infrastructure.

tals and clinics located in marginal areas closer to the populations they were supposed to cover. However, López Acuña at that time bemoaned the lack of progress toward policies which would be preventive (i.e., developmental) in nature rather than curative (i.e., remedial). The dominance of curative over preventive health care remains a feature today.

Important parallel shifts have also occurred in other areas of social welfare policy. Public-sector housing production and supports have moved away from expensive and poorly targeted project housing and resettlement programs during the 1960s, through a period of intensified production and financing of housing for salaried workers (through the National Fund for Workers' Housing, INFONAVIT, and through the State Employees' Housing Fund [FOVISSSTE), toward a multidimensional strategy that is supportive of self-help and irregular settlements (through land regularization departments or agencies, and through federal and state institutions such as the National Popular Housing Fund [FONHAPO], etc.). Recently, too, governments have begun to give some consideration to the plight of the large minority (around one-third) of renter households in Mexico, who had been almost totally ignored in the past (Coulomb 1989). As a result of this more pragmatic approach and "upgrading" policies, the levels of service deprivation nationally have declined dramatically since 1970. For example, according to national census data the proportion of dwellings without a water supply (in-house or on the plot) declined from 61 percent in 1970 to 34 percent in 1980 and to 24 percent in 1990. Moreover, the proportion of homes without a sanitary system of drainage declined from 59 to 43 to 36 percent in 1970, 1980, and 1990, respectively. Since 1990 PRONASOL has been the primary medium through which infrastructure improvements have been further extended to households, especially in rural regions and marginal urban settlements. These major improvements in servicing levels represent a considerable achievement of successive Mexican governments, and often go unrecognized. They reflect important policy shifts and changing priorities undertaken during the past two decades, which have done much to offset the slackening of social welfare as a priority for increased expenditure observed above.

POLITICAL MEDIATION AND SOCIAL WELFARE PROGRAMS

At the beginning of this chapter I suggested that social welfare policy forms an important element in the exercise of "statecraft" — what I have come to call "political mediation," by which I mean the ways in which the state attempts to placate while simultaneously maintaining social control and legitimating itself through the securement of political support for the government (Ward 1986). In the penultimate section of this chapter I want to explore the ways in which political mediation has been achieved during the past two decades and to demonstrate how it has always formed an important element in the government's project. As I intimated at the outset, I do not view that project as one of demonstrating political will toward social development in Mexico, nor as any new intent toward empowerment of local populations. Rather, the project is more one of adopting a series of palliatives and administrative and planning reforms designed to help maintain social peace (*la paz social*),[8] assist in social control, extend personal or party political support, and, most recently, seek to recast state-societal relations—the primary focus of this volume. However, while the aims remain the same, the *means* whereby this political mediation has been undertaken have changed significantly. I would identify three broad periods—four if we include PRONASOL as substantively different.

POLITICAL MEDIATION THROUGH LAISSEZ-FAIRE AND CLIENTELISM

Prior to 1970 many of the social needs of the poor, with the exception of education, were largely ignored by the state, whose economic development strategy was predicated on "stabilizing development" and "trickle down" of income and resources to the poor. It was a "grow now, distribute later" type of policy. State action in housing and infrastructure was largely inaction: it ignored the development of irregular *colonias populares,* occasionally undertaking some selective removals of fledgling settlements and occasionally providing partial servicing. The provision of social welfare goods was determined largely on an ad hoc basis and was articulated through patron-clientelist relations (Cornelius 1975; Montaño 1976; Eckstein 1988). Party-political support was mobilized through the corporatist structure of the PRI, usually through the then National Confederation of Popular Organizations (CNOP). Sometimes, too, individual politicians built up personalized constituencies and bases of support through the *colonias populares* (Montaño 1976). In exchange for goods, services, legal recognition, or the suspension of harassment by the authorities, *colonia* residents in droves supported the PRI and its candidates. It was partly through this mechanism that the clean sweep *"carro completo"* achieved by the PRI was sustained for so long. It was, however, a two-way process in which residents in effect gave their political support in return for different elements of social welfare. But relations were asymmetric, encouraged dependency, and ultimately slowed the outflow of scarce resources to a level that the state felt able to accommodate at that time (Cornelius 1975). However, by the late 1960s the economic and social strains were such that an alternative development model was adopted—so-called "shared development" (Teichman 1988; Lustig 1992).

---

[8]Several agency directors and ministers I interviewed in the late 1970s used this term to describe one of the key functions and overriding goals of their institution.

POLITICAL MEDIATION THROUGH INTERVENTION AND POPULISM

This period epitomizes the Echeverría administration. In many respects the fundamentals of clientelism and populist advocacy were largely the same; what differed was the extent to which they became the fountainhead of government policy. No longer laissez-faire, the government apparatus in a whole variety of areas of welfare provision was put on alert—"como un estado de guerra," as one agency head of the day described it to me. Social and political control was achieved through intervention in the spheres of housing, land, sanitation, and infrastructure. Some activities were more politicized than others, particularly those that were relatively "lightweight" and had little impact on production and accumulation—i.e., O'Conner's social expenses expenditures as defined earlier in this chapter (see also Gilbert and Ward 1985). Public-sector social welfare agencies proliferated, and their rationale was less to do a good job than to be seen to be actively engaged in attending to people's daily needs. It was a sort of smoke screen: it gave the impression that the state was concerned and active on the poor's behalf while, more importantly, giving the state breathing space. Often justifiably criticized for being overly demagogic, populist, and inefficient, this strategy suited President Echeverría's purpose to mobilize popular support for his government, and it also allowed the government to "buy time." The PRI, too, benefited insofar as there were ample opportunities for patronage to be exercised through the proliferation of agencies, many with budgets totally inadequate to fulfill their functions. Other highly resourced institutions offered huge potential of politically motivated patronage. The INFONAVIT was one of these; it became embattled as different groups struggled for control of the Board and, therefore, for control of the allocation of resources. As we now know, by 1977 the Confederation of Mexican Workers (the CTM) had in effect won that battle, and thereafter INFONAVIT lost its ostensibly nonpartisan stance as funding was directed almost always toward CTM-affiliated groups. In fairness to Echeverría, we should recognize that many of the improvements in social welfare that became apparent by 1980 (improved servicing levels, for example) required large-scale, "lumpy" investments of a primary nature before households could be connected through the *red domiciliaria*. Thus, just as much of the groundwork for petroleum exploration and production was undertaken by Echeverría, it was his successor who benefited.

POLITICAL MEDIATION THROUGH THE "ROUTINIZATION" OF SOCIAL WELFARE

This period began around 1977 and represented the first initiatives to develop social welfare provision through more administrative regimes of management and efficiency. Overlaps between agencies were reduced;

institutions sought to achieve a more decentralized basis for decision making (particularly after 1983); and their resourcing was put on a more stable footing. Increasingly, the aim was to achieve social peace by using scarce resources more appropriately, and by seeking to deliver social welfare benefits rather than just "appearing" to be active, as was often the case under Echeverría. In particular, decisions about who should benefit from programs became more "routinized" and subject to formal agency guidelines, rather than being based on individual decisions where positive outcomes were as likely to be determined by political affiliation or by other personal considerations as by need or position in the queue. "Technical" criteria were more likely to enter, and agencies increasingly sought to contract with individual recipients rather than through agents, be these political brokers or local leaders. The former "open-house," free-for-all relations between authorities and local groups were replaced by more structured and less partisan-political social relations (Ward 1981, 1986).[9] This coincided with the shift toward more appropriate policies noted earlier; and many statewide and municipal officials, as well as those in federal and parastatal agencies, adopted a less overtly partisan stance. Career advancement for politicians and for functionaries was increasingly predicated on doing a good job and demonstrating good management by effective handling of demands from what was becoming a much more competitive pluralist structure. Government officials were expected to at least appear to deal "fairly" with all groups, even where the individual leader or petitioner con-cerned was a militant PRIísta. However, one effect of this more rou-tinized and less partisan structure of decision making was that it closed down, somewhat, the political freedom for maneuver that the PRI had until then enjoyed (Rodríguez and Ward 1993). Tensions within the party were exacerbated, and the growing divide between so-called *técnicos* and *políticos* came precisely at a time when electoral competition at the ballot box was also intensifying. Although this competition was still not threatening to overturn the PRI's overall dominance, it was often making severe inroads in certain areas, including those where non-PRI governments were winning power. The PRI demanded privileged access to government resources in order to extend its basis of patronage and to win electoral support, but the government needed to disburse those resources more efficiently in order to head off unrest. In addition, the government was becoming sensitive to criticism from opposition parties that it might be misusing social welfare resources for partisan purposes.

During the 1980s, individuals engaged in mobilization for scarce urban resources—often articulated through social movements and/or

---

[9]Of course this was not total, and many opportunities for particularistic decisions continued to exist, especially in certain areas of administration (such as land regulariza-tion, for example), as well as in certain states whose governors continued to rely on "populist" support.

their coordinating committees—appear to have benefited more than did their 1970s counterparts. They were more likely to be successful in getting their demands met, often without the enormous losses of time and energy spent in lobbying local politicians and officials. Resources were better targeted, and programs were more in line with people's needs. Partisanship, too, appears to have been less intense during the 1980s as agencies sought increasingly to contract directly with individual households and to "sidestep" local leaders, especially the undemocratic ones. Generally speaking, social movements were better led and leaders were less likely to be co-opted, offering better representation for their followers.

Therefore, we can observe sharp changes in the way in which social welfare provision articulated the principles of statecraft in Mexico between 1970 and 1988. Although the basic aims were always to keep the lid on social unrest and to sustain political control, the means whereby these were achieved have tended to vary. It is my contention that the majority of social groups in Mexico have benefited more from social welfare programs in recent years than they did during the 1970s. Policies are more appropriate, closer to people's needs, and more easily come by; and the social costs incurred by households are less. But the progressive withdrawal of subsidies since 1983, and especially since 1989, means that benefits are also more expensive; whether or not they are becoming unaffordable has yet to be established. The view of my research group is that acquisition costs of residential land by low-income groups in Mexico remain affordable (Ward, Jiménez, and Jones 1993), but others will disagree.

A FOURTH PHASE—"PRONASOL: NEOPOPULIST SOLUTIONS TO NEOLIBERAL PROBLEMS"?

I mentioned at the beginning of the preceding section that President Salinas's social policy may herald the beginning of a fourth phase. To that extent only will I discuss PRONASOL in this chapter, in the knowledge that other contributions to this volume address this issue more fully. If Dresser's interpretation of PRONASOL is correct (from whence this subheading), then what we are observing is a return to clientelism and patronage politics. Although the Salinas government has been at pains to resist claims that the program is designed to breathe new life into the PRI's waning fortunes, there is now incontrovertible evidence to suggest that its targeting is motivated by partisan political considerations, and that this has served the PRI well (see Molinar and Weldon, this volume). The PRONASOL logo carries the PRI's colors (also those of the national flag), and subliminally at least it conflates government with PRI with nationalist sentiment (Rodríguez and Ward 1993). Moreover, PRONASOL funding has been heavily targeted at PRD strongholds, first in

México State, particularly the municipalities that form the periphery of the Mexico City metropolitan area, and more recently in the gubernatorial elections in Michoacán, where it is estimated that each vote for the PRI cost U.S. $70, compared with just over $2 per vote for the PRD (Chávez 1992). It is estimated that 12 percent of PRONASOL's entire 1992 budget went to the relatively small state of Michoacán (Fox and Moguel n.d.). However, although the criticism of partisanship is often voiced by opposition parties (especially the PRD), if there has been a bias toward the PRI then it has not been systematic. For many opposition groups, too, PRONASOL has represented something of a lifeline, offering them access to resources and benefits long denied by unsympathetic governors and state officials (Fox and Moguel n.d.).[10] Generally speaking, opposition parties outside the PRD have taken a pragmatic stance toward PRONASOL resources, seeking to tap into them while minimizing as far as possible the extent to which the PRI is able to reap local political advantage by taking the credit. The local political context shapes the way existing popular organizations can access PRONASOL resources and the extent to which local populations are likely to have any real control over resource disbursement and prioritization of projects (see Contreras and Bennett, and Haber, this volume).

Nevertheless, in terms of social welfare policy, PRONASOL represents the sectoral "flagship" and will probably remain so under the newly created Ministry of Social Development (SEDESOL),[11] even though health and education are far more important in terms of total budget. Even so, PRONASOL's resources are prodigious (U.S. $680 million in 1989, $950 million in 1990, and an estimated $1.7 billion in 1991), and these appear to be in addition to those allocated to social expenditure (Lustig 1992: 80–81). In terms of federal *investment* expenditures, PRONASOL is especially important (and disproportionate), embracing 17.6 percent of the national total in 1992 and 45 percent of that of the social development sector (Contreras and Bennett, this volume). Although not new (in some respects it is a continuation of COPLAMAR-type activities), PRONASOL is distinctive in terms of both its resources and its flexibility—originally being run directly out of the president's office. To the extent that it is a poverty alleviation program designed to target scarce resources at certain groups, then it is open to discretionary allocation procedures and runs counter to the tide of technocratization of social welfare policies and institutions that I have described. Nor does it

[10]Naturally, directing resources to opposition parties may also help the PRI in so far as it persuades people to take a more positive view of the government. It may also be directed at certain "softer" opposition groups in an attempt to strip support away from those groups that are intransigent or more threatening. Molinar and Weldon (this volume) present an interesting analysis of the potential strategies the PRI may adopt in order to "buy back the defectors," or to "reward" their primary constituents.

[11]Note, also, how this new ministry "flags" PRONASOL. Strictly speaking, the acronym should be SEDESO, but instead it conveniently embraces the "L" of *social*.

appear to be systematically strengthening and fundamentally recasting the nature of social organization in Mexican society. Of course, it may be more "systematized and routinized" as it is integrated into a formal ministry. But given that the new head-of-sector comes directly from being president of the PRI, there will undoubtedly be pressures of a partisan nature that he will have to confront. Democratic opening and pluralism have effectively raised the electoral stakes, and PRONASOL represents a key source of potential patronage with which to win friends and influence people. It also represents a key mechanism to provide more active and system-supporting modes of organization, but in ways which do not threaten the overall structure nor lead to greater empowerment at the local level.

It is probably premature to interpret PRONASOL as neopopulist. But I disagree with the current director's view that it is designed to offer a targeted *solution* to poverty in Mexico. If it is truly an antipoverty program, then there are systematic measures whereby its effectiveness may be assessed. These would include improvements in income distribution and nutritional intake, more equitable access to basic needs and resources, and so on. Few researchers have undertaken this sort of analysis, but some early evidence from one research institution in Tijuana (COLEF) suggests that PRONASOL has not led to any perceptible changes in inequality and poverty in Mexico (Contreras 1992). Rather, PRONASOL is targeted more specifically at local communities and mediated through municipal and state committees to provide a multitude of benefits which, while often necessary, do not fundamentally alter the structure of poverty in Mexico. President Salinas enunciated the nature of many of these benefits in his fourth State of the Nation address on November 1, 1992. These included an average of 1,052 title deeds handed out daily, 7,719 Mexicans per day receiving potable water supplies for the first time, and 5,263 people per day being brought into the health care system. But these are not necessarily indicative of an antipoverty program. Moreover, depending on where they fall spatially (place) and socially (by group or class), they may intensify existing patterns of social inequality as certain groups gain "windfall" benefits while others miss out (Moyao 1991; Ward 1986, 1990). In my view PRONASOL is highly targeted, but its role is one of a *palliative* designed to offset some of the inevitable social costs associated with structural readjustment and, if you like, the pursuit of neoliberal policies. Its genesis was not national, but was required by the IMF to accompany the restructuring process.[12] Its pattern of implementation, however, is firmly Mexican, and I do not see it as fundamentally contradicting my overall argument about the changing nature of social welfare policy in Mexico. Whether through clientelism of yesteryear, or through more

---

[12]I am grateful to Dr. Gustavo Verduzco for pointing this out to me.

appropriate policies and the application of more technical routines and procedures latterly, or through complementary programs such as PRO-NASOL, social policy in Mexico forms a key element in statecraft and in "papering over the cracks" of social inequality.

4

Social Reform in Mexico: Six Theses on the National Solidarity Program

Enrique González Tiburcio

The 1980s marked the end of one stage in Mexico's modern history. In the course of the decade, an economic model and a style of doing politics ended, and many of the social actors that arose and evolved under the organizational structure of the old model were marginalized. Once the sometimes difficult transition was made, the Mexican economy regained control over macroeconomic variables (inflation, public finances, and external accounts), paving the way for a gradual recovery in growth, employment, and social spending. Despite the depth of Mexico's crisis in the 1980s, the country managed to navigate the perils of adjustment with greater success than did other countries of Latin America. Mexico's success was due to the presence of a state that—notwithstanding some weaknesses—continued to show strength and historical continuity; to the ability of a set of social institutions to remain active despite diminished resources; and to family and community traditions which are deeply ingrained in the Mexican people.

Since 1988, Mexico's social policy has entered a new phase, marked by the rhythms and activities of the National Solidarity Program in the arena of social welfare policy. Solidarity emerged in a context of increasing macroeconomic stability (lost during the previous decade) and a rapid transition toward new forms of economic organization, operation, and linkage with the global economy. Despite the constraints that such a context may impose, Solidarity has successfully articulated the energies emanating from civil society, becoming a catalyst of popular demands

Translated by Aníbal Yáñez.

for welfare and institutional change. These demands presage new
public policies in the social sphere.[1]

⤙ As part of a modernization effort that comprises economic, social,
and political reform, Solidarity is inextricably linked to the national will
to move toward a more productive and equitable development stage.[2]
Unlike other countries in Latin America and elsewhere in the world,
Mexico has set a particular tempo for its reform program. Economic
reform has laid down the foundation (a healthy economy) on which to
base increased social spending. The political reform, meanwhile, makes
it possible to invite full political party participation, to improve electoral
processes, and to broaden citizens' rights, thus strengthening the state's
ability to lead.

Beginning with the PRONASOL mandate itself—to combat poverty—Solidarity has drawn nourishment from the new reformist environment, but it has also served to consolidate the overall process of
reform. PRONASOL's new style of social policy has involved a substantial change in daily operations from the typical, sometimes leisurely,
bureaucratic way of doing things. Because it is more decentralized,
participatory, and citizen based, Solidarity has opened a channel to new
actors, broadening the state's space for maneuver and thereby meeting a
fundamental need in the current Mexican transition.

SIX THESES

The following theses about Solidarity grew out of requests made to
PRONASOL, program initiatives, and demands from within PRO-
NASOL itself. The political will to promote Solidarity and the favorable
popular response to the program have coalesced in principles and
operating procedures that develop, not a priori, but as the result of

---

[1] According to the pronouncements by President Carlos Salinas in his fourth State of the
Nation address, in its four years of operation Solidarity, working in conjunction with local
communities, achieved the following: It enrolled 5,263 Mexicans per day in health systems.
It added 7,719 Mexicans per day to the population provided with a regular supply of
potable water. It conveyed an average of 1,052 land titles per day. It built forty-seven
classrooms, workshops, and laboratories and renovated fifty public schools per day. Each
day another 9,122 Mexicans received electricity. Groups of urban dwellers working in
concert paved more than 3,200 kilometers of streets in poor neighborhoods. Today 8,500
localities have rural telephone service; 5,000 rural communities and 8,500 poor neighborhoods have access to postal service. Nearly two years after the launching of the Niños en
Solidaridad program, almost 500,000 youths receive cash stipends, food baskets, and
medical attention to keep them from dropping out of school because of inadequate family
resources. Under the Programa de Servicio Social, 591,000 young people, graduates of
technical schools and institutions of higher education, joined community welfare projects.

[2] Social reform is defined as a process that seeks to strengthen the freedom of social
actors (giving them greater autonomy) as a means of increasing welfare. It involves policies
and instruments aimed at efficiently incorporating all members of society into the growth
process. This set of policies must include a better distribution of income, closing the gap
between the supply of and demand for services that are essential for the welfare of the
population (see BID/PNUD 1992).

experience and contact with communities. The theses presented below are clearly not the sum total that can be drawn from such a rich and evocative experience, but they are those that herald a new approach to improving well-being and advancing social reform.

- **Thesis 1. Solidarity introduces a leading-edge style of politics within the context of a changing relationship between the state, society, and the economy.**

Modifying social structure and individual and group behaviors in an open and plural society requires both the presence of the state and the action of markets to assign, regulate, and distribute (usually scarce) resources in the face of competing requests and demands. However, the interaction between state and market alone is insufficient for addressing many problems, and it can hinder efforts to resolve them. The search for possible solutions requires that communities and individuals, as the subjects of transformation, take an active role. Between the world of the state and that of the market lies an underexplored area where individuals function—their communities, their neighborhoods, their *colonias*— the spaces of public life (Schmitter 1992). This is one of the areas where Solidarity has been active, pointing social actors toward spaces that have been freed up in the process of reforming the state and imposing limits on the excesses of the market.

Mexico's search for new terms of economic linkage with the outside finds its complement in Solidarity. PRONASOL's social welfare expenditures aim to correct the resultant internal imbalances that could weaken the country. The fundamental challenge for the new Solidarity-led social policy is to create a certain equality of conditions. In this, Solidarity operates as an instrument for opening up public social policy to direct negotiation and shared financial and operational responsibilities (C. Rojas 1992a). It does this at various stages. One of the most important is the creation of committees, for it is through committees that new interlocutors are encouraged to come forward and give voice to their groups' needs at the federal, state, and municipal levels.

PRONASOL is a superior strategy for dealing with groups demanding social services. It fundamentally breaks the bounds of typical public policy management, the old clientelist pattern of social demands→pressure→bureaucratic and populist solutions. Solidarity marks the beginning of a supply-side policy, with contributions from those seeking satisfaction of their needs; an added benefit is that their involvement gives social groups greater independence and autonomy (Villa 1991).

The management of public policy cannot be limited to pressure and petition. The new demand is for participation in the execution and evaluation of social policy. Solidarity arises as an instrument, a method, not one more bureaucratic apparatus but a public resource, an attitude, a norm that can seep through to permeate the entire public sector.

Solidarity's operating method thus promotes a new form of publicly managing social demands. Because these demands emerge as community initiatives, the process belies the idea that the government is the only actor involved in solving social problems. The new management scheme combines social participation with the demand for government intervention, but more as partner and promoter than as the direct and only operator and/or producer.

All of this contributes to advancing toward resolution of social problems, awakening the initiative and autonomy of individuals, families, and municipalities, inducing them to define their problems and prioritize them in order to plan the distribution and investment of public spending and make it more efficient. Thus, participation opens up the possibility for making local communities more autonomous and cohesive, with a better capacity to solve their own problems. The awareness of their own needs can help them understand that public spending is a (perhaps) necessary but not sufficient condition for solving social problems: constant personal and community effort are also required (Aguilar Villanueva 1991).

Solidarity's operating method promotes concertation and a new rationality and balance in the management of public resources, and therefore in social policy itself. In this manner, the historic imbalance between the supply of public goods and social demand tends to find a new way of connecting.

In order for Solidarity's efforts to stay the course, appropriate institutional channels have been created for establishing firm, long-range social commitments, essential components in the fight against poverty. Examples include the Ministry of Social Development (SEDESOL) and the National Solidarity Institute (Instituto Nacional de Solidaridad), which will carry social policy forward with stipulated commitments, objectives, strategies, resources, and institutions inspired by the participatory social mobilization initiated by Solidarity (Bartra 1992).

• **Thesis 2. Solidarity is a unifying element and a federalist exercise in decentralization.**

Mexico has changed; new groups have arisen and social differentiation has increased. Solidarity provides the basis for national integration on renewed foundations of unity and cohesion, since it operates through shared participation, organization, and effort between the citizenry and government. The Solidarity idea can become an attribute of public affairs—that is, a public virtue—which includes mutual respect and a true sense of community. It involves the recognition on the part of each Mexican of his or her social as well as individual nature. Thus, Solidarity has become a means to renew the fabric of Mexican society, to harmoniously integrate the various groups that are emerging today alongside older and more consolidated ones.[3]

Because of the country's centralization, past policy has been decided by a national agenda (the federal government's) and hardly at all by local priorities. "Social questions" run the risk of becoming mired in a kind of government attention that often fails to produce concrete solutions through specific activities or programs. On the contrary, such government attention only belittles local problems. Solidarity helps to situate politics in the context of daily life, to deconcentrate politics and make it local, micro, and driven from below. Not all social and public problems are of national scope; usually the most active citizen politics is local, whether municipal or regional. Thus, community participation avoids the excesses of the concentration of power (centralism) that winds up drowning initiatives in administrative procedures.

Solidarity has enabled the bureaucracy to cede part of the power it previously held. This was done by first decentralizing power to the states and municipalities (as the primary levels of government) and finally to the population in general, which represents a real transfer of power and makes a renewal of federalism possible. This is the only way to explain how Solidarity has carried out 200,000 projects. This effort has been possible because it was based on a true deconcentration (C. Rojas 1992b).

Participation is the essential difference between Solidarity and similar programs. Not only is Solidarity a compensatory program for emergency works and investments; it is a substantial change in the way programs are defined, in operating methods, and in the pace for implementing projects (C. Rojas 1992b). For example, in Solidarity's road construction projects, calculations indicate that costs have been reduced by 30 percent from previous government road projects. The same is true of Solidarity programs for school repair and street paving.

Centralist public management has restrained the dynamic of many local societies' instruments and initiatives. Experience shows that any concentration results in excesses. PRONASOL promotes activities that do the reverse and that contain the seeds for democratic federalism. Programs such as Fondos Municipales, Escuela Digna, Fondos de Solidaridad para la Producción, and Niños en Solidaridad transform methods, outlook, and practices at the local level. Hence, despite its origins at the federal level, Solidarity is essentially municipal in nature, for two reasons. First, it operates in nearly all of Mexico's municipalities

---

[3]For example, Fondos Regionales de Apoyo a los Grupos Indígenas promotes community organization and participation within the new social policy framework, recovering the many and varied forms of solidarity that already exist among the Indian population: *tequio, mayordomía, mano-vuelta,* and *faena,* among others. Another example is the way that professional associations such as engineers and architects are getting involved in renovating, repairing, and maintaining schools under the Escuela Digna program.

and in most it doubles the volume of budgetary resources normally available. Second, by involving social participation in the prioritization, management, execution, evaluation, and control of projects, it promotes new relationships between municipal authorities and the population. Thus, PRONASOL is not only a provider of resources, but also a promoter of a new form of municipal management.

These considerations help explain why PRONASOL links federal institutions with state and local actions in resolving particular local and regional problems; bureaucratic preferences are not the starting point. This subjects centralist inertia to pressure from two directions. From above, presidential will paradoxically can make a more decentralized exercise of public actions possible; from below, there is a unique social mobilization demanding and imposing change on all intervening state institutions (Martínez Nateras 1992a).

Solidarity is a step toward democratic federalism. In this sense, it drives the democratic reform of the state, without which it would not be possible to eradicate poverty. Solidarity has set society in motion from below, and this movement clashes with certain rigidified structures and practices that hold back the advances that the population demands.[4]

• **Thesis 3. Solidarity is a social policy rooted in cultural traditions.**

Unlike other government social welfare practices, Solidarity is built on cultural traditions and patterns that come from Mexico's regions, neighborhoods, and communities. PRONASOL did not invent solidarity, nor does it replace it. On the contrary, it bases its practice on traditions that are rooted in Mexican society, especially among groups with the greatest needs.

Work for the common good and mutual aid are practiced in nearly all of Mexico's regions, among Indian groups, in mestizo rural communities, urban *vecindades*, and *colonias populares* (C. Rojas 1991b). Solidarity's significance is due to its similarity with the forms of social interaction that are characteristic of Mexico's cultural diversity (Portilla 1993). PRONASOL's energy and organic network are manifestations of community organization (neighbors, friends, and families helping one another through relations of real or fictive kinship). These links are a result of enduring traditions or of the simple needs of the less fortunate in the course of their daily lives or in a catastrophe, and it is on this reality that PRONASOL's vision is based (Portilla 1993).

Solidarity has found a method (co-responsible participation) for channeling Mexico's vast cultural knowledge in ways that can overcome

---

[4]Given the diversity in economic, political, and social potential within the universe of Mexico's municipalities, federalism is strengthened in practice when a federal program like Solidarity proposes activities that prioritize the poorest municipalities, since it provides them with new tools to manage and administer resources (as is the case with the Fondos Municipales and the Fondos de Solidaridad para la Producción, among others).

bureaucratic-administrative barriers. It follows time-honored social practices in rural schools and health stations. It supports progress toward social justice, where democratic participation strengthens the links between nation, culture, and justice (Portilla 1993).

In the framework of constitutional changes (such as the change in Article 4 of the Mexican Constitution dealing with indigenous populations), PRONASOL has fostered the idea that national integration can and should encompass the whole set of peoples and cultures that make up the country's social mosaic. What has become stunningly clear is the enormous potential of pluriculturalism and multiethnicity. The Mexican state has taken a key step in its social reforms by accepting that full recognition of all the different Mexicos is the only valid basis for national integration. This situation places the historical tension between tradition and modernity in a new context (Fábregas Puig 1992).

There are visions in which modernity is associated exclusively with urbanization and the market economy. On this road, societies that wish to call themselves modern must follow the example of the highly industrialized countries. In a country like Mexico, this vision must be put to a test: Would a modernizing model of this type be sufficiently capacious to embrace the great creative potential of all of Mexico's peoples and cultures, including the urban traditions themselves, in their entirety? We must consider these cultures on the basis of their own customs, traditions, and histories. Thus, modernity in Mexico seems to rest less on simple mimicry of developed Western models and more on respect for and inclusion of the strengths of traditional cultures. This implies reaching a scientific understanding of the technologies and worldviews of all of Mexico's varied cultures, and to discover from these their varied mechanisms for change. Only by taking this cultural diversity into account can we begin a process of deep-going change in Mexican society. By its very nature such change cannot be driven by government decisions alone; it is the natural sphere of social reform (Rubiell 1992).

Government understanding of this process must rest on the consensus that, for Mexico, modernity means accepting plurality and using it to achieve integral development. Otherwise the country would risk propagating inequities and losing the ancestral wisdom of these social groups. Mexico's plurality will find a full and modern outlet when it can express itself without restraint.

Through participation, national cultural diversity, with its many traditions and origins, can be respected. Through participation, popular organizations recreate and carry forward their deepest cultural values. Mexican society seems more a conglomeration of communities and extended families than simple individuals (consumers). This situation does not exclude market forces, but it places limits on them. Solidarity's experience suggests that when projects recognize and incorporate cultural traditions, social policies succeed.

- **Thesis 4. Solidarity gives a new dimension to public investment and social spending.**

Mexico has a long history of solving problems by allocating enormous amounts of abundant public monies. As Luis Aguilar noted, by dint of spending *for* people, not *on* people, bureaucracies that had been expert in popular affairs became fragmented machines when public resources became scarce (Aguilar Villanueva 1991).

Social spending has grown apace with state growth and has continued to hold a prominent role. However, simple quantitative growth was not enough, and in many ways it was not what the country needed. State expenditures and infrastructure and social projects were decided on and implemented by the state alone. This situation produced distortions of various kinds. The most important was that a very large proportion of social spending went to sectors that did not need it. This explains much of the inefficiency and opacity in public spending, which diminished the effectiveness of social spending in meeting the needs of the most vulnerable population sectors.

Many social groups with legitimate and urgent demands got no response, primarily because of the uncomplementarity between social demand and the supply of public welfare agencies. This means that it was not sufficient merely to increase public spending to reverse long-standing backwardness and the accumulated mistakes of the previous decade. What was needed was to put the country's powerful distributive instrument in motion with efficiency, transparency, and social participation.

Solidarity was the policy instrument charged with modifying the pattern of public spending, to transform it in operational, technical, and especially political terms (Warman 1992). The program provides a channel through which public spending can be directed to meet the demands of a society that has changed profoundly in political terms; though larger, more plural, and more unequal, Mexican society is also more aware and more participatory and it is raising new social demands.

Solidarity's most important qualitative contribution is that it modified the basic premise of social development in Mexico: the country has left behind the idea that more public spending translates into more social justice.[5] Solidarity offers a new approach: a focus on the how and why of spending. In other words, PRONASOL highlights the qualitative and not simply the quantitative aspects of spending. This is what is of crucial importance in social participation and civic co-responsibility to combat

[5] Abandoning this view does not mean that the inverse effects of the same equation can be minimized; the years of crisis showed that less social spending results in less social welfare.

poverty. Its vision includes more spending but only in combination with co-responsible participation. This is a distinct way to achieve social welfare; projects that are carried out are especially valued because they become part of the assets of the community itself. Thanks to Solidarity, many popular organizations have recovered confidence in their own efforts. Through their participation they pay the "dues" of co-responsibility in a program aimed at breaking the vicious circle of poverty (Vizcaíno 1992).

Co-responsibility forges new forms of interaction between bureaucracies and social organizations, and it has also made possible an increasing liberalization of social spending toward marginal groups in today's context of macroeconomic stabilization and renewed growth. The basic idea underlying Solidarity's management of resources is that these funds should not take the form of a handout or generate a relationship of dependency. The goal is for projects to have a well-defined purpose and be implemented with broad social oversight. Investment in goods and services is a means rather than an end in itself. Solidarity's ultimate objective is to promote the development of better-educated, better-organized people with the resources and abilities to cope with their problems.

The assignment of Solidarity resources makes room for new options to appear: it commits various levels and agencies of government to the program's objectives and to the priorities set by the communities; it breaks inertia rooted in "sectoral bureaucracies" and corrects inequities. The fight against poverty and Solidarity's operating procedures are the uppermost considerations in the management of resources, focusing these entirely toward investment since current spending is charged to institutional budgets.

The sum of resources assigned to Solidarity portrays an effort that is unprecedented in recent Mexican history. This effort has succeeded in large part because of a significant reform of public finances, which made possible increases in public spending, a reduction in financial encumbrances, and a budget surplus in 1991–93. Resources have come mainly from tax revenues (approximately 97 percent in 1992) and from savings achieved through various elements of Mexico's macroeconomic strategy: renegotiating the terms of the external debt, reducing the internal debt through privatization of state enterprises, selective use of the contingency fund, and fiscal reform. Underlying Solidarity's robust funding there is a macroeconomic strategy with a clear social purpose.

The income boost resulting from privatization of state enterprises has not gone directly to Solidarity's coffers. Rather, it has gone into a contingency fund, and this in turn has been used to reduce public indebtedness at home and abroad. Employing privatization income in this way allowed Mexico to reap larger margins of public savings for the medium and long term. This means that the resources resulting from privatization are used, not for short-term and finite ends, but to broaden the margins of public finances designed for stabilization and direct them toward welfare and growth (Aguilar Villanueva 1991).

Solidarity is sometimes criticized because it cannot put an end to poverty. This criticism sets up a false comparison: the amount of public social investment vis-à-vis the levels of extreme poverty. We must look rather at Solidarity's achievements; over the last four years federal investment through Solidarity has grown substantially, constituting the axis of the fight against poverty and the basic source for improving resource allocation in this battle. In its four years of operation, Solidarity has spent resources totaling nearly U.S. $8 billion, a figure that compares very favorably to amounts spent by other agencies, programs, and institutions, such as the World Bank and the Inter-American Development Bank.[6]

Not only has spending increased; by combining resources from the federal government, states and municipalities, and the citizens themselves, these actors are joined in a federal pact against poverty. This alliance of actors does not substitute for the state, but it serves to multiply investment efforts and ensure that they accord with the demands and requirements of the communities themselves. Everyone benefits from more rapid and more committed progress in the fight against poverty.

Solidarity has proven to be an appropriate instrument for thinking about and implementing social policy—on both the demand and supply sides. This new style of engaging in social policy does not take advantage of economic and social needs to extend political dependency. As Luis Aguilar put it, it does not "provide resources in exchange for political subordination; it assumes that there is initiative and some kind of supply on the part of beneficiaries and those demanding attention to their needs; it frames the particular demands of a family or group in terms of the interests and well-being of the larger social community; it is an incentive for discussion and concertation between community members to identify their collective problems, order priorities, and distribute responsibilities. This is a promising training for the citizens' culture of freedom" (in Medina A. 1992).

• **Thesis 5. Solidarity promotes the development of democratic social and political practices.**

Solidarity shows that there can be another way of doing things, and this idea has entered the public consciousness. This new consciousness, evident today in the more than 100,000 Solidarity Committees throughout Mexico, can point to its successes: potable water, electricity, sewers,

---

[6]The resources spent by Solidarity and Regional Development under Branch XXVI were (in billions of new pesos): 2,814 in 1989; 4,328 in 1990; 4,767 in 1991; 6,843 in 1992.

drains, and especially the upsurge among the citizenry and their call for democracy. It is here that Solidarity has found its primary outlet, according to Rolando Cordera (1991a): "citizenship and democracy are inherent features that define its [PRONASOL's] principles, its political and social meaning, its legitimacy."

This network of many small community social organizations makes it possible for individuals to find the exact measure of their problems, the basic reference points for support and recognition. It also gives meaning to community efforts and suggests the appropriate dimension for the solution of community problems, underscoring that not all solutions emanate from the heights of federal government. There are various solutions, various ways of fulfilling or satisfying needs. Policy becomes more consistent, decentralized, and also more autonomous.

The greater the number of individuals who come from traditional structures to face the modern state, the more likely it is that conflicts will arise. Hence the need for an institutional intermediary between the world of individuals and the world of government agencies. Solidarity offers new ways for society and government to deal with each other, thus making the state more people oriented.

Solidarity serves suprafamilial social groups: neighborhood social organizations; cultural, consumer, and civic organizations; local political organizations. Together these comprise a network that makes it possible to channel demands, represent interests, frame problems, implement projects. Supported by this network, individuals can advance their social demands without recurring to the upper levels of the federal administration. This transformation removes the obstacles imposed by centralism and also provides the appropriate dimension for resolving regional and local problems.

The reform of social policy heralded by Solidarity is based on community participation in decision making, calling communities to organize socially for their own benefit. Solidarity turns the old method of social policy on its head, promoting organization from the micro level upward, in both social and geographic terms. Because Solidarity does not work with political parties, but with citizens and social organizations, it opens a democratic political space for a more productive and beneficial relationship between the state and society. Because it is free from party domination, Solidarity has freed a good part of social demands and responses from party domination. In other words, the management of social demands is gradually ceasing to be handled through party and especially electoral negotiation, and becoming the direct province of the population and specific government agencies (Villa 1991).

A key goal in this process is that social groups recover the ability to organize social demands and to generate responses and projects to meet them. For example, trade unions and other forms of social organization may well adopt Solidarity-like models, with their own respective dynamic and autonomy, thus further advancing the process of micro-economic reform. Although Solidarity must retain its independence from political parties, it need not necessarily do so from organizations of rural and urban workers, nor from their efforts to contribute to social equity and the strengthening of citizen life.

Because of their disadvantaged position and unmet needs, poor people tend to view politics as made up of pressure and conflict, inevitable components in efforts to change their own living conditions. They use politics as a strategic activity to gain through pressure what they do not get in the market. This view favors the traditional social function of the state, because their primary goal is winning more public spending. Because their social experience does not correspond to that of full citizens,[7] they relegate civil and political rights to a secondary position.

Solidarity has made it possible to modify this traditional style of doing politics. Its call for justice dovetails with a call for democracy. Although certain social actors may give greater priority to one or the other, justice and democracy must not be posed as alternative options but rather as complementary ones (see Warman 1992).

- **Thesis 6. Solidarity opens up a possibility for building a social state with full respect for the freedom of citizens.**

The various social states created worldwide in this century are evolving toward new definitions of the role of government and the work of society. Social, political, and economic rights and freedoms, according to Albert Hirschman, are not irrenounceable values but foreseeable historical tendencies. Solidarity is only one part of a broad social policy, but it is unfolding within a transition to modernity and in response to the historic and present-day marginalization that modernization can cause among disadvantaged citizens. While it compensates for inequities and satisfies needs, it also provides a model for co-responsibility and citizen participation, through which people learn to contribute toward solving their own problems.

Through social organization, Solidarity makes it possible to close the persistent gap between inequality/poverty and the formal recognition of rights, strengthening the vitality of the state ruled by law. Solidarity has increased government transparency and responsibility, as well as exerted social control over public actions. It has opened up the possibility for establishing effective links between the agencies of public administration and the organizations of civil society, eliminating waste of resources and reducing inefficiencies. Solidarity takes advantage of

---

[7] In this case we are not speaking of an economically autonomous citizen on the supply side of politics who is relatively satisfied and avoids politicizing private issues.

civil society's co-responsibility to establish mechanisms and processes that ensure transparency, responsibility, and administrative honesty, and that make possible community and citizen control and a greater effectiveness of the law. Without a vigorous and universal rule of law, there can be no healthy relationship between society and the state, trust is diluted, and consensus fragments. Furthermore, without the effective and universal rule of law it is more difficult to achieve basic solidarity; and without solidarity the state will lack authority to call for consensus and collective commitment.

Solidarity gives Mexico an opportunity: to establish a bridge between equity and freedom. On a closer horizon it makes it possible to calibrate the tension that exists between governability and democracy. Perhaps in few spaces of public policy can this articulation be better analyzed. Far from being the exclusive preserve of centralized bureaucracies or the necessary result of economic growth, the search for social justice involves the state in a leading role within a broad co-responsibility with popular organizations. We are far removed here from visions in which the market and economic growth solve everything. It is a matter of building a new practice in social welfare, based on freedom and justice, in the framework of governability and democracy. In this sense, Solidarity has been a link between the problems of governability and those that arise from calls for democracy, fostering spaces for creativity and participation (Camou 1992).

With Solidarity, the government has gone from being a service "provider" to being a co-participant with the population in the implementation of social policy. As a strategy, PRONASOL is far removed from a statist social policy and from the policies of neoliberalism, which leave social demands free to the field of market forces. It makes possible a reform of institutions, which in turn changes the contours of resource utilization, methods of production, and public services. It also affects the profile and the behavior of municipal presidents and local public servants as sponsors of social demands. Increased spending via new channels is defining a new federal pact which makes the reform of the state more concrete at the local level. In this sense, Solidarity is a strategy to coordinate institutional efforts, bring together the resources of the three levels of government, concentrate investment toward poorer groups, and modify the relationship between institutions and citizens in programs oriented to improve the living conditions of the neediest.

As of 1982 the Mexican government began moving toward qualitative, directed intervention. In a context of scarce resources, it is necessary to adapt state intervention and optimize resource allocation. By emphasizing the role of social groups and their mediation in alleviating poverty, Solidarity marks a change in the view of the state as benefactor and owner toward a social democratic state under the rule of law (Cordera Campos 1991a). As it has increasingly broadened the bases for social participation, Solidarity has enriched the democratic foundation of national institutions. In this way, the principles that guide Solidarity can achieve permanence.

CONCLUSIONS

Mexico's corporatist social pact needs to involve new requirements, demands, and interlocutors. Though the pact supported welfare and served to link public institutions, social groupings, and broad layers of the population, the pact's capacity for mediation has been diluted and communication between government agencies and society has been altered. Solidarity proposes a renewed structure of intermediation so that demands and responses can once more flow through well-defined institutional and organizational channels (Fernández Santillán 1991).

Solidarity is not trying to weaken the organizational fabric of Mexican society, nor to replace the established organizations of the national political system. Solidarity posits that broadening democratic governability, together with state reform, requires a society with greater breadth and organizational density. In this sense, Solidarity presents a double challenge: the necessary construction of networks of interlocutors who are in tune with the country's ethnic, local, municipal, and regional complexity, and the formation of a social culture founded on respect for the autonomy of social organizations, i.e., for communities' capacity to take the initiative and execute projects, and on the concertation of political commitments. Thus, Solidarity is betting on an alternative development strategy that is participatory and co-responsible.

In this context of transformation, Solidarity is adapting to the new state-society and state-economy relationships. The program has been the axis where state restructuring intercepts efforts to meet social needs. Solidarity has been building new relationships between the state and specific groupings of civil society—a new social base which gives consistency and durability to the reforms that are in process.

Most significant is the fact that Solidarity gives an opportunity to reform the strategy for social development, thanks to PRONASOL's special position within the Ministry of Social Development; the influx of significant resources through economic modernization; and the program's orientation toward autonomy as an essential condition of intervention in participatory planning.

Within this framework of robust resources, decentralized institutions, and autonomous social organizations lies the road toward strengthening the Mexican state's commitment to a new model of social development. Under this model the state would channel the efforts of all Mexicans toward broadening opportunities, stimulating participation by organized society, and exercising firm social control over the origin and destination of resources. In Solidarity's case, institutionalization is the opposite of bureaucratization: it formalizes and gives permanence to the spaces, norms, resources, and principles that are aimed at maintaining the new relationship between the state and the popular classes by reforming the former and organizationally strengthening the latter.

Improvements in social welfare are normally the product of the interaction of various instruments, programs, and policies. The fact that each matures at its own pace makes it very difficult for their combined effects to become clear in the short term, and their efficacy may be undone by changes in administrations. Therefore it is crucial that the struggle for welfare become a policy that transcends six-year administrations; this policy must become, not a policy of a single administration, but a policy of the state.[8] The fight for access to welfare and against poverty cannot depend on the volatility of social policies, nor on the residual space that may be left by stabilization and adjustment processes. These changes and fluctuations are a source of social ineffectiveness; they waste financial, human, and institutional resources and destroy trust and credibility.

Nor can welfare be left to the impulses of economic growth. Social well-being calls for new social fabrics and forms of public action. Hence the strategic importance of a program such as Solidarity. But it is also clear that the democratization of politics and social relations becomes decisive, as does the formation of a less conjunctural and more permanent public apparatus that can receive and respond positively to the messages emanating from the growth-poverty relationship (see Cordera Campos1992).

Perceptions have changed in Mexico. Mexicans agree that they are not, nor do they wish to be, a homogeneous country. Mexico is immensely plural and diverse, and therein lies one of its great strengths; remaining united though diverse, and cherishing that diversity. As Arturo Warman (1992) reminds us, Solidarity has made it possible to combine pluralities. PRONASOL recognizes that regions have their features, that people have their plurality, that priorities are different in various regions, not only because needs are larger or smaller but because each population sets its priorities according to its own dictates.

Mexico is immensely plural, yet also unequal. Plurality and diversity imply options and decisions taken by the population. Inequality, on the other hand, implies limits on the decisions and options that the population wishes to take. To remove these restraints, Mexico's present

---

[8]It is a matter of reaching collective agreements that can function effectively. They must include a long-range temporal dimension and the social scope of the problem, besides the commitment to submit to constitutional norms at the formal level. The response must necessarily be a public one, i.e., not just from the government but from the national society. To advance along these lines it is necessary to agree on legislative consensus points; a career civil service linked to the technical leadership of social programs; widespread information regarding the results; evaluation and control of policies and programs. This would also make it possible to assure the continuity of domestic and external financing.

social policy sets out to provide the population with a basic floor, a common social base that gives real options. Hence the enormous importance of social justice. Its importance is increasing because state intervention cannot be what it used to be, nor will the world economy be the same. To a large extent the market will regulate the economy, and the market has no social conscience. Under these conditions, the state must compensate for the negative social impacts of the country's strictly economic dynamic. What is needed is a social state in a renewed relationship with all of society, a relationship based on participation and political plurality, but above all on trust.

5

Solidarity as a Strategy of Poverty Alleviation

Nora Lustig

The National Solidarity Program was launched by newly inaugurated President Salinas in December 1988 to coordinate and supervise poverty alleviation efforts undertaken by the government at the federal, state, and local levels. This umbrella organization encompasses a wide variety of projects designed to improve the income-generating capacity of the rural and urban poor and their access to basic services.

Thus far the program has been more the object of political than of economic analysis.[1] This should come as no surprise. PRONASOL is designed as much to legitimate the regime and produce a new generation of grassroots leaders as to reduce poverty. The program is also designed to address the sociological aspects of poverty, what is called *"marginalidad."* The demand-driven and participatory nature of the program is supposed to give people a sense of belonging and of their ability to shape their environment, something unseen in top-down programs.

It is difficult to fully appraise the impact of PRONASOL on poverty precisely because of its multidimensional and heterogeneous character.

I am grateful to Jonathan Fox, Antonio Martín del Campo, Darryl McLeod, and members of the Instituto Nacional de Solidaridad for their comments on an earlier draft, and to Harold Alderman, Hans Binswanger, Carmen Hamann, Carlos Hurtado, Carlos Rojas, Jean Claude Sallier, Andrea Silverman, and Sweder Van Wijnbergen for useful conversations about PRONASOL. Thanks also to Andrés Escalante and Annette Leak for their assistance.

[1] A preliminary assessment of the program's effectiveness appears in S. Levy 1991. The other chapters in this volume provide a good sample of noneconomic analyses of PRONASOL.

The program includes projects as diverse as building water supply systems and providing scholarships to schoolchildren. Strictly speaking, to judge PRONASOL's effectiveness we would need estimates of the internal rates of return or cost-effectiveness for each of its projects. Any effort to evaluate PRONASOL is complicated further by the fact that Solidarity's budget and the number and characteristics of its projects are continually expanding as the program incorporates new ideas and initiatives.[2] Bearing this in mind, this chapter will address three specific questions. First, how much is being spent on PRONASOL and how does it compare with the resources needed to eradicate the estimated poverty gap? Second, how is spending on PRONASOL allocated among the various programs and what does this imply about the strategy selected for poverty alleviation? Third, what evidence is there of PRONASOL's ability to reduce poverty and improve living conditions? The analysis will cover primarily the first two years of the program (1989 and 1990) and will use available official information. The initial section presents estimates of the incidence of poverty in Mexico and the size of the income gap in terms of GDP. The second section analyzes the program's characteristics and spending on PRONASOL projects. The third and final section elaborates on the question of PRONASOL's impact on poverty and living conditions.

ASSESSING POVERTY LEVELS IN MEXICO

Poverty can be measured in several ways, with the most common indicators grouped into two categories: those that measure poverty as the lack of access to a set of basic services, and those that define as poor anyone who falls below a preestablished income level identified as the poverty threshold. Data from the late 1970s and early 1980s showed that about nineteen million Mexicans suffered from some degree of malnutrition, 45 percent of the population (primarily poor) did not have access to the free or quasi-free health care system, 50.1 percent of Mexican households had no running water, in 32 percent of households the kitchen had to double as a bedroom, and 25 percent of households had no electricity (Lustig 1992: 66).

In terms of income shortfall, estimates based on the 1984 Household Income Expenditure Survey (the last survey taken before PRONASOL was launched) show the following results. Extreme poverty, defined as the percentage of households with incomes below the cost of a minimum food basket, measured 11.2 percent. Moderate poverty, defined as households with incomes below twice the extreme poverty line, equaled

---

[2] An example is the pilot program on health and nutrition launched in August 1991 and financed with World Bank support.

38.1 percent.[3] The incidence of poverty was substantially higher for rural households. Extreme poverty was four times higher in rural than in urban households, and moderate poverty was more than twice as high (see table 5.1).[4] Extremely poor households tend to live in rural areas, where heads of household are most likely to be engaged in agricultural activities. However, close to 30 percent of extremely poor households live in urban settings, and 33 percent of the heads of extremely poor households are engaged in nonagricultural activities.

TABLE 5.1
INCIDENCE OF POVERTY AND EXTREME POVERTY IN MEXICO IN 1984
(HOUSEHOLDS, IN PERCENTAGES)

| Poverty Lines[1] | Head-Count Ratio[2] | | | Normalized Poverty Gap Total |
	Total	Rural	Urban	
U.S. $ 50.61[3]	11.2	23.5	4.7	3.4
U.S. $108.63[4]	38.1	59.8	26.5	15.3

[1]Per capita, per quarter at constant June 1984 prices (not converted to purchasing power parity equivalent).
[2]Households with per capita (monetary plus nonmonetary) income below the poverty line as a proportion of total households.
[3]Extreme poverty line from S. Levy 1991.
[4]From CEPAL 1990.

Source: Author's calculations. Data from INEGI's Income Expenditure Survey: 1984, 3rd Quarter. For details, see Lustig 1992.

To what extent could one rely on "trickle down" to eradicate poverty in Mexico? A very straightforward exercise shows that growth alone may reduce poverty too slowly. For example, if the per capita income of the bottom 10 percent of households (the extremely poor) in 1984 were to grow steadily at the average 1988–90 per capita GDP growth rate (about 1 percent per year), the households in that group would have to wait nearly fifty years on average just to reach the income level defined as the cutoff of *extreme* poverty. Under a more optimistic scenario, assuming that the income of the bottom 10 percent grows at 3 percent per year (the per capita growth rate in Mexico's postwar period), the waiting period would drop to about sixteen years. If society's aversion to poverty is

[3]The moderate poverty line used in table 5.1 is slightly more than twice the extreme poverty line, the reason being that the former was proposed by CEPAL (see CEPAL 1990) and the latter by Santiago Levy (1991).

[4]However, part of the difference between the rural and urban incidence of poverty may be artificial because prices may be lower in rural areas. Thus, the poverty line for the rural sector should be lower. The incidence of poverty in rural households would still be higher, but the gap between rural and urban incidences of poverty would be smaller.

sizable, then some redistribution would be necessary to eliminate poverty more quickly. However, this redistribution does not mean that the rich must give up a portion of their base income, but only a portion of the *growth* in that income.

As a percentage of GDP, the income that would have to be redistributed in order for all households to have an income at least equal to the *moderate* poverty line is relatively small. Based on the normalized poverty gap estimated for 1984 (table 5.1) and using the 1990 figures for population and GDP, the proportion of income to be redistributed equals 2.24 percent of GDP. If we use the extreme poverty line as the relevant benchmark, the proportion of income would equal 0.24 percent of GDP. These figures indicate that the eradication of poverty, particularly extreme poverty, should be within reach in both political and economic terms.[5]

The previous calculation, however, is very rudimentary. We must bear in mind that the "cost" of a redistributive policy designed to eliminate poverty must take into account at least three important trade-offs.[6] First, redistribution may occur at the cost of efficiency, particularly because of distortions resulting from the fact that in the real world taxes and transfers cannot be lump sum. Such an efficiency loss would mean that the pie to be redistributed might be smaller than it would have been without the redistributive effort. Second, redistributing income today may reduce tomorrow's income. The argument is straightforward. Since the poor are likely to have a lower propensity to save, a redistribution of income to the poor will reduce overall savings. Since growth requires an increase in investment, less poverty today will—other things equal—result in less income tomorrow (and, thus, more poverty in the future). Moreover, redistributive policies may produce a negative political reaction; the rich and the middle class may try to evade a redistribution effort through capital flight or by creating artificial scarcities. In such cases, the size of the pie may also be much smaller than anticipated, and the intertemporal cost in terms of forgone output may be much higher.

SOLIDARITY: WHAT DOES IT COST, WHAT DOES IT DO?

Social spending in Mexico was severely curtailed as a result of the overall fiscal retrenchment of the 1980s. Between 1983 and 1988 social spending fell 6.2 percent per year. However, the negative impact on the availability of physical and human resources in health and education was not very significant, and in some cases it was not there at all. The reduction in

---

[5]These estimates, however, omit administrative costs and leakages to the nonpoor involved in any income redistribution process. In this sense, the shares of GDP are a lower limit for the costs involved in eradicating poverty.

[6]For an illuminating discussion of these trade-offs, see Bourguignon 1989. The remainder of this section is based on the contents of Bourguignon's article.

social spending reflected a drop in wages and investment in the social sectors rather than a drop in employment. During this period efforts to address poverty with targeted programs were largely abandoned except for continuing the health services provided by the IMSS-COPLAMAR program and introducing targeted food subsidies as general subsidies were phased out (see Friedmann, Lustig, and Legovini 1992). Upon taking office, Salinas immediately reversed the downward trend in social spending. During 1989–90 social development spending rose more than 7 percent per year, and in 1990 it was equal to 37.64 percent of total noninterest government spending. An essential component of Salinas's new social policy was PRONASOL.

WHAT IS PRONASOL?

As mentioned earlier, PRONASOL is an umbrella organization in charge of coordinating health, education, infrastructure, and productive projects designed to improve living conditions of the poor. Table 5.2 lists the projects implemented between 1989 and 1991. The bulk of these are investment projects: that is, transfers of nonresellable assets. They are designed to expand, rehabilitate, or improve the infrastructure available for the provision of basic services. This infrastructure includes things such as health posts, hospitals, schools, water supply systems, sewerage systems, electrification, roads, and food distribution stores. A small number of projects qualify as transfers of current income, such as the scholarship program (Niños en Solidaridad), the forgone interest payments on interest-free loans provided to some productive projects, and the more recently implemented one-year pilot program on nutrition and health.[7]

There are two characteristics of PRONASOL that should be underscored. First and foremost, a number of the projects are designed, executed, and supervised with the participation of the local communities (i.e., the beneficiaries). This is one of PRONASOL's strongest points because it kills five birds with one stone. As a result of this local participation: (1) the projects are implemented according to priorities established by the communities, so welfare is improved in the order preferred by the beneficiaries; (2) the government gains the gratitude of the communities because there has been an explicit link between community requests and government responses; (3) people within the communities are able to develop organizational and managerial skills, which can be used in other political and/or productive activities; (4) leakages due to corruption and carelessness are reduced, so projects

---

[7]Under certain assumptions (about growth of the economy and society's rate of discount of future consumption), this spending pattern implies that either the expected rate of return on PRONASOL's investment project is quite high or that Mexico's aversion to poverty in terms of lack of income is not very high.

TABLE 5.2
PRONASOL: A Description of the Projects

Program	Diagnosis	Item	Available Infrastructure Before Program	Additional Inputs (monetary in billion pesos)			Beneficiaries
				1989 Physical	1990 Physical	1991 (goals) Physical	
HEALTH	2.5 million children under 5 suffering from malnutrition (1988)		…	…	…	…	…
Programa IMSS-Solidaridad (Dec. 1988)		Medical Units	2362 (1988)	341	415	183	>4.0 million in 1985
		Hospitals in areas with large indigenous population			7		3.4 million persons 1989–90
Programa Solidaridad con SSA (Dec. 1988)		Clinics (new)		122	180	144	1.6 million families in 1989–90
		(rehabs)		601	458		
		Hospitals (new)		24	26		
		(rehabs)		80	34		
Hospital Digno (1991)		Hospitals	approx. 600 (1990)	…	…	30	
EDUCATION						…	
Infrastructura Educativa (1989)		Schools (new & rehabs)		14606	13801	18894	1.4 million students in 1989–90
Escuela Digna (March 1990)		Schools (basic ed) (rehab and maint.)		…	20782	84175	4 million students total

TABLE 5.2 (CONTINUED)

Program	Diagnosis	Item	Available Infrastructure Before Program	Additional Inputs (monetary in billion pesos)			Beneficiaries
				1989 Physical	1990 Physical	1991 (goals) Physical	
Niños en Solidaridad (Oct. 1990)	Potential dropout of 6.3 million students. Only 58% finish primary.	Scholarships	...	...	...	181969	...
Apoyo al Servicio Social (1990)		Scholarships		...	115067	169015	
FOOD AND NUTRITION (1989)	Bottom 10% of population's intake is 1/3 of nutritional requirement	CONASUPO stores					
		Rural	15447	1478	4368	1238	
		Urban	3172	1002	2245		
		Dairy stores	1346	476	2123	2722	
		Cocinas populares	(figures obtained by subtracting)	212	686	400	
				60	539		
INFRASTRUCTURE							
Agua Potable y Alcantarillado (1989)	30% of the population without access to running water; 51% without access to sewerage			...	...	...	5 million persons in 1989–90

TABLE 5.2 (CONTINUED)

Program	Diagnosis	Item	Available Infrastructure Before Program	Additional Inputs (monetary in billion pesos)			Beneficiaries
				1989 Physical	1990 Physical	1991 (goals) Physical	
Electrificación Rural (1989)		Water systems (new & rehab)		1197	1979 (water + sewer)	2253	> 5 million persons in 1989–90
		Sewer system					
		Sewer connections		377	338427	657	
		Wells		32			
		Water connections		24581	461750		
Urbanización (1989)	Deficit in street paving 45% and street lighting 35% (1988)			...	...	...	
				...	...	...	
Roads (1989)		Roads (km)	95119	...	...	...	
		New		3702	4038	5415	
HOUSING (1989)	Deficit of 6.1 million "viviendas"	Housing Units (New and Rehab)		50613	55418	48344	
				...	...	...	
Regularization of urban land tenure (1989)	1,787,800 plots were irregular (1988)	Land Titles		301418	450000	450000	775,000 families in 1989–90

TABLE 5.2 (CONTINUED)

Program	Diagnosis	Item	Available Infrastructure Before Program	Additional Inputs (monetary in billion pesos)			Beneficiaries
				1989 Physical	1990 Physical	1991 (goals) Physical	
AGRICULTURE							
Fondos de Solidaridad para la Producción (1990)	Credit to approx. 269,000 peasants (1.2 million hectares not covered by BANRURAL)			...	...	...	648,000 peasants (1.9 mill hectares)
Apoyo a cafeticultores (1989)				...	...	...	217,584 cafeticultores in 1990
SPECIAL PROGRAMS							
Support of indigenous population (1989)				...	...	...	
Fondos para el desarrollo (1990)							100,000 persons per year
Brigadas (1989)							118,594 persons (per year?)
Food supplement (1989)							5839 families (1989–90)
Education (1989)							45,000 children
Agricultural Workers (May 1990)							
Women in Solidaridad (1989)				...	...	...	9791 women (1989) 25146 women (1990)
Municipal Funds of Solidaridad (1990)				...	...		

tend to be less costly; and (5) by asking people in the communities to contribute with either their labor or some other input, the government is in effect able to "collect" some implicit taxes to finance the projects. Not every project in PRONASOL has a large local participation component, and the actual ratio overall is unclear to an outsider. Projects that particularly encourage local participation include, for example, Escuela Digna and Fondos Municipales. Electrification and water supply projects may be able to use much less local participation, particularly in the execution of the projects.

The second important characteristic of PRONASOL is that it has not created a parallel administrative structure. Past experience shows that the creation of parallel structures leads to unsustainable programs. This was the case with COPLAMAR, a program administered out of the president's office during López-Portillo's administration, but quickly abandoned by de la Madrid in 1982. In contrast, PRONASOL is fully integrated into the regular regional planning system of the Mexican government (see Bailey, this volume).[8]

SPENDING ON PRONASOL: HOW MUCH?

According to official statistics, total federal spending on PRONASOL equaled 0.32 percent of GDP in 1989 and 0.68 percent in 1992.[9] As a point of comparison, the entire budget allocated for social development (health, education, and regional and urban development, including PRONASOL) was 6.1 percent and 8.8 percent, respectively. In addition to federal spending, state and municipal governments contribute to PRONASOL's budget. If one adds the contributions made by state and local governments, PRONASOL's total budget was 0.45 percent of GDP in 1989 and 1.08 percent in 1992 (table 5.3).

Based on the poverty gap estimates presented at the beginning of this chapter, extreme poverty could be eliminated if an amount equivalent to 0.25 percent of the 1990 Mexican GDP was fully redistributed to the poor in direct cash transfers. To eliminate moderate poverty would require 2.24 percent. These are very rough calculations since they do not take into account any of the trade-offs discussed above. However, rough as they are, these numbers indicate that if the money spent on PRONASOL during 1990 (0.71 percent of GDP) were given directly and fully

---

[8]A third characteristic worth mentioning is that as part of its "menu," PRONASOL includes projects that are quite innovative: e.g., the use of solar or wind energy to generate electricity in areas where it would be too costly to introduce the normal electrical network.

[9]These numbers were calculated using the GDP figures in Banco de México 1992: 212. The PRONASOL spending figures come from tables 5.2 and 5.3.

TABLE 5.3
SOCIAL SPENDING AND TOTAL SPENDING ON PRONASOL
(BILLIONS OF PESOS AND PERCENTAGES)

Item	1989	1990	1991	1992
Public Spending on PRONASOL (real)	22.86	37.36	47.16	60.78
Public Spending on PRONASOL, Yearly Growth	—	63.40	26.25	28.88
Public Spending on PRONASOL as a Share of GDP	0.45	0.71	0.88	1.08
Public Spending on Social Sectors as a Share of GDP	6.14	6.40	7.85	8.79
Public Spending on PRONASOL as a Share of Total Programmable Public Spending	2.63	4.16	5.07	5.95
Public Spending on PRONASOL as a Share of Public Spending on Social Sectors	7.39	11.05	11.28	12.34
Memo Items				
Public Spending on PRONASOL (nominal)[a]	2,321.40	4,870.80	7,545.60	10,862.30
GDP[b]	511,537.50	689,091.30	852,783.20	1,001,300.00
GDP deflator[c]	10,154.00	13,039.00	15,999.00	17,871.00
Programmable Public Spending[d] (at the federal level only)	88,273.20	117,122.10	148,889.80	182,513.00
Public Spending on Social Sectors[e] (at the federal level only)	31,407.80	44,083.80	66,916.60	88,048.70

[a]Figures obtained from "Progrma Nacional de Solidaridad: Desglose Programático, Inversión Federal y Estatal, 1989–1992." Cuadro 1. Mexico 1993. Mimeo. Includes federal and state-level spending. Converted into real terms using implicit GDP deflator. Figure for 1992 is preliminary.
[b]Figures obtained from "La Política Social en México: Síntesis Gráfica y Estadística." Table Gasto Social con Respecto al PIB, 1983–1992. OAS-Solidaridad. Mexico, July 1992. Mimeo. Figure for 1992 is obtained from "Criterios Generales de Política Económica." Cuadro 6, Evolución Económica Estimada, 1991–1993, p. 56. Presidencia de la República. Mexico 1993. This figure is preliminary.
[c]The implicit GDP deflator has been calculated by author using information from "La Política Social en México: Síntesis Gráfica y Estadística." Table Gasto Social con Respecto al PIB, 1983–1992, and Table Gasto Social con Respecto al PIB, 1983–1992 (constant pesos). OAS-Solidaridad. Mexico, July 1992. Mimeo. And "Criterios Generales de Política Económica." Table 6, Evolucón Económica Estimada 1991–1993, p. 56. Presidencia de la República. Mexico, 1993.
[d]Figures obtained from "La Política Social en México: Síntesis Gráfica y Estadística." Table Gasto Social con Respecto al Gasto Programable 1983–1992. Mexico, July 1992. Mimeo. Figure for 1992 is obtained from "Informe sobre la Situación Económica, las Finanzas Públicas y la Deuda Pública." Table 8, Clasificación Económica de los Gastos Presupuestales del Gobierno Federal 1992, and Table 9, Balance Financiero de Entidades Bajo Control Directo Presupuestal en 1992. México, IV Trimestre, 1992. This figure is preliminary. Programmable spending includes the direct expenditure of the dependencies, organizations and businesses within budget. It also includes fiscal resources channeled to organizations and businesses outside budget. It excludes all interest payments on domestic and foreign public debt.
[e]Figures obtained from "La Política Social en México: Síntesis Gráfica y Estadística." Table Gasto Social con Respecto al Gasto Programable 1983–1992. Mexico, July 1992. Mimeo. Spending on social sectors includes health, education, Solidarity, and urban development.

to the beneficiaries, their incomes would rise above the extreme poverty line.[10]

Two additional considerations are germane to this discussion. First, PRONASOL is not the only government spending that benefits the poor. Part of the spending on education and health through regular administrative channels goes to the poor, as well as part of the regular spending by other agencies. The same goes for targeted food subsidies, although those go primarily to the urban poor. Second, the story is incomplete unless we bring in the government revenue side (i.e., taxation). In particular, if spending on PRONASOL is financed partly by imposing higher taxes on the poor, the net welfare effect on the poor—everything else equal—would be lower. For this purpose it would be important to estimate the level of implicit "taxation" extracted from PRONASOL beneficiaries in the form of free labor or other contributions. Some may object to calling the latter a form of taxation since these contributions are provided on a voluntary basis. However, even if they are not taxes in the conventional sense, the net benefit accruing to participants will be lower if the opportunity cost of their time is not zero. PRONASOL officials have argued that at least a part of the contributions from local recipients in the form of free labor, organization, or management should be included on the "benefit" side of the equation, since as local people participate in project implementation, they develop skills (managerial, for example) and a sense of community that they would not otherwise have. This interesting point means that an assessment of Solidarity's cost-effectiveness would have to incorporate such externalities.

SPENDING ON PRONASOL: FOR WHAT?

In table 5.4 we can observe how PRONASOL's expenditures were allocated among various broad categories during 1989 and 1990.[11] The largest share of expenditures goes to urbanization projects, especially water supply and sewerage systems, which absorbed over 40 percent of total spending on PRONASOL, on average, between 1989 and 1992.[12]

---

[10]This is so because spending on PRONASOL was more than twice the spending required to close that gap in the case of federal spending, and over four times as much if I use the larger number given by the sum of spending on individual projects presented in table 5.2. Nonetheless, people would still be below the moderate poverty line.

[11]This structure may have changed more recently as the Fondos Municipales (under Special Programs) increased.

[12]"Urbanization" does not mean that projects occur in urban settings only. There is no estimate, however, of the rural/urban disaggregation of funds. Additionally, some of the urbanization projects include more superfluous activities such as the "beautification" of central plazas and municipal buildings. Again, it would be useful to have estimates of how much funding is allocated to such projects.

TABLE 5.4A
NATIONAL SOLIDARITY PROGRAMMING STRUCTURE
FEDERAL AND STATE INVESTMENT
(BILLIONS OF PESOS AND PERCENTAGES)

Program	1989			1990		
	Expenditure	Program Share	Grand Total Share	Expenditure	Program Share	Grand Total Share
HEALTH						
Total	200.30	100.00	8.63	352.30	100.00	7.23
Federal	146.90	73.34	6.33	255.20	72.44	5.24
State	53.40	26.66	2.30	97.10	27.56	1.99
EDUCATION						
Total	220.60	100.00	9.50	565.30	100.00	11.61
Federal	141.50	64.14	6.10	324.20	57.35	6.66
State	79.10	35.86	3.41	241.10	42.65	4.95
FOOD & NUTRITION						
Total	61.10	100.00	2.63	50.40	100.00	1.03
Federal	46.90	76.76	2.02	32.70	64.88	0.67
State	14.20	23.24	0.61	17.70	35.12	0.36
URBANIZATION						
Total	1,007.30	100.00	43.39	1,836.10	100.00	37.70
Federal	634.20	62.96	27.32	1,109.60	60.43	22.78
State	373.10	37.04	16.07	726.50	39.57	14.92
RUNNING WATER						
Total	267.10	100.00	11.51	595.30	100.00	12.22
Federal	161.20	60.35	6.94	357.30	60.02	7.34
State	105.90	39.65	4.56	238.00	39.98	4.89
HOUSING & LAND RIGHTS						
Total	35.70	100.00	1.54	103.40	100.00	2.12
Federal	24.90	69.75	1.07	75.60	73.11	1.55
State	10.80	30.25	0.47	27.80	26.89	0.57
AGRICULTURE						
Total	n.a.	...	...	503.40	...	10.34
Federal	n.a.	...	...	395.40	...	8.12
State	n.a.	...	...	108.00	...	2.22
OTHER PRODUCTIVE PROGRAMS						
Total	n.a.	...	...	n.a.	...	...
Federal	n.a.	...	...	n.a.	...	...
State	n.a.	...	...	n.a.	...	...
SPECIAL PROGRAMS						
Total	238.60	100.00	10.28	826.50	100.00	16.97
Federal	191.30	80.18	8.24	627.00	75.86	12.87
State	47.30	19.82	2.04	199.50	24.14	4.10
INDIGENOUS PEOPLE						
Total	36.00	100.00	1.55	134.50	100.00	2.76
Federal	36.00	100.00	1.55	134.50	100.00	2.76
State	n.a.	...	...	n.a.	...	...
REGIONAL PROGRAMS						
Total	557.80	100.00	24.03	633.40	100.00	13.00
Federal	457.90	82.09	19.73	484.80	76.54	9.95
State	99.90	17.91	4.30	148.60	23.46	3.05
FEDERAL TOTAL	1,643.60			3,304.50		
STATE TOTAL	677.80			1,566.30		
GRAND TOTAL	2,321.40		100.00	4,870.80		100.00

Health: Salud y Hospital Digno + Solidaridad para el Servicio Social.
Education: Construccion de Espacios Educativos y Escuela digna + Niños en Solidaridad + Instalaciones Deportivas.
Food & Nutrition: Abasto y Comercializacion.
Urbanization: Solidaridad en Colonias y Comunidados + Agua Potable y Alcantarillado + Electrificacion + Caminos Rurales y Carreteras.
Housing & Land Rights: Vivienda Digna y Tenencia de Tierra.
Agriculture: Fondos de Solidaridad para la Produccion.
Other Productive Programs: Fondo Nacional para Emprsas de Solidaridad.
Special Programs: Fondos Municipales de Solidaridad y Programas de Infractura Social + Mujeres en Solidaridad + Comunidades Indigenas + Otros.
Regional Programs: Programas de Desarrollo Regional.
Source: "Programa Nacional de Solidaridad: Desgiose Programático, Inversión Federal y Estatal, 1989–1992." Cuadro 1. México, 1993. Mimeo.

TABLE 5.4B
NATIONAL SOLIDARITY PROGRAMMING STRUCTURE
FEDERAL AND STATE INVESTMENT
(BILLIONS OF PESOS AND PERCENTAGES)

	1991			1992		
Program	Expenditure	Program Share	Grand Total Share	Expenditure	Program Share	Grand Total Share
HEALTH						
Total	420.70	100.00	5.58	625.40	100.00	5.76
Federal	321.10	76.33	4.26	480.80	76.88	4.43
State	99.60	23.67	1.32	144.60	23.12	1.33
EDUCATION						
Total	1,007.10	100.00	13.35	1,504.90	100.00	13.85
Federal	654.50	64.99	8.67	984.30	65.41	9.06
State	352.60	35.01	4.67	520.60	34.59	4.79
FOOD & NUTRITION						
Total	41.00	100.00	0.54	47.40	100.00	0.44
Federal	27.00	65.85	0.36	21.40	45.15	0.20
State	14.00	34.15	0.19	26.00	54.85	0.24
URBANIZATION						
Total	3,065,70.00	100.00	40.63	5,076.00	100.00	46.73
Federal	1,943.40	63.39	25.76	2,875.20	56.64	26.47
State	1,122.30	36.61	14.87	2,200.80	43.36	20.26
RUNNING WATER						
Total	963.30	100.00	12.77	1,887.80	100.00	17.38
Federal	547.50	56.84	7.26	983.90	52.12	9.06
State	415.80	43.16	5.51	903.90	47.88	8.32
HOUSING & LAND RIGHTS						
Total	166.90	100.00	2.21	96.20	100.00	0.89
Federal	120.40	72.14	1.60	57.10	59.36	0.53
State	46.50	27.86	0.62	39.10	40.64	0.36
AGRICULTURE						
Total	478.80	...	6.35	850.80	...	7.83
Federal	378.60	...	5.02	639.00	...	5.88
State	100.20	...	1.33	211.80	...	1.95
OTHER PRODUCTIVE PROGRAMS						
Total	n.a.	...	...	369.70	...	3.40
Federal	n.a.	...	...	368.40	...	3.39
State	n.a.	...	...	1.30	...	0.01
SPECIAL PROGRAMS						
Total	1,326.90	100.00	17.59	1,326.10	100.00	12.21
Federal	977.90	73.70	12.96	830.00	62.59	7.64
State	349.00	26.30	4.63	496.10	37.41	4.57
INDIGENOUS PEOPLE						
Total	220.30	100.00	2.92	158.40	100.00	1.46
Federal	220.30	100.00	2.92	158.40	100.00	1.46
State	n.a.	...	...	n.a.	...	...
REGIONAL PROGRAMS						
Total	1,038.50	100.00	13.76	965.80	100.00	8.89
Federal	794.20	76.48	10.53	560.80	58.07	5.16
State	244.30	23.52	3.24	405.00	41.93	3.73
FEDERAL TOTAL	5,217.00			6,817.00		
STATE TOTAL	2,328.50			4,045.30		
GRAND TOTAL	7,545.60		100.00	10,862.30		100.00

Health: Salud y Hospital Digno + Solidaridad para el Servicio Social.
Education: Construccion de Espacios Educativos y Escuela digna + Niños en Solidaridad + Instalaciones Deportivas.
Food & Nutrition: Abasto y Comercializacion.
Urbanization: Solidaridad en Colonias y Comunidados + Agua Potable y Alcantarillado + Electrificacion + Caminos Rurales y Carreteras.
Housing & Land Rights: Vivienda Digna y Tenencia de Tierra.
Agriculture: Fondos de Solidaridad para la Produccion.
Other Productive Programs: Fondo Nacional para Emprsas de Solidaridad.
Special Programs: Fondos Municipales de Solidaridad y Programas de Infractura Social + Mujeres en Solidaridad + Comunidades Indigenas + Otros.
Regional Programs: Programas de Desarrollo Regional.
Source: "Programa Nacional de Solidaridad: Desgiose Programático, Inversión Federal y Estatal, 1989–1992." Cuadro 1. México, 1993. Mimeo.

Practically all PRONASOL spending is used to transfer nonresellable assets. In general, all of the projects (water supply systems, sewerage, electrification, adequate school buildings, accessible health posts) improve living conditions in the short term, and will probably increase future incomes either through their effect on human capital (improvement in health and nutrition conditions) or because they increase the value of the properties of the beneficiaries (thanks to roads, sewerage, water, electricity) or allow for the development of new productive activities or new techniques. Very little, however, is allocated to current transfers (exceptions include scholarships and the interest waivers on credit for productive projects). This means that the poverty gap in terms of current income or consumption shortfall is not really addressed in the short run.

Some analysts may argue that part of the income shortfall is addressed through two other channels: the local employment effect and the income derived from the productive projects supported by PRONASOL. Not much is known about the employment effect, but it seems that it may not be significant, for two reasons. First, the larger labor-intensive projects—such as the construction of roads, water supply systems, and electrification—probably do not rely primarily on local labor. Second, the smaller projects that do use local labor inputs usually do not pay for this labor since it is the community's contribution to the project. Nonetheless, this is an area that certainly deserves further analysis. With respect to the productive projects supported by PRONASOL, they are supposed—at least in theory—to meet the cost/benefit criterion. Although such projects may help producers who would have access to capital in the private sector if markets were perfect, it will not help those whose productive activities—whatever they may be—are not profitable. Again, it would be interesting to have an estimate of what proportion of the poor can actually move out of poverty through PRONASOL's support of productive projects.

PRONASOL AND POVERTY REDUCTION

My purpose in considering the data in table 5.2 was to be able to assess the impact of PRONASOL on poverty alleviation in terms of access to basic services. Unfortunately, published information rarely provides pre-PRONASOL figures which can be used as benchmarks against which to compare PRONASOL achievements. For example, we do not know how many health posts and schools were in need of rehabilitation prior to PRONASOL. And when estimates do exist, it is not always clear what year they refer to (this is true, for example, for the data on percentages of the population without access to potable water or sewerage). Second, when measures are available, the units in which "progress" is measured are often heterogeneous; for example, water "systems" can be of widely different scales. Third, the number of beneficiaries is often not provided, and when provided it is not always evident how it was calculated. Fourth, there are no estimates of the projects' impacts on social indicators: malnutrition, school dropout rates, health, etc. Finally, there is no assessment of the cost-effectiveness of the various projects.

According to the numbers in table 5.2, the projects that seem to have had a significant effect on large numbers (millions) of people are those directed toward investment in infrastructure, such as water supply systems, sewerage, and electrification. Next are those projects that deal with investment in health and education facilities. Projects that support productive activities rank third. In terms of spending, additional facilities, and beneficiaries, the numbers indicate that living conditions are improving. However, it is difficult to assess whether, and to what extent, the projects are cost-effective.[13]

It is sometimes argued that, because many PRONASOL projects are demand driven by the beneficiaries, the question of whether or not they are addressing poverty in the "right" way is irrelevant. If we assume that the community knows best, then we must abide by the priorities set by the communities and their decisions on how PRONASOL funds are to be used. Three comments are in order here. First, it is not clear what proportion of PRONASOL spending is actually determined by the beneficiaries' priorities. Second, even if this were the case for all projects, the question remains whether the most vocal and organized communities or groups within communities are also the poorest. It is conceivable that the poorest communities, or the most vulnerable within a community (e.g., the children), have a disadvantage in organizing themselves and expressing their priorities. This issue deserves particular attention. Third, the priorities established by the communities without experienced advice may be less than optimal. For example, communities commonly prefer hospitals and doctors over primary health care facilities and nurses or auxiliaries, even though the latter are proven to be a more cost-effective form of health care delivery.

Available evidence on the allocation of PRONASOL funds indicates that there are some problems. PRONASOL funds should go to the poorest sections of the population first. However, a recent cross-sectional analysis of PRONASOL spending by state finds that the coefficient for the level of poverty is negative: i.e., the poorer the state, the

---

[13]Currently there are several studies under way to analyze the cost-effectiveness and performance of specific projects. Also, see the chapter by Gershberg in this volume.

smaller the per capita spending on PRONASOL.[14] Another econometric study which focuses on the Escuela Digna project finds that the results show a potential failure to target the needy indigenous populations effectively at the micro, or project, level (Gershberg, this volume). At an anecdotal level, I found a similar result when visiting several sites in the state of Morelos. Of three neighborhoods I visited, the poorest had received much less in attention and resources than the other, relatively more affluent, communities.

Some authors have argued that Solidarity spending is guided by political/electoral criteria, and that this may explain why the poorest (and also the most politically marginalized) are not the first or primary beneficiaries (see Dresser and others, this volume). However, there may be less Machiavellian reasons for this spending pattern. First, as mentioned earlier, demand-driven projects may omit the poorest because they live in isolated areas or lack a capacity for self-organization. Second, the institutional process of allocating Solidarity funds may have an imbedded inertia or bias in favor of the most active state governors; this would result in a less optimal allocation of funds, in per capita terms, from the perspective of poverty reduction (see Bailey, this volume). Whatever the reason, these results call for a close review of the allocation process. To reach the poorest first, Solidarity might have to adopt a more "intentional" approach, rather than relying primarily on demand-driven projects.

As mentioned earlier, poverty can be measured using two types of indicators: lack of access to basic services, or an income below a pre-established poverty line. These two concepts are quite different and do not necessarily refer to the same population. It is quite likely that those who have no access to basic services will also be poor according to the income shortfall measure. However, it has been noted in the past that large sections of the population may continue to have access to basic services (though perhaps of poorer quality) but have incomes below the poverty line, especially during times of economic downturn.[15]

More importantly, although investment in social services is crucial and raises the welfare of the population, it will not reduce that aspect of poverty caused by the lack of adequate income. What is the advantage of having a good health post, a good school building, or running water if family income is too low to bring food intake to the acceptable nutritional minimum? Poverty that results from an income shortfall will not disappear in the short term, and, as we saw earlier, growth alone would

[14]Molinar and Weldon (this volume) use two different specifications to test this hypothesis. In one, "poverty" is measured by the proportion of the economically active population with an income below the minimum wage. In the other, the authors use as their measure of poverty the proportion of people who are fifteen years of age or older and illiterate.

[15]This was particularly notable in Argentina during the 1980s.

be extremely slow in moving people out of poverty. It is true that the Mexican government is undertaking current transfers through channels that are not part of PRONASOL, such as the targeted programs for tortillas and milk. Measured in monetary terms these transfers seem to be large enough to bring a portion of the participant families above the extreme poverty line. However, in the tortilla program, for example, the benefit is uniform for all the families with incomes below two minimum wages; therefore, this program does not concentrate on helping the poorest of the poor first.[16] But the greatest shortcoming with targeted food subsidy programs is that they primarily benefit the urban poor. The rural poor, who are the poorest of the population, probably receive a much smaller transfer through this type of subsidy.

If poverty due to inadequate income is to be addressed as well, then PRONASOL should expand or initiate projects that have a current transfer component.[17] These should not be linked to productive projects when those projects are not economically viable. Rather they should focus on transferring income (or consumption) to the more vulnerable groups within the poor. Two types of projects come to mind. One is the scholarship project (Niños en Solidaridad) and the other is the World Bank-supported health and nutrition pilot project, which transferred food to poor rural households along with health services. One way to transfer more current resources to poor families would be to expand the scholarship project. Its advantage is that it transfers income in the present and at the same time supports investment in human capital. The health and nutrition pilot program (whose results are now being examined) could be improved and expanded to allow an increasing number of the poorest families to gain access to this form of current transfer.

---

[16]The tortilla program operates primarily in urban areas. Families with incomes below two times the minimum wage are eligible to receive one kilogram of free tortillas per day. The system uses a computerized monitoring system based on an optically readable "smart card." The subsidy is estimated to be between U.S. $90–129 per family per year, or about four times the average extreme poverty gap.

[17]It would be interesting to find out what the communities would choose if given the chance: an investment project (such as a school improvement) or a current transfer.

6

Centralism and Political Change in Mexico: The Case of National Solidarity

John Bailey

President Carlos Salinas introduced the National Solidarity Program in December 1988 to confront a profound crisis of presidentialism, as discussed in the introductory chapter to this volume. Budgeted at U.S. $2.14 billion in 1992 and $2.46 billion in 1993,[1] Solidarity is probably the most ambitious and multifaceted member of the family of "compensatory" programs implemented recently in Eastern Europe, Latin America, and elsewhere for the purpose of cushioning the shocks of economic stabilization and structural adjustment policies (see Graham's chapter and the Appendix, this volume.) PRONASOL arguably alleviates poverty to some degree, but the program is more usefully viewed as an important instrument in efforts to restructure Mexico's overall political economy in ways that promote modernization while preserving centralized presidential rule.

The central issues with respect to the nature of political change in Mexico in the early 1990s concern the connections between the government's aggressive economic restructuring program and the reform of sociopolitical institutions and processes. The question from the governing elites' perspective is, How can necessary economic changes be promoted without producing an uncontrollable political backlash? From a different vantage point opposition parties ask, How can the forces set loose in the reform process be harnessed to effect a transition to genuinely competitive democracy? Obviously, in a complex centralized system with scores of agencies and hundreds of administrative groups, or teams, we should expect to find multiple, competing agendas. Some

---

[1] Estimated from budget data reported in *El Financiero Internacional*, November 23, 1992.

groups appear genuinely committed to PRONASOL's stated goals. Others use the program for their own ends. Further, the rhythm of the presidential term (the *sexenio*) implies that the innovation and reform of the first years will give way to consolidation and control as the succession approaches, in this case in late 1993 or early 1994.

The working hypothesis of this chapter is that the "real" (as opposed to the announced) goal of the Salinas administration with regard to domestic political change is not democratization, taken to mean genuine party competition and the structural requisites for procedural democracy. Rather, the goal is to reconstitute Mexico's strong centralist, presidential system on new institutional and coalitional bases.[2] This implies a strategy of relying less on existing bases of support that are deemed dysfunctional for modernization (with emphasis on the economic), while constructing new bases that are considered consistent with the broader economic and social project. It implies further that the political system envisaged will continue in Mexico's centralist tradition of weak state and municipal governments subordinated to a strong, restructured central government.

From this perspective, political change involves two simultaneous games, taking game in its common-sense meaning. In the old-style politics, the players that enjoy access to power through nationally organized, semicorporatist structures, such as labor and peasant confederations, receive sufficient rewards (and/or threats) to preserve their loyalties to the governing elite, or at least to prevent their defection to the opposition. At the same time, in the new-style politics spaces are opened to newly legitimated groups, such as business, the Church, and middle-strata actors, which are to gain "front door" access to the governing party and central government bureaucracy. With the erosion of the old architecture of centralized worker and farmer organizations, informal or loosely organized groups, such as urban and rural popular movements, take on greater importance as actors, not only in relation to public bureaucracies and programs but also as voters in "formal" democracy. This is not to suggest that the new politics is less centrally defined, at least in the early stages of the transition; in fact it seems more likely that the central government and presidency assume even more power as a prerequisite to their efforts to reconstitute their bases of support. Further, such a project for transition does not exclude limited and centrally conceded instances of genuine electoral competition or of negotiated concessions to the opposition. It does, however, impede changing the core logic from presidential authoritarianism to one of generalized, transparent rules.

---

[2]The interpretation that follows fits most closely with the scenario of "modernization of authoritarianism," as sketched by Cornelius, Gentleman, and Smith (1989b: 36–45).

SOLIDARITY'S ROLE IN THE LOGIC OF CHANGE

Sustained economic growth with low inflation is the overriding goal for the Salinas administration. Economic success is the prerequisite for regime relegitimation. Given internal and external levels of public debt, the engine of growth must necessarily be private-sector investment, much of it to be attracted from abroad. Reducing inflation implies a series of orthodox financial reforms (e.g., holding the line on public spending while expanding the tax base and intensifying tax collection; restructuring internal and external debt; restraining growth of money supply), as well as reforms to promote greater overall efficiency. The latter reforms include the privatization of "nonstrategic" public enterprises through their sale to either the private or "social" sector,[3] their transfer to the state or local level, or simply their elimination. Also important is restructuring subsidy programs away from generalized benefits (e.g., subsidized staple goods available through public markets) toward targeted benefits (e.g., requiring means tests to receive coupons, or "*tortibonos*," to exchange for food). Yet another area concerns tightening the definition of creditworthiness in allocating public credit to farmers. Most of these measures create large groups of losers in the short term.

Solidarity programs help ameliorate at least some of the negative effects of structural adjustment. For example, as the privatization of INMECAFE (the coffee institute) exposes small-scale, usually impoverished coffee growers to market forces, Solidarity can provide limited credits through revolving-fund mechanisms. Similar "production fund" arrangements can be set up for high-risk farmers who are cut from bank lending rolls. The main differences are that PRONASOL provides smaller amounts of benefits through more targeted mechanisms. That is, instead of providing benefits to whole categories of recipients, the beneficiaries must meet a series of administrative requirements as determined by central authorities and, in many cases, must also take the initiative to request assistance.

Apart from specific groups hurt directly by structural adjustment measures, PRONASOL targets benefits to the very poorest in Mexican society. The rationale is to revalidate the government's commitment to social justice, but also important is the general recognition that overall economic policy in the 1980s has worsened income distribution. Two such impoverished groups are Indian communities, located largely in the south (Chiapas, Oaxaca, Guerrero), and the urban shantytown communities present throughout the country. Solidarity also provides a

---

[3]The social sector refers mainly to cooperative factories or service enterprises (often belonging to labor unions), as well as to ejidos, which are cooperative farms making up about half of Mexico's arable land. The concept was raised to constitutional status by President de la Madrid in 1983.

number of targeted benefits to other territorially defined groups—e.g., specific regions such as La Laguna in Coahuila—as well as to disparate disadvantaged groups—e.g., lower-strata women and children, migrant workers. In fact the twenty-plus programs reach diverse populations, and a particular family in a given locale could conceivably benefit from several of them (see Appendix).

While sustained economic recovery and poverty alleviation are the government's primary goals, two other threads in the fabric of reform are grassroots participation and administrative decentralization. The first notion, popular participation in demand-based public works or social projects, is straightforward and appears in most compensatory-type programs. Lower-strata groups are encouraged to organize themselves to petition for benefits, to participate in project selection and implementation, and often to pay some portion of costs. This sort of participation should support the transition from a paternalistic state acting on a passive civil society, to a relationship of solidarity between a downsized government and a more dynamic society. Decentralization, discussed below, is more complicated.

Beyond the mechanics of programs and bureaucracies, an important challenge for the overall reform project is how to legitimate "modernization" in the context of Mexico's populist traditions, the subject of Dresser's chapter in this volume. That is, the various pacts between government and the popular strata that contributed to the success of Mexico's inclusionary form of authoritarianism suffer the direct adverse consequences of the economic restructuring. Wages, along with a whole array of subsidies, have been slashed. Solidarity contributes to the effort to legitimate the broader project, to demonstrate—as much to the middle and upper strata as to the poor—the state's commitment to marginal groups. In effect, the state moves from constitutional guarantees to labor (Article 123) and the poor (Articles 3, 27) to promises of "solidarity."[4] In sum, while PRONASOL shares some features of other compensatory programs in Latin America (e.g., grassroots participation, bureaucratic independence), it arguably plays a more important role in a well-considered logic of regime recomposition, in good part by re-legitimating presidential centralism. The reinforcement of presidentialism, however, hinders the transition to political democracy.

This chapter assesses the impact of PRONASOL on the nature of political change in Mexico, emphasizing bureaucratic structures and center-periphery relations. My goal is to simplify aspects of a complex set of programs and a dynamic political context so that the chapters that follow might be more comprehensible. I begin with a review of basic politico-administrative concepts and relationships; this is followed by a

---

[4]This issue of commitment to the poor is reflected as well in the government's emphasis on an ideology of "social liberalism," in response to criticism about its "neoliberal" bias.

description of aspects of the Mexican planning and budgeting apparatus. With this as background, I analyze the ways in which one of the more significant programs, Fondos Municipales de Solidaridad, affects relations of power between the central, state, and local governments. The question investigated is whether PRONASOL acts to reinforce presidentialism, in either a traditional or modernizing form, or whether the overall effect might promote systemic change, be it toward democracy or something else.

Lacking a comprehensive evaluation of Solidarity, or even much by way of systematic data, my discussion must be a bit formalistic and anecdotal. Like the proverbial elephant, PRONASOL presents contrasting images to the information impaired. My direct field experience with PRONASOL is limited to Nuevo León, which is not a priority state in the program, and I must rely on interviews and public sources for impressions about other states.[5] Even with these limitations, however, we can identify trends and issues more precisely. The nub of my argument is that Solidarity acts to *deconcentrate*, not to *decentralize*, administration. Yet, while the short-term effect is to bolster presidentialism, the program may help create conditions to support decentralization over the longer term.

CENTRALISM AND REGIME CHANGE

We should link Solidarity to the more general conversation about political change and democratization. Following O'Donnell and Schmitter (1986: 7), we distinguish between liberalization and democratization. The former refers to the "process of making effective certain rights that protect both individuals and social groups from arbitrary or illegal acts committed by the state or third parties." Liberalization is usually indicative of the beginning phases of a transition and deals with basic rights and freedoms, such as speech, physical integrity of the person and home, fair and impartial justice, and the like. For groups, it refers to freedoms such as communication, assembly, and lawful dissent.

Democratization centers on the notion of citizenship, involving both rights and obligations. It implies the right of participation and influence in decision-making processes that affect individual citizens. Further, democratization suggests a process of expanding participation to include persons previously excluded for reasons of poverty, youth, minority status, and the like (O'Donnell and Schmitter 1986: 8). Important to both liberalization and democratization is the shift from arbitrary government action to procedures and policy based on generalized rules.

---

[5] To the extent possible, I rely on public documents. Interviews were conducted between September 1991 and January 1993, using a journalistic equivalent of "not for attribution." With only a few lapses, I have tried to resist the temptation to use direct quotes.

And democratization ultimately assumes popular controls over ruling elites through periodic elections.

It seems apparent that liberalization and democratization are linked in historical experience, although not in a fixed and necessary sequence. That is, liberalization implies granting individual and group freedoms that may make possible the expansion of rules and obligations of citizenship. But one change need not lead to the other. In fact, authoritarian rulers may permit some degree of liberalization precisely in order to relieve pressures and/or admit new coalition members so that further steps toward democratization may be avoided; that is, so that they might survive with minimum adjustments. O'Donnell and Schmitter have called this "liberalized authoritarianism" or "dictablanda" (1986: 9). Furthermore, one can envision various degrees and mixes of liberalization and democratization; and the processes need be neither unidimensional nor irreversible.

With Mexico, we focus primarily on liberalization measures introduced by regime elites who are pursuing strategies to respond to crisis in ways that do not threaten their own rule (see Middlebrook 1986; D. Levy 1989). It is a regime characterized by impressive centralism, an ingrained distrust of the competence and even the loyalty of state and local governments, and a strong preference to manage national life from the capital city. Further, it is a form of centralism in which power is highly concentrated in the Office of the Presidency and in which other institutions and practices are designed to reinforce presidential power.

We also need to clarify basic relationships between center and periphery, and between the presidency and other institutions. Of obvious interest are degrees of centralization-decentralization with respect to decision making. Following Mexican terminology, which is consistent with general usage, we take decentralization to refer to the devolution of decision-making authority to constitutionally authorized bodies separate from the central government line ministries that operate under presidential authority. This can take the form of "functional decentralization," as when duties and powers are transferred to an autonomous agency within the national government administration. An example is the National Autonomous University of Mexico (UNAM), which enjoys an important degree of autonomy from the Ministry of Education (D. Levy 1979). The other main type of devolution is "territorial decentralization," which in a federal system like Mexico's refers to granting constitutional powers to regional subgovernments, like river valley authorities, or to state governments and municipalities (Beltrán and Portilla 1986: 92).

"Deconcentration," in contrast, refers to delegating some degree of decision-making authority from the federal ministries to their own field offices operating in the states and municipalities, or to state and local bureaucracies themselves. For example, the Ministry of Internal Affairs (Gobernación) might delegate more powers to its field office in the state of Baja California to decide particular cases of immigrant status for foreigners in that state. Or the Ministry of the Treasury might expand the administrative discretion of its officials in the state of Guerrero to issue tax exemptions to qualifying businesses. The objective usually is greater efficiency and convenience. In contrast to decentralization, though, the field offices operate under the authority and supervision of the central ministries; and powers that have been deconcentrated by executive order can be reconcentrated by a similar measure. Similarly, a federal program deconcentrated to a state or municipal agency remains under central guidance and may be reconcentrated at the central government's will.[6] For example, federally mandated health inspections conducted by state health agencies remain under federal supervision and control. Deconcentration becomes especially complicated when federal funds are blended with state and local spending, giving federal authorities some degree of control over a joint activity. *Solidarity's operating logic is one of deconcentration, not decentralization; and the distinction is critical to the nature of regime recomposition.*

Apart from center-periphery relations, another institutional dimension concerns the relationships between executive power (the national presidency, governorships, municipal presidencies) and legislative and judicial bodies. This we might think of as executive dominance versus checks and balances. To what extent do the federal legislature and supreme court operate independently and effectively from the presidency? Similar questions would apply to governors' dealings with state legislatures and courts, as well as mayors' interactions with municipal councils. *Solidarity operates to reinforce executive dominance.*

We need to rehearse these relationships in order to describe patterns of change. We should avoid the naive assumption that territorial decentralization leads necessarily to either liberalization or democratization. Nor should we assume a priori that decentralization promotes greater administrative efficiency or more equitable distribution of benefits. Consider, for example, the implications of decentralizing power from a reformist, progressive center to state or local governments dominated by authoritarian cliques (which is precisely the worry of many central actors, based on repeated experiences). On the other hand, territorial decentralization provides more opportunities for the citizenry throughout the country to participate in decision-making processes important to their daily lives. To take De Tocqueville's hypothesis, such citizen (usually elite) involvement with debate, legitimate opposition, and

---

[6]Deconcentration may in fact increase central control, as seen, for example, in the case of the Ministry of Education (SEP) in the late 1970s. "The deconcentration tightened central control . . . by establishing one delegation in each state and granting the SEP delegates— who answered directly to the education minister—control over the programming of resources and matters relating to teaching personnel, undermining the authority of the directors general" (Cook 1990: 206).

alternation in power contributes to create habits of behavior that support democratic politics on the broader scale.[7]

But liberalization can advance along routes other than decentralization. It makes intuitive sense to link checks and balances, the strengthening of legislatures and courts, with liberalization, if we take this to mean the competition among various forces (e.g., groups, organizations, bureaucracies) in a policy-making process. Institutional competition ought to reduce the arbitrary power of the executive. Such pluralism, however, would imply democratization only to the extent that the significant institutions, especially legislatures at all levels, are made accountable to mass publics through mechanisms of periodic and free elections.

Though Solidarity operates through many and diverse programs, its overall nature is presidential, executive-dominant, and centralist. PRONASOL *deconcentrates* program implementation to state governments and municipalities and to federal field offices through grant-in-aid mechanisms, but effective decision authority remains in Mexico City.[8] In this sense the program belongs to a long tradition of resilient and imaginative presidential centralism. At the same time, however, PRONASOL appears to strengthen actors (e.g., neighborhood committees, municipal administrators) that might, over the longer term, reinforce grassroots demand making. Solidarity reformists refer to this possibility as their "bet" (*apuesta*) that the program will produce significant reform (author interview, Mexico City, January 1993). Thus, the interesting question is whether PRONASOL might create or reinforce tendencies that will promote political change, perhaps in unanticipated ways, over the longer term.

DECENTRALIZATION, REGIONAL DEVELOPMENT,
AND POVERTY ALLEVIATION

Mexico rightly enjoys its reputation as perhaps the most centralized nation in a region characterized by centralization. An important dimension of this phenomenon concerns taxing and spending. Table 6.1 illustrates the relatively greater degree of central government control

---

[7]Francisco Gil Villegas (1986) provides an excellent discussion of these themes. With respect to decentralization and structural reform, Sheahan (1991: 59) suggests: "In general, [structural adjustment] favors decentralization of power: it undercuts the use of economic controls to fortify state authority and fosters a more complex, pluralistic society, less likely to tolerate authoritarian government." Thus, we should distinguish between transition, which might see centralization reinforced, and the longer-term result.

[8]To clarify terms, a grant-in-aid, in U.S. usage, is a federal grant implemented by state and local governments that carries numerous restrictions and guidelines. A block grant, in contrast, provides federal money for general purpose categories such as education, public health, transportation, and the like, allowing state and local governments considerable leeway to define specific projects. Revenue sharing allocates tax money to states without restrictions.

over revenues and expenditures in the case of Mexico in the mid-1980s. Only Chile, a formally centralist system, shows greater fiscal concentration at the national level.

TABLE 6.1
TAXING AND SPENDING BY LEVEL OF GOVERNMENT: SELECTED CASES
(% DISTRIBUTION)

	Revenues			Expenditures		
	Federal	State	Local	Federal	State	Local
Australia (1988)	60	35	5	60	35	5
Brazil (1988)	77	17	6	69	23	8
Canada (1989)	40	43	17	43	41	16
Chile (1988)	92	8*		91	9*	
Mexico (1984)	84	16*		89	12*	
U.S. (1988)	51	26	23	56	23	20
Argentina (1988)	59	41*		56	44*	

*Combined state (or department) plus local.
Source: IMF, 1990.

The obvious point, before we take up some details about bureaucracy, is that the central government virtually monopolizes taxing and spending. The main source of state and local revenues is the system of revenue sharing, which itself is centralized. Further, the vast bulk of federal spending is done by the central government ministries based on decisions taken in the capital. If decentralization were indeed a priority, the simplest measure would be to reallocate revenues more equitably between levels of government, an option which remains strictly taboo in the PRI-government system. In fact, as I have argued elsewhere (Bailey 1992b), the trend in Mexico since the late 1970s is toward even greater centralization in fiscal policy-making.[9]

The pertinent threads of Solidarity's policy history include decentralization, distribution of federal investment spending among the states, and antipoverty policies. In the de la Madrid *sexenio* (1982–88) a

---

[9]For example, the system of "fiscal coordination," which gave important powers to the states, was recentralized in 1989.

small fraction of central government investment was made available to the states under relatively looser controls through a program called "Regional Development" (Desarrollo Regional), the immediate antecedent of Solidarity. In 1988, with the advent of PRONASOL, that small amount was first "recaptured" by the central government and then substantially expanded in a strategy of reinforcing presidential power. Along with (re)centralization, we find a clearer effort to redistribute spending toward the poorer states.

Though Mexican presidents have typically advocated regional development, if not the redistribution of wealth among the regions, specific policies toward this end were not attempted until the administration of Luis Echeverría (1970–76). His government invested relatively greater resources in rural development and antipoverty initiatives and targeted industrial development as a strategy of promoting growth poles outside the Valley of Mexico. Regional development was promoted even more aggressively in the *sexenio* of José López Portillo (1976–82), whose master plan called for four industrial ports to serve as regional growth poles. Other programs, such as COPLAMAR, PIDER, and SAM, were designed to promote agricultural productivity and ameliorate malnutrition.

An important stocktaking of these efforts concludes that the Echeverría and López Portillo governments largely fell short in their efforts to promote regional development and redistribution. Two reasons are stressed: federal investment, which was the primary policy instrument during 1970–82, largely reinforced the existing maldistribution of wealth, and disincentives were not used to steer private investment away from wealthy and toward poor regions.

> There is evidence that the regional policies of the Echeverría and de la Madrid administrations were not carried out in accord with their declared objectives, given that federal public investments—their primary tool— were not directed to the geographic areas which the attainment of the policy goals would have dictated. That is, a decentralization from the Federal District toward the states, particularly those with a relatively lower level of development.
>
> Moreover, these policies were virtually ineffective in their aim to promote the decentralization of industrial investment, despite the fact that during the 1970s these two administrations established the first regionally differentiated development schemes at the national level in Mexico. This relative failure can be explained in large part by the absolute reliance of decentralization policies

on the use of incentives to capital and the refusal to
restrict industrial development in areas of high concentration, primarily the Valley of Mexico (Palacios 1989:
236–37).

President de la Madrid took apparently contradictory steps with
respect to decentralization. The severe economic crisis of the 1980s ruled
out much attention to poverty alleviation and redirected emphasis
toward such symbolic issues as anticorruption initiatives and strengthening municipal government. De la Madrid's main accomplishment had
been to author and implement López Portillo's national plan. He also
brought to the presidency a keen interest in Mexico's liberal traditions,
especially the role of the independent municipality. Thus, de la Madrid's
election campaign emphasized both central government planning and
political decentralization, and his government introduced constitutional
amendments to promote both ends. The result was an apparent contra-
diction: to strengthen a centrally controlled national planning system,
and at the same time to promote municipal independence.

One set of constitutional amendments (Articles 25–28) established
the central government as rector of the economy, defined strategic areas
of economic life to remain under public-sector control, and raised to
constitutional status the concept of a national system of democratic
planning. At the same time, Article 115 was amended to strengthen
municipal governments, in large part by spelling out the services they
are required to provide and the revenue sources to which they are legally
entitled. The probable intended effect of the clarification was to help
mayors in their budget negotiations with state governors, who had
acquired a generally deserved reputation for greater centralization and
arbitrariness than even the central government.

De la Madrid's interest in both central planning and municipal
government reflects Mexico's particular mix of the traditions of nine-
teenth-century liberalism and the twentieth-century activist, welfare
state. Overall, the latter tradition—with its attendant centralizing bias—
has typically prevailed. That is, while the Constitution calls for the
standard liberal formula of separation of powers, federalism, individual
rights and obligations, and popular suffrage, the reality is a centralized
party-state system, dominated by the presidency, which effectively
ignores Congress and the judiciary, and much prefers complex bureaucratic control mechanisms over institutional checks and balances.

With regard to de la Madrid's style of planning, this meant, for
example, continuing to ignore formally constituted legislatures and
emphasizing instead "popular consultations." These were mass meetings with varieties of groups, often with the president himself presiding,
at which public demands were recorded to help inform the centralized
planning process. In this sense, de la Madrid was continuing the

"technified" version of the activist presidency, as introduced by Echeverría and raised to extraordinary heights by López Portillo.

Put simply, de la Madrid constructed an effective planning-budgeting apparatus that marginalized formal legislatures and subordinated state and local governments to a constitutionally mandated planning system.[10] An irony was that a statist, forward-looking planning system was installed in the early 1980s just as the economy collapsed. Even so, the planning machinery served effectively as the structure within which regional development policy, and later PRONASOL, could be coordinated.

Two particular mechanisms help us understand center-state relations in terms pertinent to Solidarity: the structures created to improve bureaucratic coordination, and the method of linking central with state and local planning and budgeting. The coordinating structure, originally called the COPRODE (roughly, Promotion Committee for Economic Development), was first introduced in the poorer states (Yucatán, 1971; Chiapas and Oaxaca, 1973) and was gradually extended to the remaining states by 1975. It was intended to serve as a consultative mechanism, to include private-sector groups as well as federal and state agencies, in the formulation and implementation of plans. The Convenio Unico de Coordinación (CUC, or Single Coordinating Agreement) was a device introduced by the López Portillo government to link multiyear planning processes to annual budgeting, by coordinating the financing of projects by the federal and state governments. Negotiated annually in each of the thirty-one states (the Federal District was and is handled as a central line department), the CUC was a treaty-like document that recorded the agreements worked out by federal, state, and municipal authorities about project priorities and means of finance. Further, the newly created Ministry of Budget and Planning (SPP) channeled certain funds through the CUC-COPRODE mechanism in order that the states might implement small-scale public works under federal guidelines. Over time, the CUC proved its worth as a device useful to implement projects that did not clearly fit the central government bureaucratic scheme and in which state cooperation was useful (Ortega Lomelín 1988: 283–87). Also, starting in 1976 federal subsidies to cover financial shortfalls in states and municipalities were channeled through the CUC. By 1978 certain CUC programs became known as state investment programs to emphasize that they were considered to be deconcentrated. And the states were brought into—made co-responsible for—the administration of certain multiagency federal programs, such as COPLAMAR and PIDER. In 1981 the SAM was channeled through the CUC as well (author interviews, Mexico City, October 1991).

---

[10] As a former Nuevo León state official put it, there is *one plan*, the national plan; state and local plans have to fit within the national plan (author interview, Monterrey, October 1991).

Designed to facilitate federal-state coordination, the CUC probably had the overall effect of strengthening the presidency by forcing certain intrabureaucratic negotiations out of the hands of cabinet secretaries and state governors and into the open (although the agreements were couched rather vaguely, and we have no research about whether they were really kept). And the annual ceremonies at which the CUC was signed in the various states by the president (or by an appropriate surrogate sent from Mexico City) reminded all parties who really governed.

Along with the national planning system and free municipality, the de la Madrid government introduced significant changes in coordinating mechanisms. In 1981, while de la Madrid was still SPP secretary, the COPRODEs were renamed COPLADEs (Planning Committees for State Development) and put under the coordination of the state governors, this to emphasize their role as state mechanisms. Though the state planning-budgeting agencies typically staffed the COPLADEs, decision-making power remained with the SPP field offices in the states, whose chiefs were the principal negotiators on matters of federal spending. Also, the CUC was replaced by the CUD (Single Development Agreement) to reinforce the point about state development.

As secretary of planning and budget in the de la Madrid government, Carlos Salinas consolidated various interagency programs that López Portillo had administered out of Presidency on an ad hoc basis. These were grouped into a regular budget line, "Regional Development," or Branch (Ramo) 26 as it became known. Administered by Undersecretary Manuel Camacho Solís, Branch 26 contained the programmatic elements that later evolved into Solidarity.[11] The purpose of Branch 26 was twofold: to promote deconcentration by giving the state governments some flexibility in choosing from a mix of federally funded welfare and infrastructure programs, and to distribute federal investment money preferentially to the poorest states. The funds still came with varying degrees of guidelines, but there was a sense of pragmatic negotiation among state and federal budget officers about how to blend federal and local resources to best achieve state purposes.

To be sure, Branch 26 represented only a modest amount of federal investment, and the central ministries continued to control the great bulk of federal spending in the states. But in a period of extreme austerity, Regional Development funds could be quite significant: "in several states the funds provided to the programs for regional development and employment exceeded the investments that the state governments made with their own funds" (SPP 1988: 35).

---

[11]SPP was the bureaucratic base for the main groups of top officials in both the de la Madrid and Salinas governments. See, e.g., Hernández Rodríguez 1987.

To sum up a bit, from its halting missteps in the mid-1970s, SPP had evolved under Miguel de la Madrid and Carlos Salinas into an effective budget master, increasingly tightening its hold over state and local governments through its control of the CUD-COPLADE machinery.

Solidarity originated in December 1988 in SPP's Subministry of Regional Development, headed by Carlos Rojas and administered through SPP's field offices in the states. Rather than the product of systematic planning, PRONASOL was more the translation of certain principles (redistribution, de-bureaucratization, grassroots participation) into specific programs. Over the next four years (1989–92), programs were adapted, invented, or simply relabeled on the run. An administrative reorganization in January 1992 abolished SPP, transferred most of the budget-making powers back to Treasury, and shifted PRONASOL to the Ministry of Social Development (SEDESOL), which was created from the former Ministry of Ecology and Urban Development (SEDUE). Rather than Rojas, however, Senator Luis Donaldo Colosio, president of the PRI's national executive committee, was appointed to head SEDESOL. In the new structure, Solidarity was arguably better integrated with urban development and ecology. SPP's field offices also passed to SEDESOL, and the CUD was renamed the Social Development Agreement (CDS). Further, a new "technical cabinet of social development" was established in Presidency, bringing together the secretaries of SHCP, SEDESOL, Education, and Health, and headed by Colosio. Finally, a new legal instrument, the Concertation Agreement, was created as an annex to the CDS to permit the federal government to legally transfer funds through and around state governments to the municipalities.[12]

Even as the programmatic offspring of Regional Development, Solidarity differs from its parent in important ways. Regional Development focused mainly on the state level and the COPLADE. Though the COPLADE remains the main coordinating mechanism, PRONASOL has more options to work around the governors to deliver services directly to the grassroots. Regional Development emphasized the need for the states and municipalities to take the initiative in developing their own plans in the framework of the national planning system. Solidarity avoids any rhetoric about planning, and its rich menu of grassroots-oriented programs fills virtually all policy space. Further, Solidarity operates with more aggressive matching-fund mechanisms that tend to

[12]SEDUE's principal focus had been housing and urban infrastructure, with much of its emphasis on the Mexico City metropolitan area, especially in the aftermath of the September 1985 earthquake. Colosio's appointment to head SEDESOL reinforced speculation about an eventual convergence of Solidarity with the PRI. Regarding coordination of social policy, President Salinas retained the system of technical cabinets created by his predecessor in the Office of the Presidency. These are small coordinating staffs in areas such as foreign affairs, national security, economy, and the like, which monitor and coordinate presidential initiatives as these are implemented by the bureaucracy.

mobilize more resources than was the case with Regional Development. Finally, in the matter of presidentialism, PRONASOL reinforces Salinas's image and power much more effectively than Regional Development served de la Madrid.

SOLIDARITY, MUNICIPALITY, GRASSROOTS PARTICIPATION

PRONASOL is so complex that it is difficult to generalize. But it would appear that PRONASOL spending in the states comes with more extensive programmatic restrictions than was the case by and large with Regional Development. In effect, state-generated programs are largely squeezed out of the CUD (now CDS), and the little money that the states have left over after meeting essential spending is devoted to qualifying for PRONASOL matching funds (author interviews, Monterrey, October–November 1991; Mexico City, December 1991).

Most Solidarity programs focus on specific clienteles, though they may not necessarily involve grassroots committees or participation by municipal governments. Support for coffee growers and migrant workers, for example, appears to be funneled through SEDESOL field offices. Empresas de Solidaridad, launched in 1992, is administered through a deconcentrated entity within SEDESOL, which deals directly with applicants at the local level (SEDESOL 1992a). Mujeres en Solidaridad, at least in the case of Nuevo León, is administered jointly by SEDESOL and the state-level Ministry of Social Development.[13] Other Solidarity programs reach far beyond neighborhoods or single clienteles. Examples include the "big ticket" program, Agua Potable y Alcan-

---

[13]Mujeres en Solidaridad is in some ways the most innovative and ambitious program of social change, focusing on raising the consciousness of self-worth and participation of women from the lower social strata. It is an administratively intensive program in its efforts to devise projects to meet priorities as expressed by beneficiary groups themselves, as formulated in lengthy processes of conversations assisted by trained professional women, or *promotoras*. In Nuevo León, some eleven *promotoras*—social workers, psychologists, and the like—were based in a unit of the newly created state Ministry of Social Development and showed an impressive mix of idealism, social commitment, and hard-earned street savvy. Starved for resources, the *promotoras* typically relied on public transportation to reach their roughly sixty projects, which were scattered throughout the state. In most cases, the *promotoras* served as their own political brokers in negotiations with municipal presidents and heads of ejido councils, and they enjoyed varying degrees of cooperation. The program's main challenge in late 1991 was to focus on projects already under way in establishing economically and financially viable micro-enterprises, such as bakeries, child-care centers, and *tortillerías*. One *tortillería* I visited was successful in good part because the lead participant's husband also chaired the ejido council; another *tortillería* was struggling because of factional infighting in the ejido. A bakery run by mothers of retarded children in the kitchen of a public school could not arrange steady support from its municipality. In all, the staff thought that perhaps half of the projects showed good potential, while those remaining presented problems (author interviews, Nuevo León, December 1991).

tarillado, which is national in scope, and several regional development programs, such as Eastern Michoacán.[14]

Those Solidarity programs that most nearly approximate the popularized notion of neighborhood-oriented, grassroots programs include the following:

• Fondos Municipales de Solidaridad (which includes World Bank funding and offers a variety of social, production, and infrastructure projects).

• Urbanización (similar to Fondos Municipales in some respects, but limited to small-scale urban infrastructure and available to wealthier states that do not qualify for Fondos Municipales).

• Fondos de Solidaridad para la Producción (aimed at high-risk, dryland farmers).

• Escuela Digna, and its follow-on, Niños en Solidaridad (based in the schools and aimed at poor neighborhoods).

• Regularización de la Tenencia (which legalizes de facto land occupation in urban areas).

• Mujeres en Solidaridad (which operates on a much smaller scale than most of the above).

As noted above, PRONASOL was invented in pieces and at full gallup. In many cases specific projects and even program concepts were identified in presidential tours or election campaigns of administration favorites. In the case of Nuevo León, for example, the prime beneficiary of Solidarity was Sócrates Rizzo, mayor of Monterrey (1986–91) and subsequently elected governor for the term 1991–97. Just as the town of Chalco in México State became President Salinas's showcase, Rizzo devoted special care (and resources) to the Monterrey neighborhood of San Bernabé, which served as the venue for the third National Solidarity Week in September 1991 (Bailey n.d.2).

As Graham points out in this volume, PRONASOL should be viewed as a complement to the established bureaucracy. There appears

[14]Along with complaints about police misbehavior and lack of public safety, access to water was the most frequently and intensely voiced demand heard by Salinas in his 1988 presidential campaign. Municipalities, charged with providing water services in the 1983 reforms, proved largely incapable. Agua Potable y Alcantarillado deals with the urgent nationwide issue of constructing, consolidating, or improving water delivery systems, primarily at the municipal level. Grassroots committees are mentioned in the 1991 SPP technical guides, but they play no significant role. In the 1993 guidelines, reference to committee participation is dropped altogether. The priority is to impose greater rationality to water pricing across regions and between cities, and to enforce more realistic billing procedures for water consumption. Data from 1991 show that rates charged for water vary enormously from one city to another, and that on average some 30 percent of water supplied is lost through leaks or consumer "piracy" (PRONASOL 1991c; SEDESOL 1992c; Comisión Nacional del Agua 1992: 20; author interviews, Mexico City, September 1992).

to be an inherent tension between the presidential preference for flexibility and discretion in designating recipients of Solidarity benefits, versus the bureaucratic instinct for procedures and accountability. One dimension of this tension is the interplay between SEDESOL's program officers and accountants versus PRONASOL's more unconventional *promotores*, many of whom come from backgrounds of social activism in leftist movements and parties. For systemic purposes the tension may be positive, coupling the effectiveness of the *promotores* in reaching the grassroots with the discipline of the bureaucrats in imposing order and continuity. In the field, however, the tension tends to produce stress in both groups.[15]

By late 1992 SEDESOL had formalized procedures for virtually all the programs, although one expects considerable discretion is permitted in implementation. Even so, a brief review of the formal guidelines for one of the programs, Fondos Municipales de Solidaridad, helps illustrate the likely interplay between federal control, state-level involvement, and local initiative. An estimated 1,777 of Mexico's 2,387 municipalities suffer serious problems of administrative backwardness and rural isolation (PRONASOL 1992: 1).[16] The obvious incapacity of these municipalities to administer even simple programs has long justified centralism. Fondos Municipales is interesting for our purposes because it channels money through municipal offices and provides training and support for local officials. In this sense, Fondos Municipales contributes to create conditions that might permit decentralization in the future. In this "micro-description" we are looking for clues about decentralization and grassroots participation. For example, how is the formation of grassroots committees and selection of projects "from below" coordinated with the allocation of money and definition of guidelines "from above"?

The funding process for Fondos Municipales through a budget cycle (January–December) involves some fifteen steps.[17]

1. Treasury (SHCP) in Mexico City sets the budget "roofs" for agencies and programs, including SEDESOL and PRONASOL (September–October of the year preceding).

---

[15]To return to the example of Mujeres en Solidaridad in Monterrey (see note 13), SPP staffers grumbled about the *promotoras* as "a bunch of psychologists who need psychiatrists" (author interview, Monterrey, December 1991).

[16]Recall that "municipality" refers to something like a U.S. township. In urban areas the municipality may be coterminous with city and suburbs. In rural areas a town or village serves as the municipal "seat" which administers outlying farms and hamlets.

[17]The description is based on PRONASOL 1992; SEDESOL 1992b; and author interviews, Mexico City, September 1992 and January 1993. In principle, Fondos Municipales applies to poorer states. Thus, a state like Nuevo León, which ranks at or near the top of the states on most social indicators, does not qualify. Nuevo León, however, received federal money through the Urbanización program (see Appendix) for activities broadly similar to those of Fondos Municipales; Urbanización also operated through grassroots committees and demand-based decision making.

2. SEDESOL negotiates budget "floors" with the various states, taking into account the previous year's allocation and giving priority to the poorest regions (October–November preceding).

3. SEDESOL field offices and the state governors (and COPLADEs) determine which municipalities will be included in which of the various PRONASOL programs following general guidelines about relative poverty (January–February of the budget year).

4. SEDESOL field offices send representatives to the municipalities chosen for inclusion in the Fondos Municipales program with information on its purposes and procedures. The municipal president, along with city and state officials, convenes the *cabildo* (municipal council or legislature), explains the program, and solicits project requests from the neighborhoods (March).[18]

5. In a follow-up *cabildo* meeting, project requests are analyzed to identify those that qualify for the Fondos Municipales program (March).

6. Once project selection is done, a Municipal Solidarity Council is created, presided over by the municipal president and including state government representatives, municipal "delegates," the municipal treasurer and director of public works, and democratically elected members of the neighborhoods. Solidarity committees are then established in each locality whose proposals were accepted, and all neighbors are eligible to participate in the committees, whose executive organs are also democratically elected (March).

7. Project proposals are sent to the COPLADE for analysis and evaluation. The COPLADE forwards those it approves along to the SEDESOL delegation, "which will decide if they are approved." Once projects are approved, an agreement is signed between the neighborhood committees and the municipality (March–April).

8. With the agreement in place, the SEDESOL field office and the COPLADE release funds to the *municipio*, up to the full amount for each project approved (beginning in April).

9. The municipal treasurer opens a checking account and accounting system separate from municipal funds (also beginning in April).

---

[18]This phase is unclear in both documents and conversations, but presumably there is prior activity in the neighborhoods by which priorities are defined and projects identified. In the case of San Bernabé, Solidarity reactivated a whole network of "neighborhood boards" (*juntas vecinales*) which had considerable prior experience with cooperative activities and negotiation with government agencies. Many of the activists in the boards took leadership roles in the Solidarity committees (author interviews, Monterrey, December 1991).

10. The municipal treasurer pays contractors or neighborhood committees as needed for goods and services to implement projects (April–October).

11. Neighborhood committees report monthly (changed to quarterly, 1993) to the Municipal Solidarity Council on progress in project implementation (April–October).

12. The Municipal Solidarity Council prepares monthly (quarterly as of 1993) reports on project implementation for the COPLADE and SEDESOL field office, and a separate monthly report on difficulties encountered (April–December).

13. Once projects are completed, the municipal government turns each over to its neighborhood committee, which then administers and maintains the project (October–December).

14. A report on project completion should be presented by the Municipal Solidarity Council no later than October 31. Any work not finished by that date must be completed from state and municipal funds.

15. The state field office of the Federal Comptroller does the accounting audit of the municipality (October–December).

In terms of guidelines, Fondos Municipales combines wide selection of types of projects with clear rules. The program follows federal accounting and administrative procedures. Projects must involve neighborhood committees in implementation, and the beneficiaries must contribute at least 20 percent of the project cost (in cash, materials, or labor).[19] Funds should go toward physical projects and not to working capital. Payments by beneficiaries go to the Municipal Solidarity Council, which cannot invest the money for interest but rather must fund new projects. It is difficult to transfer money between projects, or to assign savings to new projects; approval must be granted at all levels, from the neighborhood committee to the COPLADE. A number of provisions act to force spending outside the municipal seat to the surrounding villages and farm settlements. The Municipal Solidarity Council may allocate up to 15 percent of program funds for general-purpose projects, but no money can be used for municipal or church buildings. Of the remaining 85 percent, only a maximum of 25 percent can be spent in the municipal seat unless that community has at least two-thirds of the municipality's population, in which case it can receive up to 40 percent of the money.

---

[19]Payment by beneficiaries can create conflicts. A Solidarity coordinator in Monterrey told of disputes arising as beneficiaries of physically adjoining projects found out they were paying different rates for similar works (author interviews, Monterrey, December 1991).

Therefore, between 60 and 75 percent of the money must be spent in outlying localities.

Furthermore, projects are limited to $100 million pesos (roughly U.S. $30,000). There should be no "agrarian problems" to complicate projects.[20] Money cannot go to complete work in progress but rather must be spent on new works. Projects must be completed within a fiscal year, and stages of a project cannot qualify as discrete projects. Money spent for maintenance of schools and health centers assumes that equipment and personnel are already funded and in place. No new infrastructure should be constructed when existing facilities are underutilized or poorly utilized. Projects should benefit the least wealthy in the communities.

In terms of programmatic structure, Fondos Municipales consists of two broad categories, Infraestructura de Apoyo (divided in turn into five programs and ten subprograms) and Infraestructura Social (with eight programs and sixteen subprograms). Communities can choose production projects (e.g., fruit- or vegetable-packing plants, fisheries); physical infrastructure (e.g., rural roads, electrical transmission lines); or social infrastructure (e.g., street lighting, potable water, maintenance of health care centers). Guidelines are offered more as examples, and projects not specifically mentioned may be allowed if they meet the spirit of the program. Nevertheless, Fondos Municipales, like all PRONASOL programs, comes in a grant-in-aid package, densely wrapped in red tape and thoroughly tied up in procedural strings that ultimately reach Mexico City.

What can the minutiae of a specific program tell us about center-periphery relations and institutional dynamics? First, the main points of negotiation occur at the first three steps of funding as Treasury allocates funds to SEDESOL, as this allocates among the state governors, and as the governors—in conjunction with the SEDESOL field offices and COPLADEs—designate qualifying municipalities. Despite incremental practices and some substantive criteria to benefit poorer states and municipalities, these phases are eminently discretionary.[21] Second, the procedures in effect force the governors and mayors to upgrade community involvement in project designation and implementation. SEDESOL can force the spending outside the state capital and municipal seats, and since the community involvement in the municipalities revolves around

---

[20]"Agrarian problems" is administrative shorthand for the virtually thousands of disputes over boundaries, water rights, titles, and the like, which can seriously complicate routine public works activities. If the dispute affects an ejido, it falls under separate legislation and administrative jurisdiction. A former mayor of Sabinas Hidalgo, a medium-size city in northern Nuevo León, told about PRONASOL *promotores'* innocently ignoring boundaries between public and ejido lands in designing a project, unaware of the legal morass that lay in wait (author interviews, Monterrey, December 1991).

[21]See Fox and Moguel n.d. for an illuminating discussion of the complicated relations between Solidarity and opposition-controlled municipalities in Oaxaca and Michoacán.

specific neighborhoods and projects, it complicates efforts by local bosses—at least in the medium-size and larger cities—to gain control of the spending. This is because such bosses often base their power in a particular labor union or business, which is geographically concentrated or dispersed in ways that dilute the bosses' influence in a given neighborhood.[22] Third, the form of deconcentration effectively marginalizes the state legislature,[23] and—even though the municipal *cabildo* participates in the early stages of local decision making—it is reduced to the status of equal partner with popularly elected representatives from the neighborhoods on the Municipal Solidarity Council. Fourth, the discretionary nature of PRONASOL spending reinforces uncertainty and thereby magnifies central control, exercised ultimately by the president. This control is even more impressive when we consider the deep recession of the 1980s and the fiscal destitution of local government.[24]

CONCLUSION: CENTRALISM AND GRASSROOTS MOBILIZATION

Solidarity is an important instrument in a strategy of modernizing presidential centralism. The core ethos remains that of an activist, modernizing central government which mobilizes and "tutors" civil society. If the form taken during the 1930s through the 1950s was one of constructing quasi-corporatist associations, the form in the 1990s is the dismantling or rearrangement of national-level actors and the controlled activation of the grassroots. Centralism remains the key organizing principle.

Solidarity on balance, at least in the short term, operates against liberalization, which we understood as the replacement of arbitrary government actions with generalized and transparent rules. The main effect of the program is to reconstruct the image and powers of the presidency, which had been so badly tarnished in the succession of 1987 and general elections of 1988. Assuming power under allegations of fraud, and confronting thirty-one governors—many of doubtful loyalty and even competence—President Salinas needed an immediate and

[22]Interviewees in San Bernabé emphasized this point (December 1991). In the case of Nuevo León, the main tension operated between the CTM and the reform elements of the PRI. The CTM had established deep roots in several municipalities, and the state government and party leadership were engaged in nonconfrontational (for the most part) campaigns to reduce the union's influence while retaining its overall support.

[23]In the case of Nuevo León, the state legislature was barred from oversight of programs that included Solidarity funds, because such spending was considered to be federal in nature.

[24]The impact of Solidarity on municipal finance is considerable. For example, recall that one of the features of Fondos de Producción is that loans repaid by farmers to the municipality become available for local projects. The loan repayment rate for 1992 is estimated at about 50 percent (which sounds low but is much superior to BANRURAL's recovery rate of about 15 percent), and these funds frequently exceed the income the municipality receives through the revenue-sharing system (author interview, Mexico City, January 1993).

potent response. The elements were at hand: a team and budget apparatus from SPP, and experience with grassroots-oriented programs from Regional Development. Solidarity combines wide discretion in allocating funds with fairly detailed bureaucratic procedures at the implementation stages. As we saw with Fondos Municipales, the main steps of assigning resources among the states and to the municipalities can be fairly arbitrary. Once projects are chosen, extensive procedural oversight ensures effective central control.

At the same time, incentives for grassroots participation complement the center's project to "build around" existing bureaucratic channels and corporatist structures, such as labor unions and peasant associations and local bosses, in order to create grassroots support. Governors and mayors must come to terms with new actors and forces. To the extent that these executives enjoy the president's favor and know their communities well enough to shape demand-making processes to some degree, they can use the new resources to reinforce their influence. Governors out of favor and out of touch find their situations complicated.[25]

With respect to the direction of overall political change, the presidency and executive structures benefit from PRONASOL rather to the exclusion of legislatures and political parties, even including the PRI. Thus, rather than strengthening institutional pluralism, Solidarity reinforces presidentialism. It would appear that efforts to reform the official party reached their peak in this particular *sexenio* in the party's Fourteenth Assembly, held in September 1990. The key to party reform, decentralization of candidate selection to the grassroots, was put to the test in late 1990 and the first half of 1991. By and large the reforms failed, and the party leadership retreated to a backup structure, the "political council," to choose candidates. The PRI's failure probably reinforced the position of those in the governing coalition who are least committed to democratization.

In Nuevo León and Coahuila, which—for a variety of reasons ought to have been prime candidates for institutional change—efforts to reform the PRI were unsuccessful. The party remained an appendage of the governors' offices. The official party's electoral success in 1991 was linked to Salinas's popularity and to the center's selection of popular congressional candidates. Campaigns revolved around popular personalities (Sócrates Rizzo in Nuevo León, and Rogelio Montemayor in Coahuila) and personalist coalitions. There was little or no medium-

---

[25]By way of illustration, Mariano Palacios Alcocer (governor of Querétaro, 1985–91) did not belong to the Salinas inner circle. Nevertheless, he had cultivated enough local support from a long career in city and state politics to shape PRONASOL projects in some detail. On the other hand, Eliseo Mendoza Berrueto (governor of Coahuila, 1987–93) was a relative outsider and lacked local support. PRONASOL in his state was largely managed by Rogelio Montemayor.

term benefit to the PRI as an organization from PRONASOL, and efforts to strengthen party organization at the base came largely to nought.[26]

The direction of political change, at least in the short term, appears to be the strengthening of presidentialism, bolstered by the arrival to power of an extensive team of bureaucrat-politicians who are implementing a clear agenda of structural adjustment. Coalition building with new business and middle-strata groups, as well as with foreign actors (primarily the United States), supports that agenda. PRONASOL has generated significant support for the incumbent group and reform project. My findings indicate that PRONASOL deconcentrates rather than decentralizes administration. This said, we still need to note that the program can strengthen actors that may, in the longer term, push for decentralization and liberalization. In short, while we certainly cannot accept official claims at face value, we cannot reject out of hand the official reformist "bet" that Solidarity is sowing conditions for long-term change.

---

[26]While individual PRIísta candidates capitalized on Solidarity, the PRI's state president in Nuevo León was initially indifferent, even hostile, toward the program. Rogelio Montemayor constructed an effective campaign machine in Coahuila in 1991 but showed little interest in longer-term party reform. In short, PRI as a party appeared not to benefit much from Solidarity (author interviews, Nuevo León and Coahuila, October–November 1991).

III

Political Control and State-Society Relations

7

Electoral Determinants and Consequences of National Solidarity

Juan Molinar Horcasitas and Jeffrey A. Weldon

Since its creation at the beginning of Carlos Salinas de Gortari's presidential term, the National Solidarity Program has been the center of political controversy. Criticisms of PRONASOL have come from many perspectives—so many, in fact, that they tend to be contradictory. For example, some critics reject PRONASOL, not for the specifics of the program itself, but because it forms part of an economic policy package which they oppose as a whole. Others reject it as a mere propagandistic effort on the part of the government. Yet others see benefits in the program's goals but consider its budget too small to achieve them, leading them to reject PRONASOL as ineffective as a poverty alleviation program.

Some opponents attack the program's political bases, asserting that it is antidemocratic. These attacks are twofold: One argument is that PRONASOL reflects a populist strategy that reinforces centralism and authoritarian presidentialism; that PRONASOL money and decision making bypass state and municipal authorities, thereby weakening local governments. The second of these arguments focuses on PRONASOL's presumed political purpose—to buy back votes for the PRI—a strategy which supposedly consolidates authoritarianism. Proponents of these two views fear that PRONASOL is a political tool of the regime, and a highly effective one. This criticism has spread since the 1991 midterm

We thank Rolando Cordera for providing us with the PRONASOL budget figures. We also thank John Bailey, Wayne Cornelius, Fernando Cortés, Ann Craig, Todd Eisenstadt, Federico Estévez, Jonathan Fox, and David Myhre for their comments on earlier drafts of this paper.

elections, when the PRI garnered 61 percent of the vote, 11 percentage points above its nadir in 1988.

In fact, many political analysts have claimed that PRONASOL contributed to the PRI's landslide victory in 1991 (Dresser 1991; Aziz Nassif 1992; Crespo 1992; Heredia 1992; Klesner n.d.). As plausible as this may be, we do not know of any study that provides positive evidence of the electoral efficacy of PRONASOL at the national level. The same is true for the even more plausible assertion that the allocation of PRONASOL funds is electorally targeted, a claim that has been system-atically denied by government officials. Enrique González Tiburcio (1992), secretary of PRONASOL's Consultative Council, stated that not only does PRONASOL not favor any party, "the program does not work with parties at all, but with citizens and social organizations." Against these denials, most authors have been able to produce only fragmentary evidence from case studies. Exceptions, such as Gershberg (this vol-ume), are rare and limited to one of PRONASOL's many funds or programs.

In this chapter we explore these issues. We first provide empirical evidence to support the claim that, besides its specific goals as a poverty alleviation program, PRONASOL is also driven by political and electoral considerations. We will demonstrate that PRONASOL's allocation deci-sions are better understood in terms of electoral criteria than poverty indices. In the second section we attempt to gauge the effects that PRONASOL investments in 1990 may have had in the elections of 1991.

ELECTORAL DETERMINANTS OF PRONASOL EXPENDITURES

THE MODEL

In addressing these questions, we assume that there are three variables that may affect the allocation of PRONASOL funds among the states. First, we must consider poverty and its associated variables, which are the explicit targets of the program. Second, we must account for state and municipal budgetary considerations which should restrict alloca-tion decisions. Third, we must look at political variables, specifically electoral and partisan considerations.

If PRONASOL were truly an apolitical poverty alleviation program, only the first and second variables should be considered in allocations. We assume that political considerations may also play a role. In most cases this assertion would not be controversial. For example, Barry Ames (1987) describes public spending in Brazil as a method to advance the chances of political survival of incumbent politicians. However, such models are not commonly used in the case of Mexico, where political survival is confounded by the presence of a hegemonic party, electoral fraud, and prohibitions on reelection for every office in the country. However, we believe that political considerations do play a role in the budget process in Mexico, and in fact are also important in this sup-posedly neutral program.

Therefore, we will explain the distribution of PRONASOL expendi-tures among the thirty-one Mexican states[1] as the following function:

PRONASOL = f\{Poverty, Budget Constraint, Electoral Politics\}   (1)

This function will be tested using ordinary least squares (OLS) regression.[2] We specify our dependent variable through four different per capita specifications of PRONASOL expenditures in 1990: total PRONASOL expenditure and three large subdivisions: *productivo, social,* and *apoyo*. These subdivisions are often presented by the government in literature regarding Solidarity, disaggregating Branch 26 (Solidaridad y Desarrollo Regional) of the federal budget into three general groupings: Solidaridad para la Producción, Solidaridad para el Bienestar Social, and Infraestructura Básica de Apoyo. Solidaridad Social has constituted about 60 percent of Solidarity expenditures over the last three years.

At its creation, PRONASOL was explicitly committed to alleviating poverty by attending to the basic social demands of the poorest sectors of the population. The program explicitly emphasized some areas of action, such as health, education, housing, and jobs. It also targeted some specific subgroups of the poor: indigenous groups, poor urban settlers, and inhabitants of arid regions (Peniche 1992). If these are the targets of the program, the funds should be allocated accordingly. We therefore expect, all else being equal, that more funds should be allocated to the poorest states, to states with lower educational indices, to states with higher proportions of indigenous populations, and to states with higher proportions of rural population.

We also expect the distributive decision to be limited by state and municipal financial constraints. Specifically, all else being equal, we expect that central planners would allocate more PRONASOL resources to states that have lower state and local budgets per capita.

Finally, if the allocation decisions were apolitical, we would expect to find no significant relationship between the amount of funds a state receives and its specific electoral and partisan characteristics. In particu-lar, if this were the case, all else being equal, the level of PRONASOL funds should not be affected by the electoral strength of political parties (either the PRI or opposition parties) in that state, nor by the expectation of upcoming local or state elections.

---

[1] We had to exclude the Federal District for lack of data.

[2] We employed a method that renders heteroskedasticity-consistent standard errors, using SST (Statistical Software Tools), by J.A. Dubin and R.D. Rivers.

SPECIFICATION OF VARIABLES

As mentioned earlier, the dependent variable is the state level of PRO-NASOL expenditure per capita, specified as TOTAL and as its three main components: APOYO, PRODUCTIVO, and SOCIAL. As expected, these three components are strongly correlated to TOTAL, as can be seen in table 7.1, though it also appears that some states receive greater proportions of some types of PRONASOL expenditures over others. As we will show, these differences between programs have consequences for the results of the regressions.

TABLE 7.1

CORRELATION MATRIX OF THE FOUR DIFFERENT SPECIFICATIONS OF THE DEPENDENT VARIABLE (STATE-LEVEL EXPENDITURES BY PRONASOL)

	TOTAL	APOYO	SOCIAL	PRODUCTIVO
TOTAL	xxx			
APOYO	0.670	xxx		
SOCIAL	0.831	0.294	xxx	
PRODUCTIVO	0.753	0.404	0.395	xxx

zero-order Pearson coefficients

The first set of independent variables,[3] those which are intended to tap POVERTY in equation (1), are specified as follows:

- BILINGUAL: the proportion of the state's population age five and older that speaks an indigenous language, regardless of whether they also speak Spanish.

- POOR: the proportion of the economically active population that earns less than the official minimum wage.

- ILLITERATE: the proportion of the population above fifteen years of age that cannot read.

- RURAL: the proportion of the state's total population that lives in communities of less than 2,500 inhabitants.

- METROPOLITAN: the proportion of each state's total population that lives in communities of 100,000 inhabitants or more.

The BUDGET CONSTRAINT term in equation (1) is specified by the following:

- REVENUE 86: the sum of state and municipal fiscal revenues for the state (excluding federal transfers) in 1986 (the latest date for which data are available).

---

[3] All socioeconomic data are from *XI Censo General de Población y Vivienda*, 1990.

Finally, ELECTORAL POLITICS in equation (1) is specified by the following variables:

- PRI 88: PRI votes, divided by total turnout, in the elections for federal deputies in 1988.

- CARDENAS 88: the sum of votes for PARM, PFCRN, PMS, and PPS (parties that nominated Cuauhtémoc Cárdenas for president), divided by total turnout, in the elections for federal deputies in 1988.

- PAN 88: PAN votes, divided by total turnout, in the elections for federal deputies in 1988.

- ELECTION 91: a dummy variable which assumes a value of one in the states that elected governors in 1991, and zero otherwise.

- PRI*ELECTION 91: the product of PRI 88 and ELECTION 91 (the intersection of these two variables). It is zero where there was no state gubernatorial election in 1991, and the value of PRI 88 in states that did elect governors in 1991.

- PAN*ELECTION 91: the intersection of PAN 88 and ELECTION 91. It is zero where there was no state gubernatorial election in 1991, and the value of PAN 88 in states that did elect governors in 1991.

- CARDENAS*ELECTION 91: the intersection of CARDENAS 88 and ELECTION 91. It is zero where there was no state gubernatorial election in 1991, and the value of CARDENAS 88 in states that did elect governors in 1991.

ANALYSIS OF REGRESSION RESULTS

According to the Mexican government, PRONASOL is supposed to be an apolitical poverty alleviation program. If this is the case, then we should expect to find high correlations between PRONASOL expenditures and levels of poverty in a state. PRONASOL is also supposed to be especially targeted toward indigenous groups in Mexico. We expect, therefore, that the coefficients explaining per capita PRONASOL expenditures should be positive for levels of poverty and proportion of indigenous persons in a state.

Since PRONASOL is also generally targeted toward rural areas, we have added a variable that measures urban-rural demographic characteristics of a state. Although some PRONASOL money has certainly gone to some major urban areas, such as the urban slum of Chalco southeast of Mexico City in the state of México, much of the money has gone to resolve special problems of the rural parts of the nation. Here we used two variables: METROPOLITAN (the proportion of the population that lives in municipalities with populations greater than 100,000, i.e., the proportion of population living in large cities), and RURAL (the proportion of the population living in localities with less than 2,500 inhabitants, i.e., persons living in neither cities nor small towns).

We ran the model to test if PRONASOL does in fact respond to social demands. The results are not entirely intuitive. Table 7.2 reveals that the per capita level of total PRONASOL expenditures for a state is positively correlated with the number of indigenous persons, BILINGUAL, and there is also a clear antiurban bias. We ran the same equation with RURAL instead of METROPOLITAN, but the latter parameter always performed better.

TABLE 7.2
SOCIOECONOMIC AND BUDGETARY DETERMINANTS OF PRONASOL
EXPENDITURES I
(OLS)

Dependent Variable: TOTAL PRONASOL

Variable	Coefficient	Standard error	t-stat
INTERCEPT	0.105	0.021	5.00
BILINGUAL	0.155	0.044	3.55
POOR	-0.147	0.067	-2.21
METROPOLITAN	-0.090	0.030	-3.00
REVENUE 86	0.235	0.188	1.25

No. of observations = 31
R^2 = 0.335; Corrected R^2 = 0.233

Curiously, the coefficient for POOR is negative. The greater the number of persons in a state with incomes of less than one minimum wage, the less PRONASOL money the federal government spent there in 1990. This is contrary to the expressed goals of the program. We also ran a model replacing POOR with the illiteracy rate of a state, in order to detect if our definition of poverty might be the cause of this anomalous result. However, we found similar results (table 7.3). The negative signs for both POOR and ILLITERATE hold for all three groupings of PRO-NASOL programs, and for different specifications of both variables.

Since the principal stated goal of PRONASOL is the alleviation of poverty, we will continue to use this measure instead of the illiteracy rate.[4] We are aware of the conceptual and methodological problems that the measurement of poverty presents, and we think that our model would certainly benefit from a better operationalization of this variable. This would be particularly relevant if we manage to gather more data on PRONASOL expenditures.

---

[4]Only one of the two variables (POOR or ILLITERATE) can be included in the subsequent models in order to avoid multicolinearity.

TABLE 7.3

SOCIOECONOMIC AND BUDGETARY DETERMINANTS OF PRONASOL
EXPENDITURES II
(OLS)

Dependent Variable: TOTAL PRONASOL

Variable	Coefficient	Standard error	t-stat
INTERCEPT	0.113	0.016	6.92
BILINGUAL	0.178	0.030	6.02
ILLITERATE	-0.341	0.088	-3.88
METROPOLITAN	-0.099	0.034	-2.93
REVENUE 86	0.190	0.206	0.92

No. of observations = 31
$R^2 = 0.429$; Corrected $R^2 = 0.341$

We also find that there is a slight *positive* relationship between the state's locally collected revenue (REVENUE 86) and PRONASOL expenditures. This is not what we should expect, since states with lower revenue sources should require the assistance of PRONASOL expenditures more than richer states.

We also ran the model with only political parameters as explanatory variables. These variables are the percentage of Chamber of Deputies votes for the PRI, FDN (votes for the parties that supported Cuauhtémoc Cárdenas for president in 1988), and the PAN in 1988, and a dummy variable indicating whether or not there was an election in the state in 1991. We chose 1991 because it was the first calendar year *after* the given PRONASOL expenditures. There were federal elections for the Chamber of Deputies and Senators in *all* states in 1991, but we assume that the federal government had added interest in investing in states where local governments would also be elected. It is likely that the federal government felt the PRI was more likely to lose gubernatorial offices in 1991 than its majority in either chamber.

Furthermore, we include an interaction term (the product of the party variables and the election year variable) to determine whether or not there is a change in the slope for the effects of party vote in 1988 and PRONASOL expenditures in 1990 *if* there is a local election in the state in that year. If the null hypothesis that there are no political considerations in PRONASOL expenditures is true, then all of the variables should be indistinguishable from zero. It should be noted that this method of employing an interaction term is functionally equivalent to running two separate regressions of seven and twenty-four observations each, where the former is the sample of states with concurrent gubernatorial elections, and the latter the group of states without. However, with so few cases, we would lack the degrees of freedom necessary for the analysis.

Table 7.4 reveals the political effects of the PRI vote, combined with concurrent state and federal elections, excluding social and budgetary factors, in the allocation of PRONASOL money. This table demonstrates that the greater the PRI vote in 1988, the greater the total amount of money spent by PRONASOL in the state. The variables for the ELECTION 91 and the interaction terms are essentially zero. This is evidence that the government appears to have spent more money on states where the PRI did well in 1988 (without controlling for the social variables).

TABLE 7.4
POLITICAL DETERMINANTS OF PRONASOL EXPENDITURES I
(OLS)

Dependent Variable: TOTAL PRONASOL

Variable	Coefficient	Standard error	t-stat
INTERCEPT	0.022	0.015	1.42
PRI 88	0.070	0.031	2.28
ELECTION 91	0.029	0.100	0.29
PRI*ELECTION	-0.049	0.161	-0.30

No. of observations = 31
R^2 = 0.079; Corrected R^2 = -0.023

Breaking PRONASOL down into its several parts, we find that there is really no relationship between the PRI vote and PRONASOL SOCIAL or PRONASOL PRODUCTIVO. However, with PRONASOL APOYO there is a strong positive relationship between the PRI vote in 1988 and PRONASOL expenditures when local elections *were not* held concurrently with the federal elections in the state, and a marginally significant negative relationship between PRI support and expenditures on APOYO when there *were* concurrent elections. This appears to indicate that the government rewarded PRI supporters when local elections were not held, but did not reward loyalty when there were local elections.

On the other hand, we find a very strong correlation between total PRONASOL expenditures and Cardenista support (table 7.5). In this case, there is a clear bias against states with higher support for the FDN in 1988 when there were no concurrent local elections in 1991. Yet, the slope of the coefficient changes and becomes sharply positive when elections were held. The same relationship holds for PRONASOL APOYO, though the correlation is even stronger.

TABLE 7.5
POLITICAL DETERMINANTS OF PRONASOL EXPENDITURES II
(OLS)

Dependent Variable: TOTAL PRONASOL

Variable	Coefficient	Standard error	t-stat
INTERCEPT	0.074	0.011	6.88
CARDENAS 88	-0.059	0.031	-1.91
ELECTION 91	-0.038	0.015	-2.52
CARDENAS*ELECT	0.274	0.079	3.46

No. of observations = 31
$R^2 = 0.123$; Corrected $R^2 = 0.025$

In contrast, we did not find a relationship between PRONASOL SOCIAL and the Cardenista vote when no concurrent local elections were scheduled. However, we found that when such elections were held, there is a strong positive relationship and states which were Cardenista strongholds tended to receive more funding. The same effect holds true with PRONASOL PRODUCTIVO. In all cases, it appears that there was an effort on the part of PRONASOL planners to spend more money in areas that had supported the FDN in 1988. This strategy may be one of "buying back the defectors." Or, more likely, it may be that the government wanted to reward PRI loyalists more in those states where the opposition had grown stronger.

On the basis of our data, we cannot tell which one of these alternative strategies was followed, or whether the federal government followed a mixed strategy instead. This is because any such analysis, especially a cross-sectional analysis aggregated at the state level, suffers from ecological problems.[5] Yet, there are theoretical reasons to think that it is more likely that PRONASOL planners allocate more funds in states where the opposition has gained strength, but that those funds are locally distributed more to PRI supporters than to opposition sympathizers.[6] More careful analysis of the strategic rationale of PRONASOL planners is needed, but what is clear is that politics, and elections in particular, drive the allocation of PRONASOL funds.

In the case of the PAN, there is no relationship between PAN vote and total PRONASOL expenditures when elections were not scheduled, but there is a strong negative relationship between the PAN vote and

---

[5]The ecological fallacy arises when statistical inference is performed with grouped data instead of using observations on individuals.

[6]Cox, McCubbins, and Sullivan (1984) make an insightful theoretical analysis of these kinds of strategies. They claim that when they face a "question of redistribution of welfare, risk averse politicians will attempt, not to be evenhanded toward all groups in their constituency . . . nor to direct benefits chiefly to swing groups . . . but rather, first and foremost, to maintain their current electoral coalitions, and in particular, their 'primary constituency'."

PRONASOL spending among the states where elections were held. In the case of PRONASOL SOCIAL (table 7.6), this relationship is nearly linear. The effect is identical and the coefficients significant, though weaker, in the other two PRONASOL programs.

TABLE 7.6

POLITICAL DETERMINANTS OF PRONASOL EXPENDITURES III
(OLS)

Dependent Variable: PRONASOL SOCIAL

Variable	Coefficient	Standard error	t-stat
INTERCEPT	0.031	0.005	6.30
PAN 88	-0.003	0.032	-0.11
ELECTION 91	0.076	0.008	9.43
PAN*ELECTION	-0.347	0.044	-7.80

No. of observations = 31
R^2 = 0.288; Corrected R^2 = 0.209

Could this observed political effect be an artifact of the social variables? Is it possible that the model is merely reporting the effects of a high correlation between certain social and partisan characteristics? We ran the two models together to determine the possible political influence in PRONASOL spending while controlling for the key social variables. Table 7.7 shows that there is no political effect when considering total PRONASOL expenditures and the level of PRI support in a state, with or without local elections. However, we find that this is an effect of contradictory strategies of PRONASOL spending among the different programs.

TABLE 7.7

DETERMINANTS OF PRONASOL EXPENDITURES I
(OLS)

Dependent Variable: TOTAL PRONASOL

Variable	Coefficient	Standard error	t-stat
INTERCEPT	0.092	0.024	3.85
BILINGUAL	0.151	0.046	3.24
POOR	-0.163	0.064	-2.55
METROPOLITAN	-0.086	0.029	-2.92
REVENUE 86	0.197	0.205	0.96
PRI 88	0.033	0.034	0.98
ELECTION 91	0.009	0.063	0.14
PRI*ELECTION	-0.017	0.111	-0.15

No. of observations = 31
R^2 = 0.346; Corrected R^2 = 0.147

In table 7.8, we see a strong relationship between PRI support and expenditures for PRONASOL APOYO. When elections were not scheduled, the slope between vote for the PRI in 1988 and APOYO spending is positive (0.032). However, when there are concurrent local elections scheduled in a state, the slope becomes negative (-0.030).[7] On the other hand, the slope for PRI support and spending on PRONASOL PRODUCTIVO is zero when no elections were held (0.008), but the relationship becomes significantly positive (up to 0.032) in states where there were concurrent state and federal elections in 1991. This may be because PRONASOL PRODUCTIVO is especially efficient in rewarding PRI loyalists.

TABLE 7.8
DETERMINANTS OF PRONASOL EXPENDITURES II
(OLS)

Dependent Variable: PRONASOL APOYO

Variable	Coefficient	Standard error	t-stat
INTERCEPT	0.001	0.010	0.14
BILINGUAL	0.059	0.025	2.31
POOR	-0.037	0.026	-1.44
METROPOLITAN	-0.013	0.011	-1.20
REVENUE 86	0.042	0.049	0.87
PRI 88	0.032	0.012	2.56
ELECTION 91	0.034	0.021	1.61
PRI*ELECTION	-0.062	0.034	-1.85

No. of observations = 31
R^2 = 0.521; Corrected R^2 = 0.375

Our model of the relationship between Cardenista support in 1988 and PRONASOL expenditures in 1990 shows very strong correlations when intersected with the ELECTION 91 variable. For example, the coefficient for FDN support against total PRONASOL spending (table 7.9) when concurrent state elections were not scheduled is -0.042, indicating that the government usually allocated more PRONASOL funds to those states that were loyal to the PRI, while it punished states that had voted for the opposition. However, when state elections were scheduled concurrently with the federal balloting, the slope of the coefficient for CARDENAS 88 becomes strongly positive (0.135).[8]

---

[7]This is derived by adding the coefficient of the interaction term (-0.062) to the coefficient of PRI 88 (0.032).

[8]This coefficient is derived by adding the coefficient of the interaction term (0.177) to the coefficient of CARDENAS 88 (-0.042).

TABLE 7.9
DETERMINANTS OF PRONASOL EXPENDITURES III
(OLS)

Dependent Variable: TOTAL PRONASOL

Variable	Coefficient	Standard error	t-stat
INTERCEPT	0.109	0.025	4.30
BILINGUAL	0.143	0.050	2.87
POOR	-0.132	0.060	-2.21
METROPOLITAN	-0.080	0.033	-2.40
REVENUE 86	0.219	0.204	1.07
CARDENAS 88	-0.042	0.033	-1.27
ELECTION 91	-0.027	0.015	-1.78
CARDENAS*ELECT	0.177	0.061	2.89

No. of observations = 31
R^2 = 0.385; Corrected R^2 = 0.197

As we observed earlier, it is not clear what happened locally: it is possible that these coefficients reflect a decision by the government to buy back votes directly from opposition groups when elections were to be held, or a decision to reward the remaining PRI loyalists in those states as a demonstration of what could be gained through loyalty to the PRI.

The model for Cardenista support and PRONASOL APOYO spending is even stronger (table 7.10). The government usually spent less money in states that gave more votes to Cárdenas (-0.031), but when gubernatorial elections were scheduled, the slope becomes strongly positive (0.058), again with the possible strategy of trying to reconvert these voters or to reward the remaining PRI loyalist neighbors in states that became opposition strongholds. This result for FDN partisanship, incidentally, explains the negative slope for the PRI in election years. It is not the case that the government was punishing the PRI; rather, PRONASOL planners preferred to reconvert opposition states.

The story for the PAN is quite different. When controlling for social variables, the coefficient for PAN support and total PRONASOL expenditures (table 7.11) continues to be essentially zero (0.030, though with large standard errors) when no elections were scheduled. However, when there were local elections, the states that gave more votes to the PAN in 1988 got significantly less PRONASOL money (-0.453).[9]

As before, the model for PRONASOL SOCIAL and PAN support remains quite dramatic. Less money was spent (with a coefficient of -0.034, though not significant) in states with higher PAN voting when concurrent state and federal elections were not scheduled, but signifi-

[9]This coefficient is derived by adding the coefficient of the interaction term (-0.483) to the coefficient of PAN 88 (0.030).

cantly much less money was spent in PRONASOL programs in those states where gubernatorial elections were held in 1991 (with a coefficient of -0.301).

TABLE 7.10

DETERMINANTS OF PRONASOL EXPENDITURES IV

(OLS)

Dependent Variable: PRONASOL APOYO

Variable	Coefficient	Standard error	t-stat
INTERCEPT	0.022	0.011	2.10
BILINGUAL	0.053	0.020	2.60
POOR	-0.021	0.025	-0.85
METROPOLITAN	-0.017	0.011	-1.47
REVENUE 86	0.054	0.044	1.23
CARDENAS 88	-0.031	0.012	-2.51
ELECTION 91	-0.016	0.005	-3.50
CARDENAS*ELECT	0.089	0.026	3.44

No. of observations = 31
$R^2 = 0.560$; Corrected $R^2 = 0.426$

TABLE 7.11

DETERMINANTS OF PRONASOL EXPENDITURES V

(OLS)

Dependent Variable: TOTAL PRONASOL

Variable	Coefficient	Standard error	t-stat
INTERCEPT	0.090	0.021	4.28
BILINGUAL	0.125	0.046	2.69
POOR	-0.106	0.066	-1.61
METROPOLITAN	-0.069	0.034	-2.06
REVENUE 86	0.134	0.186	0.72
PAN 88	0.030	0.055	0.54
ELECTION 91	0.095	0.024	3.93
PAN*ELECTION	-0.483	0.112	-4.32

No. of observations = 31
$R^2 = 0.463$; Corrected $R^2 = 0.300$

The findings in table 7.11 appear to reflect less a strategy of conversion than one of punishing states that had not been loyal to the PRI. According to this strategy, PANistas are not as easily converted as Cardenistas, especially since many of the latter had once voted for the PRI, while the former have long voted for the opposition. It is much more efficient to try to reconvert to the official party those who were recently lost.

DETERMINANTS OF PRONASOL EXPENDITURES

From the preceding results it is clear that PRONASOL is not an apolitical program, designed solely for the alleviation of poverty, as its representatives claim. On the contrary, we have evidence that the central planners make electoral and partisan calculations. The question of the program's efficacy as an electoral instrument is distinct, however. We will tackle it in the next section of this chapter.

ELECTORAL EFFECTS OF PRONASOL

Several analysts have claimed that PRONASOL is an effective political program, and that indeed it was a key instrument in the 1991 electoral recovery of the PRI. Yet only fragmentary or impressionistic evidence has been offered to bolster this claim. In this section we will provide supporting evidence, using a statistical model similar to the one used in the previous section.

We know from various studies (e.g., Klesner 1988; Molinar and Weldon 1991) that for many years there have been strong relationships between party vote and certain socioeconomic characteristics of the population. In particular, we know that party vote has been strongly related with variables measuring the rural-urban continuum, educational levels, ethnicity, type of economic activity, and so on. We also know that the party vote is affected by regional variables. Thus, we will test a model that measures the impact of PRONASOL expenditures in explaining the change in party vote between 1988 and 1991, controlling for a battery of socioeconomic and regional variables.[10] In other words:

$$\text{Change in Party Vote} = f\{\text{Socioeconomics, Regions, PRONASOL}\} \quad (2)$$

However, from equation (1), we assume that PRONASOL is a function of socioeconomic variables; therefore, equation (2) suffers from endogeneity. This can be corrected,[11] but for the sake of simplicity we will assume that PRONASOL expenditures are fixed. The regional variables are specified as follows:

- BORDER: states bordering the United States (Baja California Norte, Sonora, Chihuahua, Coahuila, Nuevo León, and Tamaulipas).

- CENTER: Aguascalientes, Guanajuato, Jalisco, México, Michoacán, Querétaro, and Tlaxcala.

---

[10]Most recent works on the subject used data disaggregated at the electoral district level (N varying from almost 200 to 290). In this work we use a model with only state-level disaggregation, because we have been unable to obtain more detailed data of PRONASOL expenditures.

[11]However, the fact that our model assumes nonlinearity in the endogenous variable (PRONASOL expenditures) complicates matters.

- SOUTH: Campeche, Chiapas, Guerrero, Oaxaca, Quintana Roo, Tabasco, and Yucatán.

Tables 7.12 through 7.14 show the results of the regression models including only the regional variables, the dummy variable for the presence of concurrent local and federal elections in a state (ELECTION 91), and total PRONASOL expenditure per capita in each state (PRONASOL TOTAL). Finally, we introduced an interactive term (ELECTION*PRONASOL), which is the product of ELECTION 91 and PRONASOL TOTAL. This parameter is zero when there are only federal elections in the state, and takes on the value of PRONASOL TOTAL when gubernatorial elections are also held in the same year.

TABLE 7.12
ELECTORAL EFFICACY OF PRONASOL SPENDING I
(OLS)

Dependent Variable: CHANGE IN PRI VOTE 1988–1991

Variable	Coefficient	Standard error	t-stat
INTERCEPT	0.280	0.099	2.83
BILINGUAL	0.257	0.194	1.32
POOR	-0.398	0.215	-1.84
METROPOLITAN	-0.033	0.072	-0.46
BORDER	-0.117	0.032	-3.61
CENTER	0.022	0.032	0.69
SOUTH	-0.136	0.041	-3.30
ELECTION 91	-0.190	0.041	-4.56
PRONASOL TOTAL	-0.692	0.425	-1.63
ELECTION*PRONASOL	2.006	0.607	3.30

No. of observations = 31
R^2 = 0.614; Corrected R^2 = 0.448

Table 7.12 shows that regions were an important factor in explaining the changes in the PRI vote between the 1988 and 1991 elections. Controlling for socioeconomic variables and PRONASOL spending, the official party did relatively worse in 1991 in the border and southern states. Table 7.12 also shows an interesting pattern of relationship between the role of concurrent local elections, PRONASOL expenditure, and the recovery of PRI vote. In states where elections for governor were not scheduled in 1991, the PRI did somewhat *worse* in the federal elections for every extra peso spent on PRONASOL (the coefficient is -0.692). However, in states where gubernatorial elections were held, the sign of the slope becomes strongly positive (1.314)[12] and the PRI received more votes with greater expenditures by Solidarity.

---

[12]This coefficient is derived by adding the coefficient of the interaction term ELECTION*PRONASOL (2.006) to the coefficient of PRONASOL TOTAL (-0.692).

TABLE 7.13
ELECTORAL EFFICACY OF PRONASOL SPENDING II
(OLS)

Dependent Variable: CHANGE IN FDN-PRD VOTE 1988–1991

Variable	Coefficient	Standard error	t-stat
INTERCEPT	-0.222	0.093	-2.39
BILINGUAL	-0.154	0.122	-1.26
POOR	0.375	0.167	2.24
METROPOLITAN	0.047	0.093	0.50
BORDER	0.059	0.040	1.47
CENTER	-0.009	0.028	-0.31
SOUTH	0.096	0.033	2.95
ELECTION 91	0.070	0.035	2.02
PRONASOL TOTAL	-0.086	0.408	-0.21
ELECTION*PRONASOL	-0.222	0.436	-0.59

No. of observations = 31
R^2 = 0.478; Corrected R^2 = 0.254

TABLE 7.14
ELECTORAL EFFICACY OF PRONASOL SPENDING III
(OLS)

Dependent Variable: CHANGE IN PAN VOTE 1988–1991

Variable	Coefficient	Standard error	t-stat
INTERCEPT	-0.016	0.048	-0.34
BILINGUAL	0.175	0.066	2.65
POOR	-0.009	0.080	-0.11
METROPOLITAN	0.004	0.071	0.59
BORDER	0.042	0.029	1.44
CENTER	-0.027	0.017	-1.56
SOUTH	-0.035	0.015	-2.31
ELECTION 91	0.079	0.032	2.47
PRONASOL TOTAL	0.288	0.271	1.06
ELECTION*PRONASOL	-1.149	0.359	-3.20

No. of observations = 31
R^2 = 0.376; Corrected R^2 = 0.108

We should remember that more PRONASOL money was spent in those states with greater Cardenista strength that were holding local elections in 1991, and the evidence in table 7.12 suggests that the efforts at reconverting were generally successful. In states with concurrent elections, PRONASOL was indeed effective in improving the level of PRI vote. This table also demonstrates that spending money on reconverting (the strategy used in states with local elections) seems to be a more effective strategy than spending money on loyalists (in states without local elections).

How did PRONASOL expenditures affect the voting patterns for the opposition parties? After controlling for socioeconomic and regional differences, there appears to be no effect of PRONASOL spending on the FDN vote (table 7.13). The Cardenista parties did do relatively better in the poorer states and in southern states.

There appears to be a slightly positive relationship between PRO-NASOL expenditures and the change in vote for the PAN (table 7.14) in states where gubernatorial elections were not scheduled in the same year as the federal midterm polling (0.288, though the coefficient is not significant). However, in states that did have local elections, there is a strongly negative correlation between PRONASOL spending and the PANista vote (-0.861). In these states, the greater the PAN support in 1988, the less money spent on PRONASOL by the government in 1991 (according to table 7.12); the less PRONASOL money spent, the greater the support for the PAN in 1991 (table 7.14). Therefore, whatever was spent did have an effect on reducing PANista vote totals in states where gubernatorial elections were scheduled.

Although the preceding findings are limited by the ecological nature of the analysis and by the highly aggregated level of the available data, there remains strong evidence to support the claim that PRONASOL is not only electorally driven, but that it is also electorally effective.

CONCLUSIONS

Our analysis supports the claim that PRONASOL is something more than a poverty alleviation program. This chapter confirms that the allocation of federal resources to the states through PRONASOL cannot be explained solely on the basis of the explicit goals of the program, but that electoral considerations weigh in the minds of the decision makers. The results of the 1988 elections and the concurrence of state elections certainly had some effect on the levels of PRONASOL spending in different states. In general, planners decided to spend more where there were concurrent local and federal elections; they also decided to spend more where Cárdenas was strong in 1988 and less in PANista strong-holds.

Furthermore, there is evidence to support the claim that these political decisions were fruitful for the government decision makers, since at least a part of the PRI recovery in 1991 can be explained by these revealed patterns of PRONASOL spending.

Given these conclusions about the politics of PRONASOL, what can we deduce about Mexican electoral politics and political change? Is this proof that PRONASOL advances authoritarianism in Mexico? First, we differ with most critics of PRONASOL when they equate the program with clientelism, and thus with authoritarianism. We take issue with the idea that PRONASOL is clientelistic. PRONASOL clearly deals mostly with the exchange of public goods, shared by a community, for electoral support. Some may consider this to be clientelistic, but when similar patterns of political exchange are used in democratic regimes we do not call it clientelism. We call it "pork-barrel politics."

In other words, the political efficacy of PRONASOL does not necessarily equate with the strengthening of authoritarianism. In fact, it is possible to come to the opposite conclusion: by allocating resources according to electoral outcomes, the federal government is incorporating the population's politically expressed demands. This amounts to a considerable decentralization of decision making, since it is electoral competition and popular demands expressed through the vote that drive the process. This would be the case even if the true motives of the government planners were only to remain in power (and this is not a motive that we deny to governments in more democratic regimes).

Second, the hypothesized link between PRONASOL and political centralism in Mexico remains a complex issue. On the one hand, it may be true that the alleged bypassing of municipal governments (if not municipal officials) by PRONASOL promoters and Solidarity Committees may be detrimental to efforts to institutionalize subnational government in Mexico, since these governments lose control of resources they might otherwise receive in federal transfers. However, it cannot be denied that many people are receiving goods from the federal government more rapidly and efficiently than before, which we must consider as good in itself. Furthermore, local officials are able, as members of Solidarity Committees, to claim credit for PRONASOL "pork." In fact, the evidence suggests that PRIísta gubernatorial candidates benefit from increased PRONASOL expenditures.

Third, we should consider that PRONASOL is not only "pork," it is also relatively efficient "pork." It is clear that the intended beneficiaries of the program are the federal government (particularly the executive) and the targeted constituents. The actual procedures of PRONASOL planning and expenditures make both beneficiaries better off (the government receives political credit in the form of votes, while the people receive public goods), thus rendering the program efficient for those involved. It is important to consider that PRONASOL is only one of several methods of delivering public goods in return for votes. The usual method is through huge federal agencies, such as Mexico's Ministry of Health, Department of Roads and Bridges, and Federal Program for School Construction. In this system, the federal government assigns tasks to the ministries, but has less control over agency loss by the bureaucracy since monitoring is expensive. The agencies decide where to invest, often for their own reasons. In such cases, the recipients do not always know what they are *not* getting, nor will they always want what they receive. Since this system does not address political demands well and much money is lost along the way, the federal government does not receive the political credit for its expenditures.

Under PRONASOL, however, the recipients ask the federal executive directly for what they need from the government. The federal government decides by whatever criteria it prefers (including political guidelines, evidently) and invests directly through the Solidarity Committees. The money bypasses federal agencies (and agency losses as well). The Solidarity Committees monitor the expenditures and report mishandling of the money to the executive, since they want the project to be funded, know how much is to be spent, and know how it is to be spent. Therefore, agency losses are reduced, the project is funded and completed, and the federal government receives electoral credit. Both of the key beneficiaries are better off. It is a more efficiently designed program, despite—indeed, because of—its decentralization.

Finally, we argue that PRONASOL expresses the Mexican government's *electoral responsiveness*. Despite its decades-long history of noncompetitive elections, the regime is demonstrating that it is willing to compete for votes with methods common to all electoral democracies. Resorting to the pork barrel is much more "fair" than other methods the government has relied on. In this light, PRONASOL could be considered a positive sign for political change in Mexico. To put it bluntly: Mexican elections fall far below democratic standards of fairness and competitiveness, but PRONASOL reveals that when the people vote, the government listens.

8

Bringing the Poor Back In: National Solidarity as a Strategy of Regime Legitimation

Denise Dresser

Just one day before a coup attempt in Venezuela in early 1992, President Carlos Andrés Pérez boasted about the success of his country's economic reform program. "The spirit of the reforms is no longer a subject of controversy," he declared (*New York Times*, February 9, 1992). Yet twenty-four hours later, violence in the streets of Caracas revealed the limits to Venezuela's incipient recovery from a decade of economic crisis. Venezuela is not unique. The history of attempts to institute economic reform in Latin America is one of beleaguered presidents heading uncertain regimes. Many attempts to change development models floundered when political elites relied too heavily on market forces. Latin American leaders have often gambled on the magic of the market, rather than construct alliances or design new forms of state intervention to promote development and social equity. As a result, many governments now find themselves isolated and vulnerable.

Mexico, in contrast, emerges as a paragon of stability. Mexican political elites have been able to carry out far-reaching economic reforms without provoking the social unrest and political upheaval that have been endemic throughout the continent. Why is this so? Mexico's stability has usually been attributed to the authoritarian nature of its political regime and to the corporatist grip that the ruling party maintains over society. This still holds true; however, Mexican authoritarianism is not static. Broad-based economic reforms undertaken during the last decade have affected the reach of the state, the legitimacy of the PRI, the composition of the ruling elite, and the organizational abilities of groups within civil society. To maintain its legitimacy in these changing circumstances, the Mexican state elite has been forced to restructure the terms of its domination.

In the era of the retrenching state, Mexico's leaders have opted for a new kind of "statism" in order to assure political survival. The day after the aborted revolt in Venezuela, Carlos Salinas de Gortari announced that Mexico's economic reform would not be based on the retreat of the state, but on a new form of "socially determined" interventionism, through the National Solidarity Program (*La Jornada*, February 6, 1992). PRONASOL is the linchpin of a governability strategy that seeks to redefine the state's task and its relationship with society. According to Salinas, the country's new development model will be led by a leaner and more efficient state, which promotes economic growth through private power but does not abandon its distributive commitments. PRONASOL aims to construct a political consensus that will allow the continuation and deepening of the economic adjustment program.

This chapter argues that PRONASOL provides the political conditions necessary to sustain the neoliberal model. By redefining the members of the old corporatist coalition as consumers of PRONASOL benefits, the program has helped rebuild the state's constituencies. By incorporating social reformers into the ranks of the bureaucracy, PRONASOL has enhanced the representativeness of the political elite and reinforced its ties with autonomous social groups. By reinstating the PRI's role as a welfare machine, PRONASOL has enabled the PRI to regain its position as centerpiece of the party system. By strengthening the powers of presidentialism, PRONASOL has allowed the government to establish centralized control over the policy process. Neoliberalism demands an aggressive political and ideological remaking, not simply the implementation of economic measures. PRONASOL entails both. The Salinas administration is presenting neoliberalism as a hegemonic project, and at the same time it is using Solidarity to create a durable base of support for the project in civil society. PRONASOL constitutes the political web within which Mexico's neoliberal reform program is being spun.

PRONASOL AS A POLITICAL CONSTRUCTION

> *The task of most of the nation's politically active population is to create problems: demand rights, demand a role, mobilize the dissatisfied. . . . The task of government is the opposite: to resolve those problems, to keep them from exploding, so that you can continue addressing problems in a climate of peace and institutional harmony.*
> —Aguilar Camín (1991: 156)

Political power rests on explicit or implicit coalitions.[1] The system of resource allocation that evolved during Mexico's period of import-substitution industrialization (ISI) created a broad-based "populist-distributive" coalition of organized interests.[2] Its membership comprised the state bureaucracy and its beneficiaries: private enterprise protected from international competition, the organized working class, and the intelligentsia. This alliance was maintained through increasing use of the state's regulatory apparatus to protect organized interests. Thus, the coalition flourished on state business such as public credit, production subsidies, tariff protection, tax incentives, and purchasing contracts. As the state arena expanded in size, it also became an extremely porous arena of distributive conflict, through which state elites forged a wide variety of alliances with groups based in civil society.[3] The resulting institutional network became known as the "social pact," and that pact provided the cornerstone of regime stability.

During the 1980s, the ISI development model, which had both created and destroyed the "Mexican miracle," began to change in response to external pressures combined with an internal "paradigmatic shift." The international context provided an impetus for change, while Mexico's external debt crisis brought to the fore critical analyses of the ISI model. For the first time Mexico's state elites judged their statist strategies and policies for economic growth deficient and implemented an ambitious structural reform program to rationalize and modernize the country's statist experiment. As a result, after 1982 Mexico witnessed diverse efforts to replace redistributive state interventionism with efficient market-led capitalism.

Structural adjustments have proceeded at a varied pace and with varying degrees of zeal. Change within the de la Madrid government (1982–88) tended to be incremental and system sustaining, aiming toward new equilibria within existing arrangements. As the country's conjunctural crisis unfolded, the initial response was "cosmetic structural tinkering"—efforts to reform existing arrangements to make them more efficient. In this first reform phase, the aim of Mexico's leadership was to bring about change without seriously disrupting coalition partners. De la Madrid—a trial-and-error statist—did little to shake his coalitional pillars, though inflation severely impaired their foundations. The new strategy, despite it stop-and-go approach, carried very high

---

[1] This section draws from Waterbury n.d.

[2] Mancur Olson (1982) defines distributional coalitions as alliances of special interest groups that can reduce the rate of economic growth by taking for their own consumption resources that could otherwise be used for investment purposes. The distributional coalitions associated with ISI are usually composed of urban wage earners, organized labor, public-sector enterprise employees, and manufacturers.

[3] This argument draws from Kaufman 1990.

political costs. By July 1988 the traditional alliance of interests and loyalties had begun to crumble.

As a result, Carlos Salinas's strategies show sharp discontinuities with previous political arrangements. Pragmatic problem solving has given way to pragmatic transformation. Under Salinas, Mexico entered a second phase, where the goal is not so much system maintenance as system renewal. Mexico's leadership is trying to remake its coalition. A shift away from ISI necessarily leads to a recasting of supportive coalitions at a time when public resources are extremely limited due to state streamlining policies (Nelson et al. 1989). The move toward export-led growth implies a new framework of tense interdependencies between the "winners" and the "losers" of the new development model.

Mexico's development shift marks important changes in the context of political struggles and economic trade-offs. The costs of economic restructuring have been both concentrated and disperse. Devaluation, curtailed public expenditures, and stagflation affected the bulk of the population, while the costs of public-sector reform and privatization have fallen primarily on the shoulders of organized labor (Schneider 1988). The initial benefits of structural reforms have been highly concentrated, confined primarily to the export sector. The new development model is not likely in the medium term to improve income distribution, create many new jobs, or appeal to a broad range of social interests. Additionally, the 1988 election revealed that top-down change without the support of organized constituencies could probably not be sustained. In an intuitive manner, the Salinas team has groped for strategies that would allow it to survive this process. One effort to assure political survival has been to direct resources to trouble spots with the minimum amount of fuss, in order to shore up political support and develop new alliances. This is the genealogy of PRONASOL.

PRONASOL permits political survival and at the same time entails the fundamental restructuring of the state's constituencies.[4] Under Salinas we are witnessing a marked change in coalitional strategy. State leaders are reaching out to all segments of the private and informal sectors, consumers as opposed to public-sector employees, and market-oriented farmers as opposed to *ejidatarios*.

The fundamental tactic in this coalition building has been to concentrate as much power as possible in the hands of the executive, in order to channel resources to politically turbulent zones or disaffected groups.[5]

---

[4]For two comparative discussions of political survival (i.e., the drive of politicians to retain their jobs), see Migdal 1988; Ames 1987.

[5]As one PRONASOL ideologue pointed out, the program emerged in the context of "a political economy with clear and long-term fiscal restrictions that incorporated strict efficiency criteria. This generated problems for state organization and administration, as well as a host of demands that emerged out of the wave of democratization and citizen action that has swept Mexico over the last decade" (Cordera Campos 1991c).

The political elite see PRONASOL as the backbone of a neocorporatist structure that incorporates lower-middle-class and informal-sector interests. PRONASOL was created as a discretionary fund designed to construct new patronage networks with low-income groups across the country, particularly those with electoral weight. Through "modernizing centralization," the country's social pact is being rewritten.

In order to refashion domestic alliances, the Salinas team has worked diligently and effectively to establish a host of new relationships outside of traditional corporatist mechanisms. By promoting a general context of *concertación*, the political elite has been able to infuse neoliberal economic reforms and austerity measures with a new, more popular, and inclusionary face. What has changed is the governing style. PRONASOL activities promote the impression that more people are participating in the construction of the new development model.[6]

PRONASOL's strategy is to build a new coalition of support by denying the concept of class as an organizational factor of political life. The program attempts to transcend class differences and forge links of social solidarity on the basis of other forms of collective identification.[7] PRONASOL redefines the members of the traditional corporatist coalition essentially as consumers, and creates majorities by slicing the social spectrum in a horizontal fashion. In the ISI era, members of the distributive coalition were defined according to their economic functions: they were campesinos, capitalists, blue-collar workers, and bureaucrats. These functions, however, were progressively eroded by the economic crisis. The deterioration of working conditions, layoffs resulting from the privatization of state enterprises, and dramatic wage losses weakened the organized labor movement. The critical situation in the Mexican countryside impaired the effectiveness of campesino organizations. The explosion of the informal economy and the growing presence of self-organized urban popular movements placed numerous groups beyond the reach of the PRI's traditional control apparatus.

Economic crisis affected most systems of representation and the economic functions associated with them; as a result, their traditional members were recast by the state elite essentially as consumers of PRONASOL benefits—electricity, scholarships, paved streets—instead of as beneficiaries of traditional state protection in the form of wage increases, subsidies, and agrarian reform.

Redefining members of traditional corporatist organizations as consumers helps the Mexican political elite in various ways. Consumers had

[6]For an analysis of concertation strategies developed by the Salinas administration, see Haber n.d.1.

[7]According to Gibson (1992), the strategy of minimizing social class as an organizational factor is crucial for the survival of conservative political movements. Given that their support base is so narrow, they must forge multiclass alliances based on "solidarity" or "the nation" as a unifying factor among disparate groups.

been victimized by the old regulatory and predatory institutions operating under ISI, especially the PRI. PRONASOL places the consumer and his/her aspirations at center stage, and consequently strikes a responsive chord. Second, consumers' aspirations tend to be uniform across groups, while the interests of the old functionally defined corps were often at odds with each other. Although wages are repressed and the ejido sector becomes ever less viable, compensatory resources flow back to workers through PRONASOL in their capacity as consumers, residents of certain regions, and squatters in search of legal land titles (Waterbury n.d.).

During the 1980s, many independent groups grew up outside the realm of political parties. Large sectors of Mexican society today earn their living outside the formal economy and are marginalized from formal legal and political institutions. The existence of widespread social organizations that escape party control is threatening to parties that are used to monopolizing political representation (see Graham 1991c). PRONASOL reduces this threat by simultaneously constructing Salinas's hegemony among popular sectors and incorporating new actors like urban popular movements — born outside the PRI fold — into the political system (see Zepeda 1991). Solidarity links into an array of measures devised by state elites to reincorporate disaffected constituents, particularly urban groups, into formal political organizations.[8] Through targeted disbursements and off-budget funds, PRONASOL is neutralizing, if not co-opting, significant segments of the urban population. As an ex-member of Salinas's team at the Ministry of Budget and Planning (SPP) declared:

> The intention behind PRONASOL is to create, through public works and services, a new urban base for the Mexican state. By the end of the 1980s the social bases of the Mexican state were unraveling. We were confronted with an unfamiliar urban scenario that we had to organize politically. . . . What's new about PRONASOL is its political dimension, the political importance Salinas gives it (author interview, February 14, 1992).

---

[8]The political implications of the priority given to urban sectors are clear. Most urban-based organizations developed in an autonomous fashion and have no established links with the PRI. The Salinas team is seeking to tie into these organizations by avowedly respecting their independence while incorporating them into the state's distributional network through PRONASOL and concertation strategies. During the closing ceremony of the International Urban Society Meeting, Salinas assured these organizations that urban reform would not be conducted without popular participation, because "many people from the cities and countryside do not belong to political parties, and they demand that their initiatives, organizations, and forms of expression be respected" (*La Jornada*, May 23, 1992).

PRONASOL's political importance has been underscored by the resources allocated to it. From 1991 to 1992 Solidarity's budget increased from U.S. $1.6 million to $2.1 million dollars. Solidarity investment as a percentage of GDP grew from 0.45 percent in 1989 to 1.0 in 1991 (*Epoca*, September 7, 1992). Sixteen subprograms currently appear under the "Solidarity and Regional Development" rubric of the federal government's budget, signaling the extension of PRONASOL beyond the originally contemplated sectors and activities.

PRONASOL was not initially intended to be a comprehensive solution to social-sector problems, but rather a temporary mechanism to protect the needy. It was set up to provide short-term relief to those most affected by the adjustment program. During its first two and a half years, persistent criticisms pointed to Solidarity's inability to address the fundamental problems of poverty. Throughout this period Salinas carefully and consistently promised only to "improve the standard of living" of the neediest Mexicans. At no time did the Solidarity elite declare that the program would generate employment or increase the income of Mexico's impoverished masses.[9]

As Solidarity expanded in both size and popularity, however, it began to generate expectations that exceeded the program's initial capacity to deliver. Its evolution from a compensatory relief program into a formula for regime legitimacy prompted Carlos Rojas, Solidarity's coordinator, to describe the program as an octopus "that extends its reach as we speak." This assessment accurately indicates the changes that PRONASOL underwent as it increasingly focused on promoting productive activities, especially among the rural poor.

Members of PRONASOL's Consultative Council have frequently underscored the need to add a productive dimension to the state's poverty alleviation efforts. As its first director stated:

> A central axis of poverty alleviation relates to productive projects, and it entails promoting specific projects that have a direct impact on the living conditions of the neediest. In other words, incorporating the poorest sectors not only as consumers but as producers, and creating the necessary infrastructure to facilitate productive tasks . . . so that, at the end of the *sexenio* we may have more than a series of disperse actions that may have solved some specific problems but only acted as

---

[9]In September 1991, *Mexico Service* reported that "Some Solidarity programs and funds back production efforts (support for coffee growers, some women's programs, some indigenous programs). But the vast majority of activities are public works that have a less direct effect on improving incomes for the poor, although they presumably benefit workers in the sectors directly impacted by the pickup in construction."

momentary palliatives and did not solve the problem of
poverty (Carlos Tello, in *Expansión*, August 15, 1990).

PRONASOL's productive effort has been carried out primarily
through the Fondo Nacional de Apoyo a Empresas de Solidaridad,
which channels credit to small and micro enterprises that have demonstrated their economic viability (see PRONASOL 1990a). By providing
risk capital, the state has attempted to enter into productive alliances
with the social sector of the economy in order to generate income and
employment at the micro level.[10] Mexico's 1988 economic census reported that more than 85 percent of all enterprises in Mexico had fewer
than ten employees, and Solidarity officials were quick to recognize the
importance of addressing the needs of this sector (Carrasco Licea and
Hernández Puente 1992). According to the head of the new Ministry of
Social Development (SEDESOL), a thousand industries have already
been created, and the Fondo expects to consolidate ten thousand more
by the end of Salinas's term in office (*La Jornada*, September 13, 1992).

In January 1992 the federal agricultural bank, BANRURAL, announced that it would transfer its outstanding loans of U.S. $1 million to
Solidarity. PRONASOL is now in charge of determining payment conditions and opening up new credit lines for campesinos. The state has also
expanded the coverage of Fondos de Solidaridad para la Producción,
whose purpose is to aid peasants who own low-productivity and high-
risk plots, and is offering nonguaranteed loans (*crédito a la palabra*).
During a whirlwind tour during Mexico's third National Solidarity
Week, Salinas reiterated that campesinos and micro-producers were not
alone. He promised to allocate more resources to bolster productive
activities in the countryside: U.S. $225 million to *crédito a la palabra*, $69
million to indigenous funds, $80 million for agricultural infrastructure,
and $161 million for the Fondo Nacional de Apoyo a Empresas de
Solidaridad (*La Jornada*, September 10, 1992).

Solidarity's recent emphasis on productivity and employment explains the paradoxical character of state spending policies over the
course of 1992. The Salinas team declared that the government's chief
macroeconomic goal for the year was single-digit inflation. In order to
achieve this objective, public spending was tightly controlled, producing an economic slowdown beginning in January 1992. In April, however, the government reactivated public spending through PRONASOL,
particularly in allocations for infrastructure. Most productive sectors,
with the exception of PRONASOL-related activities, suffered important
decreases. Economic policy was redirected toward expanding public

[10]According to official documents, the Fondo Nacional de Apoyo a Empresas de
Solidaridad will assist ejidos, workers' organizations, cooperatives, worker-owned businesses, and all forms of social organizations for production, distribution, and consumption of needed social services. The Fondo received an initial budget of 500 billion pesos.

spending to counteract the fall in private investment and manufactured exports. According to a report issued by the private consulting firm Bufete de Investigación Económica, the logic behind the expansion of public allocations is fundamentally political: "public spending is being redirected to guarantee positive results in the current electoral year and to assure a manageable political transition in 1993, when the PRI's candidate for the presidency will be announced" (Acevedo Pesquera 1992).

PRONASOL's expansiveness, particularly during electoral contests, dovetails nicely with "political survival" arguments that explain policy options as choices that rational policymakers undertake to maximize their goals. Political survival involves calculating the costs of attracting new supporters and maintaining old ones. Barry Ames, one of the few to apply rational choice theory to policy-making in Latin America, argues that his theory of political survival explains variations in public spending patterns (Ames 1987). Politicians will use the budget to reward and recruit followers. In particular, Ames discusses an "electoral-expenditure cycle" in Latin America: spending, in response to elections, designed to provide jobs and projects for supporters and allies. The ubiquitous nature of Solidarity programs in Mexico and its budgetary link to elections reveal the program's usefulness as a tool for political survival.

THE MARRIAGE OF TECHNOCRATS AND SOCIAL REFORMERS

> *I would put my talent to the service of that absurd and frustrating task of constructing Mexican civilization. It must be done step by step, even at the price of our convictions.*
> —Aguilar Camín (1991: 564)

Recent analyses of the Mexican political class point out the emergence of a new dominant group within the political elite—the technobureaucrats (Centeno and Maxfield 1992). This new group combines technical and political skills, is more closely tied to the private sector than its predecessors, and is supported by a group of political bureaucrats who manage the political control apparatus on which the regime depends for order and stability. Both the PRI's power and the power of traditional politicos vis-à-vis the bureaucracy have declined.

During this phase of systemic transformation, Mexico is drawing on its best and brightest to engineer substantive reforms. "Change teams" are not unique to Mexico. Risk takers committed to the reform strategy, and to varying degrees insulated from societal pressures, have sprouted throughout Latin America during the neoliberal decade. What distinguishes the Mexican team is the marriage of convenience between determined "can-do" technocrats and social reformers. While the former group speaks of rational management practices, generating profits, and competing effectively, the latter emphasizes growth with redistribution and popular participation. These two groups, with different institutional bases and backgrounds, struck an alliance from which emerged a hybrid political elite combining technical skills, political savvy, and insulation from societal pressures with "hands on" experience. The economists may be in power but they are not alone in this administration. Despite their different professional profiles, the technocrats of Mexico's change team need PRONASOL's social reformers and vice versa. By stabilizing the economy, the technocrats can make the PRONASOL reformers look good, allowing them to move up the political ladder. At the same time, the social reformers can dole out the resources and carry out the privileged political deals that assure regime legitimacy and thus allow the technocrats to do their job effectively. Planners and financiers were able to provide a solution to the central problem facing the regime in the 1980s: the economic crisis resulting from the exhaustion of the ISI model and exacerbated by the debt. During the 1988 election, however, the regime suddenly faced an unprecedented legitimacy crisis, which "technically correct" policies seemed insufficient to resolve. Cornered by electoral challenges, the political elite searched for and found a survival strategy: the incorporation of social reformers into the bureaucracy.

The PRONASOL network includes figures who, sincerely or not, insist on the transformative role of the state and its obligation to promote social equity. Many served at some point in their professional careers in institutions promoting social welfare, such as CONASUPO and the National Indigenous Institute (INI). A member of PRONASOL's Consultative Council described its affiliates as:

> individuals with a great deal of legitimacy among social groups. They are committed to doing things differently. They are militants who have worked with the community, and they are very well known at the grassroots level. The Salinas project seems credible to people like Hugo Andrés Araujo, Rolando Cordera, Gustavo Gordillo, Armando Labra, Enrique del Val, Arturo Warman, and Carlos Rojas (author interview, January 21, 1992).

Salinas had begun to construct working relationships with leaders of social organizations while a student in the Economics Department of the National University and while conducting fieldwork for his dissertation in the Mexican countryside. As Luis Hernández, adviser and consultant to many grassroots organizations, explained: "Solidarity simply institutionalizes at the level of public policy an organizational effort that already existed. Solidarity has a long history under other names."[11]

Salinas's choice of Carlos Tello as Solidarity's first coordinator was significant. Tello, secretary of budget and planning during the first half of the López Portillo administration, had been a key supporter of the 1982 bank nationalization and had headed the Banco de México for three months afterward in an unsuccessful attempt to build a banking system concerned more with social welfare and less with profits. He was subsequently removed by incoming president Miguel de la Madrid. Thus, the decision by Salinas—who is much closer ideologically to de la Madrid than to López Portillo—to appoint Tello as head of Solidarity surprised most political observers. It indicated Salinas's tendency to build ties with political figures of a more populist past. It should be no surprise that PRONASOL programs are designed and/or executed by individuals whose professional backgrounds lie in left-wing political organizations, including members of the Mexican Communist Party and the Unified Socialist Party. The recruitment of social organizers undoubtedly has contributed to Solidarity's efficacy and endowed the program with the human capital necessary to carry out its directives. As a consultant to PRONASOL stated:

> When PRONASOL leaders recruit personnel, they know exactly where to look: organizers, promoters, people with social sensibility, who know how to understand, interpret, and channel the demands of the inhabitants of poor regions. These are people accustomed to working in the countryside, accustomed to grassroots politics and to negotiation—people who don't mind traveling to the most obscure and inhospitable places, like the mountains, the most remote communities. . . . The Harvard or Stanford boys couldn't do that kind of work. Nor are they interested in it (Emilio Romero Polanco, in Acosta 1992: 18).

As Kathryn Sikkink (1991: 2) has argued, for successful implementation, ideas have to "fit in" with preexisting ideologies and become embedded in state institutions. Solidarity built on previous developmentalist ideas and organizations devoted to poverty alleviation and provided them with an institutional home. PRONASOL's antecedents lie in the organizational structure that Salinas established during his tenure at the Ministry of Budget and Planning. Under his leadership programmatic and financial guidelines for the disbursement of public resources

[11]Comments at the seminar on "The Politics of Economic Restructuring in Mexico," Mexico City, June 16–17, 1992.

were established, as well as norms to govern the flow of funds from Los Pinos (the presidential residence). The eight regional employment coordinators at SPP designed and undertook many of the activities currently assigned to PRONASOL at the state level. As a figure at the apex of the power structure—and a presidential contender—Salinas surrounded himself with individuals able to promote his influence. Even before PRONASOL was created as a state institution, Salinas had laid down its foundations through a network of support throughout the country, based on the management of public resources.

As a mid-level official at SPP, Carlos Rojas, the coordinator of PRONASOL, occupied a relatively low-profile position. During Salinas's presidential campaign he was in charge of coordinating "social acts," i.e., the candidate's infrequent visits to marginal areas like the Sierra Tarahumara. According to a Rojas colleague from that period: "After the elections, when all hell broke loose, Rojas's programs became crucial" (author interview, February 17, 1992). The election revealed the degree of discontent fermenting in popular *colonias* and poverty-stricken areas, as the state abandoned its social policy because of the acute fiscal crisis. The state elite's response was the enactment of a poverty alleviation program under direct presidential supervision, although formally a part of SPP. In May 1992 PRONASOL was incorporated into the new Ministry of Social Development (SEDESOL).

According to the Salinas team, the institutionalization of Solidarity in SEDESOL "is part of the current government's modernization strategy and state reform . . . that seeks to promote the efficacy and efficiency of social welfare policies" (*La Jornada*, May 9, 1992). This measure, however, also indicates a desire to extend PRONASOL's life span beyond the remainder of the Salinas term. By providing PRONASOL with a full-fledged institutional sponsor, the state elite hope to perpetuate and "lock in" the hybrid policy package—neoliberal economic policies combined with neopopulist welfare policies—that has characterized Mexico's reform. As an influential political observer pointed out: "The economic cabinet and the new ministry (SEDESOL) constitute the institutional cuff links of the political philosophy of *salinismo*. The former is in charge of neoliberal matters, and SEDESOL takes charge of social matters" (Granados Chapa 1992).

The close collaboration between the economic cabinet and SE-DESOL, and between technocrats and social reformers, suggests that the Mexican state will continue to pursue politically determined objectives that may contradict the imperatives of fiscal and economic efficiency. In order for the efficiency-oriented fraction of the state to deepen the economic reform process and retain power, it will have to keep channeling selective state resources through PRONASOL to compensate the poor and win allies. Contrary to what analysts have suggested (e.g., Centeno and Maxfield 1992), this hybrid political elite will not fight patronage politics with vigor. The technocrats will rely on the social reformers and political "experts" to dole out political slush in order to preserve the stability judged critical for the success of their project. Even though neoliberal policy currents underscore the importance of reducing the economic power of the state, the Mexican case reveals that the imperatives of political survival will often dictate the need for continued state intervention through discretionary compensation policies.

PRI AND PRONASOL: ALLIES OR CONTENDERS?

> *The defenders of immobility undermine the regime more than do its*
> *critics.*
> —Aguilar Camín (1992)

As I have argued elsewhere (Dresser 1991), reversing the 1988 electoral victories of the PRD appeared to be a significant part of PRONASOL's political agenda. The results of the August 1991 midterm elections — which renewed the PRI's hegemonic status, particularly in urban areas — indicate that deactivating the left-wing opposition has been largely achieved. From "stealing the enemy's thunder," PRONASOL seems to have moved to a new, more proactive and constructive phase designed to promote coalitional realignment. Instead of deactivation, PRONASOL will encourage "mobilized participation" via a preemptive model whereby state elites extend participation before it is demanded, in a way that co-opts the new participants.[12]

In many ways PRONASOL has acted as an important impetus to independent local initiative and organization. Indeed, PRONASOL oftentimes has been able to reverse the deep-seated mistrust in government that resulted from a long record of unfulfilled state promises. By responding to proposals from community organizations and local governments instead of imposing top-down directives, PRONASOL narrowed an age-old divide between state and society. However, Solidarity has been immune to political pressure or to the "poverty alleviation cycle." In many regions, the PRI has harnessed the new-found trust engendered by a demand-driven program and channeled it in support of partisan objectives.

The Alvaro Obregón District in Mexico City, which boasts 1,700 Solidarity Committees,[13] is a telling example in microcosm of what Solidarity can accomplish and what PRONASOL officials would like to institute throughout Mexico. Out of 170 *colonias* there, 140 are classified as in "extreme poverty." Four hundred thousand inhabitants lack access to any public service. With Solidarity's assistance (50 billion pesos from

---

[12]For an analysis of earlier forms of popular-sector incorporation, see Collier 1982.

[13]According to statements made by the *delegado* from the Department of the Federal District, Oscar Levín Coppel.

1990 to 1992) the community has constructed 56 kilometers of sewerage and 50 kilometers of pipeline for potable water. The PRI lost all sub-districts here in 1988, but won them all back in 1991.

The key to Solidarity's success lies largely in the ties that the program's *delegado* has forged with autonomous organizations in civil society, like CONAMUP and ANAMUP. When interviewed, the *delegado* openly discussed the essence of the Solidarity strategy:

> Those NGOs that overwhelmed the government after the 1985 earthquakes and during the 1988 elections became the basis of PRONASOL. We turned these organizations into instruments of change, into an engine driving our efforts. To the extent that we addressed some popular needs, we solved the Alvaro Obregón District's political problem.[14]

In the 1930s the mobilization of popular sectors was introduced as a tactic in intrafactional elite rivalry: workers and campesinos were rallied against a landed elite. In the 1990s this strategy has been reenacted: the Salinas team can muster the support of urban popular movements and the disenfranchised in the struggle for power and patronage between "modernizing" factions of the state elite and traditional brokers in the official party. Solidarity Committees were conceived explicitly to replace traditional PRI-affiliated corporatist organizations like the CNC and the CTM as vehicles for political incorporation, organization, and, ultimately, control. As an ex-director of regional development during Salinas's tenure at the Ministry of Budget and Planning stated: "Solidarity Committees were designed to become political cells. . . . In Mexico, unlike the rest of Latin America, we are creating institutions. That explains why nothing like Venezuela has happened here."[15]

The same scheme of pitting Solidarity organizations and beneficiaries against local PRI networks has been extended beyond Mexico City. Indeed, the country appears to be witnessing a renewed rivalry for the heart of the nation. Insofar as PRONASOL has displaced traditional sources of patronage, it has engendered divisiveness and disruption among Mexico's political elite. Many PRONASOL organizers complain about top-level PRI officials' lack of understanding about and support for Solidarity. In regions where Solidarity appears to be most effective—

---

[14]Comments made during a tour of the Alvaro Obregón District, February 1992.

[15]Author interview, February 14, 1992. Candid comments by José Alberto Lozoya, former technical secretary of the foreign policy cabinet, may have cost him his job; they also underscore the mobilizing drive behind PRONASOL: "PRONASOL has multiplied the potential and capacity for self-organization of popular sectors in a colossal way. . . . It made the entire political system shake, because the left lost its traditional constituency and the bureaucrats who used to be intermediaries of decisions and benefits are losing their jobs" (*El Universal*, September 9, 1992).

such as Yucatán, Oaxaca, and the Federal District—PRONASOL leaders emphasize that positive outcomes were assured only by marginalizing traditional PRI leaders, and that "it's easier to count on the opposition than on the PRI. Party leaders are afraid that the institutional PRI may be coming to an end."[16] PRONASOL reformers argue that the population voted for Solidarity and Salinas (*La Jornada* 1991a), and that to gain the trust of popular groups they had to "corner the PRI and sweep it away."

PRI leaders, meanwhile, respond that despite PRONASOL's growing presence and organizational abilities, Solidarity alone cannot explain the PRI's electoral recovery. From the PRI's perspective, PRONASOL will never play electoral politics effectively or supersede the party. According to Enrique Jackson, the PRI's secretary of organization, the party has regained its hegemonic position thanks to its capacity for electoral mobilization (author interview, February 11, 1992). During the August 1991 elections, the PRI experimented with new tactics which ranged from training and assigning "vote promoters" to coaching PRI candidates on how to dress and speak in public. According to party officials, the PRI won as a result of its effort, not because of its links with Solidarity's welfare apparatus.

These contrasting interpretations of the political clout exercised by PRONASOL and the PRI merely reveal the contours of what has become a growing struggle over power and patronage. Solidarity has engendered numerous institutional conflicts, particularly between federal and state governments. Political control in Mexico has rested traditionally on a vast web of structured clienteles. With the arrival of PRONASOL to a particular state, suddenly 30 percent or more of the governor's or the municipal presidents' budgets must be redirected to Solidarity projects, often making governors reluctant to participate in the program. Given the way its resources are allocated, Solidarity tends to weaken traditional forms of political control.[17]

PRI leaders feel threatened because PRONASOL often appears to function as a parallel political party, more closely linked to presidential interests than to PRI affairs. PRI party sections have lost ground vis-à-vis Solidarity Committees, which are in direct contact with the federal authorities who assign and disburse public resources (Ramírez 1992). During the last PRI assembly in September 1991, PRI militants opposed the suggestion of changing the party's name to Solidarity; the negative implications for the traditional corporatist coalition seemed all too clear.

---

[16]During a tour of the Alvaro Obregón District, a PRONASOL official explained that in order to carry out Solidarity works, his team had to confront a traditional PRI leader who had established an alliance with the most conservative forces in the city government.

[17]The Mexican press has reported conflicts over the allocation of resources between Heladio Ramírez, governor of Oaxaca, and PRONASOL *delegado* Carlos Villalba, and between Dulce María Sauri, governor of Yucatán, and PRONASOL *delegado* Carlos Sobrino, among others (*El Financiero, Informe Especial* 91 [February 7, 1992]).

But during the midterm electoral campaigns, Solidarity effectively functioned as a partisan political organization, leading voters to declare, "We voted for the PRI, but our vote really is for Solidarity because it's better than the PRI" (*La Jornada* 1991a). It may be no coincidence that exactly the same number of people—thirteen million—participated in events related to Mexico's second National Solidarity Week and voted for the PRI in the August 1991 elections.[18] Salinas's third State of the Nation address may someday be compared to President Calles's announcement of the creation of the official party in the 1930s. Salinas said: "Solidarity is the democratic reform of the popular bases throughout our country that gives a new dimension to our nationalism. It provides the stability and social peace that we deserve; it has created new ties between institutions and public officials, ties that are part of the state reform that I proposed to bring government closer to the people."

In light of these statements, PRIístas can be legitimately concerned about whether Solidarity will replace the PRI if the president decides that the party has fulfilled its historic mission and can now be discarded. Salinas's impassioned promotion of PRONASOL could form part of a deliberate strategy undertaken by the state elite—a variant of the "orthodox paradox" whereby the "old PRI" is used to create the "new PRI." But then, if PRONASOL was created to replace the PRI, why have Solidarity's daily activities been so explicitly intertwined with those of the PRI? And why has former PRI president Luis Donaldo Colosio been named to head the ministry that will supervise PRONASOL activities in the future?

One critic observed that "PRONASOL funding is not much to alleviate poverty with, but it is a lot when it is given to the PRI" (author interview, October 20, 1991). The 1992 gubernatorial race in Michoacán highlighted the politicized nature of PRONASOL disbursements and revealed the close linkages between public spending and electoral contests. Of all the races scheduled for that year, Michoacán and Chihuahua were the most troublesome for the official party because of opposition strength in both states. However, these two opposition groups hold different political positions, and this has made all the difference. In Chihuahua, the Salinas team was willing to recognize the victory of the right-wing PAN; the PAN's anti-statist and free market record, as well as its support for key legislative modifications, provided the basis for political accord. But Salinas refused to make concessions to the left-wing PRD in Michoacán, a party which continues to challenge the legitimacy of his government and demands radical changes that would undermine the neoliberal economic model. For the PRI the electoral race in Michoacán was an opportunity to prove that the party

---

[18]Thirteen million is the government's official vote count; I use this figure with the usual trepidation.

had regained its electoral hegemony even in a left-wing stronghold; for the PRD, it was a last chance to reestablish itself as a viable political force.

Since the beginning of Salinas's term, PRONASOL authorities have devoted special attention to Michoacán, where the PRD governed 52 out of 113 municipalities. According to journalistic accounts, PRONASOL channeled over 12 percent of its national budget to the state and deployed one-fourth of its national promoters there during the 1992 governor's race (*La Jornada*, July 4, 1992). Assisted by PRONASOL funds, the PRI spent nearly twice as much to combat the PRD in Michoacán as it did to run against the PAN in Chihuahua.[19] According to independent electoral observers, none of the ten characteristics of a clean electoral process was present in Michoacán, putting the PRD at a severe disadvantage.[20]

As the Michoacán case underscored, PRONASOL funds infuse energy into the PRI's middle ranks during electoral contests. Solidarity *delegados* are PRI officials one day and poverty alleviation experts the next. This symbiosis between the PRI and PRONASOL has functioned successfully until now, but it could encounter serious problems in the future. The informal sector and urban popular groups linked to PRONASOL tend to vote pragmatically. They support democrats, dictators, or populists—whoever takes their needs into account—and they withdraw their support just as easily when ignored (see Graham 1991c). As long as the PRI acts as a welfare machine, it will hold the electoral support of these groups. But renewed clientelism can be a double-edged sword. Patronage may win votes and the exchange of favors may generate political support, but clientelism can never create legitimacy (see Mainwaring 1991). Clientelism discredits political parties, the political class, and the political system itself. It contributes to the cynicism and depoliticization of a populace which asks: Why participate in politics if politics amounts to little more than a corrupt exchange of goods and favors? Clientelism flourishes when parties are weak, and it weakens parties even more by undermining regime legitimacy. When legitimacy is lacking, governments are fragile. This is the risk that the Mexican political elite has taken by renewing the PRI's license as a clientelist apparatus.

PRONASOL could also exacerbate the troubled relationship between opposition parties and the PRI. Solidarity has been severely criticized by both the PRD and the PAN, who denounce it as "political bait" and claim it "perverts national politics" (*El Financiero*, November 6, 1991). PAN officials in Chihuahua complained about the politicized use of PRO-

---

[19]The PRI spent 100 billion pesos in Michoacán and only 52 billion in Chihuahua (*El Financiero*, July 27, 1992).

[20]Both the Movimiento Ciudadano por la Democracia and ACUDE charged the federal and state governments for paying the PRI's campaign with PRONASOL funds (*La Jornada*, June 22, 1992).

NASOL resources by the municipal president of Ciudad Juárez (*Proceso*, April 6, 1992). Campesinos from Michoacán protested the channeling of PRONASOL funds exclusively to PRIísta municipalities (*La Jornada*, May 28, 1992). Victims of the Guadalajara earthquake criticized PRONASOL state authorities for trying to divide independent organizations by selectively doling out "reconstruction funds"(*La Jornada*, May 29, 1992). And in the July 1992 gubernatorial race in Durango, the PRD-PAN coalition candidate charged that PRONASOL authorities had threatened to withhold PRONASOL benefits from groups that intended to vote for the opposition. This sampling of complaints underscores that corruption, clientelism, selectivity in resource delivery, and the promotion of partisan goals appear to have become part of PRONASOL's standard operating procedure in many regions.

Solidarity appears at minimum to have become an important element in Salinas's efforts to establish a political base outside the PRI's traditional power structures, even as it emerges as a useful tool in shoring up PRI support nationwide (Haber n.d.1). Whether PRONASOL weakens or strengthens the PRI in the long term will depend on how Salinas resolves his political ambiguity toward the party: at times he appears to want to govern without the PRI, yet at other junctures he seems to throw his (somewhat qualified) support behind the party (Dresser 1992a). Salinas wants enough change within the PRI to sustain the economic reform model, but no more. With Solidarity's support the PRI may achieve a "modernized" form of dominant party rule, whereby it wins in an apparently less corrupt and more competitive fashion, but always wins. Consequently, initiatives to level the playing field for all parties—by limiting PRONASOL's support of PRI crusades, for example—have been temporarily discarded. Beyond the imperative of maintaining centralized control, for Salinas the PRI-PRONASOL relationship appears to be subordinate to assuring the political stability necessary to institutionalize the country's economic reform.

PRESIDENTIALISM AND SYMBOLIC POLITICS

> *In this republic, you don't say no to the president. . . .*
> *Presidentialism is like a habit of our soul. . . . We carry the mark of*
> *that branding iron in our heart, in our sensibility. Worse yet: in our*
> *spinal chord.*
> —Aguilar Camín (1991: 313)

Solidarity has become a vehicle for reasserting presidential power in Mexico. Underscoring that there are no formal ties between Solidarity and the PRI, Salinas bypassed the PRI and the government itself in order to legitimize the regime. Leadership and effective styles of governance are crucial for the adoption of new economic models. Redeployed presidentialism and an effective use of symbolic politics constitute, in many ways, essential ingredients of Mexico's reform program.

For a new development model to become consolidated, a high level of consensus must emerge around it (Sikkink 1991). Coalition building and political survival entail not only "buying off" different groups but also mobilizing political support. One of the most effective means for mobilizing support is an appeal to commonly held ideas, a "project" that captivates and inspires people, that binds otherwise disparate coalitions together. In this sense, PRONASOL has served as a mixing bowl for ideas, inspiration, leadership, and the unquantifiable qualities that motivate people to believe and to act. Solidarity has become Mexico's "captivating social metaphor" for the 1990s — or at least for the remainder of Salinas's term.

During each of the three National Solidarity Weeks, the peripatetic Salinas toured over ten states. His helicopter touched down in at least three towns each day, and the president led a dizzying series of meetings where he inaugurated public works and announced budget increases for Solidarity. At each of these outdoor rallies, carefully organized and orchestrated by Solidarity officials and the president's advance team, Salinas delivered a "personalized" statement — alluding to concerns of the specific locality — *and* a generic speech on the political philosophy of Solidarity. Thanks to PRONASOL's information machinery, Salinas always knows exactly what constituency he is facing and what are its expectations and problems.

Through this PRONASOL-related activism, Salinas appears to be reconstructing society's relationship with the state. His most frequent message in the countryside is: "You are not alone. You have the support of your friend, the president." Salinas also goes to great lengths to establish a sort of antibureaucratic complicity between the president and popular sectors. Early in his term, Salinas ordered that PRI logos not be displayed at Solidarity meetings, and neither the PRI nor local governments are mentioned on Salinas's tours. These moves dissociate Solidarity from party politics and also link Salinas and PRONASOL in the public mind. The president's willingness to make and follow up on promises has imbued Solidarity with a high degree of efficacy (Hinojosa 1992). Because of Salinas's follow-up, local governments are forced to deliver what the president promised. This presidential effort to reach out and touch popular sectors was described by a PRONASOL beneficiary in the following terms:

> President Salinas received us with open arms. Just like
> he says, he doesn't make distinctions among people,
> and like the great national authority he is, he treated us
> very well and he didn't tell us he didn't have time for
> us. . . . He listened to us. In that interview he told us:

"Huehuetla will no longer be forgotten. Maybe that
happened in the past, but from now on it will no longer
be forgotten" (municipal president of Huehuetla, in
México Indígena, August 1991).

The president's PRONASOL-related activities are highly publicized
nationwide. During Solidarity Week, publicity for Salinas and the
program airs on the two official national television channels: daily
coverage of the latest government statistics on PRONASOL, man-in-the-
street interviews about the program, and comprehensive coverage of the
president's tours (*Mexico Service*, September 18, 1991).

In a strong presidentialist system like Mexico's, ideas held by the
president and his economic advisers are crucial for determining what
political-economic model is adopted. Mexico's intellectual entrepreneur
president is disseminating a new developmentalist ideology contained in
Solidarity. Its messages are that the government fulfills its promises and
that Solidarity can accomplish what may seem impossible. Solidarity
officials describe PRONASOL as "citizen's mobilization without populism or paternalism." The government's basic premise is that by encouraging the creation of local Solidarity Committees, PRONASOL is fostering democracy and strengthening sovereignty. As Salinas told
slumdwellers in Michoacán, "Solidarity is democratic reform through
popular groups, democracy at the grassroots." Or as he argued in a
speech delivered to health workers in Michoacán, "When we combine
justice and democracy, we strengthen Mexico's sovereignty and independence. This is the new way of doing things" (in *Mexico Service*, September 18, 1991). The term solidarity has become ingrained in the national
consciousness: in a recent poll conducted by Mexico's National Public
Opinion Institute, 96 percent of the population identified "solidarity" as
a "very important" political concept, versus 76 percent for "democracy."

This contrasts markedly with the situation shortly after Salinas's
second State of the Nation address in November 1990, when 78 percent
of the Mexican population was not yet familiar with PRONASOL. To
remedy the situation, the administration commissioned a massive,
multimillion-dollar publicity campaign (see Gómez Leyva 1991). Ten
"chronicles" were produced for movie, television, and radio spots.
Within a matter of days, the entire country learned of a young boy who
would become an engineer thanks to a Solidarity scholarship, of the
grandmother who finally received her land title from the hands of the
president himself, of the child who helped rebuild his school through
the Escuela Digna program, and of the young woman who could finally
invite her boyfriend home after electric lighting, installed with Solidarity
funds, convinced her father that "it wasn't too dark in the house
anymore." By the following July, a survey revealed that 72 percent of
Mexicans knew what PRONASOL was, and 63 percent remembered its

slogan: "Joined in Progress." One Solidarity official acknowledged that perhaps PRONASOL's propaganda has been excessive, but "all political movements need propaganda. . . . Only through propaganda do people feel that they participate and that they are taken into account" (author interview, February 10, 1992).

During the golden age of import-substitution industrialization, the political class developed several ideological justifications for expanding public enterprise and state interventionism in order to promote social justice. In the era of the modest state and market-led growth, state elites have replaced these "rusty weapons" with a heterogeneous mix of ideas called "social liberalism." The "old" revolutionary is he who supports the large, proprietary, and subsidizing state. The "new" revolutionary, in contrast, proclaims the virtues of the small, lean, and fiscally responsible state which channels resources to the neediest through Solidarity.

In this sense, state elites are transforming Solidarity into what Albert Hirschman (1979) defined as an ideology of economic development: a set of distinctive beliefs, principles, and attitudes which give meaning to a political-economic situation and permit purposeful action within it. In the past, developmentalist ideologies captivated the population with the concept of state-supported heavy industry as a route to autonomy and with the mystique of planning and technification as tools that would allow the country to leap into the future. The shift toward neoliberalism in the 1980s, however, entailed the search for new developmentalist ideas that fit better with the ideologies of the new model's beneficiaries. The Salinas team has demonstrated remarkable success in advancing an economic platform that builds on traditional nationalist symbols and institutions, while simultaneously orienting them toward North American integration, privatization, deregulation, and public-sector reform (Haber n.d.1). Thus, perhaps the most important shift in Mexico's political economy over the last ten years is a perceptual one, from national populism to the new ideological framework of social liberalism.[21]

CONCLUSION: ON THE TIGHTROPE

> *Nothing can harm this country more than the truth. . . . We are a hunchback, but a century ago we were a sewer. Tomorrow we will merely be lame, and one day we will be normal, as long as we keep on doing little by little what we have done up to now: hide our deformity, tell ourselves that we were born for something else . . . put ourselves in the place of normal beings.*
> —Aguilar Camín (1991: 326)

---

[21] Salinas defined "social liberalism" as the new ideology of the Mexican state in a speech that celebrated the sixty-third anniversary of the PRI (*Epoca*, March 9, 1992).

PRONASOL reflects the sometimes contradictory demands of economic strategy and political survival. Mexico's market-oriented reforms of the 1980s and 1990s argue for selling off public assets, promoting automaticity in economic transactions, and ending social welfare entitlements for privileged members of the populist-distributive ISI coalition. By contrast, the need to control public resources for coalition restructuring, compensatory payments, and pre-election pump-priming dictates continued state intervention, large doses of presidentialism and discretionality, a hybrid "change team," and a new ideological framework designed to hold a disparate reform package together.

This tension between economic strategy and political control can be sustained over long periods as long as there is growth in the economy.[22] The sustainability of Mexico's hybrid policy mix of neoliberalism and neopopulism is anchored in performance. As long as there is growth, the state can continue to engage in selective compensation, via PRONASOL, for some of the many victims of privatization, layoffs, and inflation who litter the shining path of neoliberal reform.

Nonetheless, the political challenge facing state elites is as important as is the need for economic growth: in the shift from ISI to market-oriented reforms, Mexico's leaders are dealing with established distributional coalitions (like the PRI) with legitimized claims to resources. The Salinas team will find it difficult to disengage from them and may opt not to do so entirely. Potential and new allies who benefit from the recently implemented policies have not yet fully consolidated. Political survival entails assuring an equilibrium between groups. PRONASOL, meanwhile, allows the political elite to survive this impasse and gives it enough political resources to ensure regime stability.

However, Solidarity's essential feature—its symbiotic relationship with presidential power—awakens the age-old question about the impact of presidentialism on political evolution. Vigorous presidentialism appears to be both the key to the success of Mexico's neoliberal program and its Achilles' heel. The concentration of power in the executive allows effective discretionality but also entails the risk of arbitrary heavy-handedness. Presidentialism reinforces personalist politics at the expense of institution building (Mainwaring 1990). There is no guarantee that Salinas's successor will have the talent or vision to administer PRONASOL effectively. In the wrong hands or the wrong context, the vast discretionary power that PRONASOL places in the president's hands might jeopardize the stability of the reform process itself. In turbulent political times—including, perhaps, the presidential succession—the temptation to pass from selective and fiscally responsible compensation to massive and populist transfers might be irresistible.

---

[22]For an analysis of the Japanese case, see Calder 1988.

Thus, the challenge will be to maintain the precarious balance between economic growth and compensatory payments, between coalition destruction and coalition construction, between the strengthening of the government and the weakening of the PRI, between presidentialism and institutionalization, and between the two polarities that Albert Hirschman (1979) defined as accumulation and distribution. And the balancing act must hold the line of least popular dissatisfaction. To accomplish this, PRONASOL has been and will continue to be instrumental. What Salinas has going for him currently are expectations. For the thousands who cheer him when he inaugurates public works, Solidarity represents a hope that, after long decline, living conditions will finally improve (Sarmiento 1991b). Hope is the stuff votes are made of. But unfulfilled hopes are the stuff revolts are made of—and if PRONASOL offers more than it can deliver, Salinas's successors may yet discover that the streets of Mexico City can resemble those of Caracas, or Lima, or São Paulo, and that perhaps Mexico is not so exceptional after all.

9

The Mexican Left and the Social Program of Salinismo

Julio Moguel

"To create a new relationship between the people and the state": this is
how Carlos Salinas de Gortari defined one principal objective of the
National Solidarity Program. The context was an unprecedented political event, the National Meeting of Urban Settlers, which took place in
Monterrey during Mexico's second National Solidarity Week, in 1991.
The president's words openly signaled what up to that point had only
been hinted at: PRONASOL was to become the axis for the state's "new
mass politics," which would particularly target the peasantry and
impoverished urban populations. The program's primary objective
would be to channel financial resources to combat extreme poverty. Its
instruments would be the Solidarity Committees, organizations with no
links to the old corporatist structures. The ideology of this new antipoverty strategy was a combination of mass politics, autonomous organization, and horizontal coordination, along with transparency, direct
democracy, development "from the bottom up," community participation, concertation, and solidarity.[1]

Translated by Aníbal Yáñez.

[1] The new relationship between government and civil society is based on four main
principles: respect for the wishes, initiatives, and organizational structures of individuals
and communities; a strong community role in organizing and implementing PRONASOL
projects; co-responsibility; and transparency, honesty, and efficiency in the resource
management. These four principles are to "eliminate any vestiges of paternalism, clientelism, political strings, or pretense in programs designed to improve the well-being of the
poor. Solidarity belongs to all Mexicans; it does not require or encourage beneficiaries to
alter their political position. The program promotes social mobilization on behalf of those
who have the least; this is the shared premise that supports an active and pluralistic
consensus for development and social justice" (PRONASOL 1991a: 5–6).

PRONASOL is a program of co-responsibility; operationally it begins with the selection of an investment project or public work and extends through its construction and implementation in co-participation with the beneficiaries. Throughout the process, the Solidarity Committee serves as a direct link between PRONASOL officials and the co-participants through a community or neighborhood assembly. This assembly is completely autonomous and is the highest authority for the regulation and oversight of the sharing of responsibilities. At a second level, Solidarity Committees can link and coordinate locally and regionally. In theory, they could then become part of a national organizational structure by sector (as Salinas proposed in Monterrey, when he urged those attending the National Solidarity Week event to form a national coordinating committee for popular neighborhoods). According to the formal model of PRONASOL, a point is ultimately reached where there are two national organizational networks (one rural, the other urban). These networks may be more or less formalized, but all are linked very directly to the state, articulated through PRONASOL. As Salinas declared in Monterrey, "Solidarity belongs permanently to the people."

The PRONASOL strategy carries two significant social and political implications: First, through PRONASOL the government is challenging the so-called social left's influence and leadership role among urban popular sectors, to a large extent by using the left's own formulas and methods. It does the same among the rural population by strengthening the organization of Solidarity Committees vis-à-vis what are called autonomous organizations. Second, traditional corporatist co-optation is often bypassed or circumvented: new structures arise that are parallel to or independent of the PRI's traditional sectors. These often place PRONASOL in open conflict with local and regional forces organized in the League of Agrarian Communities, in rank-and-file committees of officialist organizations (e.g., the CNC, CCI), or through other forms of traditional political control.

By official count, in 1991 there were more than three thousand Solidarity Committees in the coffee-growing zones of Mexico, about five thousand in popular neighborhoods, and no less than sixty-four thousand in Mexico as a whole. By the third National Solidarity Week in 1992, there were more than 100,000 committees, described as the cells in the tissue of a new relationship between the people and the state.

This chapter will not debate whether a social spending program such as Solidarity can modify the state-society relationship or attempt to gauge to what extent this changing relationship has gained entrance in rural and urban areas of Mexico. Nor will it consider the real or apparent paradoxes which arise in the application of a "neoliberal" model accompanied by "neopopulist" solutions (see Dresser 1991). My interests are the ideology and practices put forward to build new links between the state and the people and, more specifically, those points of intersection when an important sector of the Mexican left joined hands with PRO-NASOL (and through it, with Salinismo) or, in another iteration, has come fully and militantly to adopt the colors of Solidarity.

THE RECENT DEVELOPMENT OF THE MEXICAN LEFT: POSITIVE UTOPIA

What today we call the Mexican left bears little resemblance to that of the 1970s or 1980s, and even less to the left of earlier, more turbulent years. Its sheddings of skin have been many and deep. The 1968 student movement was the great watershed which forged an entire generation of militants. The next event of this magnitude was the FDN's call to electoral battle in 1987–88.[2]

The twenty years between 1968 and 1988 correspond to the second golden era of the Mexican left.[3] The popular struggles of the late 1950s and early 1960s, along with the impact of the Cuban revolution, had already revitalized the left and made it a significant political presence on the national scene. But it was not until the 1968 student struggles that this ideological and political current once again had a profound impact on the policy of the Mexican state, to such a degree, in fact, that we could not explain Echeverría's Neocardenismo (1970–76) or López Portillo's political reform (1977) without it.

The political nuclei that would make up the new left appeared in the early 1970s. Although qualitatively different from the left of the 1960s and earlier, the new left retained some symbols, organizational forms, and lines of action that dated back to the previous decade. Most older leftist groups, including the Mexican Communist Party (PCM), founded in 1919, consolidated their social bases and organizational policies with nuclei of youth whose political apprenticeship took place in 1968, and, with Mexico's universities serving as the laboratories, a new organizational body took shape.

The ascendance of popular movements of peasants, workers, and squatters throughout the first half of the 1970s provided a favorable environment for these new organisms to spread to other levels of society. Preexisting and emerging political organizations were able to carry out

---

[2]Neither case (1968 and 1988) represented an abrupt change; each built on a preceding period of maturing practices and ideas among certain sectors of the left. The struggles carried out by the National Liberation Movement (MLN) or political organizations like the Mexican Communist Party (PCM) or the Liga Leninista Espártaco help explain the events of 1968. The antecedents of the 1988 watershed lie in civic and popular movements such as those that arose in reaction to the 1985 Mexico City earthquakes, in the municipal struggles that developed during the first half of the 1980s, and in the 1986–87 student movement (see Moguel 1987; Bennett 1992b).

[3]The first golden era covered the 1920s and 1930s, when the Mexican left had considerable influence in the mass movement of peasants and workers and other struggles such as the Veracruz renters' movement, and even came to have a decisive influence on government policymaking (as during the Cárdenas administration, 1934–40).

unprecedented, sometimes very successful, efforts to link with and become part of some popular sectors.

All the organizational nuclei that would appear in the political struggles of the next ten or twelve years emerged between 1970 and 1976 (with the exception of the PCM). The National Consultation and Coordination Committee (CNAC), formed in 1971, gave rise to the Mexican Workers' Party (PMT), the Socialist Workers' Party (PST), the Revolutionary Socialist Party (PSR), and the Socialist Action and Unity Movement (MAUS). The Internationalist Communist Group (GCI), formed in 1970, was the ideological and political source of the Trotskyist Revolutionary Workers' Party (PRT), founded in 1976. The magazine *Punto Crítico*, which appeared in 1971, was the nucleus that would later split to form two new currents: the Union Council (*Consejo Sindical*) group of Mexico's National Autonomous University (UNAM) and the Revolutionary Organization Punto Crítico (ORPC). Years later, the former would help make up the Popular Action Movement (MAP) and the United Mexican Socialist Party (PSUM).

The Coalition of Workers, Peasants, and Students of the Isthmus (COCEI) was formed in 1974. Notwithstanding its regional character and its popular front structure, this organization gained enormous importance through the early 1980s. In 1975, a group led by Gascón Mercado split from the Popular Socialist Party (PPS) and later founded the Mexican People's Party (PPM) in 1977. (The PPM would later join the PSUM's unification project.) A process that began in 1969 and continued into the early 1970s led to the formation of significant Maoist groups such as Popular Politics (Política Popular) and the Ho Chi Minh Section (Seccional Ho-chi-min), which years later would lead to the formation of the People's Revolutionary Movement (MRP), the Organization of the Revolutionary Left-Mass Line (OIR-LM), and Proletarian Line (LP). Those same years saw the birth and development of the main nuclei that would later join together as the National Revolutionary Civic Association (ACNR).

In this hodgepodge of acronyms we can discern several main currents: the communist (later, socialist) current, basically represented at that time by the Mexican Communist Party; the Cardenista-Lombardista current, fed by tributaries from the old PPS, the PPM, the PMT, and the PST; the radical Marxist current with Trotskyist origins organized around the PRT; the radical Marxist current with a Leninist or pro-Cuban profile, represented by the group around *Estrategia* magazine, by the ORPC, the COCEI, or the ACNR; and the radical Marxist current with Maoist origins (better known as the Mass Line current), with branches in Popular Politics, the MRP, or the OIR-LM.[4]

---

[4]Elsewhere (Moguel 1987) I consider the Lombardista current separately from the Cardenista current, but this distinction is not significant here.

MASS LINE'S SOCIAL STRENGTH AND IDENTITY

Over time, all the left currents underwent splits and fusions which led to more clearly demarcated broad tendencies. Toward the second half of the 1980s, two large blocs became important. One followed a formal socialist line and culminated in the formation of the Mexican Socialist Party (PMS).[5] The other was a network of organizations with Maoist or Leninist origins organized around nuclei such as OIR-LM, MRP, LP, or ACNR. This network also claimed to pursue the goal of socialism.

Even with all their programmatic or doctrinal differences, the Leninists and Maoists shared some points of convergence and unity which occasionally led them to present themselves as a single bloc vis-à-vis other currents. Most importantly, they rejected the "reformism" of the current that was grouped around the PCM-PSUM-PMS axis, criticized their "bureaucratic apparatism and top-down politics," and refused to participate in high-level negotiations with the government. Instead, they focused on "mass politics": political activity completely divorced from electoral processes or electoral participation rooted in social organizations, almost always confined to the level of municipal presidencies. To distinguish themselves from the "reformist left," this current began to define itself as the "revolutionary left."

It was the current with Maoist origins that most radically criticized the bureaucratic apparatism mentality of the old Communists or new Socialists.[6] They went so far as to accuse the PCM-PSUM-PMS of promoting a USSR type of socialism, which, the Maoists claimed, was just a new overlay on state capitalism. In addition, an important sector of the Maoists refused to participate in electoral processes because they viewed them as the arena of bourgeois and reformist politics.

One major tendency of this Maoism was first represented by organizations such as Popular Politics or the Independent Popular Front (FPI). Despite diverse paths of development, their common denominator was

---

[5]The Mexican Communist Party joined with other left parties and groups to form the United Mexican Socialist Party (PSUM) in 1979, and through fusion with still other groups—most notably those that came out of the Mexican Workers' Party, led by Heberto Castillo—formed the Mexican Socialist Party (PMS) in 1987. The Trotskyist Revolutionary Workers' Party (PRT) entered an unresolvable crisis in 1988, when it lost its registration as a national political party by failing to win 1.5 percent of the national vote, the minimum needed to retain registration.

[6]Unlike the case of Peru and other Latin American countries, Mexican Maoism did not adhere to a guerrilla program. Further, its cult of the masses, its rejection of bureaucratic apparatism, and its assumption that the party would develop as a product of the mass movement to a large extent shielded its militants from the sectarian and conspiratorial nature of small groups. The Maoists of one of Mexico's main currents (that which comes from Popular Politics, Ho Chi Minh Section, and Proletarian Line) were actually somewhat unorthodox. They were very much influenced by Charles Bettelheim and the Althusserian school. They held ideas reminiscent of anarchism, and a not insignificant number of their theorists and leaders quickly evolved toward a more Gramscian concept of revolution (see Macciocchi 1975).

their origin among university professors and students committed to an ambitious project, a "turn to the people."[7] They emphasized political work with the peasantry and squatters' movements, believing that the trajectory of the socialist revolution would carry the Mexican movement (which shared features with prerevolutionary China) from the country-side to the cities, creating "liberated zones" of popular power which would eventually challenge the global power of the bourgeoisie.

While much of what these militants defended may now seem remote or even risible, what is important is not whether their positions were correct or their outlook realistic. What is important is how their beliefs were expressed and translated into given political practices; how they reflected a certain state of mind and the social or political consciousness of specific popular sectors; how they represented a debate which, whatever its interpretive value, gave rise to an interweaving of standards and identity whose political effectiveness cannot be overestimated.

These groups can take credit for building important regional organizations such as the COCEI in Oaxaca and the ACNR in Guerrero, and mass fronts such as the Committees for Popular Defense (CDPs) in Chihuahua and Durango, and the "Land and Liberty" Popular Front (FPTyL) in Monterrey. A significant number of the entities that made up the National Union of Regional Peasant Organizations (UNORCA) were built by this type of organization, as were those that later formed the National Coordinating Committee of Coffee-Producers' Organizations (CNOC). But their highest achievement was establishing the National Coordinating Committee of the Urban Popular Movement (CONAMUP), the National Coordinating Committee of Education Workers (CNTE), the National Union Coordinating Committee (COSINA), and the National Front Against Repression (FNCR), all between the late 1970s and the early 1980s.

Three years after the CNTE appeared in 1979, to give but one example, it had established central struggle committees in Guerrero, Hidalgo, Morelos, Chiapas, and the Valley of Mexico, and sectional executive committees in Chiapas, in the National Institute of Anthropology and History (INAH), and in the National Polytechnic Institute (IPN). Committees were also at work building central struggle committees in Baja California Sur, Tlaxcala, Querétaro, San Luis Potosí, Sinaloa, Puebla, Michoacán, Guanajuato, Baja California Norte, the La Laguna region in Coahuila, and the Federal District (Hernández Navarro 1983; Moguel 1987: 29–31).

When CONAMUP was formally constituted in 1981, it already included more than sixty popular organizations in Mexico's major cities. After its third national meeting in May 1982, CONAMUP spread to

---

[7]In the nineteenth century, populist Russian students and professors (the Narodniks) carried out a mass "turn to the people," to "live with the masses . . . make the revolution." A similar political romanticism motivated the Mexican "Narodniks."

Guerrero, Sinaloa, Durango, México State, and Baja California, and included more than one hundred regional social organizations. The National "Plan de Ayala" Coordinating Committee (CNPA), formed in 1979, would come to lead the national process of peasant convergence around struggles for land which had been under way since the early 1970s. In 1983–84, these forces together formed the National Front for the Defense of Salaries and in Opposition to Austerity and Shortages (FNDSCAC) and the National Popular Assembly of Workers and Peasants (ANOCP) to launch what were without doubt the most important popular mobilizations of that period.

I have already discussed some of the basic tenets of the social left: 1) building autonomous organizations, self-managed and free of corporatist forms of state control;[8] 2) developing networks or social and political organizations which are neither vertical nor bureaucratic but are based on the concept of coordinating committees (rather than a set, hierarchical structure) and mass fronts; 3) mass politics; 4) direct or assembly democracy as the basis on which to build popular power today and a socialist democracy in the future, one that rejects on principle delegated or representative democracy as reformist and bourgeois; 5) concertation as a means of negotiating specific demands of the popular sectors with the state, with no loss of political independence or autonomy; and 6) a separation between the work arena and the arena of politics, achieved paradoxically by politicizing what relates specifically to work (the preferred context in which to carry out counterhegemonic practice and discourse), while rejecting what is specifically political (elections and parliamentary activity) because it is characteristic of reformism and the bourgeoisie and therefore alien to the mass movement.

THE INTERSECTION OF THE SOCIAL LEFT AND PRONASOL

The similarities between certain ideas held by the social left and incorporated in PRONASOL are not coincidental. The ingredients that the social left has contributed to PRONASOL are as visible as are the members of the social left who now hold key posts in the Salinas team, beginning with Carlos Rojas, the individual directly responsible for PRONASOL.[9]

PRONASOL is not the first government program to involve participation from the left. Members of the social left may join an administration to make a short-term contribution to a high-minded cause, or they

---

[8]As Gustavo Gordillo and others have noted, the concept of autonomy meant dropping the earlier sectarian and not very useful idea of independence, which the left and some organized popular sectors used in the 1970s.

[9]Before joining the government, Carlos Rojas worked closely with a sector of the social left in research and community development activities. As a student, Carlos Salinas associated with the Popular Politics nuclei, and later his brother Raúl was an active promoter of or sympathizer with some ideas of this left while he was in various government posts (particularly while at DICONSA).

may do so seeking a long-lasting relationship and political commitment with a faction of the ruling team. Luis Echeverría (1970–76) was able to attract sectors of the Mexican left to some of his programs, particularly his project of ejido collectivization. José López Portillo (1976–82) opened the door to the left with his Mexican Food System (SAM) and the CONASUPO-COPLAMAR program.[10] Nevertheless, with only one exception (Cárdenas's policies in the 1930s), PRONASOL has attracted the most significant contingent of left militants.

Various factors help explain this particularly strong relationship between the left and the government in PRONASOL. First, PRONASOL has an explicit ideological component, unlike the redistributive or social policy programs of previous administrations. Not limited to addressing given economic and social problems affecting the population, this ideological component poses the transformation of the relationship between society and the state. Second, PRONASOL's target population—peasants and the urban poor—are those sectors where the social left has had a decisive influence in recent years. Third, as we have seen, the very structure of Solidarity incorporates fundamental elements of the left's discourse, such as direct or assembly democracy, concertation, noncorporatist organization, horizontal coordinating committees, mass politics, etc. Fourth is the separation between the arenas of work and politics, which underlies PRONASOL's noncorporatist design, attractive to a large number of left militants who maintained just such a separation—at times quite sharp—in their own action programs. The fifth element, introduced above, is the political and personal links between theoreticians and leaders of the Mass Line and the Salinas team.

One additional factor is relevant: the social left (as well as the core of the "other" left) underwent a severe organizational and identity crisis beginning in the latter half of the 1980s. This was due, first, to the growing importance of electoral processes and of specifically civic (not sectoral) struggles in the country's social and political conflicts. Between 1983 and 1985 the PAN party headed several significant electoral mobilizations and was able to gain control of important municipal governments. The 1985 earthquakes in Mexico City generated spontaneous citizen participation which went beyond all calculations of the government and

---

[10]The contingent of field promoters recruited for the CONASUPO-COPLAMAR program "tended to be nonparty activists who saw the consolidation of autonomous peasant organizations, rather than electoral politics, as key to greater social justice and the democratization of Mexican society" (Fox 1993: 165). Fox also tells how "the pressures on CONASUPO-COPLAMAR to limit its promotion efforts began to mount soon after the program was launched. . . . By May 1981, 65 percent of the promoters in the central highlands states of Puebla, México, Tlaxcala, and Hidalgo either had been fired or had resigned to protest 'actions contrary to the philosophy of the program.' . . . The reformists at the top had to give in or lose their positions. . . . CONASUPO-COPLAMAR managers decided to try to handle the political pressure through evasive action, without resisting directly. At first fifty members of the original field staff of three hundred were fired, but by the end of the SAM period four hundred of a total of six hundred were replaced" (171–73).

the left; in the main this participation did not stay within the channels preestablished by those organizational entities. In 1986, Mexico's National Autonomous University (UNAM) was the scene of a new and combative student movement which led to the formation of the Council of University Students (CEU), whose symbols and tactics of struggle had little connection with previous experiences of the university-based left. And in 1987 and 1988 the Democratic Current headed by Cuauhtémoc Cárdenas and Porfirio Muñoz Ledo split from the PRI. This rupture opened up a struggle that shifted the axes and action priorities for broad sectors of the left: from social movement to electoral politics, from a sectoral focus to a citizen focus, from popular struggle to civic struggle.

The second element that drove the social left to its organizational and identity crisis was the deafening collapse of the socialist ideal throughout the world. This process reached its apex in 1989 with Gorbachev's *glasnost* and *perestroika* policies and with the fall of the Berlin Wall. Many of Mexico's Maoists or Mass Line activists had long before abandoned any reference to Chinese socialism, and there was no other model to replace it.

Some of the left, disconcerted by the failure of their models and the increasing inefficiency of their political and ideological instruments, adopted pragmatism as their new creed. Within one current that did not join the PRONASOL project, there was soon a process of conceptual substitution: the idea of a struggle for democracy began to appear where before there had been a struggle for socialism. The idea of direct and assembly democracy, of popular power, was gradually exchanged for those of effective suffrage, social and popular control, political representation in civil government and state bodies. Poor urban residents were no longer innate or potential proletarians, but rather part of a civil society in the process of organizing itself. Pluralism began to be seen as something more than an inevitable challenge to Mexico's one-party system.

CONCLUSIONS

Beginning in 1988, Mexico's social left broke with its previous pattern of development and split into four main currents: one that abandoned its independence to join the Salinas administration at its highest command levels (the Ministry of Agriculture and Water Resources, the National Indigenous Institute, PRONASOL) or at intermediate and operational management levels; one that joined the Party of the Democratic Revolution (PRD) or kept up its militant activities in social movements while maintaining its formal independence from the PRD but supporting— and voting for—Cárdenas; one that remained in the mass movement and steadfastly rejected any direct or indirect party commitments; and one that regrouped to form the Labor Party (PT), an organization which is still seeking its legal registration to participate in the electoral process.

The links between PRONASOL and those sectors of the left that joined the program or decidedly allied themselves with it (as one current of the PT did) were more than a matter of pragmatism and a temporary coincidence of particular interests. Nor were PRONASOL's ideological elements a mere conjunctural adoption from the left of symbols without content. Along the way, they represented some points of real unity. This was true of the common struggle against corporatist and cacique interests, and in a shared language: "to change the relationship between society and the state."

A key element in integrating militants from the social left into PRONASOL was the fact that Solidarity reproduced the idea of sharply differentiating what is work related from politics. In this way PRONASOL could turn to its advantage the left's rejection of what it viewed as the terrain for bourgeois and reformist politics.

The collapse of socialism undoubtedly contributed to the fact that a part of the social left joined PRONASOL. But their participation was not merely the result of this defeat. In a process of conceptual substitution, many on the left who today participate in or ally themselves with PRONASOL firmly and honestly believe that they are carrying forward a cause that transcends Salinas's six-year presidential term, and that Salinismo may be for the twenty-first century what Cardenismo was for the twentieth.

IV

Case Studies of
Programs and Regions

10

Targeting the Poorest: The Role of the National Indigenous Institute in Mexico's Solidarity Program

Jonathan Fox

INTRODUCTION

Is Mexico's National Solidarity Program really a "new way of doing things?" The government claims that it is abandoning its past populist paternalism, making antipoverty policy more targeted and accountable by promoting pluralistic grassroots mobilization. Program decisions are now supposed to be demand-driven, based on "co-responsibility" between policymakers and low-income communities rather than partisan clientelism. Solidarity's innovative public discourse is the linchpin of President Salinas's new ideology of "social liberalism," which commits the state to buffering the social costs of economic liberalization and structural adjustment. More broadly, Solidarity promises a profound change in state-society relations, renovating the social foundations of Mexico's long-standing political stability.

In practice, generalizing about Solidarity is complicated by the diversity of programs carried out under the same label. Implementation styles vary greatly by program and by region, as Solidarity's more

Field research for this project was carried out in 1991 and 1992, partially funded by a grant from the Howard Heinz Endowment. I am very grateful to the INI officials, indigenous leaders, and nongovernmental development organizations who shared their insights and experiences with me. I especially appreciate conversations with Josefina Aranda, Helga Baitenmann, Alejandro de Avila, Denise Dresser, Manuel Fernández, Amadeo García, Lucio García, Paul Haber, Judy Harper, Luis Hernández, Julio Moguel, and Miguel Tejero. A shorter and substantially different version of this paper appears in *World Politics* 46:2 (January 1994).

sophisticated advocates recognize.[1] Elements of the program certainly
are innovative, but it is not difficult to find implementation experiences
that also contradict program goals. Indeed, coexisting within the Solidarity "apparatus" are both genuine reformists and others more concerned with using social policy to maintain ruling party control. For
researchers concerned with understanding the prospects for more effective and pluralistic antipoverty programs, the challenge is to determine
the relative weights of Solidarity's diverse implementation experiences,
ranging from "more of the same" clientelism to those that actually
respect poor people's associational autonomy, with many shades of grey
in between.

The range of possible Solidarity policy implementation scenarios
can be cast along a continuum with three distinct categories.[2] At one
extreme are those social policies that are "captured" by traditional
political elites. Their style is associated with clientelism, corporatism,
and corruption. At the other extreme are Solidarity's most innovative
elements, associated with the official discourse of equity, "transparency," pluralism, and power sharing with civil society. In between are
those Solidarity activities whose targeting and policy style are most
ambiguous. They are not traditional, in the sense that they do not
condition access to benefits with crude partisan electoral manipulation.
Nor are they completely pluralistic, in the sense of respecting the
political diversity of civil society, since beneficiaries are obliged to
organize through certain official channels, to petition within predeter-
mined constraints, and, most notably, to avoid public criticism of the
government's broader policies. In this intermediate scenario, all politics
is required to remain local; to gain access to social programs, citizens are
discouraged from exercising their right to political dissent. Grassroots
participation in the program varies, but it is limited to *implementation of
projects*, while Solidarity policy decisions are made at the discretion of
the executive branch of government.

This study will explain varying degrees of pluralism in practice by
analyzing the achievements and limits of one of the Solidarity programs

---

[1] For example, as one government journalist put it, "Not everything, of course,
corresponds to this [official, reformist] orientation. In the state governments, in the
municipalities, and even in some levels of the federal government in charge of implementing the program (such as the state delegations of the Ministry of Social Development), there
are still important relics of the old political culture of patrimonialism and control . . . there
are still corporatist practices that try to make the committees into transmission belts for a
PRIísmo which still has not managed to reform itself. But this is not, *as far as we know*, the
main tendency in Solidarity (Hirales 1992: 7–8, emphasis added).

[2] See Fox 1994 for theoretical elaboration. This approach frames Solidarity as a case of the
difficult transition from clientelism to citizenship. In contrast to explanations of democratization that are limited to "high politics" and electoral competition, this process is posed
as inherently uneven, involving three distinct patterns of state-society relations within the
same nation-state: redoubts of persistent authoritarian clientelism can coexist with new
enclaves of pluralist tolerance, as well as large grey areas of "semi-clientelism" in between.

that was *most* likely to promote qualitative reform—the only one that actually tried to transfer *resource allocation decision making* to representative organizations of civil society. Remarkably, this ambitious policy opening was undertaken on behalf of Mexico's indigenous peoples— precisely the social groups that are the most systematically victimized by state-sanctioned authoritarian abuse. With political and economic support from the Solidarity program, the federal government's National Indigenous Institute (INI) created the Regional Solidarity Funds. Their goal was to turn local development investment decision making over to autonomous regional councils of representative indigenous social and economic organizations. In contrast to most Solidarity programs, where the state creates its own interlocutors, the Regional Funds attempt to bolster *existing* representative organizations.

This chapter begins by situating Solidarity in the context of the last two decades of changing patterns of bargaining between the state and poor people's movements. After a brief overview of Solidarity, the analysis of the INI Regional Funds program combines a national overview with a more systematic survey of experiences in the state of Oaxaca.

SOLIDARITY AND THE ROOTS OF *CONCERTACIÓN SOCIAL*

Solidarity's political and ideological roots reach back to the 1968 student movement, when the president's use of massive repression provoked a legitimacy crisis.[3] Mexican reformist policymakers have been concerned with the renegotiation of the state's relationship with society ever since, leaving a long heritage of efforts to carry out both partial electoral reforms and more flexible social programs. The result has been recurrent cycles of conflict over the terms of state-society bargaining relations. From below, organizations of civil society have pressured the state to respect their associational autonomy. From above, reformists within the federal government have sought to displace more authoritarian politicians by creating alternative bargaining channels that bypassed parties—both official and opposition.

In Mexico, machine-style political brokers have long played the key role in mediating state-society relations, both inside and outside the scope of the corporatist apparatus. The classic political bargain required official incorporation of social groups under state tutelage in exchange for access to social programs. Mass protest was sometimes tolerated, as long as it was strictly "social," but if it was perceived as "political" (i.e., questioning ruling party hegemony) the usual mix of partial concessions with repression shifted toward the latter. Movements were more likely to

---

[3]Most of Solidarity's key architects and cadres were affected, since they were students themselves in the late 1960s and early 1970s.

be labeled as "political" if they expressed their autonomy by publicly rejecting official subordination.[4]

The pyramid of brokers managed challenges to stability for decades, but as they became increasingly ossified and provoked growing resentment, social groups sought greater autonomy. By the 1980s, ascendent technocrats who viewed the old-fashioned brokers as both expensive and politically ineffective moved social policy away from reliance on traditional patronage and generalized subsidies toward measures ostensibly more targeted directly to the poor. This targeting process deliberately favored a mix of official and nonpartisan social movements. In contrast to the government's past rejection of autonomous movement leaders, this new bargaining style recognized them as legitimate interlocutors as long as they steered clear of overt political opposition.[5]

These new targeted channels shifted the mix of clientelistic carrots and sticks faced by social movements. Where state managers replaced their traditional crude insistence on ruling party control with more subtle forms of conditioning access to the system, one can speak of emerging "semi-clientelist" relations. Such relationships do not depend on the threat of coercion, as with classic authoritarian clientelism, but nor are they pluralistic, in that they still strongly discourage criticism of the government's broader socioeconomic policies and its controversial electoral practices.[6]

During the post-1982 economic crisis, social policymakers tried to manage a transition away from traditional patronage and generalized subsidies while strengthening the more targeted social programs that held up what was left of Mexico's social safety net. A new bargaining relationship between federal reformists and social movements began to

---

[4]This "official vs. independent" social movement dichotomy was especially pronounced in the 1970s and 1980s, as collective resistance to the state grew. By the 1990s, social movements increasingly stressed autonomy from political parties in general, since contestational "independence" had often involved subordination to opposition parties. See Fox and Gordillo 1989; Foweraker and Craig 1990; Hellman 1992.

[5]It is important to point out that Mexico's ruling political class has a long tradition of mobilizing contending social groups to settle its own internal conflicts, most notably during the radical populist phase in the 1930s. What began to change in the 1970s and 1980s was that social movements increased their capacity to retain some degree of autonomy in the course of bargaining with the state. These small increases in tolerance for autonomy left movements a crucial political resource which, if conserved in the troughs between waves of mobilization, could permit them to take advantage of the next political opportunity.

[6]While the transition from clientelism to semi-clientelism may appear to be a step in the direction of responsive government, the erosion of strict controls on voter compliance may also *increase* the incentives for some state managers to rely on electoral fraud to minimize uncertainty. Distributing patronage widely through semi-clientelistic means (i.e., nonenforceable deals) can also make fraudulent electoral outcomes more politically plausible to much of the electorate, since many people will think that others sold their votes even if many of those who accepted the incentives actually vote their conscience. This uncertainty among voters in turn undermines the potential for collective action in defense of clean elections (see Fox 1994).

emerge, known by the mid-1980s as *concertación social*, a new bargaining relationship between "mature" interlocutors in state and society.[7] The first national experience with the creation of more pluralistic institutional channels for state-society bargaining over antipoverty policy was the rural village store program which began in 1979, run by CONASUPO's distribution arm (National Subsidized Staple Products Company) which began in late 1979. This highly innovative program encouraged accountable policy implementation by creating citizens' oversight mechanisms in Mexico's poorest, largely indigenous rural regions.[8]

By the mid-1980s, under unprecedented pressure in the electoral arena, some federal reformists ceded new space in the nonelectoral sphere. The most important new *concertación* experience during this period was the largely positive-sum bargaining between the state and Mexico City's post-earthquake housing movements.[9] State managers began to demonstrate a limited but still unprecedented willingness to cede legitimacy to autonomous citizens' groups by establishing both formal and informal *concertación social* agreements. While traditional corporatist pact making was also brought under the rubric of *concertación*, the more open and pluralistic variant also made inroads in agricultural production policy, urban social services, and public-sector labor relations.[10]

The reformist advocates of this potentially pluralistic style of interest group politics worked within a ruling coalition dominated by conservative economists and the "dinosaurs" who continued to handle the electoral system. The more pro-pluralism reform officials did not challenge the dominant economic or electoral strategies; instead they tried to buffer their political impact by experimenting with new bargaining

---

[7] An official food policy publication used the term "mature" in this way as early as 1985 (Ramos 1985).

[8] This pro-accountability impulse came from COPLAMAR (1979–82), which in turn had roots in a previous cycle of rural development reform, PIDER. Like Solidarity, these programs tried to reach the rural poor by reorienting the actions of regular line agencies. They tried to change what conventional functionaries did by both bypassing them and competing with them. By offering these agencies fresh resources from above while deploying their own community organizers from below, they combined carrots and sticks. Within both PIDER and COPLAMAR, reformist policymakers who were influential but not dominant pursued deliberate "sandwich strategies" designed to activate poor people's movements which could reinforce their efforts to reform the state apparatus from above (Fox 1993). As a result, each program recruited operational and outreach staff largely from outside the conventional state and party apparatus. More specifically, each of these programs recruited significant numbers of community organizers from the ranks of the "social left," the post-1968 generation of student movement veterans who rejected traditional political parties and emphasized independent poor people's organizations as the path to social change in Mexico (see Moguel, this volume).

[9] The government's low-income housing agency was quite akin to the village food store program in its reformist orientation. The post-earthquake housing negotiations came to be led by one of the most important architects of *concertación*, then-secretary of urban development and ecology Manuel Camacho (later appointed mayor of Mexico City).

[10] On *concertación* policy in agriculture, see Harvey 1993; Moguel and Aranda 1992.

relationships. In the late 1980s, reformists ceded small but significant political space to some representative social organizations, while at other times attempting to limit their growth or recover lost political ground. At the same time, however, more traditional policymakers used the new rhetoric and funding of *concertación social* in an effort to inject new life into the ossified official political apparatus.

After Mexico's electoral earthquake of 1988, the new president had to deal with the accumulated political costs of the post-1982 economic crisis. President Salinas claimed the mantle of reform, vowing to "modernize" Mexico's economic and political system. He sought to revive citizen confidence by bypassing both the political opposition and the traditional corporatist political apparatus. To carry this out, however, he needed to buffer the social and economic crisis that had helped to drive the 1988 political opposition. But the budgetary constraints imposed by economic adjustment priorities meant that it was "inefficient" for the state to distribute social spending through traditional channels; the intermediate layers consumed huge amounts of revenue before services actually reached those poor people who managed to gain access.

Under Solidarity's umbrella, the president significantly increased social spending, but to improve the likelihood that high-profile basic infrastructure services would actually be delivered, Solidarity either bypassed or reoriented many traditional government agencies to maximize the number of beneficiaries.[11] They got results; by 1991 the president and Solidarity both received very high opinion poll ratings—much higher than the official party itself.[12]

SOLIDARITY IN PRACTICE

Solidarity's target groups are poor peasants, indigenous people, and the urban poor. Programs focus on potable water and sewerage, electrification, health clinic construction, school repair, distribution, street paving, road building, housing, and specific supports for rainfed peasant producers, women, and indigenous groups. Solidarity's rapid accom-

---

[11] As Rojas put it, Solidarity's "new dynamic . . . breaks with bureaucratic atavism and administrative rigidity. Public servants increasingly share a vocation for dialogue, agreement, *concertación* and direct, co-responsible work with the citizenry, which also assumes an increasingly active and leading role in the actions intended to improve their standard of living" (C. Rojas 1991: 23).

[12] See Dresser 1991, 1992c. According to one poll, by late 1991 83 percent of Mexicans thought that Salinas was doing a good job, even though only 36 percent said they were better off than when he took office. More than half of those who said they supported Salinas mentioned Solidarity as one of the reasons. One-third of those interviewed said they or a family member had benefited personally from a Solidarity project. Those who called themselves PRIístas also increased, from one in three in 1989 to almost one in two (*Los Angeles Times*, October 22, 1991). On Solidarity's massive public relations campaign preceding the August 1991 national legislative elections, see Gómez Leyva 1991. For journalistic accounts of direct electoral use of Solidarity funding, see, among others, Beltrán del Río 1990a, 1990b; Correa 1990.

plishments in the construction of physical infrastructure have been quite notable, delivering electricity, piped water, and paved streets to literally thousands of communities (see Appendix). To understand how state-society relations change, however, the focus is on how institutions operate.

From a national point of view, the geography of Solidarity resource allocation indicates some degree of electoral motivation (see the statistical analysis in Molinar and Weldon, this volume).[13] The issue of which groups and regions are favored by Solidarity funding is distinct, however, from the question of to what degree the *process* of policy implementation changed. Electoral targeting from above does not necessarily mean, from the point of view of low-income citizens, that access to the program's benefits involved systematic clientelism or vote buying in the traditional sense. Even where government officials did attempt to recover electoral support with Solidarity projects, they may have lacked the control mechanisms needed to effectively condition citizen access.[14] To get at the question of how the politics of *access* actually changed, one must disentangle the precise mix of clientelistic controls and pluralistic openings through detailed study of Solidarity's implementation mechanisms.

Most Solidarity funding is distributed through federal block grants to state and municipal governments (see Bailey, this volume).[15] Officially, "in this way, Solidarity has articulated with traditional social policy, but adding an important modification in the attitude, the way of acting and thinking of the institutions" (González Tiburcio 1991: 9). The actual degree of responsiveness, accountability, and targeting of the

[13]The program's official regional development priorities, for example, appeared to channel disproportionate resources to "recover" areas contested with the center-left opposition, such as La Laguna, eastern Michoacán, Oaxaca's Isthmus of Tehuantepec and coast, the southern state of México, and Tierra Caliente of Guerrero. Solidarity spending in Michoacán in 1992, the year of a major governor's race, was perhaps the most extreme case, reportedly accounting for 12 percent of Solidarity spending nationally that year (Golden 1992b). This spending was in addition to the almost U.S. $80 per official vote spent in campaign expenses defined more narrowly (Chávez 1992).

[14]Many Solidarity projects involve public goods, for example, which would complicate distinctions between official and opposition voters within a locality. Much more research is needed on the mechanisms that do effectively condition access. For example, how is the widespread lack of ballot secrecy related to the distribution of Solidarity benefits, which programs are most likely to be electorally linked, and where? For one of the few discussions of this issue in print, see J. Cantú 1992. Even in this news report, the title's claim that Solidarity "coerced" electoral support for the government is not supported by the information actually reported, which indicates instead a more subtle process of *attempted* conditioning of access.

[15]This component, called "Solidarity for Social Welfare," falls under the budgetary category of "Regional Development," allocated by the Ministry of Budget and Planning (later merged into the Ministry of Social Development). Solidarity and Regional Development represented 60 percent of total federal investment in 1990, up from an annual range of 18–28 percent during the de la Madrid administration. For background on budgetary flows between different levels of government, see Rodríguez n.d.

spending carried out through state and municipal governments depended at least in part, however, on the nature of those subnational governments. Some states and municipalities are more democratic and accountable than others, but virtually all face trade-offs between the more influential urban areas and the poorer outlying rural areas. Even in democratically elected municipalities, there is no guarantee that Solidarity funding will be clearly targeted to the poorest of the poor. Bridges, town squares, road paving, and other traditional public works projects all promise electoral benefits but do not necessarily favor the poor. Much more systematic empirical research is needed, but at this point it is sufficient to note that the complex bargaining process between (and within) federal, state, and municipal governments that determines how resources are actually allocated in practice does not guarantee targeting to Mexico's poorest citizens.[16]

One of Solidarity's most notable characteristics, and one of the features which differs most from past antipoverty reforms, is its explicit emphasis on strengthening the municipality, in an effort to decentralize responsibility for service delivery. Where municipal governments are democratically elected, Solidarity funding may well have such an impact. Municipal governments play especially important roles in several Solidarity programs, including the school renovation program, the children's scholarships, the peasant production loans, and the Municipal Funds, which permit communities to choose from a wide range of small-scale local public works.[17]

Where opposition political parties manage to both win over the majority of voters and succeed in defending their municipal ballot victories, federal Solidarity funders do not discriminate in obvious ways.

---

[16] According to one top policymaker, of PRONASOL's 1991 budget of M $5.2 billion, no more than $2 billion should really be counted as targeted antipoverty spending. The rest consisted of untargeted public works (i.e., relabeled "regional development" revenue sharing).

[17] While most Solidarity funding consists of tied block grants for various public works and services, some smaller programs focus on employment creation. Solidarity funding targeted to crop loans for poor peasants is channeled to individuals as "on your word" crop loans, but they were only $100 per hectare, essentially partial consumption support until harvest time. Reaching 600,000 producers in 1991, the loans were an important symbolic substitute after the withdrawal of most other federal rural development agencies from the peasant economy (see Fox n.d.). In contrast to the official discourse of community participation, however, these loans were distributed discretionally by mayors, and often by local PRI officials who used them as electoral patronage. The delivery process often bypassed existing autonomous producer organizations. One top Solidarity official estimated that 40 percent of the Production Funds "operated well," 20 percent were "so-so," and 40 percent worked badly. In the state of Yucatán, for example, an internal government survey of the program opened up "a Pandora's box." As they convened village-to-village assemblies to verify who really existed, they found in many cases that mayors had signed up children and dead people as producers. By mid-1993, internal evaluations within the Ministry of Social Development led to a proposal to change the production loan policy, to put the loan allocation process in the hands of community assemblies rather than the mayors.

According to Solidarity coordinator Carlos Rojas, Solidarity worked with 171 of 173 opposition municipalities (*El Universal*, September 5, 1991). But spending federal money *in* municipalities does not necessarily mean that the local authorities are actually ceded the power to decide how to allocate those funds. Many opposition mayors in Michoacán charged, for example, that monies came to them already allocated to particular individuals or for specific projects not of their choosing. In this scenario, Solidarity funding undermined rather than strengthened local government. Not all opposition municipalities faced this problem, however—Oaxaca had fewer such problems than Michoacán, for example.[18] Some state governments were more hard-line than others, and almost all federal Solidarity funds go through state budget planning commissions before they get allocated to municipalities. This process poses a dilemma for those Solidarity policymakers who are genuinely *municipalista*, since it is difficult to strengthen municipalities by funding them through the states when there has often been a conflictive relationship between the two levels of government.

At the receiving end, Solidarity usually requires that beneficiaries form local Solidarity Committees, which in turn choose from a set menu of possible public works projects (i.e., electrification, paved roads, school repair, etc.). As of mid-1993, high-level Solidarity officials reported that over 120,000 local committees had been formed. The officials confided that as many as 60 percent of the committees were short-lived, formed only to distribute funding, but that 40 percent had gained real presence, developing some capacity to demand accountability from below.[19]

Organizing grassroots participation in Solidarity projects is more complex in areas where poor people have already created their own organizations. Solidarity had a mixed record with the more consolidated autonomous social organizations, bargaining with some while bypassing others in the name of working "directly with the base" (for example, see Hernández and Celis, this volume). In some cases, Solidarity agreements with the federal government have permitted independent poor people's organizations to bypass hostile governors (see Haber, this volume). In cases where governors managed to deny access to autonomous community development organizations, as in Guerrero, the most authoritarian elements in the ruling party used Solidarity programs to promote competing welfare projects.

In most of the country, the Solidarity Committees were controversial within the ruling party. The first years of the program provoked serious behind-the-scenes conflicts between Salinistas at the federal level and

---

[18] Juchitán had a much more positive experience than Morelia, for example (see Fox and Moguel n.d.).

[19] This diversity is confirmed by Contreras and Bennett's findings (this volume).

more traditional PRIísta state authorities, especially those inherited from the previous presidency and not beholden to President Salinas.[20] Solidarity became one of several key issues that refracted these deeper tensions within the political system. Especially during the first half of his term, Salinas appeared to use Solidarity groups as a deliberate counterweight to the official party structure, encouraging their scaling up to statewide and possibly national organizations with what he called the "new mass politics of the Mexican state."[21]

THE NATIONAL INDIGENOUS INSTITUTE

The National Indigenous Institute (INI) carries out some of Solidarity's most innovative projects. Mexico's indigenous population is the largest in the hemisphere, variously estimated at between 9 and 15 percent of the population. Officially, the census reports that over seven million Mexicans actively speak an indigenous language, accounting for 9 percent of the national population and one in six rural people.[22] INI estimated that almost one-third of the fourteen million Mexicans officially considered to be in "extreme poverty" are indigenous people (INI 1990). Confidential government surveys found that the percentage of rural indigenous people considered malnourished rose from 66 percent in 1979 to 71 percent in 1989 (Consejo Consultivo del Programa Nacional de Solidaridad/API Consultores 1992).

In an effort to make up for years of neglect of Mexico's poorest citizens, INI's budget increased *eighteen-fold* during the first three years of the Salinas government.[23] One of INI's most important initiatives was the creation of revolving credit funds, to be managed

---

[20] According to one credible report, a top PRONASOL official confided that in October 1991, just before the president defined PRONASOL as the "political base" of his government, twenty governors "did not accept PRONASOL and differed with its strategies and principles." The commentator observed that "we are speaking of two-thirds of the country's governors, most toward the end of their terms, who owe their careers and their posts to the old political system and the party that sustained it" (Fernández 1991; see also Dresser 1991, 1992c).

[21] In this context, as the president once told a long-time friend, a historic radical leader of the urban popular movement: "You were my teacher. [I learned from you that]: everywhere I go I leave a base of support." At a meeting of 500 representatives of 5000 urban Solidarity Committees, the president called for the creation of the Coordinadora Nacional de Colonias Populares, appearing to ignore the PRI's own efforts to modernize the official "popular" sector. See Lomas (1991a, 1991b), who also reported that the *colonos* chanted "Salinas, otra vez." This gathering was an extreme example of Salinismo in action, as distinct from PRIísmo.

[22] The census definition is biased, excluding Mexicans under five years of age from the possibility of being counted as indigenous.

[23] According to INI's annual report, its 1991 (fiscal year) budget was M$419,477,686,000 (approximately U.S. $140 million).

by regional councils of socioeconomic community-based indigenous groups.[24]

INI's other main strategic initiatives during the Salinas administration included a new human rights program,[25] support for the large indigenous population of Mexico City, increased emphasis on research in indigenous languages and bilingual training, and a continuation of its ongoing health and education efforts. INI also played a key role in supporting the president's constitutional amendment of Article 4, which officially recognized Mexico as a multicultural society for the first time.[26] In addition, after the coffee crisis broke in 1989, INI also tried to buffer the combined effects of a severe frost, a collapse in the international price, and the abrupt withdrawal of the government regulatory agency from the market (see Hernández and Celis, this volume).[27]

With Solidarity funding, INI transformed itself from a service provider into an economic development agency.[28] INI had previously spent most of its budget on maintaining staff and educational programs (e.g., rural boarding schools), and its few economic programs

---

[24]Indigenous organizations that defined themselves in exclusively ethnic or political-ideological terms were not invited to join. See Ruiz 1993 for a critique. After many years of corporatist control through the government-sponsored *consejos supremos* created for each ethnic group since the early 1970s, several different efforts to form independent pan-ethnic indigenous networks and movements have emerged in recent years. See Sarmiento 1985, 1991a; see also Consejo Mexicano 500 Años 1991.

[25]INI's human rights program facilitated the release of over 4,120 indigenous prisoners during its first three years, though over 5,000 remained (Llanos Samaniego 1992). On INI's efforts to reform the judicial system, see R. Rojas 1991a, 1991b. According to Warman, between 1984 and 1989 INI had assisted in the release of over 3000 prisoners (Rico 1989), but this earlier effort apparently had little effect on the causes of unjust imprisonment. See also America's Watch 1990, 1991; Amnesty International 1986; Concha 1988. There is a strong consensus among human rights advocates that anti-indigenous bias greatly aggravates entrenched state-sanctioned violence and impunity.

[26]The Senate delayed approval of the amendment until the end of 1991. Strong resistance to this presidential initiative from all across the political spectrum provoked the formation of an unusual de facto alliance between Salinistas and indigenous rights advocates within the left opposition. The best coverage was in the journal *México Indígena*, later known as *Ojarasca*. As of mid-1993, however, the enabling legislation needed to actually put the reform into effect was tabled indefinitely.

[27]Two-thirds of coffee producers are indigenous smallholders, accounting for 30 percent of national production and one-third of coffee lands (INI 1990: 17).

[28]PRONASOL funding accounted for 64 percent of INI's 1991 budget. President Salinas began his emphasis on INI by naming one of Mexico's most distinguished anthropologists, Dr. Arturo Warman, as its director. In addition to his university career, Warman had also worked closely with PIDER development project evaluation in the mid-1970s. See his discussion of INI's limitations in Rico 1989.

had little development impact.[29] In terms of Solidarity's reorientation of existing line agencies, the INI experience appears to be one of the most successful. This could occur, however, only because of the long-standing presence within INI of a policy current that supported autonomous self-organization of indigenous peoples.[30] The agency was also more insulated from the electoral arena than other Solidarity implementation channels. INI's room for pluralistic maneuver may have also been facilitated by the ruling party's perception that its electoral base in indigenous regions was not seriously at risk, since opposition parties have yet to become viable alternatives in most of these areas.[31]

The history of the postrevolutionary Mexican state's relationship with indigenous peoples is one of conflict between factions that consider themselves allies of indigenous people, versus opponents of indigenous self-determination. The INI's history since its founding in 1948 can be understood in terms of a shifting internal balance of forces between the faction primarily identified with the PRI and often with local elites, those currents that oppose local elite domination of indigenous peoples

---

[29]See González, Valdivia, and Rees 1987. They found that INI's economic development projects were chosen in communities based on proximity, and occasionally to head off opposition. For an example of an indigenous leader's critique of INI's traditional development projects, known as "ethnodevelopment" during the mid-1980s (regarding the state of México): "The INI technicians think they are owners of the programs. They think they are the bosses and treat the indigenous population worse than peons, like beggars. The public works are poorly built. In summary, the programs designed for indigenous people are turned over to the mestizos and caciques in the region, because they [the technicians] will have sure results and there won't be any failures. For the indigenous people, who need these programs the most, the INI technicians don't take them into account; they see that they might fail. So the policy of the state government and INI is to make the rich richer and the poor poorer. That is why the *mexiquense* Indians see the INI director as just as much an inept cacique as the rest of the technical staff that works there" (Flores 1991).

[30]This process has yet to receive systematic research attention. The Mexican government created its first agency for dealing with indigenous peoples in 1934, with the Autonomous Department of Indigenous Affairs. Until the 1970s, official "*indigenista*" policy saw indigenous problems in terms of the lack of education and cultural assimilation rather than discrimination. For related discussions of "*indigenista*" policy, see, for example, Barre 1983; Bataillon 1988; Bonfil 1990; Collin and Báez Jorge 1979; Drucker-Brown 1985; Hewitt de Alcántara 1984; INI 1978; Limón 1988; Mejía Pineros and Sarmiento 1987; Nachmad n.d.; Ruiz 1993; Stavenhagen and Nolasco 1988; Warman et al. 1970.

[31]The vast majority of votes in indigenous areas are reportedly cast for the ruling party, even in 1988. Guillermo Bonfil, who was one of Mexico's most prominent indigenous self-determination advocates, supported Warman's interpretation, which is that they vote "*en corto.*" That is, "based on short-term considerations which have nothing to do with political programs that propose alternative models for the society of the future. The vote is seen more as a resource for here and now, exercised toward the promise of finishing a road, building a school or a drinking water system, moving forward a land titling process, and other small benefits which help to resolve ancestral problems which shape their daily lives" (Bonfil 1990: iii; see also Rico 1989). It may also be true that indigenous voters do not so much lack national political preferences as they lack reasons for sacrificing short-term benefits in favor of what often appear to be unviable longer-term alternatives. In other words, no opposition political party has made organizing around specifically indigenous concerns a major national priority.

but do not support independent demand making, and a third group that supports autonomous self-organization for indigenous rights. All three policy currents have been embedded within the INI since its founding.[32]

According to Jesús Rubiell, a former top development official at INI, the agency could become one of Solidarity's most targeted instruments for four main reasons.[33] First, INI is the only agency that specializes in dealing with one of Solidarity's target populations. For example, in the case of poor peasants, there are many agricultural agencies, and most do not specialize in reaching the poor. In the case of the urban poor, the government's low-cost housing work is highly targeted but it does not influence the many other policies that relate to urban poverty. INI, in contrast, has an experienced, specialized staff with an overview of the population's problems.

Second, there is little competition with other existing agencies working in indigenous territories. In contrast to those working with peasants or the urban poor, the INI does not have to share indigenous political and policy space with other government agencies. Less inter-agency competition, Rubiell suggested, "leads to greater capacity to implement Solidarity programs according to their principles, with trans-parency."

Third, INI is different because its staff are "usually not in any political party. It's very unusual that INI personnel are in the PRI or CNC—but they aren't in the PRD either [the opposition Party of the Democratic Revolution]. They aren't people who are going to manipu-late or condition [access]." Working in such remote, culturally distinct areas, "they will work with existing organizations—they can't invent others."

Fourth, INI is able to carry out Solidarity principles of participation, respect, pluralism, and transparency "with orthodoxy" because most of its development funds are distributed directly, not through municipal or state governments. The Regional Funds, Rubiell stressed, have the greatest transparency because development funds are actually turned over to the indigenous organizations. Along these lines, he continued, most of the organizations INI supports are actually preexisting groups, with roots, and INI does not oblige them to change their structure (although INI encourages them to call themselves local Solidarity Com-mittees).

The general principle officially guiding INI's development work is that indigenous peoples should be the subjects, rather than the objects,

---

[32]While indigenous rights advocates have accounted for a minority of INI outreach staff since the beginning, they gained input into INI policy-making only during the Echeverría presidency, the first six months of the de la Madrid presidency, and under Salinas. On policy currents, see Fox 1993.

[33]Author interview, October 1991. For an interview with Warman along similar lines, see Rico 1989.

of development policy (INI 1978; Limón 1988). INI has officially encouraged "participation" since 1977, but the current approach has become
much more precise and pluralistic, committing INI to promoting:

> The participation of the indigenous peoples and com-
> munities, through their representative organizations, in
> the planning and execution of all the actions in [INI's]
> program. The forms of participation will be varied and
> flexible, adjusted to the organizational diversity that
> exists among indigenous peoples, but all will be con-
> certed and will contribute to *the strengthening of indige-
> nous organization, increasing their autonomy and their ca-
> pacity for representation and [project] management
> [gestión]*. . . . All the representative and legally constitu-
> ted organizations can be subjects of these *concertación*
> processes, without any political or religious discrimina-
> tion. Without forcing the process, support will be given
> to the self-managed formation of higher-level represen-
> tative and democratic organizations [i.e., regional and
> statewide], with greater development management ca-
> pacity. *Public institutions will abstain from intervening in
> the internal decisions of the organizations with which INI has
> concerted actions* (INI 1990: 41–42, emphasis added).

It should be noted that major indigenous organizations have been
calling for greater involvement in INI decision making since at least the
mid-1970s.[34] INI director Arturo Warman clarified the role envisioned
for indigenous organizations. When asked whether he saw an increased
role for them in INI policy-making, he said:

> I think not. Our proposal is that the indigenous organi-
> zations should receive support of public institutions in
> their area of influence. They need to increase their
> management capacity. . . . Our Regional Development
> Funds [however] are indigenous entities where the
> decision making, the repayments, the oversight, the
> operation is done by the indigenous people, and INI
> only provides technical advice (*La Jornada* 1991b).

INI's declared goal of transferring certain agency functions to
indigenous groups does not, therefore, mean turning *policy* decisions
over to indigenous organizations. Indeed, pro-indigenous-organization

---

[34]For example, this became an issue when the INI-promoted National Council of
Indigenous Peoples tried to become autonomous of government at a key 1979 conference.
See Mejía Pineros and Sarmiento 1987; Sarmiento 1985.

INI policymakers were purged when they tried this in 1983, convincing many of the political inviability of this strategy.[35]

How did INI put its explicitly pluralistic policy guidelines into practice? This question is best answered by analyzing INI's two main economic development programs, the coffee program and the Regional Solidarity Funds. INI's credit supports for small-scale coffee producers combine some funding via pluralistic channels to existing, autonomous producer organizations with semi-clientelist relations with much more funding via INI-sponsored local Solidarity Committees (see Hernández and Celis, this volume). The coffee program's relative pluralism evolved through a very ad hoc process of sectoral economic collapse, grassroots protest, and policy response. The Regional Funds program, in contrast, involved a deliberate institutional reform strategy from the beginning. INI framed this process in explicitly political terms. As stated in the first Regional Fund operations manual:

> The funds are an innovative process to increase the participatory role of civil society in decision making and in the definition of policy, which reflects a change in state-society relations. The relationship of co-responsibility established between the government and the indigenous population implies a change [*giro*] in the role of [government] institutions to avoid reproducing paternalistic and vertical attitudes which interfere with indigenous peoples' development (INI 1991: 2).[36]

The main challenge was to carry out this transfer of control over development projects with as much pluralism as possible, and to build up the managerial capacity of the organizations without compromising their autonomy. In principle, the Regional Funds program goes further than most Solidarity programs in developing a pluralistic relationship between the state and organized citizens, as table 10.1 indicates. First, the state devolves *regional* development decision making to civil society, rather than overseeing each project and imposing forms of local organization. Second, the interlocutors are supposed to be autonomous coun-

---

[35]This was actually tried at the beginning of the de la Madrid administration, when INI's incoming director, Salomón Nachmad, took the new president's pro-indigenous campaign promises to heart and began turning over regional INI centers to the more consolidated indigenous organizations. He also promoted the planning of a national conference of indigenous organizations outside the corporatist control channels of the National Peasants' Confederation (CNC). This pluralist initiative was perceived as a threat by both the secretary of Gobernación (internal affairs) and the CNC, leading to Nachmad's imprisonment on trumped-up charges of corruption—later dropped after international protests (see Nachmad n.d.).

[36]This paragraph changed when the manual went from internal photocopy form to publication for mass distribution (INI 1993).

cils made up of representative organizations, in contrast to the ad hoc and discretionary relationships with autonomous groups which characterize other Solidarity programs. Ostensibly, elected officials are not involved, and the corporatist organizations participate in the Regional Funds just like any other producer group. INI also encouraged the Regional Funds to go beyond economic support for production projects and become advocates for indigenous communities in the public investment allocation process more generally. Specifically, INI tried to help the leadership councils of the funds gain access to the Planning Committees for State Development, known as COPLADES, as recognized interlocutors and de facto counterweights to traditionally privileged interests, though largely without success.[37]

REGIONAL SOLIDARITY FUND OPERATIONS

During their first three years of operation, the Regional Funds received M $280,000 million (U.S. $93 million), starting with M $500 million each during the first year (R. Rojas 1992a). Second-year funding varied for each Regional Fund, from a floor of M $500 million to a ceiling of M $1,700–2,000 million in most cases, depending on INI's evaluation of their degree of consolidation. After a brief description of Regional Fund operations, the rest of the study will focus on how implementation unfolded in the state of Oaxaca. Oaxaca is one of Mexico's poorest states and accounted for one-fifth of the total number of Regional Funds nationally as of 1991.[38]

The funds were launched by INI's main outreach apparatus, the Indigenista Coordinating Centers. Starting in 1990, the almost 100 centers were charged with convening general assemblies of the socioeconomic indigenous organizations in their respective "areas of influence." This meant that organizations of the social sector (e.g., unions of ejidos and agrarian communities) were invited, as well as local community subgroups formed through past INI outreach efforts (e.g., CO-COPLAS), while strictly political actors, such as municipal authorities or

[37]The idea that autonomous social organizations should manage development projects has been on the Mexican antipoverty policy agenda at least since the community food councils, beginning in 1979 (Fox 1993). The main difference was that the community food councils oversaw policy implementation rather than managing project selection. Nevertheless, the most consolidated councils began proposing that the government transfer the direct operation of the regional warehouses to them as early as 1982. The first full transfer to community management was in Alcochoa, Guerrero, in 1988 (Cobo and Paz Paredes 1992). Beginning in 1993, the government began proposing the transfer of rural food supply programs to the regional councils, but most were probably not sufficiently consolidated to successfully manage such large-scale logistical and administrative responsibilities.

[38]According to the 1980 census, 44 percent of the state's population speaks one of the state's seventeen indigenous languages (Blanco Rivera 1991; see also Barabás and Bartolomé 1986).

TABLE 10.1
OFFICIAL GOALS OF THE REGIONAL SOLIDARITY FUNDS
FOR INDIGENOUS PEOPLES' DEVELOPMENT

- To strengthen the autonomy of the indigenous organizations and communities so that they can manage, directly and independently, their resources.

- To encourage the indigenous organizations and communities to participate actively in the planning, programming, execution, oversight, and evaluation of all the projects oriented toward their development.

- To promote [*desatar*] organizing processes in the weakest communities and strengthen them where required, to avoid the concentration of resources in the most organized communities, which often already have access to diverse funding sources.

- To establish profitable, self-sustaining productive projects, based on true co-responsibility with indigenous communities.

- To encourage productive diversification and to increase the productivity of indigenous communities through the delivery of resources and the training of their members.

- To encourage the formal recognition of the associational figures that the communities choose, so that they can have access to other existing funding sources.

- To support the tendency for the benefits of the productive actions to capitalize the indigenous organizations and communities.

- To generate more employment in the communities, to improve the standard of living of the indigenous population.

Note: The name of the program in Spanish refers to *"pueblos indígenas,"* and is translated in the title above as "indigenous peoples." In Mexico, however, the term *pueblos* refers primarily to village communities rather than ethnic groups. To reflect actual official usage more accurately, the term is therefore also translated above as "indigenous communities." *Source*: INI, "Manual de Operación de los Fondos Regionales de Solidaridad para el Desarrollo de los Pueblos Indígenas," 1991, p. 5.

political parties, were excluded. This general assembly was charged with electing a leadership council (*consejo directivo*).

The leadership council was to actually operate the fund, allocating loans based on its evaluation of project proposals submitted by the organizations of the region. Loan periods could range from one crop cycle to several years, depending on the nature of the projects. INI technical staff were to provide support in the evaluation process, as well as in project elaboration, but were not to intervene in the actual decision-making process. Nevertheless, the Regional Fund financial procedures require that the INI center director co-sign the project loan checks. This gave each INI director potential veto power over leadership council decisions, provoking serious debate where representative organizations felt constrained by INI directors who did not "understand" the goals of the program (as INI's internal program evaluators put it).

There were few official constraints on the types of projects eligible for funding, though in principle preference was given to those that had the greatest potential for multiplier effects and job creation within the region (table 10.1). One of INI's criteria for determining the degree of Regional Fund consolidation, and therefore the amount of annual renewal funding, was precisely its evaluation of the potential regional impact of the projects chosen. Table 10.2 shows the range of types of projects supported in the state of Oaxaca. At one extreme, in terms of social impact, were some of the *mezcal* (liquor) producers which were reportedly small family businesses where the employees were signed up as project beneficiaries. At the other extreme were some of the trucks, which played a crucial role in the development of peasant-managed coffee marketing, perhaps the single most important cash crop for Oaxaca smallholders.

Defining regional project impact is not always straightforward. It could involve ethnic and institution-building, as well as economic, criteria, as in the case of the Oaxaca Regional Fund based in Jamiltepec and managed by the Organizaciones Unidas de la Costa (OUC) leadership council. INI evaluators differed over how to rate its progress because most of the funding was divided up between a large number of relatively small projects. In this case, however, participants knew that a past effort to form a regionwide organization had foundered because it concentrated all its efforts on a small number of large projects. The region is simply too diverse—ethnically, politically, and agroclimatically—to unify many communities around just a few projects. The OUC decided instead to provide immediate benefits for as many participants as possible, to build trust and pluralism as a prerequisite for institutional consolidation.[39]

---

[39]The bulletin jointly published by INI and OUC is one of the most impressive efforts to democratize access to information about Regional Fund activities. Each of the thirty-two projects is explained in detail, including remarkably frank discussions of their problems.

TABLE 10.2
REGIONAL FUND INVESTMENT PROJECTS: OAXACA, 1991

Subsector	Type of Project	Amount (M $ Millions)	Number of Projects
Agriculture	Vegetables	550,000	12
	Fruit	280,000	7
	Coffee	2,742,000	39
	Basic grains	4,033,000	39
	Fertilizer	1,383,000	16
	Infrastructure	1,531,000	20
	Marketing	2,945,000	34
Livestock	Cattle	2,462,000	45
	Poultry	79,000	4
	Bee-keeping	431,000	5
Fishing	Infrastructure	865,000	15
	Marketing	183,000	5
Crafts	Textiles	65,000	3
	Palm	64,000	2
Forestry	Project design	462,000	4
	Infrastructure	356,000	2
Food Supply	Community store	113,000	4
Small Industry	Carpentry	67,000	3
	Mezcal	279,000	5
	Tortillería	187,000	4
	Sewing	101,000	2
	Brick-making	11,300	1
	Salt-works	195,000	5
	Sandal-making	29,000	2
Infrastructure	Parts supply	141,000	1
	Trucks	1,717,000	13
	Gas station	90,000	1
Mining	Exploration	26,000	1
Regional Funds	Operations	53,204	
Totals		**21,443,000**	**294**

Source: INI, Coordinadora Estatal Oaxaca, "Análisis de la Información sobre los Fondos Regionales de Solidaridad," Subcoordinación de Organización y Capacitación, July 1991.

The national distribution of Regional Funds is shown in table 10.3. The number of INI centers in each state is broadly reflective of the relative weight of their indigenous populations. While all were funded equally in 1990, varying average 1991 budgets for each Regional Fund reflected the results of INI's evaluation of relative degrees of consolidation, including such factors as institutional development of indigenous organizations in each region, breadth of inclusion and representation in the leadership council, and project quality and scope.

In 1992, INI's preliminary internal evaluation of the Regional Funds indicated that, in very approximate terms, between one-fourth and one-third of the Regional Funds were consolidating, a comparable share were failing, and a plurality were still operating as funding arms of the local INI center directors. Most of the Regional Funds that INI considered to be doing well were located in Veracruz, Chiapas, and Oaxaca, while those in the Huasteca, Chihuahua, and the Peninsula were doing quite poorly. Tabasco was especially disastrous; the governor vetoed any development aid that could reach potential opposition sympathizers.[40] The mixed performance is due to a variety of factors to be discussed further below, including outright political exclusion and conflict, continuing INI paternalism, and "low" levels of indigenous organizational development in some regions.

LEADERSHIP COUNCILS: SIZE AND SCOPE

The breadth of the social base of the organizations represented in the leadership councils varied widely. Table 10.4 shows the official INI leadership council membership figures for Oaxaca as of 1991. One must treat the categories of "number of organizations" and "number of members" with caution. The "number of organizations" is a difficult category to deal with because it includes organizations of so many different sizes, some with many constituent subgroups. This list gives as much weight to one large network of multiple communities as to each small community subgroup of six or eight families. For example, Cuicatlán's apparently lone member was the Unión de Ejidos y Comunidades de Cuicatlán, which credibly claimed to represent sixty-four communities in its region. Both INI and independent observers agreed that it was quite appropriate for this network to control the leadership council, since they were the only broad, representative group in the

---

[40]In response to the Tabasco governor's effort to impose a corrupt local politician as INI director, the Chontales occupied the INI center in protest in 1990. Perhaps not coincidentally, the state PRD leader, Manuel López Obrador, had won a broad following among Tabasco's indigenous peoples during his tenure as local INI director in the early 1980s. The situation remained stalemated until grassroots civic protest reversed fraudulent municipal election results and led to the governor's resignation. After a new, more flexible governor was appointed, a Regional Fund began operating in the state in 1993.

TABLE 10.3
REGIONAL SOLIDARITY FUNDS: BUDGET DISTRIBUTION BY STATE, 1991

State	INI Centers[1]	State Budget[2] (millions)	Average/ Regional Fund
Pacific/South			
Chiapas	11 (16)	20,000	1,250
Guerrero	5	7,150	1,430
Morelos	1	1,000	1,000
Oaxaca	20	23,170	1,160
North/Center			
Baja California	1	650	650
Chihuahua	4	3,400	850
Durango	1	1,510	1,510
Nayarit/Jalisco	5	8,200	1,640
Sonora/Sinaloa	4	3,500	870
Querétaro/Guanajuato	3	3,100	1,030
Michoacán	3	2,700	900
México	1	5,100	5,100
Gulf/Peninsula			
Hidalgo	4	4,200	1,050
San Luis Potosí	3	2,270	760
Veracruz	7	12,510	1,790
Tabasco	1	30	30
Campeche	4	5,580	1,320
Yucatán/Q.Roo	8	9,600	1,200
Puebla	8	9,670	1,200
Total	99	126,850	1,280

[1]A few INI centers did not create Regional Funds, while some INI outposts did ("modules" and "residences"). The count here reflects those Regional Funds that INI budget data show were funded in 1991. In the Chiapas case, one fund divided into five to improve coverage and representation. The state of México seems to be an outlyer. Tabasco was frozen because of political conflict.

[2]The budget figures are rounded, and are based on funds transferred through October, plus increases already approved for the rest of the year.

Source: INI Development Office.

TABLE 10.4

OAXACA REGIONAL FUND LEADERSHIP COUNCILS: SIZE AND SCOPE
(IN DESCENDING ORDER OF MEMBERSHIP, ACCORDING TO INI ESTIMATES)

Leadership Council	Groups[1]	Members
Guichicovi	12	20,000
Miahuatlán	28	18,500
San Mateo	15	17,800
Tlacolula	27	15,500
Guelatao	14	15,300
Jamiltepec	33	14,400
Cuicatlán	1	11,700
Lombardo	23	10,800
Tlaxiaco	8	9,000
Huautla	13	8,800
Ecatepec	12	8,500
Ayutla	8	8,100
Tuxtepec	30	7,800
Nochixtlan	7	5,100
Huamelula	24	4,700
Juquila	6	3,700
Temascal	35	3,200
Laollaga	7	2,700
Copala	3	900
Silacayoapan	2	900
Totals	**305**	**187,500**

[1]The organizations range in size from small, kinship-based groups to small INI-promoted work groups, community-wide organizations, and larger, multi-community networks, such as ejido unions. Most are small and informal.

Source: INI, Coordinadora Estatal Oaxaca, "Análisis de la Información sobre los Fondos Regionales de Solidaridad," Subcoordinación de Organización y Capacitación, July 1991.

area.[41] In Lombardo, in contrast, one network that reportedly united eight entire communities had a vote equal to any of twenty-odd tiny community subgroups. This imbalance reportedly facilitated INI domination of the leadership council there.

The leadership councils gave one vote to each group regardless of size, but larger groups sometimes carried corresponding "moral authority." In some cases, the mix of large and small groups was the intended result of INI efforts, both to make sure that some local-level interests

[41]The union was dominated by autonomous community groups but included the official CNC as well. This was also one of the few cases in Oaxaca where municipal and agrarian authorities worked well together regionally. The movement began as a a community food council in the early 1980s, spilling over to form a broad municipal democratization coalition between 1984 and 1987, when the president was assassinated. After a period of demobilization, the movement reemerged in the regional political space created by the Regional Fund leadership council (author interview with Eliseo Cruz Arellanes of the Cuicatlán leadership council and former president of the community food council, 1984–86, December 1991).

were represented as well as to have counterweights to the larger and more powerful leadership council members. The official data summarized in table 10.4 appear to underestimate the base membership of some of the larger autonomous organizations, at least in the two regions studied most intensively. The largest member of the Miahuatlán leadership council, for example, the Unión de Comunidades Indígenas "Cien Años de Soledad," was listed as having a mere 679 members, when experienced INI officials themselves estimated privately that it has between 1,600 and 2,000 members and the Unión's own membership claims were much higher (Vera 1990). In the Mazateca highlands, the membership of the five smallholder coffee-grower associations that dominated the leadership council was systematically undercounted on INI's lists, compared to their own quite detailed membership figures. These associations were members of CEPCO, a statewide network which pushed for greater leadership council autonomy from INI.[42] At least in this particular case, INI seemed to bolster smaller groups as a counterweight to the autonomous grower associations.

LEADERSHIP COUNCIL CONSOLIDATION

INI itself used evaluation categories that corresponded to the traditional clientelist, semi-clientelist, and pluralistic scenarios proposed at the outset. The agency's training department used the following three general categories to rate the Regional Funds in Oaxaca:

• Regional Funds that gained autonomy from the INI coordinating center that convened them, where the leadership councils actually used the fund to consolidate their organizing process and pursue regional development strategies. These regions were usually characterized by a relatively high degree of prior development of autonomous organizations.

• Regional Funds that were used as a complementary funding source by the INI coordinating center. They may or may not have leadership councils that reflect the diversity of representative indigenous economic organizations.

• Regional Funds whose development was constrained by conflicts between organizations or the intervention of political parties, or was taken over by local economic or political elites.

According to the Oaxaca office of INI's training department, toward the end of their first year, the twenty Regional Funds' performance emerged as follows: five were consolidating, ten were still INI-con-

[42]See Moguel and Aranda 1992. CEPCO is a key member of CNOC, one of the major actors discussed in the Hernández and Celis chapter in this volume.

trolled, and five were lagging behind, taken over by caciques or political parties. In principle, it is not controversial to propose that three such categories exist (although quite unusual for a government agency). In practice, however, such distinctions are quite difficult for outsiders to determine conclusively, whether they be INI evaluators or independent researchers. Contrasting evaluations from different independent sources can help to clarify some of the subtleties. First, differences among INI's own evaluators will be discussed, followed by a comparison of INI's results with an independent study of leadership council development in Oaxaca.

The differences between INI's Mexico City and Oaxaca offices were notable. After INI's mid-1991 national evaluation of the Regional Funds, for example, these two offices differed in their evaluation of the Oaxaca Regional Funds in thirteen of the twenty cases. There was no clearly consistent pattern to these differences, since they went in both directions (i.e., INI-Oaxaca rated different Regional Fund performances both higher and lower than did INI-Mexico City).

The debate between INI's Mexico City and Oaxaca offices over how to evaluate—and therefore how to fund—was especially revealing in the case of the Regional Fund of Huautla, in Oaxaca's Mazateca highlands region. It was notable because virtually all independent observers and many INI personnel agreed that Huautla's leadership council was among the most representative, consolidated, and autonomous. This was implied, for example, by INI-Mexico City's proposal that Huautla's 1991 funding be increased by M $1,400 million. INI-Oaxaca disagreed, and managed to bring it down to $800 million in the internal INI negotiations. Since the 1991 Regional Fund increases for Oaxaca ranged from $500 to $1,700 million, this pushed Huautla closer to the "floor" than the "ceiling" of the implicit ranking (see table 10.5).

INI's evaluation had rated the Huautla leadership council performance as "fair." The main complaints were: poor coordination between the leadership council and INI personnel (except for the INI center director); bilingual teachers rather than INI personnel led the organizing of the leadership council;[43] certain official documents were not prepared; some of the original organizations left; and only two of the three subcommittees were functioning. Finally, INI evaluators asserted that "the leadership council is controlled by a few indigenous professionals who have managed to support their own coffee-producer organizations (which are the largest) with Regional Funds resources, leaving the smaller groups without funding." The evaluation acknowledged that four coffee-marketing projects did achieve regional impact. The thrust of the criticisms stemmed from local INI staff feeling bypassed by an

---

[43]Note the presumption by government officials that bilingual teachers were inherently unrepresentative of their communities.

TABLE 10.5

OAXACA REGIONAL FUND LEADERSHIP COUNCILS:

DEGREES OF CONSOLIDATION

Leadership Council	INI 1991 Budget (M $ million) (implicit ranking)	Independent Confirmation of INI Ranking[1]	Pluralistic[2]
Jamiltepec	1,700	Yes	Yes*
Miahuatlán	1,700	Yes	Yes*
Guichicovi	1,350	Yes	Yes*
San Mateo	1,300	No (too high)	0
Cuicatlán	1,250	Yes	Yes
Tlacolula	1,250	Yes	Yes*
Guelatao	1,200	Yes	Yes*
Juquila	1,200	No (too high)	0
Nochixtlan	1,200	No (too high)	0
Huamelula	1,100	No (too high)	0
Tuxtepec	1,000	Yes	No*
Huautla	800	No (very low)	Yes*
Laollaga	800	No (too low)	Yes*
Copala	700	Yes	No*
Ecatepec	700	No (too high)	No
Silacayoapan	650	Yes	?
Temascal	600	Yes	Yes*
Lombardo	600	Yes	Yes*
Ayutla	500	Yes	Yes*
Tlaxiaco	500	Yes	Yes*

[1]Independent confirmation means that there was a "good fit" between INI's implicit leadership council ranking and the results of a survey of twelve Oaxaca-based grassroots development experts (as of March 1992).

[2]"Yes" means that the representative, autonomous organizations in the region had some access to the leadership council. "No" means that significant groups were excluded or seriously underrepresented. "0" means that there were virtually no strong representative producer organizations reported in the region, and the fund was INI-run. Asterisks (*) indicate the presence in the region of groups in the autonomous Coordinadora Estatal de Productores de Café de Oaxaca (CEPCO) network.

empowered leadership council. Moreover, there was no qualitative distinction in the evaluation between the leadership council's lack of interest in relying on INI's bureaucratic procedures and actual development work. Several factors converged to explain this "underrating" of the Huautla leadership council:

- *Internal bureaucratic resistance.* The INI center director in Huautla initially sided with the autonomous organizations that dominated the leadership council. Because of the paternalism associated with the regular INI "technical" staff, this made a great deal of sense if he wanted to actually carry out the goals of the Regional Funds program, but in the process both he and the leadership council alienated the regular staff, who in turn influenced the evaluators.[44]

- *Competition from the state government and its corporatist allies.* Oaxaca state government authorities felt threatened by the Regional Funds program. The governor resented being bypassed by the direct federal funding channel to the grassroots, especially since autonomous organizations were among the beneficiaries. Complaints from the official National Peasants' Confederation (CNC) in the region added to state government pressure on INI's Oaxaca office to reduce support for the Huautla Regional Fund. CNC affiliates had received significant project funding during the first year, but independent members of the leadership council charged that these projects were not actually carried out.[45] They further alleged that the local CNC continued to receive INI funding from Mexico City and Solidarity funding from the state and municipal governments. According to INI officials, the CNC pushed for the removal of the INI director. In response, he encouraged both sides to have the CNC return, leading leadership council members to wonder about his reliability as an ally.

The main independent organizations in the Huautla leadership council were members of the Oaxaca State Coffee Producers' Network (CEPCO), whose success at providing an alternative to the corporatist producer groups was perceived as a threat by both the CNC and the state government. By 1992, CEPCO represented about one-third of small coffee producers in Oaxaca, and both the state government and the CNC have had to recognize their capacity for "interlocution" in other arenas, including the official Oaxaca State Coffee Council and a joint coffee-processing venture between the CNC and CEPCO.

- *INI-Oaxaca rejects full leadership council autonomy.* The Huautla leadership council was one of the most autonomous in the state. Unlike the groups in the Miahuatlán region mentioned above, it did not have a high-level back channel to Mexico City INI and Solidarity officials. Unlike the Jamiltepec region, its key leaders were CEPCO members and bargained hard with INI on the coffee policy front. Moreover, one of the leaders of the Huautla leadership council, Professor Lucio García, a bilingual teacher, developed a great deal of credibility among other Regional Fund leaders throughout the state. They regularly elected him their spokesperson, and he encouraged them to form a

---

[44]One possible alternative, if the local staff were not respected by the most representative organizations, would have been to involve more state- or federal-level INI staff in the outreach process, but INI assigned few resources to organizing and training.

[45]For example, there is a large honey warehouse along the road from Teotitlán to Huautla, co-financed for the CNC by the state government and the Regional Funds, which is a white elephant.

statewide network of Regional Funds. They began to challenge INI on the issue of financial procedures, asking why INI center directors were required to co-sign Regional Funds checks for development projects when the leadership councils were supposed to be empowered to allocate the resources.

REPRESENTATIVE LEADERSHIP

These three mutually reinforcing explanations for INI's underrating the development accomplishments of the Huautla leadership council do not directly address the possibility that the leaders of the leadership council are indeed unrepresentative, as some INI officials claim. In principle, independent leaders could well be autonomous of INI and other authorities but clientelistic in relation to their rank and file. The Regional Fund operations manual draws attention to this issue:

> It is important to stress that dialogue and *concertación* with the indigenous communities should be two basic instruments in the relations they establish with the organs of government. This implies serious review of the quality of interlocution, paying special attention to the authenticity of the leaders, the truthfulness of their pronouncements, and the transparency of their relations with those they represent (INI 1991: 3).

Nevertheless, it is not clear whose job it is to make sure that indigenous leaders are representative, especially given INI's long history of creating or recognizing its own preferred interlocutors, sometimes at the expense of more representative leaders (Ruiz Hernández 1993).

Much more extensive field research would be required to come to strong conclusions about representation *within* leadership council member organizations in any given region. For this study, the Mazateca leadership was observed in action at the village level, in the regional town center, in the state capital, and in Mexico City. The most notable occasion was an annual "profit-sharing" assembly of the Local Agricultural Association (AAL) of the remote municipality of Santa María Chilchotla, which brought together about three hundred delegates and rank and file from almost sixty communities, representing more than one thousand families. Insofar as one could tell from unconstrained observation (with disinterested translation from Mazateco to Spanish), the all-day meeting involved considerable heated criticism of the leadership. The majority of those present spoke up at one time or another. Members were extremely frustrated that the price of coffee was so low, and the leadership struggled to explain why it was due to factors beyond their control and why the members should not give up on the idea of cooperative marketing and processing now that the government had pulled out of the market. Elders recalled the days before the government company came in to regulate monopolistic private buyers. It is certainly possible that this observer was unable to perceive some hidden manipulation, in spite of apparently broad and open debate, especially given the language barrier. But the views expressed and the issues raised certainly indicated that the interaction between members and leaders was quite balanced. Tellingly, leaders confessed afterward that they felt they had barely survived a serious challenge.

In terms of the development impact of the funds—perhaps the most "objective" criterion for inclusion—four of the Huautla leadership council coffee-producing organizations used Regional Fund loans to buy trucks which have had widespread spillover effects through setting a price floor for coffee—the region's principal crop.[46] More recently, the Huautla leadership council became a key arena for negotiating the transition to new leadership in the INI center.[47] In other words, in spite of the INI evaluators' qualms, the Huautla leadership council was putting the Regional Fund policy into practice, transforming the regional economy while developing into a new, representative interlocutor to bargain more broadly in defense of the interests of the people of the Mazateca highlands.

LEADERSHIP COUNCIL CONSOLIDATION:
ARE ADVERSARIES INCLUDED?

The general three-scenario pattern of INI's own internal evaluation was confirmed by the author's direct field checks of leadership councils, together with a survey of independent indigenous leaders and non-

---

[46]This does not mean that loan recipients necessarily paid them back to the Regional Fund. On the contrary, grassroots skepticism about the government's commitment to the future support for the Regional Funds greatly undermined the incentive to pay back loans, at least in the short term.

[47]The council successfully vetoed INI's first candidate for director, but INI also vetoed the leadership council's first candidate. This spillover effect, whereby the leadership council becomes an effective body for negotiated "co-responsibility" between indigenous groups and INI officials beyond the scope of the Regional Funds themselves, went even further in the Sierra de Juárez region. Here, in Oaxaca's northern mountains, the INI director became a key ally of autonomous groups. When the assassination of a key regional Zapotec leader (allegedly on orders of a top state government official) provoked the first regionwide grassroots human rights campaign, the INI director allowed the movement to use his offices to paint protest banners. This gave the state government the pretext to have him removed. In the process, not only did the leadership council lead the mobilization to protest the murder of one of its own members, it also became the forum for negotiating with INI over who would become the new outreach center director. The eventual consensus candidate was a veteran indigenous grassroots leader from the region, representing a face-saving step in the direction of INI's proposed "transfer" of its functions to indigenous organization themselves.

governmental development experts from throughout the state. Table 10.5 shows where the independent observers concurred or differed with INI's implicit ranking of leadership councils.[48] This survey also found a consensus that after the first two years of Regional Fund operations, at least six leadership councils had reached "consolidation," meaning that autonomous groups played a leading role in resource allocation decisions (table 10.6).[49] Only three of the twenty Oaxaca leadership councils were found to have directly excluded representative indigenous organizations.

In terms of pluralism, it was notable that relatively few Oaxaca leadership councils exclude important representative indigenous organizations, as table 10.7 indicates. The cases reported are in especially conflictive areas. The Triqui and Tuxtepec regions are among the most violent and polarized in the country. The cooperatives in Yautepec were embattled with the Subdelegada de Gobierno, the representative of the state government who had purged the group from the region's community food council in 1989.[50]

Perhaps the single most powerful indicator of pluralism was the consistent presence of CEPCO affiliates in the leadership councils. CEPCO was the most consolidated, autonomous grassroots economic network in Oaxaca; its member groups represented approximately 20,000 families statewide. The CEPCO network was fervently nonpartisan; most member groups operated within the PRI or were not involved in party politics, although a few affiliates sympathized with the center-left opposition Party of the Democratic Revolution (PRD).[51] Several CEPCO affiliates claimed to be underrepresented, as in Lombardo, but in only two Regional Funds out of thirteen were they actually excluded. In most cases they shared power (and therefore funds) with both other autonomous organizations and CNC affiliates.

To put the Regional Funds in context, they constituted a small fraction of overall Solidarity funding, even in largely indigenous rural areas. Overall, they were only one of many entry points for autonomous

---

[48]The broad array of "participant observers" disagreed over how to rate particular leadership councils less often than one might have expected. As table 10.5 shows, the seven cases where they disagree tend to be the more ambiguous "intermediate" leadership councils.

[49]"Consolidation" means that autonomous groups played a leading role in making resource allocation decisions. It does *not* imply that all or even most leadership council members came from broad-based grassroots groups. Even in regions where the groups that led a leadership council were solid, most of the rest of the leadership council members could well still be fragile, overnight creations (e.g., Jamiltepec).

[50]Author interview with the former president of the food council.

[51]CEPCO's main activity was buying, processing, and selling coffee, both setting a floor price after the state withdrew from the market and increasing the value added retained by peasant producers. In 1991, CEPCO estimated that it bought 8 percent of the coffee produced in the state.

TABLE 10.6
REGIONAL FUND LEADERSHIP COUNCILS:
CONFIRMED CASES OF RELATIVE CONSOLIDATION IN OAXACA

Leadership Council
Jamiltepec*
Miahuatlán*
Huautla*
Tlacolula
Guelatao*
Cuicatlán*

Note: Consolidation is defined in INI's own terms, but the list is based on independent cross-checking of those criteria. There are wide-ranging differences within INI over how to evaluate consolidation. This table shows the least ambiguous cases, based on a survey of twelve Oaxaca-based independent rural development experts, as well as INI officials and indigenous leaders. Asterisks indicate cases where the evaluation was based on direct interviews with leadership council members.

TABLE 10.7
REGIONAL FUND LEADERSHIP COUNCILS:
CASES OF APPARENT EXCLUSION IN OAXACA

Leadership Council	Groups excluded
Tuxtepec	UGOCP[1], CORECHIMAC[2], CCC,[3] MN-400,[4] and CEPCO affiliates
Copala	MULT[5]
Ecatepec	Unión de Comunidades de la Región de Yautepec[6]

Note: As of March 1992.

[1]The Unión General Obrera, Campesina y Popular has a significant base in the region. Led by a former Trotskyist, UGOCP is a land rights group which combines militant tactics against local elites with alliances with national government officials.

[2]Consejo Regional Chinanteco, Mazateco y Cuicateco (an affiliate of the Frente Independiente de Pueblos Indios, FIPI). Ruiz, a national FIPI founder, noted that the Tuxtepec council twice denied or tried to condition CORECHIMAC access (1993: 35).

[3]The Central Campesina Cardenista is a semi-official peasant organization.

[4]The Movimiento de los 400 Pueblos is a semi-official organization centered on a charismatic populist leader.

[5]Movimiento de Unificación y Lucha Triqui, affiliated with both the Coordinadora Nacional "Plan de Ayala" (CNPA) and CEPCO.

[6]Promoted by a liberation theology-oriented priest.

social organizations to gain access to Solidarity funding, depending on the particular program and group involved. Autonomous social organizations could bargain for access to other Solidarity programs, but the terms were completely ad hoc, depending on past bargaining relations, personal ties, and the intensity of traditional corporatist opposition.

PROPORTIONAL REPRESENTATION

Compared to most government rural development programs, relatively few of the Regional Solidarity Funds in Oaxaca clearly excluded representative organizations. A more robust notion of pluralism would involve not simply inclusion but measures that would encourage some degree of proportional representation. Again, the Huautla leadership council experience offered instructive lessons. By late 1991, the official peasant federation complained loudly to the state government and to INI that it lacked sufficient voice in the Mazateca highlands leadership council. Several CNC representatives had left, leaving vacancies which put the restructuring of the leadership council on the agenda.[52] The leadership council first launched its own "renovation" process in late 1991, and several of the more independent veteran leaders remained on the council. INI had the power to reject the new council, with its control over the fund checkbook, and called its own restructuring process in March 1992—just before President Salinas was due to inaugurate local public works projects and focus media attention on the Mazateca highlands. This new process marked the first time that the general assembly used a proportional representation formula to elect a leadership council. Each local community-based group would get one delegate, but each organization that encompassed many villages would have one representative for each three hundred members, elected by local assemblies. If carried out fairly, this new electoral process would be a real test of the "representativeness" of CEPCO affiliates in the region. They accepted the challenge.

Out of the eight regional organizations present, six were CEPCO affiliates. Of the eighty-two delegates chosen, forty-five were from CEPCO groups or their local allies. This general assembly voted in a twelve-member leadership council with six CEPCO members, two likely CEPCO allies, two from the CNC, and one likely ally. The most articulate CEPCO leaders were reelected, in spite of strong opposition from the CNC and the INI. As one put it, however,

> They really treated me something awful, they really
> didn't want me on the council. But the producers had

---

[52] The small local affiliate of one independent national peasant organization also lacked representation (UNCAFAECSA).

named me, and they had to respect the producers'
decision. The official groups just came with the idea of
dividing up the money, but we also want to carry out a
regional development plan—not just projects, but
something for the region as a whole. But our intention is
to overcome our differences.[53]

He expressed support for INI's proposal that the leadership council
become a broader regional development advocate, defending indigenous peoples' interests to other government agencies as well as the INI.
After all, "if the organizations don't say what the communities need,
then the government agencies will do whatever they want."

INI's first experiment in proportional representation turned out
quite well from the point of view of those very leaders who seemed to be
targeted for exclusion. The representation of the autonomous leadership
survived the government's test. As of mid-1993, however, there were no
signs that this experiment in proportional representation would be
replicated elsewhere. On the contrary, the government's support for the
program as a whole began to weaken.

THE "WAR OF POSITION" FOR PLURALIST INCLUSION

Within this "most likely" case for inclusion, both state and societal actors
willing to share power were distributed unevenly throughout the country, and possibilities for respect for associational autonomy were greatest
where they overlapped. Where consolidated, representative organizations already existed and INI directors were willing to devolve effective
power over Regional Fund resource allocation, "virtuous circles" of
pluralistic policy implementation emerged. These nascent processes
nevertheless faced two major obstacles at higher levels in the political
system. The first was resistance from more authoritarian political elites,
often entrenched in state governments, and the second was INI's own
semi-clientelistic tendencies.

The potential distribution of pluralistic leadership councils depended, fundamentally, on the varying "thickness" of Mexico's organized indigenous civil society—in some regions richly textured, in
others quite thin or still heavily structured by clientelism. Some regions
had experienced two decades of ebb and flow of protest and mobilization, often beginning with land rights and then focusing on ethnic
identity and human rights issues.[54] Most of the movements that man-

---

[53] Author interview with Professor Lucio García, Asociación Agrícola Local-Huautla,
member of both the original and new Mazateca Regional Fund leadership council, April 12,
1992.

[54] Indigenous mobilizations have been strongest in Chiapas, Oaxaca, Hidalgo, Veracruz, and Guerrero. See Mejía Pineros and Sarmiento 1987; Nagengast and Kearney 1990;
Sarmiento 1991a; and the journals *Ojarasca* (formerly *México Indígena*) and *Etnias*.

aged to offset entrenched regional political and economic elites had previously received some kind of support, or at least tolerance, from past rural development reform programs like PIDER or CONASUPO-COPLAMAR; each brief and partial opening of political space for new levels of regionwide collective action left the movements better able to take advantage of future cracks in the system. This "accumulation of forces" was very uneven, however, and many regions still lacked autonomous groups with the bargaining power and organizational capacity needed to handle development projects. In these regions, INI officials continued to control the Regional Funds, according to both nongovernment development organizations and INI's own internal evaluations.

If the map of representative societal groups was uneven, so was INI's commitment to the program's pluralist principles. Many INI officials encouraged groups to form overnight (*"al vapor"*), whether to facilitate their "unloading" of resources or to generate a local clientele. It was not always because of INI paternalism or political polarization that leadership councils or member groups failed to "take off," however. There may simply have been few representative societal partners with effective "absorptive capacity." In these regions, INI is in the position of either allocating less money or investing it less effectively.[55]

For INI's part of the bargain, the agency was characterized by a mix of personnel. The directors of each of the almost one hundred outreach centers were among the most strategic actors, since they were the ones most responsible for convening their corresponding leadership councils, and they retained the power to co-sign the development project checks. Both indigenous leaders and INI officials agreed that INI director attitudes were crucial. Those INI staff who support leadership council autonomy referred to INI directors in terms of whether they "understood" the goals of the program. The fundamental question was whether they were willing to see their budgets increase while giving up their traditional discretional authority. According to high-level INI staff, less than half of INI directors "understood" the Regional Funds program.[56]

Lower-level INI staff were also a major obstacle. Often paternalistic or corrupt, many were frustrated at seeing Indians seem to get more money than they did. Even the honest officials were often unwilling to work beyond the conventional urban 9 a.m. to 3 p.m. weekday schedule. This meant that most INI staff almost never went to outlying communities, and certainly not on days when assemblies were held. Evaluators repeatedly referred to a "shocking inertia." Relative to the scope of the Regional Funds

---

[55]Even within relatively consolidated leadership councils, some observers thought that the more fragile groups and those created *"al vapor"* got more than their share of project lending (e.g., Jamiltepec). See also Ruiz 1993.

[56]For example, eight of the twenty INI directors in Oaxaca were reported to "understand" the Regional Funds program. For the Gulf-Peninsula region as a whole, the proportion was similar (40 percent).

program, INI devoted relatively little attention to outreach and reorganization of staff to encourage a truly pluralistic policy style.[57]

Governors are strategic authoritarian elements within the regime, in part because they can resist reform efforts in the name of federalism.[58] In states where indigenous citizens joined the electoral opposition, authoritarian elites usually managed to block the Regional Funds program (e.g., Tabasco, Michoacán, Guerrero). INI may have had more room for maneuver in Oaxaca in part because there was no threat of a statewide electoral challenge. Yet the most authoritarian response to the program was in a state with virtually no electoral competition at all—Chiapas. Governors of Chiapas, one of Mexico's most socially polarized states, are among Mexico's most repressive and patrimonial. Indigenous organizations in Chiapas were nevertheless highly developed in as many as half the state's regions. Remarkably, this view was shared both by INI's own internal evaluators and by one of INI's sharpest critics, Margarito Ruiz.[59] As he put it:

> The situation in Chiapas is exceptional, since the majority of the so-called "independent" and "political" organizations are in the Regional Funds. This has been achieved because of the maturity of the Chiapas indigenous movement, and a certain separation between INI's political clientele and the governor's clientele, which have set up parallel *indigenismos*. As a result, the independent indigenous organizations have an important presence in the Regional Funds, while the other organizations work with the municipalities and the state government's indigenous offices, so they do not compete for the same spaces. At this moment the organizations and 123 communities which are members of the Frente Independiente de Pueblos Indios in Chiapas are incorporated in the Regional Funds. . . . When indigenous organizations are able to effectively take the Regional Funds into their own hands, they really can become an important space for participation and decision making, and *can facilitate the*

---

[57]Several veteran Oaxaca-based community organizers contrasted the rather staid process of organizing the Regional Funds with the idealistic enthusiasm and esprit de corps of the village food supply networks back in the early 1980s, which involved a major commitment of institutional resources and recruited several hundred committed grassroots organizers (Fox 1993).

[58]The rate at which presidents remove governors is an excellent indicator of the degree of intra-state conflict in Mexico. During the first three years of the Salinas administration, nine of thirty-one governors resigned because of political problems. See also Fernández 1991.

[59]Ruiz, a Tojolobal leader from Chiapas, was a founder of the national Frente Independiente de Pueblos Indios. He was also elected as an opposition representative to Congress in 1988, on the PRD ticket, where he played a key role in the Article 4 reform.

> *creation of a phase of "transition"* —not transfer—from *indi-genismo* to *"postindigenismo"* (Ruiz Hernández 1993: 35, emphasis in original).

Indeed, INI and indigenous producer organizations in Chiapas were so successful at building pluralistic relationships that the governor jailed three top INI officials in the state on trumped-up charges of fraud. Not only was this clear evidence of state government hostility to federal reform activities, but it also provoked a large protest march by indigenous organizations in the defense of the INI officials and their efforts. As leaders of one grassroots delegation put it:

> Their only crime was to work with everyone, whether or not they are sympathizers of the government. We indige-nous people are disturbed by their detention; it's clear that there was no fraud or sin. We demand that they respect us, now that we're learning [to carry out development projects], that they don't block our work. . . . This is a political problem, they blame the INI for everything that happens in Chiapas, but we want to make it very clear that these are our decisions.[60]

Only the governors of Nayarit and Veracruz supported the Regional Funds program, and the leadership councils were relatively consolidated in both states. The Oaxaca and Chiapas cases point in opposite directions. In both cases governors opposed the Regional Funds and in both cases they managed to blunt their reform thrust, but the Oaxaca state government's strategy was more subtle than that of the Chiapas hard-liners. The former waited until INI was politically weakened by a change in national leader-ship in late 1992 to move to reduce INI's autonomy in the state.

Another risk to the consolidation of a pluralistic relationship with the leadership councils lay within INI but outside the Regional Funds program. INI's national agenda involves policy debates about human rights, culture, education, and constitutional amendments—includ-ing the controversy over Article 27 of the Constitution, which deals with land tenure. A major internal INI study was leaked to the press at the height of the brief public debate about changing the land tenure system—the only major official voice to highlight the possible nega-tive social impact of ejido privatization.[61] It is very unlikely that INI's director approved of this leak, but when the primarily pro-privatiza-tion proposal emerged Warman appeared to have "lost" the internal

---

[60]R. Rojas 1992b. Six INI officials were arrested at first, but three were released quickly.

[61]See, for example, Pérez 1991, as well as the October 20, 1991, lead editorial in *La Jornada*.

policy debate. He quickly moved to announce his strong public support for the reform. In his zeal to demonstrate the depth of his support for the ejido reform during the peak of the national debate, Warman called an urgent, last-minute meeting of five hundred Regional Fund leaders from all over the country. INI officials first proposed the gathering as an "interview" with the president, but after gauging the depth of skepticism among leadership council members regarding the constitutional amendment, the event was quickly repackaged as "informational." On several days' notice, the INI convened meetings throughout the country to pick state delegations to bus to Los Pinos (the Mexican "White House").

In a meeting of all twenty Oaxaca leadership councils, the first reaction was to reject the "invitation." The leaders felt that since their membership had yet to have an opportunity to learn about and discuss the proposed reform, they were in no position to go to a national meeting of de facto acclamation. Some even expressed concern for their physical safety in their home communities if they were perceived as having supported the reform. After much discussion, an extended open debate led to a 14-6 vote in favor of going to Los Pinos. A desperate appeal from INI's Oaxaca state director made the difference. He clearly risked his job if he proved unable to "deliver his base" in a major INI effort to show its loyalty to the presidential project. Most of Oaxaca's leadership councils had seen the state director as an ally, at least until this strong pressure to go to Los Pinos, and they were concerned that if he were removed, his replacement could well be worse. In the spirit of unity, the losing side went with the majority to the capital. Regardless of their vote, most felt betrayed. They had trusted INI's promise of treating them like citizens.

The INI's "roundup" of its leadership councils for the November 29, 1991, presidential meeting seemed to resonate with traditional election-time clientelism and obligatory "mobilization," but it was actually more semi-clientelist in content. The threat was the withdrawal of carrots, not the use of the stick. This process of state structuring of representation had nothing whatsoever to do with the official political party or elections. Instead, reformists were indirectly conditioning access to their most innovative antipoverty program, imposing "consent" to its land tenure policy change.[62]

As of mid-1993, a new threat overshadowed both the hostility of the governors and INI's own limitations. Most of the 1992 Regional Fund budget allocations had still not been released by the federal Ministry of Social Development (SEDESOL). SEDESOL officials complained about lagging repayment rates and the program's lack of fit

---

[62]With the government majority in Congress, there was no question as to the proposal's legislative prospects, so the presidential speech to the leadership councils seems to have been political overkill.

with official project funding procedures. Repayment problems were not surprising, given the critical problems of profitability throughout the countryside; but since the federal government was very flexible with much larger debts from other agricultural borrowers, such as large coffee plantation owners or the buyers of privatized sugar mills, slow repayment rates alone were not a credible explanation for freezing program funding.

On SEDESOL's second point, the Regional Funds are indeed vulnerable to the charge that they violate official disbursement procedures. In practice, this complicated *"normatividad"* requires that all Solidarity-funded projects be approved by the central Ministry of Social Development (PRONASOL 1993). Community organizations are free to propose, implement, and supervise projects, but the key decision about *whether to fund them* remains in the hands of the government. The whole point of the Regional Funds program, in contrast, was to *transfer* this decision-making power to the leadership councils. If SEDESOL's main concern were fiscal accountability, then INI's check co-signing powers would presumably have been sufficient, but that was not enough for SEDESOL officials. Meanwhile, INI had been politically weakened by the transfer of its influential director to fill the newly created post of agrarian attorney general. This left INI's Regional Funds vulnerable to opposition from powerful antipluralist elements within the Ministry of Social Development itself.[63]

CONCLUSIONS

Since the early 1970s, successive waves of rural development reform opened small but significant cracks in the system, permitting greater space for more pluralistic development policy in some of Mexico's poorest regions. The openings were small because they were limited to those few regions and policy areas where reformists effectively intervened in the implementation of rural development policy. The openings were significant because they offered political and economic resources which helped the consolidation of representative and au-

---

[63] A combination of bureaucratic and political motives may help to explain why SEDESOL undermined the Regional Funds program. First, central bureaucracies generally tend to oppose co-responsibility between state and society. Indeed, at one internal meeting with INI officials, SEDESOL's representative wondered, "why should indigenous people get special treatment?" (i.e., be allowed to control Solidarity resource allocation when they hold all the other purse strings). For many SEDESOL officials, community participation should be limited to a narrow set of local choices from a set menu, and then providing manual labor. While this explanation may be sufficient, it is compounded by the complexities of presidential succession politics. The secretary of social development, a former president of the ruling party, was a leading candidate for the official presidential nomination. It was therefore not in his interest to promote Solidarity programs that irritated state governors, who play important roles in the behind-the-scenes jockeying that determines the nomination.

tonomous social organizations. Through waves of mobilization and partial reforms, representatives of society's most oppressed groups— rural indigenous movements—increased their capacity to bargain with the state while retaining important degrees of autonomy. Some chose to abstain from overt electoral challenges, mainly to avoid losing semi-clientelistic access to significant resources. But if representative leadership remained in place, then they could choose to engage in open opposition politics if and when the political opportunity structure should change in the future. In a gradual "war of position," social movements and state reformists pushed back the boundaries of the politically possible.[64]

With the National Solidarity Program, political action from both above and below further eroded classic clientelism, in urban as well as rural areas. Semi-clientelism largely took its place, along with enclaves of pluralist bargaining. The National Indigenous Institute carried out one of Solidarity's most pluralistic development programs. The geographic distribution of reformist INI officials and consolidated community-based organizations was quite uneven throughout Mexico. Possibilities for respect for associational autonomy and Regional Fund success were greatest where they overlapped. Where consolidated and representative organizations already existed and INI directors were willing to devolve effective power over Regional Fund resource allocation, "virtuous circles" of pluralistic development policy implementation emerged. This process also led to the creation of unique instances of power sharing among indigenous organizations themselves, within and across ethnic groups. Nevertheless, the Regional Funds lagged behind in much of the country because of continued paternalism entrenched in the INI apparatus, opposition from traditional authoritarian elites and their federal government allies, and uneven degrees of consolidation among autonomous indigenous movements themselves.

---

[64]Distributive reform thus became political reform, as Przeworski defines it: "a modification of the organization of conflicts that alters the prior probabilities of realizing group interests given their resources" (1986).

11

Solidarity and the New Campesino Movements: The Case of Coffee Production

Luis Hernández Navarro and Fernando Célis Callejas

A NEW REGULATORY FRAMEWORK

Between 1973 and 1989, the production model governing coffee cultivation in Mexico was regulated by extensive state intervention. The 1989 collapse of the quota system of the International Coffee Organization (ICO), in combination with Mexico's economic stabilization policy, hit the Mexican coffee sector particularly hard. In response, the old form of state intervention disappeared, replaced by a new framework for the relationship between the state, producers, and the market. However, this new framework arose in the coffee sector more as a result of a series of chaotic and disarticulated policies than of clear and mutually compatible rules to govern the relationship between the various actors in the sector. Those principally affected by this transition were the 194,000 small producers who jointly produce in excess of 100,000 tons annually.

The National Solidarity Program has been a fundamental part of this new regulatory model. This chapter seeks to describe how Solidarity has operated in the coffee sector, and how it both resembles and departs from the old forms of state intervention.

A preliminary version of this chapter appeared in *El Cotidiano* (July–August 1992). The authors would like to thank Josefina Aranda, Gabriela Ejea, Arturo García, Zohelio Jaimes, José Juárez, Fidel Morales, and Miguel Tejero for their comments and information on Mexican coffee production. The opinions expressed are, however, the responsibility of the authors alone. Translation by Aníbal Yáñez.

The Collapse of Mexican Coffee Production

For years coffee production was one of Mexico's "healthy agricultural sectors": it maintained a steady rate of growth; it competed successfully in international markets, bringing in significant foreign exchange (nearly U.S. $600 million in the 1988–89 season); it broadened its agroindustrial and productive base; it developed new technologies; and it provided an income for broad segments of producers.

This situation began to change dramatically after the 1987–88 cycle. Drought, rain, and frost led to a drop in the production of coffee beans, and producers were burdened with three additional hindrances as well: the economic stabilization policy; the breakdown of the price-supporting quota system of the ICO in July 1989; and the restructuring of IN-MECAFE, the government agency responsible for the coffee sector, which withdrew from financing, storage, and marketing activities. The consequences for producers' incomes have been drastic, with coffee prices falling by more than 60 percent since 1989.

The economic stabilization policy severely affected coffee producers. As inflation outpaced exchange rate adjustments by a factor of five, producers' incomes per 100 lbs. of coffee exported dropped. Furthermore, they found themselves facing extremely high interest rates and a virtual freeze on the price of ground and roasted coffee in the domestic market. The cost of credit, fertilizers, and other inputs rose, and these increases could not be covered by the selling price.

Both U.S. and Mexican representatives strongly supported the dissolution of the ICO system of national quotas because of the large gap between coffee supply and demand. Mexico saw this as a means to free its high-quality coffee from restrictive export quotas. With stockpiles of close to 2.2 million sacks of coffee (valued at about U.S. $33 million) from the previous cycle and an additional 3.5 million sacks from the new crop, Mexico was seeking ways to improve the country's ability to market such large quantities and increase foreign earnings at the same time. Instead, the end of the quota system led immediately to a sharp drop in the price of aromatic coffee. Previously at $130–140 per 100 lbs., the price fell to an average $70 per 100 lbs. Although Mexican exporters were able to place their coffee on the international market faster and in larger quantities, abandoning the quota system did not benefit the country. While there were savings in the cost of stockpiling inventories, the lower selling price implied a revenue loss of U.S. $300 million.

For years, INMECAFE was the main instrument of state intervention in coffee production. It was founded in 1958 to protect and improve the cultivation, processing, industrialization, and marketing of Mexican coffee, both at home and abroad. After 1973 it assumed a key role in the coffee sector's organization, financing, storage, and exports as well, significantly transforming its previous role as intermediary between production and sale (see Hernández Navarro 1991b). However, after 1989 INMECAFE underwent a structural change designed to withdraw the state from the coffee storage, financing, and marketing functions while simultaneously fostering peasant self-management in the coffee sector. To achieve this end, the government freed up the internal market, limiting INMECAFE's role to assisting marginalized producers, and put parastatal coffee-roasting companies up for sale (INMECAFE 1989b). INMECAFE's restructuring has had far-reaching consequences for the relationship between small coffee producers and the state.

SMALL PRODUCERS AND STATE INTERVENTION: THE INMECAFE MODEL

Close to two million people in Mexico make a living from coffee, cultivating about 750,000 hectares. Mexico is the fourth largest exporter of coffee, and the second largest exporter of the Arabica variety. According to INMECAFE's 1992 census of coffee-producing states, more than 194,500 producers with up to two hectares apiece produce over 100,000 tons of coffee. More than 64,500 producers cultivate between two and five hectares and together harvest nearly 100,000 tons, and just over 5,000 producers have more than ten hectares and produce nearly 75,000 tons. What we have is a highly polarized production structure, in which 70 percent of the producers have less than two hectares and produce about 30 percent of national output.

This concentration of productive resources extends to other areas. The private sector stores 90.4 percent of the coffee produced, owns 75 percent of the existing processing plants, as well as almost all the roasting and instant coffee industry, and controls the bulk of credit available for coffee marketing.

INMECAFE's intervention in the financing, storing, and marketing of coffee after 1973 created a peculiar relationship between producers, the market, and the state. The basic organizational axis of this model were the Economic Units for Production and Marketing (UEPCs). INMECAFE defined these organizations as firms made up of small coffee producers organized to solve problems related to the production, industrialization, and marketing of coffee, as well as problems related to the integral development of coffee-producing communities (F. Cantú 1976). In reality, the UEPCs were community instruments which granted advance payments in order to halt the sale of coffee crops to intermediaries. This advance payment, in effect a form of credit, was granted in fertilizer or in cash; the producer offered part of his crop as collateral, which allowed INMECAFE to reach repayment rates above 90 percent, paid in marketable coffee (INMECAFE 1989a).

INMECAFE fostered the formation of the UEPCs through promoters who were warned in advance to avoid the "dangers of manipulating peasants under the guise of addressing their problems and conscious or unconscious paternalism, which supposedly would make peasants passive and conformist" (INMECAFE 1974). Promoters organized the UEPCs and also visited them about twice a year. In practice, their role was limited to granting and collecting credits.

The credits granted by INMECAFE went to groups, not individuals. Although they were not legal entities, the UEPCs were in fact credit associations in which all members were collectively responsible for the loans. Selling coffee to INMECAFE was the condition for obtaining credit, due after six to eight months at an annual interest rate of 10 percent, below the rate charged by development banks. In fact, besides covering inputs such as fertilizer, these credits allowed the producers to subsist until their crops matured.

When it began in 1973–74, INMECAFE granted 34 million pesos in advance payments; in the two following cycles it distributed 145 and 138 million pesos, respectively. It recovered 99 and 85 percent of the advance payments in the first cycles (INMECAFE 1975). These high repayment rates reflect the fact that these loans were guaranteed by the producers' crops, which were then marketed by INMECAFE. The credit was a short-term cash advance only, and was not sufficient to increase farm productivity. Nor was it sufficient to cover all necessary phases of cultivation. Worse, these credits usually arrived late. (Because of these considerations, the credit program did not eliminate the moneylenders who advanced usurious loans against the crop.) In some places, caciques took control of the UEPCs, and the regional power structure was merged with the structure built by INMECAFE; only where the local bosses had been weakened could INMECAFE impose its control (Flores de la Vega and León López 1979). Nevertheless, the UEPCs' insertion among the organized small producers was an undeniable fact. By the end of 1976, more than 78,000 coffee producers were organized in over two thousand UEPCs.

INMECAFE's involvement in storage and marketing activities also permitted a certain degree of control over the price of coffee while it was in storage in the internal market. This translated into a relatively higher level of income for the small producers, and in the possibility of placing part of their production without having to go through traditional middlemen (coyotes).

INMECAFE's intervention was far from idyllic, however. From 1982 on, producers organized important mobilizations against INMECAFE because it represented detested government policies. Peasants wanted better prices; they also wanted credits to arrive on time, fair weighing, and less downgrading of their product. They wanted a more efficient and less bureaucratic agency. They wanted an agency that was less involved with local bosses and more in touch with peasants. As the struggle continued, producers built important regional organizations which stored, processed, and marketed the coffee directly. Thus, when the Salinas administration announced that INMECAFE would be downsized and certain of its functions would disappear, most autonomous organizations applauded the move. Almost no one argued in support of INMECAFE (see Ejea and Hernández 1991).

THE STRINGS UNRAVEL

With restructuring, INMECAFE ceased to be the instrument regulating coffee cultivation in Mexico. This change created turmoil in the coffee sector, for a number of reasons. First, restructuring was carried out precipitously, with no clear model for the new relationship between the state, producers, and the market. Second, it occurred concurrently with the dissolution of the ICO agreement on quotas, when prices fell dramatically. And third, at the time of restructuring, INMECAFE was suffering from institutional instability.

During the first three years of the Salinas administration INMECAFE had four different directors. Two went on to political posts; one became a PRI candidate for Congress; and the fourth became head of the PRI. With such mobility at the top, it was virtually impossible to guarantee policy continuity in the coffee sector. Beyond the internal instability caused by changes in administrative leadership positions during those first three years, INMECAFE failed to focus on setting a national coffee policy; instead it emphasized finding ways to eliminate its old functions and transfer ownership of its storage and processing facilities.

While INMECAFE was withdrawing from financing, storage, and marketing, the government failed to advance a model that would define the role of the various institutions involved in the coffee sector. Thus, INMECAFE, the National Indigenous Institute (INI), the Ministries of Agriculture and Water Resources and Agrarian Reform (SARH and SRA), the Rural Credit Bank (BANRURAL), the Foreign Trade Bank (BANCOMEXT), and the state governments pursued their coffee-related activities with little coordination among them. It was not until April 1991 that officials from most of these institutions met at a seminar to discuss an integrated national coffee production policy aimed at increasing coordination among national programs and creating the programmatic bases for a national policy for this subsector (Memorias 1991). The seminar resulted in an interesting but disjointed array of diagnoses and proposals for action and policy. There is still no integrated national coffee policy (which is not to say that there are no guides for action), and the interinstitutional conflicts are still alive despite the SARH's indication that it would take responsibility for coordinating the coffee sector.

Who is fulfilling the functions of financing, storage, and marketing previously covered by INMECAFE? PRONASOL provides part of the old financing, though through new mechanisms. Storage and marketing have been organized, in part, by autonomous social organizations that have grown up in the free market juncture. But the largest portion of these functions has been taken over by reemerging middlemen and by large transnational companies which now operate directly in this area they once relegated to intermediaries. As noted by José Juárez, a leader of the Unión de Ejidos de la Selva in Chiapas (in Ejea 1992):

> Two years ago we pushed hard to market our coffee crop, but we were stopped by lack of resources. Sales do not yield enough to recapitalize. You are left with nothing. In the best of cases you don't lose in accounting terms, but you are left just as you started. Last year all of us together were able to market only 800 tons, compared to 11,500 tons two years ago.

THE PRODUCERS' PLIGHT

Small producers' problems are not limited to adverse weather, falling prices, or middlemen as the only route for marketing their coffee. Producers are also stymied by debt, inadequate credit, declining productivity, and obstacles that make it difficult for them to acquire the infrastructure previously belonging to INMECAFE, which would give them entry into coffee roasting and industrialization.

Producers' accumulated debts are enormous. By the end of January 1991, coffee producers had run up 77 billion pesos in loans with BANRURAL and owed 18 billion pesos to INMECAFE. During the 1989–90 growing cycle, producers, especially large ones, accumulated a debt of more than 10 billion pesos with FIDECAFE. Even so, producers' total debt with commercial banks is far larger still than the sum owed to BANRURAL, INMECAFE, and FIDECAFE together.

The lack of credit is also a serious problem. During the 1990–91 cycle, BANRURAL loaned 51 billion pesos to support production on 70,647 hectares. This represents 18.4 percent of the area worked by producers with between two and ten hectares. More than 80 percent of producers in this range were left without financing. PRONASOL provided 185,000 smaller producers (those with under two hectares) with 81 billion pesos from its land renewal and revitalization programs, granting producers between 200,000 and 400,000 pesos each—a significant but insufficient amount. Insofar as credits for storage, marketing, and industrialization, during that same cycle BANRURAL provided 27.2 billion pesos. PRONASOL, for its part, allocated 20 billion pesos to several organizations. Once again, the resources allocated were clearly insufficient.

The limited availability of financial resources has slowed the transfer of the agroindustrial plant to producers. Although 70 percent of IN-MECAFE's agroindustrial plant is now administered by the social sector, producers lacked the resources necessary to consolidate the storage and industrialization processes, which is a prerequisite for realizing a profit in the sector (Consejo Consultivo del Sector Social 1991). Years of low prices and lack of credit have left coffee farms uncultivated and unfertilized. According to INMECAFE's director, there was a progressive reduction in yields per hectare between 1986 and 1989 and a further 20 percent drop in the 1990–91 growing cycle (Funes 1991).

A NEW PLAN FOR STATE INTERVENTION

What role does PRONASOL play in this context? What is its function? Has it provided producers with a basic social floor? Is it indeed a new way of doing things? Is it an instrument for state reform?

Carlos Rojas, the first director of PRONASOL, stressed the importance of the coffee sector for PRONASOL: "Coffee producers stand out among [PRONASOL's] most important projects" (C. Rojas 1991b). PRO-NASOL began to work in the coffee sector at the end of 1989, establishing the Programa de Apoyo a los Productores de Café in Mexico's twelve coffee-producing states (Dirección de Desarrollo 1991). Its first institutional action was to support coffee producers affected by a freeze in December 1989 in the states of Hidalgo, San Luis Potosí, Puebla, and Veracruz. It carried out activities to revive the coffee plants and supported the planting of basic crops; it also established 919 Solidarity Committees (C. Rojas 1991b).

The coffee sector is one of Solidarity's target populations: 60 percent of coffee producers live in extreme poverty, and 60 percent are indigenous. This explains Solidarity's close collaboration with the INI in its work in the coffee sector.

Although the forms of providing support to producers varied broadly in terms of their practical aspects when Solidarity began, they always followed two basic norms:

- Resources should go to producers who are considered to be in extreme poverty, and in some cases to local and regional coffee organizations that can guarantee a transparent use of the resources.

- Resources should be unencumbered by paternalist and populist practices so that they can be recovered on a schedule dictated by the program, project, or activity, thus guaranteeing a revolving Solidarity fund for the benefiting organization or community (Dirección de Desarrollo 1991).

Three thousand Solidarity Committees were established to implement the former policy, with the support of some local and regional organizations. Some confusion arose regarding the implementation of the second policy. Since substantial portions of these funds were channeled to producers hurt by the December 1989 freeze, there was a question whether monies earmarked for reviving the coffee plants need be repaid. Fund administrators eventually decided that they should be, but on a schedule set by the affected communities. In the case of credit provided for planting basic crops, administrators decided that these should be repaid after the harvest. And loans provided to support coffee production, storage, and marketing would be due at the end of the 1990–91 harvesting and marketing cycle.

PRONASOL AND INMECAFE

When INMECAFE cut back its activities, PRONASOL stepped in to cover some of them by providing credit for production. However, PRONASOL functioned in a very different manner from INMECAFE. First, INMECAFE granted credit through the UEPCs, while PRO-NASOL channels funds through local Solidarity Committees. Second, INMECAFE granted credit to a group, and the group was jointly responsible for it; PRONASOL grants credit to individuals. Third, INMECAFE's credits were paid in kind, while PRONASOL's must be paid in cash. Fourth, INMECAFE charged interest rates below those of development banks; PRONASOL charges no interest. In both cases the credits fulfill the function of supporting the producer's subsistence. Both institutions created associations that were not legal entities and that could not enter into credit contracts by other means. Further, both institutions achieved high repayment rates during their early operations.

The first question that arises from this brief comparison of these two institutions is, why did PRONASOL create its own organizational forms if there were already organizations in the coffee sector, not only the UEPCs but also ejido and community unions, cooperatives, rural production societies, local agricultural associations, etc.? The answer is closely tied to two issues. The first is the negative opinion that many coffee-sector officials held regarding the existing second-tier organizations as nontransparent and overly vertical in structure. The second was the need to provide PRONASOL with a social base of its own, with a new profile that distinguished it from other poverty programs. Some UEPCs went on to become Solidarity Committees; others did not.

The second question has to do with the ease with which credit relations can be handled with a group versus an individual. Clearly, handling credit collectively implies much lower operating costs than handling it on an individual basis. The bureaucracy required to grant, supervise, and recover individual credit is much greater than that required for collective credit. Also, while managing credit collectively may allow some individual abuses, it forces the group to develop a set of solidarity practices to deal with it.

The third question has to do with payment in kind. If peasants can pay with coffee, the task of collecting payment is much easier than if they pay in cash. Cash payment forces producers to sell their crops as individuals to whoever can pay cash for it on the spot—that is, to the intermediary. And it makes it difficult for the peasant to "invest" his coffee as part of a larger-volume marketing effort in association with other peasants. To address this problem, PRONASOL—unlike IN-MECAFE—has opened a second credit line which provides resources for storage and marketing and is granted through Regional Solidarity Funds and through this program to the Solidarity Committees and second-tier organizations (see Fox, this volume). This credit line, however, has limited funds (21.5 billion pesos in 1991), far short of what is required for the sector. Further, stipulating that credits must be repaid in kind means that the recipient must be a producer. Making this interest-free credit repayable in cash opens access to community members not involved in coffee growing. At the same time, the fact that peasants must repay credits in kind restricts their freedom to sell their coffee to whomever they choose, thus reducing their profits when market conditions are favorable.

PRONASOL AND FINANCING

Solidarity's coverage of coffee producers has increased. In 1990 the program reportedly reached approximately 187,000 small producers from 2,878 communities. The total area covered in 1990 was 238,334 hectares (C. Rojas 1991b). In 1990–91 PRONASOL paid out 91.6 billion pesos: 37.6 billion for fertilizing and harvesting; 30.4 billion for areas damaged by frosts; 21 billion for storage and marketing; and 2.6 billion for other activities.

Do these resources meet the financial needs of small producers? Clearly not. If the average cost per 100 lbs. of harvested coffee beans is 170,000 pesos and producers with less than five hectares produce 241,000 tons, then 819 billion pesos are needed to meet the sector's financial requirements. In other words, the resources that PRONASOL provided met about 11 percent of the credit needs of the coffee sector's small producers.

How then do small producers meet their credit needs? Those who can "double dip" by contracting for credit as an association with BAN-RURAL or commercial banks and also with PRONASOL as a Solidarity Committee, do so. Those who cannot must resort to the usurer-intermediary or work as day laborers off their land, or simply not invest in their land.

One financial instrument available to coffee producers is FIDECAFE. This trust fund was established in 1988 with contributions that coffee producers made between 1982–83 and 1986–87. Its goal is to provide resources for projects and programs that promote the development and improvement of coffee growing, thereby improving socioeconomic conditions for Mexico's coffee growers (Arellanes Caballero 1992). The trust currently holds 323 billion pesos, though it has outstanding loans to INMECAFE, large producers, and the National Peasants' Confederation (CNC) for nearly 164 billion pesos. Since it was established, FIDECAFE has undertaken three basic financial programs: support for the 1989–90 crop, with a recovery rate of 50 percent; guarantees of up to 100 percent for BANRURAL outlays of 60 billion pesos in loans for the 1991–92 coffee cycle; and a 22.5 billion peso emergency program for the 1991–92 harvest.

Following an intense internal debate over PRONASOL's proposal to become the institutional conduit for 100 billion pesos for production loans from the FIDECAFE trust fund, FIDECAFE decided to hand over only 25 billion. This proposal was rejected by producers, who saw no reason to finance PRONASOL and felt instead the trust should serve as a guarantee for leveraging larger loans.

PRONASOL AND THE APPROPRIATION OF THE PRODUCTION CYCLE

Among Solidarity's goals is to help producers gain control over coffee production through increasingly active participation in every phase of the process (Dirección de Desarrollo 1991). There is a problem here, however. Solidarity tries to concentrate resources in organizations like the local Solidarity Committees, which cannot fully undertake projects of this sort because of problems of scale. Controlling regional markets or building coffee marketing and roasting companies, for example, can only be undertaken successfully by second-tier organizations or national organizations. Although Solidarity addressed this problem in the 1992–93 cycle, it was already three years too late.

During the first phase of PRONASOL, various officials suggested that the coffee sector's main problem was productivity. According to an internal document prepared during Solidarity's takeoff phase: "[In the coffee sector] Solidarity must focus its attention along two tracks—supporting production alternatives for peasants who have no chance of becoming part of the market; and promoting substantial productivity increases in high-yield areas through improved organization, inputs, infrastructure, or financial resources" (PRONASOL n.d.). INMECAFE's director noted in August 1991 that "the challenge for the Mexican coffee-growing sector is to achieve new levels of efficiency and productivity in every one of the activities that make up the chain of production" (Funes 1991).

This fixation on productivity as a fundamental problem in coffee cultivation arises both from the overall approach the Salinas administration adopted in its governmental program and from the real fact of low productivity levels in the coffee sector. However, it loses sight of the fact that decapitalization in the coffee sector—above all among small producers—is such that it is practically impossible to improve the situation given current low coffee prices and a monopolized marketing structure. A Oaxacan peasant pays the equivalent of U.S. $85 in production costs per 100 lbs. of coffee he produces. With an international selling price of under $70 per 100 lbs., where are peasants to get the resources necessary to break the cycle of low productivity?

INSTITUTIONAL FRAGMENTATION AND PEASANT MOBILIZATION

The lack of a national coffee policy has not meant a lack of *any* coffee policy. Each of the government institutions that intervene in the coffee sector has its own agenda.

In reality, two large blocs, each with its own proposal for the coffee sector, have been taking shape within government institutions. The first, which assumed formal responsibility for the coffee sector in early 1992, is the SECOFI-BANCOMEXT-SARH-INMECAFE axis; the second involves INI and PRONASOL. Although no interinstitutional conflicts appear publicly, the views of these blocs clash daily over budgets and strategies.

The first bloc proposes separating producers with less than two hectares from profitable or potentially profitable producers, and throwing the bulk of resources available to the coffee sector behind the latter group. This bloc decided early on that the free market alone would produce the reordering; and although they spoke of not providing "subsidies," they restructured the overdue loans of the large producers on such favorable terms as to make them virtual subsidies. To wit, they restructured a debt totaling U.S. $250 million per year (some say close to $400 million with accumulated interest) to a nine-year term with a two-year grace period, subject to a rise in the dollar price of coffee. Underlying this strategy is the assumption that Mexico's coffee sector will receive preferential treatment from the United States under NAFTA. The second bloc of agencies concentrated on supporting production and, to a lesser extent, marketing, regardless of whether growers were small producers or members of indigenous groups.

A key moment in the relationship between the institutions came with the varied responses of the two blocs to the national coffee producers' mobilization from February to August 1992. The mobilization spread to almost every coffee-producing zone in Mexico. Producers marched and organized sit-ins; they attended every public forum where their views might be heard. They sent cards and delegations to the president during his tour of the coffee-growing states, to the heads of SARH and SEDESOL, and to governors or gubernatorial candidates.

Although these mobilizations were initiated by the National Coordinating Committee for Coffee-Producers' Organizations (CNOC), they quickly became unified actions which brought together coffee producers belonging to the CIOAC, the UGOCP, and even the CNC. The CNC and the UGOCP participated in the last two Encuentros de Organizaciones Económicas in order to promote their positions from those platforms. The CNOC went so far as to propose building a united national coffee producers' federation, open to all.

The words spoken at these meetings and public forums were strong and clear: coffee policy needed to change course. Autonomous coffee producers not only requested satisfaction of specific demands; they also offered many elements of an alternative policy and marshalled statistics to demonstrate the disasters that had resulted from the lack of a coherent national policy. The national press covered the mobilizations and the producers' proposals, helping to create a current of opinion in support of the measures. Little by little, a consensus began to take shape around the autonomous producers' proposals. Their positions began to show up in briefing notes that advisers prepared for coffee-sector officials. Little by little, the positions drawn up from below began to emerge as possible policies.

Over time, both the mobilizations and producers' discontent grew more intense. Under these pressures, the contradictions within the ministries responsible for the coffee sector (SARH and SEDESOL) identified institutional channels for their resolution. To a large extent these differences indicated the diversity of the "clienteles" that the two institutional blocs were supposed to service and of their respective policy orientations.

For example, in March 1992, coffee producers belonging to the CNOC carried out mobilizations in front of the SARH offices in Oaxaca, Veracruz, Guerrero, and Chiapas, and were granted a meeting with the secretary of agriculture in Mexico City to present a package of demands from Mexican coffee growers. Among these demands were: to support a return to the quota system in the international coffee market; to implement a plan to support coffee production; to renegotiate overdue loans; to create an institution to direct national production with the participation of all involved in the chain of production; to institute a program to promote Mexican coffee. The government response was blunt: in a free market a return to the quota system was not feasible; any kind of support program ran contrary to the administration's policy to eliminate subsidies; renegotiating overdue loans to the coffee sector would be dealt with as part of the renegotiation of overdue loans nationwide; an organization to oversee national coffee production was unnecessary given the role played by INMECAFE and the coffee-sector policy developed by SARH. The only positive outcome was the government's offer of a program to restructure the coffee-producing sector, already announced by the head of SARH on January 29, 1992.

The coffee producers' mobilizations against INMECAFE in the first half of the 1980s followed a relatively simple and comprehensible plan: getting INMECAFE to pay more for coffee. The 1992 mobilizations were much more complex. Instead of a single pressure action in one region, producers made an effort to open various fronts of the struggle in several regions and states, relying on a series of actions over time instead of betting everything on a single decisive action. Theirs was an attempt to unleash broad convergences from below directed at the leadership level of the organizations. Instead of focusing on a single, narrow demand, they proposed an alternative policy, and their proposal was publicized among all sectors interested in agricultural policy. Not wanting to confront government institutions in a bloc, they sought to influence those that were more receptive to their demands. In PRONASOL they found an instrument that could support some of their proposals.

Eight months after the struggle began, officials in the coffee sector were forced to admit that they had been wrong; that, in fact, there was no adequate plan for the Mexican coffee sector. In October the government accepted some of the independent organizations' positions: support for a return to the quota system; an emergency program to support coffee production with additional federal government resources; creation of a Consejo Mexicano del Café to replace the sidelined INMECAFE. Salinas recently underscored the changes in coffee policy when he signaled support for the quota system and launched a special program for coffee production.

Throughout this policy-making process, PRONASOL served as a channel for peasants' proposals and, to a limited degree, as their spokesperson within government institutions.

PRONASOL: A CRITICAL APPRAISAL

Has PRONASOL been successful in combating extreme poverty in the coffee sector? In the 1989–90 season, a small producer with two hectares in coffee, producing a crop of 500 lbs., earned the equivalent of 369 days of work at the minimum wage. In 1991–92, that same producer earned the equivalent of 195 days of work at the minimum wage. Thus, the answer to our question must be "no." Small coffee producers are poorer today than when Solidarity began. Clearly PRONASOL is not to blame for this situation, though it did not prevent it either. It is true that, given the withdrawal of INMECAFE, without PRONASOL things would be worse. But the situation is, nevertheless, far from good.

Will the repayment rates on PRONASOL loans in the coffee sector remain high? No; the strong economic recovery in the 1989–90 and 1990–

91 cycles did not carry over to 1991–92, when Solidarity recovered barely 40 percent of what it financed. Moreover, what repayment was made came only in response to the offer of additional financing of 175,000 pesos per hectare to producers who paid 25 percent of their previous debt. What happened? The brutal fall in the price of coffee in that cycle — to below $50 per 100 lbs. — canceled out any possibility for an immediate and broad recovery.

Earlier, when organizations suffered serious financial problems and failed to repay loans, Solidarity officials pointed to their lack of transparency and strongly vertical structure. Many Solidarity Committees now find themselves in the same financial straits, having been good repayers for years until the 1989 collapse in prices plunged them into a circle of insolvency and bankruptcy. When the Solidarity Committees began disbursing credit, coffee prices were low but stable, and while the price held they paid their debts. With coffee prices falling again, it will be very difficult for them to continue repayment. This suggests that we should look again at the regional producer organizations. While no doubt there were problems of corruption in some, including the UEPCs, their failure to repay loans may be the result of falling prices, and the Solidarity Committees' almost "magical" repayment track record may result less from PRONASOL's methods, however laudable, than from the circumstances prevailing when the committees appeared. Today we see that their "magic" has its limitations.

Has PRONASOL democratized rural Mexico? Very little. It has not strengthened the regional producer organizations which are a key factor in democratization. In order for their members to have access to Solidarity resources, they have had to operate as if they were organized only at a community level. However, in rural Mexico caciques function at a regional level, and it is only at that level that they can be defeated. While the community level is important, it is not decisive. What is required are structured regional forces able to take control of production, storage, and marketing. Nor do Regional Solidarity Funds solve this problem despite their support for the development of new peasant leaderships. As José Juárez points out (in Ejea 1992):

> We saw PRONASOL as important for bringing our organizations back into the process. We saw it not as a checkbook but as a new space in which to build a new relationship between producers and the state . . . a relationship in which producers would be taken into account in designing a regional, state, and national coffee policy. . . . But PRONASOL has spent more time trying to figure out how to help us than in actually helping us.

These weaknesses do not mean that PRONASOL has done nothing of importance in the coffee sector. Far from it. Solidarity has permitted the survival of many thousands of producers. In the heated interinstitutional conflict over an emergency program for coffee production, PRONASOL officials gave some support to small producers. However, the program has not solved the underlying problems in the coffee sector. Some of these problems are not its responsibility. Others are. If PRONASOL is to be more effective, it must redirect its activities; its intervention in the coffee sector must be based on a new policy that addresses underlying problems. This implies interinstitutional coordination to develop a new government plan for the rural sector that incorporates the interests of small producers. Pursuing this argument, PRONASOL must shift its main emphasis from organizational bodies like the Solidarity Committees that emerged under the current administration to provide more support for regional or national organizations with full capacity to direct coffee roasting and marketing activities. Where there are no organizational bodies other than the Solidarity Committees, these should continue to function. But where committees have been superimposed on organizations that have proven themselves through years of work, the committees should no longer be supported.

12

Distributing Resources in the Education Sector: Solidarity's Escuela Digna Program

Alec Ian Gershberg

INTRODUCTION

The Mexican federal government's Solidarity program has grown rapidly under the Salinas administration into one of the most powerful and important development programs in the nation's history. Funds channeled through Solidarity represented nearly 8 percent of total public-sector spending in 1990 (Salinas de Gotari 1991: 517), and this figure has continued to grow. Considering the fixed nature of most public expenditure (in that the most important factor in a given year's budgeting is last year's budget), Solidarity represents a very significant portion of the government's flexible resources. It is, thus, very important to analyze the manner in which the program distributes resources throughout the country in order to judge its potential effectiveness as a development and poverty alleviation tool.

In this chapter I analyze the way Solidarity distributes resources through two programs in the education sector—Escuela Digna and Niños en Solidaridad. Initially, analysis is performed on the distribution of resources to the thirty-one states, through both Solidarity and

I would like to thank Andrew Foster, Robert Inman, Andrew Haughwout, Boris Graizbord, Tony Smith, two anonymous referees, and especially Til Schuermann for helpful comments. I also gratefully acknowledge the generous support of the Center for Demographic and Urban Studies (CEDDU) at El Colegio de México, where much of the research for this study was conducted.

the Ministry of Education (SEP),[1] followed by important analysis at the municipal level for one state, the state of México. While this may appear limited in scope, the analysis provides a window into the operations of Solidarity which might easily be generalized to other sectors and, at the municipal level, to other states. Analyzing expenditure streams through Solidarity's education programs allows for a clearer definition of outputs and outcomes, both of which are critical to the proper analysis of any government program.[2]

In this manner, the analysis may shed light on how Solidarity is fighting poverty in Mexico as well as the types of policy changes that may make it more effective in this endeavor. In addition, most studies of this nature in Mexico have been limited to the national or, at best, the state level. Municipal-level analysis is critical, since it is much closer to the level at which resources are targeted. More aggregate studies cannot help missing the locational characteristics that affect resource allocation decisions.

The chapter has seven main sections. The first briefly describes the current condition of Mexico's education system, with a particular emphasis on the effect of poverty on educational outputs and on the growing interregional disparities in educational performance. This section thus paints the picture with which Solidarity is dealing in the education sector. The second outlines Escuela Digna and, briefly, Niños en Solidaridad, fitting these programs into the context of Solidarity and the larger program's functions and goals. The third section develops an econometric model to analyze the distribution of resources by a central authority (such as Solidarity or SEP) to subcentral jurisdictions with respect to the outcomes resulting from the investment, as opposed to the distribution of financial resources alone. The fourth section describes the variables chosen to represent both schooling inputs and outcomes as well as the state characteristics in the state-level model. The fifth section presents the statistical results of this model and the appropriate analysis for funds flowing through both Solidarity and SEP. The sixth section follows with a similar analysis of the allocation of Solidarity educational resources to municipalities in México State. Finally, the seventh section

---

[1] The Federal District (D.F.) is excluded from the analysis because its population size and aberrant fiscal relationship with the federal government would unnecessarily skew the results. More specifically, the budgeting system and transfer mechanisms for Solidarity funds invested in the D.F. are different enough, particularly given the assumptions of the model employed, that it may not be proper to include it in a study that is primarily interested in resource distribution to states.

[2] That is, an analysis of the Solidarity expenditure streams in aggregate leaves cloudy what variable(s) ought to be used for output. This touches on the common debate of what is meant by development. Would one, for instance, use GDP per capita or some poverty index? By restricting the current analysis to the education sector, the choice for the type of output becomes much better defined. Of course, problems exist with choosing educational outputs (e.g., literacy, completion rates, test scores, etc.), and none is perfect. But the scope of this debate is narrower and the potential errors not nearly as great.

presents the current study's implications for policies affecting Solidarity's investment in states and the potential impact this investment may have on poverty alleviation.

EDUCATION AND POVERTY IN MEXICO

The disparities in income between classes in Mexico have been well documented, as have (more recently) the disparities between educational levels and achievements between the classes[3]—and the concomitant connection to income and earning potential.[4] In addition, similar disparities exist between different states and regions. Reducing these differences is one of Solidarity's primary and most intensely articulated goals. Educational policies and investments are widely viewed as a major means by which to reduce these disparities, both interclass and interregional.

Such policies hold particular importance given certain trends in Mexico over the past two decades. Muñoz has shown that the gap in indicators of educational achievement between wealthier states (in terms of income) in 1970 and relatively poorer states has widened drastically. That is, improvement of educational indicators in poor states has stagnated in relation to rich states. Poverty levels of the states directly influence educational indicators, and educational policies have done little to reverse or slow the trend (Muñoz 1992: 10).[5] Interregional equity in education has gotten worse, not better.[6]

---

[3]The information in this section draws on two studies: Muñoz Izquierdo and Ulloa Herrero et al. 1992 and García Rocha and Szekely Pardo 1992, referred to in the text as Muñoz and García, respectively.

[4]García (1992) provides convincing and detailed evidence of the returns to education (particularly primary and secondary) in Mexico with respect to incomes and earning potential.

[5]These facts indicate that any decentralization of the educational finance system must be sure to include some mechanism that does not place the states more at the mercy of their endowments, thus diminishing interregional equity even further. This highlights the need to coordinate poverty alleviation programs like Escuela Digna with those policies and programs of the line ministries, in this case the Ministry of Education. This is true for all programs in Solidarity.

[6]An anonymous referee has pointed out that while the gap between indicators in rich and poor states has widened, all states have in fact improved since the 1970s. Thus, one could question the benefits of a policy to reduce the gap. While this discussion is clearly beyond the scope of this chapter, it seems clear that, especially given richer states' greater ability to invest in their own education programs, some attempt at interregional redistribution of educational outcomes would be beneficial. Poorly educated states currently exhibit educational achievement at levels too substandard to deny the need to invest in them, perhaps at the expense of richer states. Clearly, though, a fuller picture of the behavioral trends (such as migration) and the demographic trends (such as decreasing fertility rates in wealthier states) affecting the gap between the states would help both analysts and planners to design more effective educational investment programs. The present study simply attempts to paint the picture as it is perceived by SEP and Solidarity officials, and to test how funds are allocated as a result.

In addition, inequality in the level of educational service provision and outcomes stems mostly from the *quality* of the teaching and education system at the local level. Unfortunately, local data are insufficient for a comprehensive study of this phenomenon, and analysts are reduced to individual case studies of states or municipalities. Muñoz shows that in the state of Puebla in 1991, for instance, there existed large differences in educational achievement between urban and rural areas, as well as between wealthier and poorer districts, with the latter portion of each group faring worse.

THE ESCUELA DIGNA PROGRAM

In recognition of Mexico's need to improve its educational infrastructure, Solidarity established the Escuela Digna program in 1989. This program provides support for rehabilitating and maintaining school buildings and other infrastructure, with a focus on poor localities. According to government literature, the program is intended to work in a decentralized manner, relying heavily in each locality on the Solidarity School Committee (Comité Escolar de Solidaridad), which is in large part made up of parents and teachers in the community, for the execution of works and projects. There is some technical support provided by the federal and state governments, and the state's Committee for Planning and Development (COPLADE) oversees and supports all projects.[7] In fact, most expenditure decisions are made centrally, from the federal government to states, and then from each state's COPLADE to municipalities, localities, communities, or Solidarity School Committees. For Escuela Digna, it appears that the municipal presidents act as a conduit for funds for most projects.

The stated priorities for projects include school buildings and/or facilities suffering from serious physical deterioration, infrastructure that is used intensively, and classrooms. A factor in all cases is a high level of interest and participation on the part of the respective School Committee.

As with all programs in Solidarity, project financing is a mix of federal Solidarity funds, state resources, and local resources (in cash or kind). States are divided into two categories, essentially rich and poor, in order to determine the level of federal participation in projects. Projects in rich states may receive up to 50 percent federal funding through Solidarity, while those in poor states may receive up to 75 percent. The remainder must be state or local resources, although the federal govern-

---

[7]The COPLADEs, well described in Campbell et al. 1991, consist of high-level state and federal authorities who meet to negotiate expenditure decisions. Importantly for this study, the decisions are, from the point of view of a municipal or other substate jurisdiction, centralized.

ment still seems to play a leading role in determining where investments occur and maintains a good deal of discretionary authority.

In 1990 Escuela Digna affected 22,365 schools in 1,810 municipalities nationally,[8] with a total investment of 182.6 billion pesos (Escuela Digna 1992). This amount represented nearly 7 percent of all funds invested through Solidarity in all sectors and over 2.8 percent of public-sector expenditure on primary and secondary eductation.[9] As a proportion of reconstruction and rehabilitation of school infrastructure, the figure would be much higher.

The Niños en Solidaridad program provides scholarships to students in the first three years of primary school. It targets those marginalized students most likely to drop out of school and provides them with support aimed at preventing that outcome. The support comprises a small stipend, a package of food and other household goods for the child's family, and medical care. To retain a scholarship, the student must stay in good standing at school and report for regular medical checkups. Scholarships are only awarded to students in schools that already have an Escuela Digna project, but the number of scholarships is not tied to the size of the support from Escuela Digna. As with Escuela Digna, the Solidarity School Committee, in conjunction with the municipal president, must solicit the funds that the state allocates to municipalities and localities. It is important to emphasize that these committees—their competence, level of organization, and connections with the state and federal authorities allocating resources—play a significant role in soliciting funds successfully.

A MODEL OF RESOURCE DISTRIBUTION THROUGH ESCUELA DIGNA

This section attempts to explain how a central or federal government allocates resources to states in the education sector.[10] It develops a model to analyze two criteria often considered relevant in the decision-making process: the *equity-efficiency trade-off,* and *unequal concern* with respect to

---

[8]Roughly one out of six of the nation's schools in three-fourths of its municipalities. The program has the goal of reaching over ninety thousand schools.

[9]It must be noted that Solidarity investments are essentially separate from those made through SEP. This figure simply gives an idea of Escuela Digna's importance, in terms of magnitude, with respect to educational resources available for distribution in any given year.

[10]This section is an abbreviated presentation of a simplified version of a model developed in Gershberg and Schuermann 1992. Less technically oriented readers may wish to skip to the next section or skim this section to glean the basic goals of the current analysis. Note also that the same model is employed for the Niños en Solidaridad program and SEP expenditures. For simplicity, the following section refers only to Escuela Digna by name. Again for simplicity, this section refers to federal allocation to states, but the mechanism is the same for state-to-municipal allocation. In addition, while the section refers to Escuela Digna expenditures, one could substitute SEP or Niños en Solidaridad.

the characteristics of the subnational jurisdictions to which the federal government allocates resources.

The model closely follows one developed by Behrman and Craig (1987) and S. Craig (1987), as well as Gershberg and Schuermann (1992), in which a government with central authority allocates fixed total resources in a sector or program among the various localities under its control. It is hypothesized, then, that the federal government, through Solidarity, allocates resources through the Escuela Digna program *as if* to maximize a social welfare function, considering public service *outcomes* as a function of inputs.[11] The model yields the distributional concerns (vis-à-vis localities under its control) of the federal government implicit in the observed choice of "outcome allocation." The model thus offers an analysis that reveals Solidarity's distributional concerns through analyzing the allocation of resources in Escuela Digna to states in relation to the outcomes in those states.

The federal government maximizes a social welfare function that considers the outputs in each state from schooling:

$$W = W(S \ ; N) \tag{1}$$

subject to the following sectoral budget constraint:

$$\underline{E} \geq \sum_{i=1}^{n} E_i N_i \, , \tag{2}$$

where S is the vector of state outputs per capita from schooling (e.g., the primary efficiency rate); N is the vector of state school-age populations; $\underline{E}$ is the total national expenditure through Escuela Digna for the time period; E_i is the per student expenditure through Escuela Digna in each state; and N_i is the state school-age population.[12]

---

[11]Tony Smith has noted that if it seems anti-intuitive to conceive of the government maximizing a social welfare function, the problem may be rewritten as a government maximizing its own utility function. The results would not change.

[12]Note that this assumes the national amount of expenditure in the Escuela Digna program is fixed in the time period, and that the government simply allocates these resources among jurisdictions according to the social welfare function. Also note that this model fails to account for endogeneity that exists with respect to educational expenditures in a given time period, outcomes in that time period, and student endowments. A more subtle version of this model is developed by Gershberg and Schuermann (1992) for general Mexican educational expenditures by the Ministry of Education for 1980. This model corrects for such endogeneity through instrumentation, and the authors find little difference in the results obtained with or without the instrumentation.

In addition to the government expenditure constraint (equation 2), one must consider the production of the public service. The schooling production constraint is assumed to have partial log-linear form:

$$\ln S_i = \delta \ln E_i + h(x_i), \tag{3}$$

where δ is a production function elasticity and h can be any functional form as long as it exhibits positive marginal productivities over the vector x.[13]

Following S. Craig (1987) and Behrman and Craig (1987), a Kohm-Pollak welfare function is specified for equation (1). Note that doing so "allows a test of whether the [government] is concerned only with aggregate output, or whether there is some distributional concern over absolute differences" in outcomes from the service being provided (S. Craig 1987: 200). The analysis tests whether the government has distributional concerns for outcomes from schooling expressed in the way it allocates Escuela Digna resources. Outputs are, after all, what planners are interested in, and the model specified shows how the distribution of outputs by the central authority could occur in the opposite direction from inputs because of the inherent characteristics of the states' residents involved. This specification has proven more robust in similar applications than, say, the more familiar Cobb-Douglas or CES functions.

The Kohm-Pollak welfare function tests for two kinds of distributional concern: the first, *inequality aversion*, reveals the extent to which the government attempts to trade efficiency for equity; the second, *unequal concern*, reveals the extent to which particular state characteristics influence the allocation of resources (based upon the resulting outcome the government expects from those resources).[14] It takes the following form:

$$W = \frac{1}{q} \ln \left[\sum_{i=1}^{n} \alpha_i \frac{N_i}{N} e^{qS_i} \right], \; N = \sum_{i=1}^{n} \alpha_i N_i , \tag{4}$$

---

[13]By not modeling the production function more explicitly and solving a system of equations, this approach fails to account for the simultaneity that exists between expenditures and schooling. Again, Gershberg and Schuermann (1992) did so and found no significant differences from the less explicit formulation.

[14]Geometrically, inequality aversion is reflected by the degree of curvature (concavity) of the welfare surface: the more sharply curved, the higher the degree of inequality aversion. Unequal concern is reflected by the degree of asymmetry of the welfare surface about the 45° ray from the origin.

where q is the measure of inequality aversion (which grows stronger the smaller, or more negative, the value for the parameter), and the α_i are the parameters of unequal concern.

Specifically, $q \in (-\infty, 0)$ such that as q approaches zero, the government has no inequality concern and is purely concerned with efficiency (the utilitarian outcome); thus the government simply sums productivity over weighted individual outcomes. Likewise, as q approaches negative infinity, the government is purely concerned with equity (the Rawlsian outcome).[15]

The government maximizes equation (1) subject to equations (2) and (3). This yields the following first-order condition:

$$\frac{\partial W}{\partial S_i} \cdot \frac{\partial S_i}{\partial E_i} - \lambda N_i \leq 0, \tag{5}$$

where λ is the Lagrange multiplier associated with the sectoral budget constraint. In the case of the Kohm-Pollak welfare function and the partially log-linear production constraint, the first-order conditions take on the following form:

$$\frac{\partial W}{\partial S_i} = K\alpha_i N_i e^{qS_i}, \ K = \left[\sum_j \alpha_j N_j e^{qS_j} \right]^{-1}$$

$$\frac{\partial S_i}{\partial E_i} = \delta \frac{S_i}{E_i}. \tag{6}$$

Combining, we obtain an explicit form for equation (5):

$$\left[K\alpha_i N_i e^{qS_i} \right] \cdot \left[\delta \frac{S_i}{E_i} \right] = \lambda N_i. \tag{7}$$

Canceling N_i on both sides and taking logs we get:

$$\ln\left[K\alpha_i e^{qS_i} \right] + \ln\left[\delta \frac{S_i}{E_i} \right] = \ln\lambda. \tag{8}$$

---

[15]For a proof of this proposition, please see the appendix in Gershberg and Schuermann 1992.

Rearranging terms yields an equation that can be readily estimated:[16]

$$lnE_i = lnK - ln\lambda + ln\delta + ln\alpha_i + lnS_i + qS_i. \tag{9}$$

The first three terms make up the intercept term in the regression equation and are therefore not individually identifiable.

We assume that the unequal concern parameters α_i depend in logarithmic form on the state characteristics, and we can now estimate:

$$\ln\left(\frac{E_i}{S_i}\right) = \beta_0 + \beta_1 lnZ_{1i} + \beta_2 lnZ_{2i} + \ldots + qS_i + \varepsilon \tag{10}$$

where the Z_{ki} are as many characteristics of unequal concern as the analyst specifies and the last term is a disturbance. Importantly, these characteristics have been chosen specifically to fit the Mexican context, a step of crucial importance to obtaining reasonable results. The next section and the section on municipal-level investment in México State describe the variables selected.

VARIABLES FOR INPUTS, OUTPUTS, AND STATE CHARACTERISTICS

STATE-LEVEL VARIABLES[17]

- ESCDIGX: This variable is expenditure through the Escuela Digna program per student-age population in a state for 1990. It is the dependent variable in the regression analysis of Solidarity expenditure to states.

- SEP_EXP: This represents expenditure by SEP for basic education in each state, again per student-age population. It is the dependent variable in the regression analysis of SEP expenditures, which is performed to give a benchmark from which to judge Solidarity's investment patterns.

- PRIM_EFF: This is the state's primary school efficiency rate; that is, the proportion of students entering primary school that finish within six years. It is the basic educational outcome variable used in the state-

---

[16]Note that this is not the completed solution to the maximization problem. Rather, we assume that the government acts in the manner described (*as if* to maximize the specified social welfare function) and the model tests for the factors that influence its actions within the given framework. We can do so because both S and E are observable, as are the variables of unequal concern.

[17]All data are adapted from the 1990 Mexican census except for OPPOSITION (Gómez Tagle 1990), ESCDIGX (Escuela Digna 1992), and GDP/CAP (García 1992). Also, municipal-level Solidarity expenditures for the state of México were provided directly by the state's secretary of budget and planning. All data are for 1990 unless otherwise stated.

level study, and it yields the coefficient of inequality aversion. Ideally, of course, one would want a much more accurate and less aggregate measure of educational outcomes—one that more clearly combines both quantity and quality, such as standardized test results. However, since these data are not available, the analysis is forced into a second-best solution.

Interestingly, literacy rates, a very basic measure of quality, did not give significant results, indicating that literacy for the relevant age group is not such a big problem nationally. In fact, while a few states are far below the national average literacy rate, there is little variance among the rest of the states. With respect to the outcome variable chosen here, however, there is higher variance between states. In sum, while this outcome variable is clearly imperfect, especially in the sense that it measures quantity more than quality of education,[18] it does seem to represent an important educational goal for both SEP and Solidarity.

The remaining variables represent a set of basic characteristics intended to describe the states with respect to the way they are viewed by planners in government, in particular in Solidarity. These variables then represent the characteristics of unequal concern. Some are standard choices from public economics literature, while others have been chosen to fit the unique situation in Mexico.

- IND_PCT: This is the percentage of each state's population considered indigenous. The term indigenous is difficult to define, but the data used are the proportion of a state's population older than age five that speaks an indigenous language, according to the 1990 census.

- GDP/CAP: This is gross domestic product per capita and serves as a proxy for the average income of a state's residents. The most recent year for which all data are available is 1988, but the changes in the two years should not prove so great as to change the basic results.

- %URBAN: This is the proportion of a state's population living in smaller urban areas, defined as communities of over 2,500 and less than 100,000 inhabitants.

- URB>100G: This is the proportion of a state's population residing in large urban areas, greater than 100,000 inhabitants. While previous studies of Mexico, before the urban explosion of the 1980s, did not need to differentiate among types of urban areas, the great difference in the nature of areas with more than 100,000 as opposed to 2,500 inhabitants (as well as the rapid increase in the number of such large urban

---

[18]One might note, however, that the rate at which students in a state complete primary school certainly is a strong reflection of the quality of education in the state. In addition, this measure does provide a yardstick for the quality of education since higher-quality education will inspire more students to stay in school longer, given that the returns they expect to reap from doing so will be higher.

agglomerations) necessitates making the distinction in almost any state-level study.

- OPPOSITION: This is the proportion of votes cast for the main opposition party candidate, Cuauhtémoc Cárdenas, in the 1988 presidential election. It is clearly the most controversial variable with respect to state characteristics, but it is included because Solidarity programs (as well as line ministries like SEP) have come under a great deal of criticism for possibly distributing funds for political goals. In particular, the program has been accused of, in essence, attempting to buy back the electorate in areas that voted against President Salinas and the PRI in the previous election. This variable seeks to get at the accuracy of such charges.

- MIGRATION: This variable represents the portion of total migrants to Mexico City (the D.F.) in the years 1985 to 1990 that came from a given state; that is, the contribution of a given state to the overall migration to the D.F. The population explosion in Mexico City, currently the world's largest urban agglomeration, has been well documented. Naturally, then, it is reasonable to expect the federal government to perceive migrant flows to the D.F. from the states and to base policy and budgeting decisions on them.

Table 12.1 presents the mean, standard deviation, maximum, and minimum of each of the above variables.

TABLE 12.1
SUMMARY STATISTICS FOR STATE-LEVEL VARIABLES

Variable	Mean	Std. Dev.	Min–Max
ESCDIGX (1990 pesos)	12220	6890	2940 – 31950
SEP_EXP (1990 pesos)	429200	104000	248500 – 756300
PRIM_EFF (%)	57.4	12.0	27.5 – 76.2
IND_PCT (%)	8.6	12.1	0.1 – 44.2
OPPOSITION (%)	25.0	14.6	1.6 – 63.4
MIGRATION (%)	3.2	5.3	0.26 – 27.1
GDP/CAP (1000s 1988 pesos)	4868	1688	2445 – 9627
%URBAN (%)	67.8	15.1	39.4 – 91.2
URB>100G	35.2	20.1	0.0 – 78.7

Note that while percentages here and in table 13.3 are presented as running from 0 to 100, in the regression the data used run from 0 to 1.

REGRESSION RESULTS AND ANALYSIS

Table 12.2 presents the results of the ordinary least squares (OLS) regressions of equation (10), using the two different expenditure variables. In other words, we perform the analysis first on SEP basic educational expenditures and then on Solidarity's educational expenditures.[19] Columns 1 and 3 refer to the regressions using SEP_EXP as the expenditure variable, while columns 2 and 4 refer to regressions of the model using ESCDIGX.

TABLE 12.2

REGRESSION RESULTS OF FEDERAL EDUCATION RESOURCE DISTRIBUTION
DEPENDENT VARIABLE [COLUMNS (1) AND (3)]: = SEP_EXP
DEPENDENT VARIABLE [COLUMNS (2) AND (4)]: = ESCDIGX

	(1)	(2)	(3)	(4)
PRIM_EFF S	−0.017**	−0.010	−0.014**	−0.009
	(0.004)	(0.008)	(0.005)	(0.010)
IND_PCT	—	—	0.06**	0.099*
			(0.029)	(0.050)
OPPOSITION	—	—	0.13**	0.063
			(0.048)	(0.11)
MIGRATION	—	—	−0.179**	−0.29**
			(0.030)	(0.064)
GDP/CAP	—	—	−0.173	−0.039
			(0.143)	(0.310)
%URBAN	—	—	−0.552	1.25*
			(0.290)	(0.630)
URB>100G	—	—	−0.009	−0.421*
			(0.116)	(0.250)
CONSTANT	9.94**	−5.96**	3.69*	−0.906
	(0.221)	(0.448)	(1.92)	(4.16)
F VALUE [P Value]	22.4 [0.0001]	1.63 [0.212]	12.5 [0.0001]	4.94 [0.0018]
Adjusted R^2	0.42	0.02	0.74	0.49

* indicates significance at the 90% level of confidence
** indicates significance at the 95% level of confidence

Figures in parentheses are standard errors.

[19]The first regression is done to lay a benchmark and to examine how the model will perform on more general federal government expenditures.

Column 1 of table 12.2 presents the results of the regression, assuming equal treatment of states by SEP (equal concern).[20] The estimation results provide support for the hypothesis that the federal government sacrifices some efficiency in educational resource allocation for its concern for equity because q is significant and negative. Put simply, this means that, all else equal, a higher level of educational output causes the government to allocate resources in such a way as to produce less total output as a national average; thus, aggregate national schooling output is not maximized. This sacrifice is tolerated nationally to achieve the distributional aims of the government with respect to different states.

Column 3 shows the regression results allowing for the possibility of unequal concern with respect to states. Once again, the significant and negative coefficient for q indicates that educational resources are allocated to states in a manner that sacrifices educational outcomes in more well-educated states in order to achieve its stated goal of redistributing resources to help achieve interregional equity.[21] This result thus holds true even though the government apparently does not treat states equally in other respects.

Turning to the state characteristics, the positive and significant coefficient on IND_PCT indicates that the government possibly targets the traditionally marginalized indigenous populations and attempts to give them additional resources. While this is a stated goal of the government in general, it is interesting to note that traditionally (up to the late 1970s) this was not the case, and in fact the failure of indigenous populations to plug themselves into the Mexican political machine often meant that they got less than their fair share of funds. The current result is thus notable and encouraging.[22]

The lack of significance of the GDP/CAP variable is neither surprising nor alarming, although the fact that at least the sign is negative is encouraging as far as redistribution is concerned. Given that the model includes several variables (such as schooling achievement and indigenous population) which would clearly be correlated closely with income, we can interpret this result to mean that related

---

[20]By equal treatment we mean that $\alpha_i = \alpha A_i$, or that α cannot be separately identified from the intercept. In addition, recall that the log of the outcome variable is included in all estimated equations, and that coefficient is restricted to unity.

[21]Unfortunately, q is a unitless parameter. It can only tell us that redistribution is in fact taking place. It cannot tell us to what degree. This clearly provides a springboard for further study. Note that all other variables are in logs, so their coefficients may be interpreted as elasticities.

[22]Since the model includes proxies for income and urban population, it seems reasonable that it is not simply the fact that indigenous groups tend to be poorer and/or rural that drives this result.

factors other than pure income level seem to drive educational invest-ment.[23]

While urban population seems to have little effect on allocations through SEP, the positive and significant coefficient on OPPOSITION is indeed salient. This provides some evidence that the federal government may indeed have tried to, in effect, buy back those states where it felt little support during the 1988 elections. In fact, the coefficient on OPPOSITION is one of the largest in terms of magnitude, indicating that the effect of voting behavior on expenditure is quite strong.[24]

The interpretation of the last variable representing a characteristic of unequal concern is a little more difficult. It is hard to believe that the negative and significant coefficient on MIGRATION indicates a con-scious policy of punishing states that have large migration rates. If anything, one might expect the opposite to be true, that the federal government would want in essence to bribe folks not to migrate to the D.F., as Gershberg and Schuermann (1992) found for 1980 data. More research in this area could clarify why states contributing relatively more to the migration to Mexico City seem to be receiving relatively fewer resources.[25]

I now turn to a brief interpretation of the results from using the model to analyze expenditures to states through the Escuela Digna program. The fact that we cannot determine that q is different from zero means that we cannot say that Solidarity is redistributing outcomes through the manner in which it redistributes resources to states, even though the matching rate is more favorable for poor states than rich states. In fact, the results of the regression presented in columns 2 and 4

---

[23]Median income is a consistently better proxy for income in studies such as this one. For instance, in the case of 1980 data, Gershberg and Schuermann (1992) find that the coefficient on median income is significantly negative. Since those data are not available for a recent enough year, we must use GDP/CAP.

[24]Also, correlation tests showed OPPOSITION does not appear to be significantly correlated with income levels or other indices of poverty, so the result cannot be reasoned away in this manner. Nor is it troublingly correlated with the other variables in this model.

[25]An anonymous referee has pointed out that the result may come from the govern-ment's decision to support disadvantaged groups, but among them to support those with higher expected returns. Migrants tend to fit this description. Thus, if the government is ignoring 1985–1990 migration altogether and simply looking at what segments of the population are located where in 1990, an attempt to target the disadvantaged groups with high enough expected returns to avoid a very high efficiency cost could very well yield a negative coefficient on the MIGRATION variable. In addition, if the government is targeting areas with high population growth, we could obtain this same result.

Also, contrary to 1980, when migration to Mexico City presented a grave problem, the capital's population growth rate slowed considerably in the late 1980s, and the government would no longer seem to have a specific policy of paying migrants to stay put, as the results in Gershberg and Schuermann 1992 indicated. In addition, the same referee points out that Mexico City now receives most of the rural migrants, while medium-sized cities receive most interurban migration. If the government were targeting these urban migrants, at either point of origin or point of destination, the urban variables in the model might affect this variable's significance.

allow us to say much less about Solidarity's investment priorities with respect to states than we could about SEP's. While we can make some initial interpretations of the results, perhaps the most important result of the current analysis is that the state level is simply not specific enough to determine what is happening within Solidarity.

Nonetheless, it appears that the program could be targeting indigenous populations, as indicated by the positive and significant coefficient on IND_PCT. The MIGRATION result is also similar to that obtained when the model was run with SEP expenditure streams.

The results with respect to urban populations in the states are, however, intriguing and potentially informative. The coefficient on %URBAN is positive and significant—and has the largest magnitude of any coefficient in the analysis. The fact that it has a different sign from URB>100G indicates that it is indeed important to separate the two effects. This result should prove important for all future state- and municipal-level studies of Mexican public investment. In the context of Solidarity's Escuela Digna program, the results indicate a possible concern for communities with between 2,500 and 100,000 inhabitants.

Care should be taken in this interpretation,[26] for while the results show clearly that relatively more urban states receive more funding (and that states with very large urban agglomerations may receive less), this says nothing about where the investments are actually being made at the micro level. This is the inherent weakness of state-level studies. Investments may be occurring, for instance, in rural areas of urban states. Nonetheless, the result calls into question the program's claimed emphasis on rural populations and may reflect the greater political muscle of nonrural areas. The negative sign on the coefficient for URB>100G makes sense given that Mexico's largest cities have the country's better public schools and would have less need for Escuela Digna funds. In addition, those states with separate state (as opposed to federal) systems have traditionally focused on large urban areas, which would also leave less need for Escuela Digna funds in such areas.

The interpretation of the OPPOSITION variable is again difficult. The results fail to provide statistical evidence for the widely rumored practice within Solidarity of trying to buy back states that voted for the leading opposition candidate in the 1988 presidential elections. This indicates that if the government was in fact reacting to the 1988 election results in the way in which it allocated 1990 Escuela Digna funds, it did so in a manner too subtle to be picked up by a state-level study. This once again points out the problems of a state-level study. This result simply tells us that allocations to states were not uniformly affected by 1988 voting behavior. Thus, the only conclusion we can currently draw is

---

[26]In fact, I stress the preliminary nature of the state-level results, given that the number of states leaves a cross-section analysis perilously close to pushing the limit of degrees of freedom.

that this state-level study is too general to interpret the true allocation process: it provides an initial evaluation and points to the urgent need for municipal-level studies.

MUNICIPAL-LEVEL INVESTMENT IN MÉXICO STATE

We now turn to the way in which educational resources are allocated to municipalities in one state—México State, which comprises 121 municipalities. This much more local analysis allows us more confidence in our results, even though we can only draw conclusions for one state. Each of the other independent states will have different priorities and allocate resources accordingly. We employ the same social welfare model developed in the section on the model of resource distribution through Escuela Digna.

MUNICIPAL-LEVEL VARIABLES FOR MÉXICO STATE[27]

- ESCDIGMEX: This is 1991 Escuela Digna expenditure divided by the school-age population. It is the dependent variable in the regression analysis of Escuela Digna investment by municipality.

- NINOSMEX: This is the same as ESCDIGMEX, except for investment through Niños en Solidaridad.

- POSTPRIM: This is the proportion of each state's population aged fourteen to nineteen that has had at least some secondary schooling. This is the basic educational outcome variable, and it once again yields the coefficient of inequality aversion. It is a very similar measure to PRIM_EFF and has similar advantages and disadvantages.

- IND_PCT: This is the same as IND_PCT in the state-level regressions.

- OPPOSITION: This is the percentage of votes cast for PRD candidates in the 1990 elections for municipal presidents. Including this variable as a municipal characteristic attempts to provide a measure of opposition to the PRI in the municipality in order to determine how the COPLADE and other central (with respect to the state) authorities responsible for investment of Solidarity resources reacted to such opposition. Did they, for instance, punish opposition voting patterns or attempt to buy back votes for the PRI?

- LOWEARN: This is the percentage of wages earned below the *salario mínimo*, an approximation of a poverty line.[28] This is the proxy for

---

[27]The characteristics used differ from those in the state-level analysis partly because of data availability and partly because the difference in jurisdiction dictates doing so.

[28]Note that while *salario mínimo* is directly translated as minimum salary, it means the salary determined by the government as necessary to live above poverty, given the local consumer price index. Actually the figure is usually too low for this purpose.

income since GDP per capita figures are not available at the municipal level: the higher the figure, the lower the income in the municipality. Table 12.3 presents the means and standard deviations of these variables for the state of México.

TABLE 12.3
SUMMARY STATISTICS FOR MUNICIPAL-LEVEL VARIABLES

Variable	Mean	Std. Dev.	Min – Max
ESCDIGMEX (1991 Pesos)	16043.14	11998.23	3110.77 – 74145.19
NINOSMEX (1991 Pesos)	9183.58	6949.62	2363.45 – 41176.09
POSTPRIM (%)	63.1	18.6	20.3 – 91.0
IND_PCT (%)	4.2	8.7	0.1 – 48.4
OPPOSITION (%)	15.9	12.4	0.0 – 57.1
LOWEARN (%)	18.1	6.8	6.0 – 47.4

Table 12.4 presents the OLS regression results of equation (10) for these data. Columns 1 and 2 show the runs of the regression assuming equal concern for educational investment through Escuela Digna and Niños en Solidaridad, respectively. Since q is significant and negative, the model yields robust results that in fact the programs seek to redistribute educational outcomes to municipalities that have fared poorly in schooling outcomes over those that have fared better. The results also indicate that allocation patterns for Niños en Solidaridad are more redistributive in this respect than for Escuela Digna, since the coefficient q is larger for the former.[29]

We can now turn to columns 3 and 4, which show the results of the regressions when the municipal characteristics may be different from zero. Once again, the results with respect to the measure of inequality aversion are replicated. In addition, the significance of the coefficient on LOWEARN indicates that the programs redistribute educational resources to poorer municipalities even further: all other things equal, a state with more low-wage earners will get more resources. And the absolute value of the coefficient is the largest of all the characteristics of unequal concern.

Interestingly, the coefficient on IND_PCT is negative and significant, indicating that the program may fail to reach indigenous populations effectively. One traditional explanation would be that these populations are not plugged into the political machine, which then

---

[29] Also, while emphasizing once again that q is a unitless parameter, one should note that its magnitude here is much closer to similar studies. Intuitively, the magnitude for SEP in the previous regressions seems very small.

discriminates against them overtly. However, given the program's well-articulated concern for targeting such populations—and the fact that the federal government seems to distribute resources to states in a manner to make this a priority—the result may point to a breakdown in the process by which resources are allocated. The importance of the Solidarity School Committees may come into play here. If indigenous populations are less capable—because of technical capabilities, language barriers, or other social or economic factors—of organizing, lobbying, and submitting proposals properly through these committees, then the government may be failing to recognize this and support such groups productively.

TABLE 12.4

REGRESSION RESULTS OF MÉXICO STATE'S SOLIDARITY EDUCATION RESOURCE DISTRIBUTION

DEPENDENT VARIABLE [COLUMNS (1) AND (3)]: = ESCDIGMEX
DEPENDENT VARIABLE [COLUMNS (2) AND (4)]: = NINOSMEX

	(1)	(2)	(3)	(4)
POSTPRIM S	−1.75**	−2.53**	−1.56**	−2.20**
	(0.291)	(0.288)	(0.313)	(0.333)
IND_PCT	—	—	−0.16**	−0.087*
			(0.033)	(0.035)
OPPOSITION	—	—	−0.08**	−0.070*
			(0.019)	(0.020)
LOWEARN	—	—	0.288*	0.350*
			(0.176)	(0.187)
CONSTANT	11.11**	11.04**	10.57**	10.85**
	(0.191)	(0.190)	(0.271)	(0.289)
F VALUE	36.1	77.11	24.8	30.13
[P Value]	[0.0001]	[0.0001]	[0.0001]	[0.0001]
Adjusted R^2	0.23	0.39	0.44	0.49

* indicates significance at the 90% level of confidence
** indicates significance at the 99% level of confidence

Figures in parentheses are standard errors.

Finally, the negative sign on the OPPOSITION variable's coefficient indicates that the system punishes those municipalities that showed less support for the ruling party in the previous municipal elections.[30] This

---

[30]One possibility would be that the OPPOSITION variable might be correlated with some other important variable. Correlation tests failed to show significant correlation with *any* of the other independent variables, including income. This is true for both the state- and municipal-level analyses. Also, at least nationally, OPPOSITION is not correlated significantly with %URBAN.

does not eliminate the possibility that Solidarity investment is being or has been made in such a manner as to buy back areas that voted for Cárdenas. After all, the expenditure streams analyzed data from three years after the presidential elections, and the voting data used are for municipal, not presidential, elections. But this result does call into question, at least for the state of México, the investment dynamic described by many political analysts currently. Opposition seems *on average* to hurt a municipality's chances of receiving Solidarity educational investment.

CONCLUSIONS AND POLICY RECOMMENDATIONS

The results of this study are mixed with respect to the investment streams through Solidarity in the education sector and their potential effects with respect to development and poverty alleviation. Or rather, the results foster guarded optimism for a program much criticized by social and political analysts. As a whole, the government seems to recognize the critical nature of redistributing resources in the education sector. Given the clear relation between education and welfare outlined in our discussion of the Escuela Digna program, the redistributive goals *and* the results from the analysis of SEP state-level expenditures and municipal-level expenditures through Solidarity in one state are quite positive. This success ought to be promoted and stimulated further. The federal government should, however, investigate why there appears to be little redistribution of Escuela Digna funds between states, even though the favorable matching rate for poorer states should assure it.

The results do show a potential failure to target the needy indigenous populations effectively at the micro, project level. Both federal and state governments (as well as independent analysts) ought to investigate and document this failure and its causes, and then amend the processes of project design and resource allocation to better target these populations. In particular, indigenous populations' ability to form effective Solidarity School Committees may be a major obstacle.

While the study fails to yield definitive results with respect to politicization of resource allocation through SEP or Solidarity nationally, it does indicate that voting behavior may affect government investments in education through the line ministry and Solidarity, though both entities may use varying political criteria to allocate resources. One must still raise several questions with respect to such potential forces acting within Solidarity. Of course, being a government program of significant proportions, Solidarity is a political animal, and in this sense the following debate deserves substantial consideration: if, for the most part, funds channeled through the program are in fact redistributing resources substantially, how much does the politics at the fringe of the allocation process (or even at the center of it) matter? Analysts ought to be careful in expecting political factors to play a minimal role. It is common in all democracies, including the United States, for expenditure decisions to be at least partly influenced by electoral and other political needs of the party in power—and for expenditures to rise significantly before elections. The critical questions remain: what is the end result of a program such as Solidarity, and how does it compare to the programs that came before it or other politically feasible alternatives? For instance, the results with respect to the indigenous population in the state of México concern me more than do those with respect to political opposition.

Studies like this one ought to be encouraged; identifying possible flaws in the allocation process is a first step in promoting changes. In particular, analyzing Solidarity allocations at the most local and direct level in other states and sectors will prove critical in understanding whether, and how much, politics drive investment. One major policy recommendation is, then, to give independent analysts freer access to Solidarity expenditure data, especially data at the municipal level. Most available government publications cleverly hide sectoral-level allocations even to states and most certainly to municipalities,[31] making the kind of analysis performed here impossible or difficult at best. Solidarity ought to be required to release full details regarding its expenditure streams to states and municipalities by sector. Independent analysts can then verify that Solidarity programs back up their rhetoric with resources. Such an open forum would go a long way toward ensuring that allocations were made along less political lines and more successfully targeted to poverty alleviation in Mexico.

Because Solidarity resources are relatively free from traditional allocation patterns, the program can play a critical role in alleviating poverty, perhaps making up for line ministries' past failures in this regard. However, if funds flowing through Solidarity are to continue to grow, federal and state governments' discretion in the way they are distributed ought perhaps to diminish, or at least be closely monitored. Resource allocation could be based more on communities meeting various guidelines (a "checklist" process for project approval), taking discretionary resource allocation out of government's hands and leaving Solidarity with more of a role of oversight and ensuring accountability. In addition, more transparent guidelines for communities to qualify for funds could help. The results of this study indicate that such improvements might considerably improve indigenous populations' access to needed resources.

Overall, Solidarity has become a powerful development program, redistributing educational investment with relative success. The pro-

---

[31] For instance, the president's yearly State of the Nation address, as well as data available through the national legislature.

gram also seems to operate with a well-articulated concern for both interregional and interpersonal equity, and could play a major role in strengthening Mexico's recent moves toward fiscal federalism. Certainly more studies are necessary for additional sectors and states, and at a more local level, in order to generalize the results of the present analysis. For the moment this study yields no damning evidence, while indicating room for improvement. Some bridled praise is, however, due to Solidarity's redistribution of educational resources.

13

Political Change in Durango: The Role of National Solidarity

Paul Haber

The National Solidarity Program means different things to different people. President Salinas, a staunch supporter, has referred to PRONASOL as "la nueva política de masas del Estado mexicano."[1] The administration, and PRONASOL allies, champion the program as vital to Mexico's economic development and democratization. Some observers and program participants recognize PRONASOL's ability to partially meet the demands of the poor, and credit the program for at least mitigating what would otherwise have been a dramatic increase in poverty since 1988. However, they also point out that the flip side of programs designed to improve the majority's economic well-being (through agrarian reform, rural credit, the ejido system, education, social security, health services, housing, etc.) is that they also serve as mechanisms of political control (see, e.g., Blanco 1992). Others are more harsh, referring to Solidarity as the *neopopulismo* that controls and co-opts the opposition, as "the complement of *neoliberalismo*." Critics of this persuasion emphasize that while PRONASOL funds are hopelessly inadequate to resolve Mexico's poverty, they are more than sufficient to co-opt and manipulate social movements, groups, and individuals that previously played important opposition roles.[2]

This essay explores one of the crucial stories of PRONASOL: its effect on the political fortunes of popular movements that choose to participate actively in the program. In analyzing this question with primary reference to one of the most important urban popular movements in Mex-

---

[1]Speech given during the third National Solidarity Week, September 1992.

[2]Leaders of the PRD-affiliated urban popular movement, the Asamblea de Barrios, have been particularly outspoken on this issue. See, for example, Rascón and Hidalgo 1992.

ico—the Committee for Popular Defense (CDP) in the northwestern state of Durango—I will also attempt to answer the related question of what effect this active participation has had on the Mexican political system at both the local and national levels. In particular, does this participation represent a positive step in the difficult transition from clientelism to citizenship, or does it represent a strengthening of the Mexican authoritarian regime?

Attention to changing relations between state and society in Mexico has increased dramatically over the last decade. Academics, politicians, journalists, and the citizenry at large have recognized the change and attempted to understand it. While few would deny that change is both present and important, the type of academic consensus that once held sway regarding the nature of state/society relations has been replaced by uncertainty and debate. Solidarity is a crucial ingredient in this complex and perhaps paradoxical process: Is it possible that Solidarity is both strengthening Mexican authoritarianism, at least in the short term, and also promoting greater pluralism by empowering social actors more representative of their bases than the official party or other existing alternatives?

There have always been subtle interactions between electoral and nonelectoral politics in Mexico. The postrevolutionary Mexican state has for decades designed and implemented public policy with electoral objectives as a significant criterion. Solidarity continues this practice and brings innovation to a vital function that lost some of its capacity during the 1980s. The changing politics of the CDP, and Durango politics in general, represent an opportunity to observe an interesting example of a process at work throughout the country. And, as observers of popular movements in Mexico are already aware, the CDP is not only important in its own region; it is an important influence on the political strategies and decisions of state actors, political parties, and other social movements throughout the country.

BACKGROUND

CDP activities are centered in the capital city of Durango in the state of Durango.[3] With a municipal population of half a million, it is one of the population centers of northern Mexico, a region characterized generally by low population density. Despite a history of riches (Durango was one

---

[3] It is outside the scope of this chapter to provide a detailed historical account of the CDP. Nonetheless, a brief discussion of the 1972–88 period provides essential background information, and illustrates how recent CDP involvement in PRONASOL is not so much a sharp departure from past practice as a continuation of movement strategy dating back to the 1970s. For more extensive discussions of the CDP's history as a social movement organization and its involvement in Mexican movement politics on the national level, see Haber 1990, n.d.2, and 1992: chap. 6). Sections of the present text draw from these earlier works.

of the silver capitals of New Spain) and the potential for extensive timber and mineral exploitation in the future (more about this later), Durango is an economic backwater, producing less than 1.5 percent of Mexico's GDP and receiving less than 1 percent of total federal investment (Canudas 1991: tables 3, 8, 9). The state of Durango, with a population of 1,352,156, contains only 1.67 percent of the country's population, down from 2.4 percent in 1950 (Gobierno 1987).

The origins of the CDP can be traced to the crushing of the 1968 student movement and the creation of the political current known as Política Popular (see Moguel, this volume). The membership of Política Popular was dedicated to Marxist revolutionary tenets; but upon deciding that armed revolution was not a realistic strategy, they set out to develop popular movements in the provinces. Política Popular, founded by Adolfo Oribe Berlinguer, adopted a Maoist stance and dedicated itself to living among the poor, creating autonomous social movements in the countryside and in urban peripheries. Small focus groups were sent out to begin clandestine work in Zacatecas, San Luis Potosí, Tlaxcala, Monterrey, Nayarit, México State, and Durango. While many of these initial efforts were relatively short-lived, the cadres sent to Durango overcame initial setbacks, adjusted to local conditions, and built a permanent, mass-based movement.

Like other efforts in the early 1970s, the small group of students sent to Durango began their work in the countryside. When organizing efforts in rural areas failed to produce a following, they moved their base of operations to the state capital (in 1972) and began establishing *colonias populares*, neighborhoods located on the outer limits of the urban center, where land invasions were easier to defend than in the more valuable downtown areas. In February and March 1973 the movement organized its first land invasions. State police violently evicted the land invaders on their first attempt, and the second invasion was abandoned under threats from state police and federal soldiers. In September 1973, after lengthy negotiations with the National Institute for Community Development (INDECO), the CDP secured an agreement whereby it would receive twenty hectares paid for over five years. With this land it created Durango's first *colonia popular*, División del Norte.

Expansion came slowly, but in 1976 what are today the key CDPista *colonias* of Emiliano Zapata (2,000 parcels, about 12,000 people) and Lucío Cabañas (800 parcels, about 4,800 people) were established. Between 1980 and 1986, ten new *colonias* were founded through invasions of private, ejido, and public land. Over the course of this period, the CDP became increasingly skillful in its negotiations with federal and state authorities. Very often negotiations would be held prior to or simultaneous with mass mobilizations. Through negotiations, extensions of preexisting *colonias* were achieved and advances were made in the extension of low-interest housing credits and services, principally water, electricity, and drainage. The CDP developed working relationships with federal, state, and local governmental agencies. The CDP strategy always combined militancy and the threat of disruption with negotiation.

The lesson learned from these experiences remains central to the CDP's political strategy today: the importance of building working relations with federal agencies and negotiating agreements in concert with mass mobilizations. The CDP's close working relationship with state elites in the current context of PRONASOL does not represent a departure from its long-term strategy; the CDP views negotiating for state concessions as a realistic and primary goal of movement activity. How concessions are gained, the mixture of negotiation and militancy, changes over time. As we shall see, the CDP is convinced that the Salinas administration represents an opportunity for concessions and movement empowerment to be realized through consultation with state reformers and with a minimum of movement militancy and institutional disruption.

In common with many if not most popular movements in Mexico, the CDP has not fostered collaborative decision-making processes as much as it counts on rank-and-file support for the leadership decisions it sends down through the organization for consultation and ratification. More crucial to the organizational life of the CDP—again like most other large and successful popular movements in Mexico—is not democratic decision-making processes but rather the persistent ability to form broad-based consensus within the organization. On those rare occasions when consensus cannot be built around leadership decisions, changes are made. The CDP has thus far avoided a scenario all too common in the history of popular movements: forging ahead without a rank-and-file consensus, which can lead to serious internal problems or even extinction.

The decision to enter electoral politics was crucial to the CDP in a number of respects, not least being that it moderated movement behavior. Prior to this decision, militant leadership and political culture characterized many CDP *colonias*. Beginning in 1986 and continuing through the present, the CDP has worked to change its image from one of an organization of confrontation and fear to one of a responsible social movement and, today, to a political party which actively solicits the support of government officials, the media, and the middle class. What the CDP has lost in traditional revolutionary enthusiasm has been made up for in multiclass support gained through the CDP's ability to deliver the public services that Durango's citizens badly need and want. The CDP as a promoter of *colonias populares* through land invasions has been replaced by an organization which is both a social movement and a political party presenting itself, with increasing success, as the best organizational alternative for taking Durango into the twenty-first century.[4]

THE 1989 CONVENIO DE CONCERTACIÓN

Urban popular movements, along with the nonunionized urban poor, increased exponentially during the administrations of López Portillo (1976–82) and de la Madrid (1982–88). Neither administration effectively incorporated the urban poor or their movement representatives into the system, allowing autonomous development outside the ailing state corporatist National Confederation of Popular Organizations (CNOP). This challenged the system in two fundamental ways. First, it created several movements that radicalized large numbers of the urban poor to press their demands outside existing institutional channels and cost the state a degree of control in setting the national political agenda. Second, by losing the political monopoly over state access for the urban poor, the PRI lost its ability to dominate electoral outcomes in poor urban neighborhoods.

The defining characteristics of Mexico's inclusionary authoritarian regime, and its relationship with the dominant Institutional Revolutionary Party (PRI), were formed during the 1930s. The PRI has maintained three corporatist institutions responsible for maintaining political control and the electoral allegiance of labor, the peasantry, and the more heterogeneous grouping, the so-called popular sectors. The CNOP was designed when the urban poor was not a particularly large population sector, and most certainly not a political threat. As the urban poor grew and autonomous urban movements gained a political foothold during the 1970s, the CNOP began to show signs of weakness. This process accelerated during the late 1970s and 1980s, but no effective reform of the corporatist CNOP mechanism was forthcoming.[5]

The nationalist populist appeal of Cuauhtémoc Cárdenas caught the country by surprise. His allure and strength were most evident in urban

---

[4]The CDP's territorial base has held constant at about twenty *colonias* since the late 1980s, containing about 12,000 lots, or about 70,000 people. In addition, the CDP has functioning committees in twenty-seven other *colonias* with about 1,100 committee activists in the capital city alone. While CDP strength remains centered in the capital, it has been active in at least eleven other municipalities as well, through the establishment of *colonias* and/or electoral victories. The CDP has also formed a peasant organization (the Unión de los Pueblos de Emiliano Zapata), the Unión de Comerciantes (made up of street vendors and small business owners), and a legal service.

[5]In the early years of the Salinas administration, steps were taken to transform the PRI's popular sector. It changed its name and declared a new mission. Most importantly, the urban poor were identified as being important to the popular sector's mission and steps were taken to recapture their electoral fidelity to the party. The 1988 election was a rude awakening to the CNOP which failed to deliver the urban poor vote as expected. The "modernization" of the party's popular sector has run into problems, however, and been somewhat overtaken by events. In essence, PRONASOL has been the undisputed lead effort vis-à-vis the urban poor. For more details, see Haber 1992.

areas, including many poor neighborhoods that responded favorably to the possibility of returning to the kind of leadership exerted by Cuauhtémoc's father, Lázaro Cárdenas, during the 1930s. The electoral shock of 1988 demonstrated that state institutions and programs, in combination with the CNOP, were inadequate for maintaining minimal acceptable levels of political control and development initiatives among the urban poor, now the single largest population sector in Mexico. Cárdenas was able to build on the work of urban popular movements to gain a high percentage of the urban poor vote. Left unchecked, the trend threatened to continue during the Salinas years, with possibly dire consequences for the regime.

It did not take long for Salinas to demonstrate that his policy of neoliberal economic transformation would be accompanied by new political languages and institutions able to build legitimacy for the president's programs. These would also aim to incorporate, or reincorporate, a substantial percentage of the political opposition. Even before his inauguration, Salinas signaled that he was planning a new and aggressive popular movement policy directed toward recovering political ground lost during the economic crisis. Thus, just as Cárdenas was consolidating priorities behind an electoral strategy, Salinas was reaching out with a program that offered political and economic resources to popular movements willing to participate in a "new relationship" of *concertación* with the president.

The twin decisions to enter into a formal and highly public agreement with President Salinas (February 1989) and to form a state-level political party (spring 1989), in lieu of entering into a political alliance with the PRD, launched the CDP on a strategic course which has had monumental consequences for the CDP and changed the political landscape for popular movements in Mexico.

The CDP was the first of many Mexican popular movements to sign a *convenio* with the new president. The stated goal of these agreements between federal and local governments and social actors was to mitigate extreme poverty via democratically designed and implemented development projects. Under the CDP *convenio*, federal, state, municipal, and CDP resources were combined in order to implement public works projects and create CDP-owned and operated businesses. Of a total investment of 3.2 billion pesos outlined in the 1989 agreement, two-thirds was federal funding, with 1.95 billion (61 percent) through the Ministry of Budget and Planning (SPP) and 112.5 million pesos (4 percent) through DICONSA. The Durango state government committed 150.3 million pesos (5 percent), and the CDP almost 1 billion (30 percent).

It is important to note that CDP communities are able to contribute their matching funds in one of three ways: in cash, materials, or labor. The overwhelming majority of the CDP commitment was met by providing manual labor in the implementation of the public works projects.[6] This option was not unique to Durango or to the CDP. Allowing poor people to make their mandatory contribution to "shared development" via manual labor was vital to the program, for it allowed many more groups to participate than otherwise would have been the case. This type of labor puts a premium on being able to organize local people to do the work, something that many independent movements were in a better position to do than were their PRIísta counterparts.

The initial *convenio* was but the first of several signed in 1989. For example, in September the Unión de Pueblos Emiliano Zapata (the organization of rural communities within the CDP) signed a *convenio* pledging over 1 billion pesos, divided roughly into thirds between the Ministry of Agriculture and Water Resources (SARH), the Rural Credit Bank (BANRURAL), and community resources.

An ecology project was also implemented to reduce contamination in the Tunal River caused by the large wood-products plant, Celulósico Centauro. This began what was billed as the CDP's long-term commitment to reverse the damages incurred as a result of past development plans and government actions that ignored environmental concerns. The ecology project was particularly significant not only because it sought to clean up existing problems, but also because it was an important pilot effort by the CDP to establish its credentials as a responsible participant in Durango's future economic development. An interesting aspect of the ecology project is that in addition to government funds, the CDP also received funds from the owners of Celulósico Centauro as well as the Inter-American Foundation.[7]

These CDP actions provided the basis upon which the urban popular movement (and popular movements more generally) split, openly and deeply, only months after joining in support of the National Democratic Front (FDN) and Cárdenas's presidential bid. Gaining concessions was one thing; openly signing agreements that legitimated the president and his administration, if not the political system itself, was quite another. As the benefits of adopting a strategy of "cooperation without co-optation" with the Salinas administration and the development of new electoral identities independent of the PRD manifested themselves, many other movements were inspired to take similar actions. While the PRD has managed to maintain some social movement support, many poor people's movements have ceased to actively support Cárdenas. A

---

[6]The *convenio* provided funding for a long list of small projects, including the construction of fourteen primary classrooms; electrification in six CDP *colonias*; housing improvements in seven CDP *colonias*; basketball courts; potable water projects in seven CDP *colonias*; child care centers; six small tortilla factories; a construction materials supply house; construction of six kitchens which would provide subsidized food in CDP *colonias*; and a carpentry workshop.

[7]For a more complete history of the Comité de Defensa y Preservación Ecológica (Committee for Ecological Protection and Preservation), see Moguel 1991: 39–50.

smaller but still significant number have become critics of the PRD and even of Cárdenas himself.

Different priorities—and distinctive strategies designed to pursue those priorities—result from diverse locations in the political system, giving rise to conflictive agendas, even between actors that assert common political goals. It was relatively easy for left-leaning political parties and social movements to form a strong consensus behind Cárdenas's 1988 presidential bid. It was not long after the election, however, before differing priorities and strategies emerged between many popular movements and what was to become the PRD. While it was uncertain during the FDN period to what extent Cárdenas would head a social movement and/or political party, as the PRD took shape in 1989 and 1990 it became clear that its priorities were electoral. In addition to contesting the 1988 election results, PRD attention turned toward state elections and the federal elections of August 1991. While there are instances of popular movements remaining formally within the Cárdenas/PRD fold while also actively seeking and receiving PRONASOL funds (see Fox and Moguel n.d.)—such as the Coalition of Workers, Peasants, and Students of the Isthmus (COCEI) of Juchitán, Oaxaca, and the UCIS VER of Veracruz—many others felt that their movement interests could be better served by severing their formal links to the PRD.

The oftentimes contrasting priorities of political parties and social movements are well illustrated by relations between the PRD and the CDP. Immediately following the announcement of the July 1988 election results, Cárdenas and what was to become the PRD took the position of "nonnegotiation" with Salinas. Positioning the PRD for future elections, they refused to deal with an "illegitimate" president, who had gained his office through electoral fraud. The CDP saw things in a different light. As the Salinas administration began making overtures to popular movements regarding what would become known as *convenios de concertación*, the CDP found itself competing with other political organizations, not least of all the PRI, to deliver material benefits to its constituents. Its prosperity, and ultimately its very survival, depend on its ability to deliver such services. Salinas was offering the type of resources and concessions that the CDP and other popular movements had long advocated. The decision to modify some independent behaviors in exchange for resources via PRONASOL was not a difficult one for the CDP. Nor was it a radical departure from past positions. Indeed, for the CDP, PRONASOL signified an important victory, the culmination of years of effort to force state recognition of popular movements as representatives for those disadvantaged by the Mexican development model and outside the traditional corporatist institutions.

In Mexico, access to political and economic resources varies, even among like actors (urban popular movements, industrialists, academic elites, etc.). Thus, different urban popular movements cultivate different relationships with elites and institutions that provide access to desired goods. People in high places are a key movement resource in Mexico, and movements work hard to convince powerful state actors that their support is to their mutual advantage.

Throughout the crucial year of 1988, Durango's governor and state-level PRI were out of favor with Salinas and key modernizers in his administration. The governor had aggressively backed the losing presidential contender, and Salinas viewed the state's party elite as opposing new reforms and modernization. Many local political observers conclude that this situation led Salinas to take the risk inherent in building up an alternative political power base in Durango. Furthermore, the CDP had personal ties to Salinas and PRONASOL director Carlos Rojas, principally through the CDP's ties to Alberto Anaya of the "Land and Liberty" Popular Front (FPTyL) in the state of Monterrey. Moreover, unlike some urban popular movements, the CDP faced stiff opposition from the federal representatives who controlled federal spending in Durango and had close ties to Governor Ramírez Gamero, then a declared enemy of the CDP. To remain within the PRD fold carried no financial or political support in dealings with local adversaries. Indeed, remaining loyal to Cárdenas would have endangered what the CDP then enjoyed, not to mention compromising its ability to extend its power base in future.

Many on the left characterized the warming between Salinas and the CDP leadership as an act of treason: the CDP had joined forces with the authoritarian enemy and abandoned the revolutionary and democratic left. But the CDP had no undying allegiance to the "Mexican left." Indeed, once the black box of the left is opened up for inspection, deep ideological, strategic, and personal divisions are found between what are commonly referred to as the "political left" and the "social left." The political left refers to party activity, electoral and otherwise. It centers on and around the Mexican Communist Party (PCM). Popular movements like the CDP are identified with the Maoist current within the social left that comprises rural and urban social movements. Cooperation and coalition formation within the social left, let alone with the political left, have been problematic at best. The fact that the PRD was dominated, in order of importance, by ex-PRIístas such as Cárdenas, the political left, and non-Maoist sectors of the social left did little to inspire obligation and loyalty on the part of the CDP.

By summer 1989, it was clear that Durango was a prime location for observing Salinas's *concertación social* in action. Social concertation was not new to Mexico. The López Portillo administration announced such a policy as part of its efforts to increase and coordinate local participation in the design and implementation of federal programs. The concept and its practice had then gone into disrepair during the de la Madrid years; Salinas moved aggressively to bring it back to life. It quickly became, along with modernization, a code word of the new administration. From the beginning, PRONASOL was fundamental to *concertación*. In more recent years Solidarity has replaced *concertación social* as the driving conceptual force behind the administration's state/society mode of operation.

Salinas has been willing to use PRONASOL funds and associated political interventions in support of those popular movements willing and able to participate in programs that address, at least in limited fashion, the needs of the poor. But the CDP's changing political fortunes in Durango raise an even more significant political question: Is it possible that Salinas and like-minded elites both within and outside the state are willing to support the political empowerment of at least a limited number of popular movements that are in a position to contribute to the political system's legitimacy and stability?

The answer to this question appears to be yes. Durango's political power has been concentrated in the hands of traditional politicians who were unwilling or unable to introduce innovative new directions for the state's economic growth and political modernization. While the Salinas administration is demonstrating that political modernization need not be equated with the creation of formal democratic institutions, it does call for the development of political institutions and leaders capable of introducing legislation and reforms that enhance the system's legitimacy and create a more desirable investment environment for both domestic and foreign capital. Politics in Durango have long functioned in a way that stifles new political talent that enjoys public support, is capable of mobilizing and organizing citizens of all classes behind government development initiatives, and introduces new ideas for meeting basic needs and generating economic growth.

To Salinas, Durango is an area in drastic need of political and economic renewal. Though it is one of Mexico's poorest states, it possesses significant potential for economic growth. Its large mineral and timber deposits go underexploited due to a poor transportation system. Durango has no ports, and its rail and highway systems are poor by Mexican standards. Plans are under way to construct a highway linking Mexico City with Culiacán on the Pacific Coast via Durango. Should this be built—and a broad range of influential interests, including economic elites in Monterrey and Mexico City, support it—Durango's economic potential will be significantly altered. Developing a strong working relationship with the CDP appears not only compatible with but conducive to Durango's political and economic modernization.

THE PARTY OF THE CDP (PCDP) AND THE JULY 1989 ELECTION

Although the CDP's signing of the *convenio* did not lead to an immediate and formal rupture with Cárdenas, it certainly changed the relationship and put its long-term health in jeopardy. On the state level, the PRD leadership responded publicly with harsh and open criticism. Once the *convenio* was signed, the possibilities for electoral alliance were probably over.

Not unexpectedly, interviews with CDP and PRD leadership yield different accounts of how and why the alliance faltered. Each side blames the other for the break. While continuing to operate within the PRD would have been difficult at best for the CDP, given the negative fallout from the *convenio* signing, it seems unlikely that an enduring alliance was possible. There are several compelling explanations for the CDP leadership's decision to form their own party, independent of the PRD response to the *convenio*. One is that it proved impossible to come to a power-sharing agreement within the alliance. The specific issue which tore the CDP and PRD apart was candidate selection. Although the July 1989 elections were for municipalities and state deputies, the thorniest issue was who would receive the legislative seats awarded on the basis of proportional voting. The CDP has long maintained that the PRD (and before that, the PMS) had received undeserved influence in the alliance simply because they held the party registration. (In addition to political rewards, the PMS received 100 percent of the federal matching funds associated with the 1988 election.) According to the CDP leadership, it was the CDP that had the popular support; if the current party leadership would not accept a position as junior partner in the alliance, the alliance was over. The fact that the PCDP received more than twice as many votes as the PRD (7.62 percent and 3.16 percent, respectively) supports that claim.

The CDP claims that it broke with the PRD at the state level over how to register the party for the 1989 election (see Haber 1992, n.d.2). The CDP favored running on either a PRD ticket using the PMS registration (this would have been legal under Mexican law) or a provisional PCDP ticket if the PRD insisted on going through the lengthy process of gaining its own national registration. Both the national and local-level PRD structures disagreed, insisting that the CDP combine forces with the local PRD and run on the PMS ticket, an option unacceptable to the CDP.

Many observers of Durango politics take another view, resolutely denied by the CDP: that breaking with Cárdenas was an explicit prerequisite for receiving PRONASOL benefits and other favorable political interventions from the Salinas administration. These observers dismiss the registration dispute as political theater; the CDP was affecting goodwill toward the popular Cárdenas, knowing full well that its proposals would be rejected. According to this version of events, in an agreement between the central organization of the Maoist social left, the Organization of the Revolutionary Left-Mass Line (OIR-LM) and the Trotskyist political party (PRT), OIR-LM members (including the CDP) pledged to support only PRT candidates. But the agreement created discontent; many OIRistas felt they were being used by an arrogant PRT. This led to negotiations with the PMS in 1988, in which it was agreed that the OIRistas would support the PMS slate in exchange for two federal deputyships, one for Alberto Anaya of the "Land and Liberty" Popular Front (FPTyL) of Monterrey and one for Marcos Cruz of the CDP. However, when Heberto Castillo relinquished his position as PMS candidate for president and threw his support behind Cárdenas and the FDN, the situation was complicated. Fortunately, Castillo's announcement came very late, and thus pressure on the CDP to campaign for Cárdenas, and pressure for them not to do so, did not reach crisis proportions.

Problems avoided during the campaign could not be so easily sidestepped after the election. The CDP had to choose between Cárdenas and Salinas. According to observers, this was not a particularly difficult choice, given the CDP's predisposition toward garnering the best deal possible with the state and always attempting to exploit elite splits to its own organizational advantage. Thus, the CDP had to find a way to cut its ties with the PRD. The formation of the state-level party accomplished this very well.

In order to award the CDP temporary party registration, the state legislature had to amend the state electoral code. This prompted some opponents and observers, including the PAN, to allege that the administration, if not Salinas himself, had played a role in pushing through the registration.[8] Soon after the CDP gained its temporary registration[9] it moved to develop an interparty electoral alliance with the PRD. The PRD formally refused, insisting it would enter an alliance only if the CDP rescinded its independent registration, a condition clearly unacceptable to

---

[8]The reader should note that relations between the governor and the PRI vis-à-vis the CDP were very strained at this point. It is unlikely that the registration would have been approved without pressure from above. The perception was indeed widespread among political observers in Durango that Salinas had intervened in the PCDP registration, despite the absence of a smoking gun to prove the claim. Without such intervention, it is impossible to account for the fact that the CDP got the registration through a special session in February (the state congress is usually out of session from January to March). All PRI members voted for the registration, with only PAN representatives voting against it, claiming that the process by which the temporary registration was being passed violated state constitutional law. Observers argue that, while the registration might have been legal, without presidential intervention there is no way to account for the PRI majority voting in favor of holding a special session to consider the CDP registration only two weeks after Salinas had visited the state, and then voting for it.

[9]Permanent registration was contingent on the PCDP receiving 4 percent of the vote in the July 1989 election.

the CDP. At a formal meeting between the two local leaderships, Cárdenas repeated his much-publicized position that state-level organizations make alliance decisions independent of national leadership. The state-level leadership refused, nevertheless, on the grounds that the CDP had been "captured" by the official ruling party/state. It was in the context of strained relations with the PRD that the CDP made a series of agreements with the PFCRN, PPS, and PARM to support common candidates.

PRONASOL, 1990–1991

Nineteen eighty-nine was the year of *convenios*. In 1990, the situation began to change. *Convenios* gave way to the early formation of Solidarity Committees across the country and the targeting of resources to specific programs (for example, health, education, or groups such as the CDP).

Federal and state officials charged with administering PRONASOL funds in Durango are at pains to illustrate that programmatic and funding changes have made the program more systematic and rational (i.e., less politicized), and that the state government has retained more responsibility (author interviews). However, this last assertion is undermined by the fact that PRONASOL's original authorization of 63 billion pesos grew to 194 billion through subsequent presidential authorizations for specific projects. While the state government (i.e., the governor) was perhaps able to exert a degree of discretion in project selection at the initial funding level, the subsequent authorization (twice the original amount!) suggests that project selection was still highly centralized in the Office of the Presidency, at least for the state of Durango.[10]

This supports the contention that PRONASOL is a centralizing action, that it has served in particular to take power away from those governors in Salinas's disfavor. What has gone largely unnoticed by independent observers is that there are elements of decentralization involved as well, at least in Durango, where PRONASOL funds have been delivered into the hands of municipal governments. While PRONASOL officials oversee the use of funds, the Durango case suggests that municipal presidents have exercised a large degree of autonomy in determining which public works projects will be funded (not an apolitical decision). According to official PRONASOL documents which detail the budget project by project, over 92

---

[10]Many political observers have ridiculed the notion that Salinas has encouraged decentralization in the state of Durango. Constant references are made to a reoccurring Salinas habit: Upon arriving in Durango Salinas holds meetings with groups of businessmen, in which he exhorts them to enter into joint investments with the federal government and foreign capital. An excellent example of this is the Forestry Development Project, being implemented in the forested areas of southern Chihuahua and northern Durango, assisted by a World Bank loan (37 percent of the coniferous forests in Mexico are in this area). Many political observers in Durango believe that the region's development is being increasingly engineered, financed, and controlled by local and foreign capital, along with the executive branch (author interviews). In this view, the state government is being increasingly left out of the process.

billion pesos (out of a total budget of 194 billion) were spent by municipal governments in the state of Durango.

Of course, a substantial portion of these funds would have been spent in the municipalities under the previous rubric of "regional development" and thus cannot be seen simply as budgetary increases. However, under PRONASOL these funds can now be directed to municipalities more in keeping with federal priorities. So, while the overall funding level may not have changed much, the distribution of funding by municipalities may well have.[11] In addition, the allocation of those funds within the municipality in many instances changes when responsibility for project selection moves from the state government to the municipal president.

Consider the municipality of Nombre de Dios, where the CDP won municipal elections twice in a row, in 1989 and again in 1992. In 1991 the municipal budget was 1.1 billion pesos, and PRONASOL funds were 1.2 billion pesos. Although then CDP municipal president Octavio Martínez stated that this was not a significant increase over previous allocations under regional development entitlements, he did note that he was free to allocate the new money without state interference, no small matter in a state whose governor was at odds with the CDP (author interviews).

Another element of PRONASOL's decentralization is the amount of state resources handed over to popular movements. The CDP's budgetary allocation for PRONASOL in 1990 was 5.7 billion pesos under the special "CDP Program." The federal share was even higher than in 1989, rising from 65 to 85 percent. The state contribution was to be 8 percent, and the CDP's contribution dropped sharply from 30 percent in 1989 to 6 percent. This total was supplemented by an additional 1.8 billion pesos allocated as part of the La Laguna Regional Development Project. While the 1990 allocation was a significant increase over the 1989 *convenio*, problems of implementation resulted in the cancellation of projects valued at a total of 3.5 billion. (The silver lining to the cancellations is that resources not spent in 1990 rolled over to 1991.)

Technical and organizational impediments to completing PRONASOL projects are much discussed by those charged with implementing the programs on the local level. Problems encountered by the CDP are duplicated by the increased responsibilities put on the municipalities. Interviews with technical personnel both in the CDP and within several municipalities revealed a common criticism which transcended political affiliation. While PRONASOL has channeled increased funding to popular movements and municipalities across the country, it has not authorized funding for the technical staff and equipment (including typewriters, photocopiers, phones, and computers) needed to successfully implement

---

[11] To my knowledge, no available study has analyzed the impact of PRONASOL on the distribution of funding by municipality, on either a national or state level. The most likely source of such information would of course be the government, and in this, as in so many areas, officials have not been forthcoming in the dissemination of detailed statistical data.

the programs. Opinions vary as to the reasons for this problem, which remains unresolved despite three years of complaints to state and federal authorities. Some think it is an unintentional bureaucratic problem, while others say it favors the PRI, which is relatively weak in its ability to organize community involvement in projects but relatively strong on technical expertise and equipment. In other words, failing to "technically empower" popular movements and municipal offices is a political subsidy to the national and state leaders of PRI machines who have an interest in maintaining control over PRIísta municipal presidents, and of course are interested in undermining confrontational popular movements. To the extent that this is happening, it runs counter to Salinas's stated goals of decentralization and PRI reform through political competition.

THE LABOR PARTY (PT) AND CHANGING CDP POLITICS, 1990–1992: CO-OPTATION OR DEMOCRATIC EMPOWERMENT?

There is no denying that the relationship between the CDP and the Mexican state has undergone dramatic changes associated with the CDP's tacit support for *concertación social* and its active participation in PRONASOL. The CDP has progressively lessened its criticism of government officials, first and foremost of Salinas and his administration, and eventually of the governor of Durango as well, though it remains vocal in its opposition to the PRI and its relationship to the state. Regarding presidential policies, such as the North American Free Trade Agreement, the CDP either supports the president or remains noncommittal.

The debate here is whether or not the CDP's behavior can and should be defined as co-optation, or whether its relationship with the state is better understood as a means of gaining empowerment through improved relationships with government officials. A related question is whether this contributes to the democratization process by empowering an organization that represents sectors whose interests have not been well reflected in public policy (primarily the urban poor but extending also to peasants) and has recently made gains in garnering votes from the middle class.

Co-optation of a popular movement as commonly defined in Mexico—loss of autonomy and incorporation into state corporatist relations—does not adequately describe the process or implications of CDP political behavior since 1988. But should we view this behavior as a modified form of clientelism and co-optation? Before responding to this question in the conclusion section, let's look at the evidence, assessing the behavior and its implications for state/society relations, and the impact of CDP behavior on the social movement sector itself.

On the municipal level, the CDP's record has been quite positive. Both CDP municipal presidents—Octavio Martínez Alvarez of Nombre de Dios, and Jaime Sarmiento Minchaca of Suchil—built credibility for the CDP through their successful administrations. By establishing themselves as able and honest administrators, they contributed to the image of the CDP as an organization capable of governing. By so doing, these municipal governments advanced the CDP effort to build multiclass support, to transcend its role as an urban popular movement working solely on behalf of the poor.

Including other party representatives in the municipal administration and fairly distributing public projects (not just to benefit CDPistas, which would merely substitute one corporatist political machine for another) have furthered the CDP's mission of establishing itself as a mature, responsible political organization worthy of a level of support that transcends social movement membership. In my view, the municipalities' increased control over public spending and the CDP leaders' capable administration of these funds, including PRONASOL funding, are positive contributions to political liberalization in Durango.

The formation of CDP municipal governments has not been without problems. Both were headed by local men recruited to the CDP ticket. Following each election the task began of establishing power relations between the new municipal presidents and the CDP leadership in Durango. The process proved difficult: each municipal president combined forces with CDP members outside the inner circle in an effort to decentralize decision making and expand autonomy for people in "the second tier." Eventually this internal dispute went public. The CDP municipal administrations—along with other decentralized projects, such as the "CDP" newspaper, *Cambio*, headed by former state congressman Gabino Martínez Guzmán, and ecological and other development projects headed by *técnicos* imported from Mexico City—challenged the CDP's top-down power structure and decision-making process. The CDP leadership had consented to—in fact, encouraged—the creation of relatively autonomous instances of participation and decision making within the CDP. However, efforts by those operating within the CDP's new "free spaces" to assert this autonomy engendered tensions within the CDP hierarchy. This culminated in early 1991 in the publication of an open letter signed by Martínez Alvarez, Sarmiento Minchaca, and Martínez Guzmán, which appeared in several Durango publications and was commented on throughout the country. In the letter, the authors expressed in no uncertain terms their displeasure with the CDP's management of PRONASOL funds and the CDP leadership's autocratic practices. A case in point was the charge that *Cambio* was "discontinued" after running a series of articles that debated leadership decisions on a number of key issues.

The dispute was resolved with some internal dissenters staying and others leaving the CDP. However, the question of pluralism within the CDP remains in dynamic tension. As the CDP moved from a militant urban movement to an organization focused on implementing economic development projects in collaboration with state agencies, the CDP had to expand its technical capabilities. It responded to the development mandate of new

PRONASOL funding in part by importing people from Mexico City with technical and managerial experience. These individuals, along with the CDP municipal presidents, brought greater needs for decision-making power than is traditionally accepted by those outside the inner circle.

In summary, both electoral success and the expansion of development activity related to PRONASOL have created pressures for the CDP to democratize internally, with uneven results. PRONASOL has introduced new resources which have expanded the scope of CDP activities and influence. This, in turn, has exerted pressure on top CDP leadership to allow second-tier leadership more decision-making autonomy. PRO-NASOL has also generated debates within the CDP about how best to incorporate the new funds, and about the implications of new movement/ state relations. The CDP leadership has demonstrated, however, that they will continue trying to control the pace of such changes. My own view is that this is to be expected, and that the CDP should be viewed as a movement in process.

On the state level, the CDP is increasingly willing and able to come to agreements with Governor Ramírez Gamero. In a published interview, Alejandro González Yáñez, CDP leader and PCDP state deputy, reported that:

> While the first three years of the governor's administration were tense due to his policy of repression and efforts aimed at "disappearing" the CDP, we nevertheless weathered the storm, and I can say that a relationship of mature dialogue now exists between the CDP and the Ramírez Gamero administration. We understand that it doesn't make sense to continue fighting because wear and tear is suffered on both sides, and in this context we have presented various demands; some have been answered satisfactorily, others not. Nevertheless this indicates maturity in both the state administration and the CDP to manage social problems as they arise (Yáñez 1991: 21–22).

In December 1990, the two CDP deputies in the state congress, Yáñez and Alfonso Primitivo Ríos, voted in favor of the governor's 1991 budget. In a personal interview, Yáñez explained that they had voted for this bill in exchange for the following concessions from the governor:

• One billion pesos initial investment by the state for a land fund. The fund would buy land, which would be sold to *colonos*, under the supervision of the CDP. Payments on the initial investment of land would be reinvested, creating a revolving fund.

- The governor's continued assistance in the successful implementation of PRONASOL programs, and his assurance that the state government would not create unnecessary delays.

- Electricity for every CDP rural and urban area, an idea advanced by the governor. (Providing universal electrification underscores the governor's democratic and benefactor credentials for a minimum investment since most communities already have electricity, certainly more than have running water to individual house sites.) Also, instead of the community paying 33 percent of the cost (the level recently contributed in CDP *colonias*), future electrification projects will require only a 10 percent donation from the community.

- $300 million pesos to buy uniforms for a program called Deportes para Todos. Originally the program was to be handled by a central agency, but the governor changed the plan; now each of the twenty-three state deputies will get a percentage of the fund and be charged with implementing the program. While Yáñez recognized that this would mean a percentage of the money would now be lost to graft, the CDP's image would be enhanced as they used the money to buy uniforms and organize teams; other parties would be held accountable for not using the money correctly.

- Up to one billion pesos to complete two preschool facilities in two CDP *colonias*.

- Renegotiation of the governor's debt before he left office so as not to saddle the next administration with an undue financial burden.

In 1989, the CDP had abstained on the budget vote. Its 1990 "yea" vote on the governor's budget was the first time the CDP had so forcefully supported the party/state in the state legislature. While the CDP argues that its support demonstrates maturity and a move from empty rhetoric toward a more realistic assessment of what is politically possible (and reaps more rewards for the poor), others view it as a significant indication of co-optation.[12]

The CDP has moved aggressively to improve its relations with state government, extending to the governor, formerly its arch enemy. While we

[12]Many political commentators observed that Ramírez Gamero came to political agreement with the CDP because he wishes to remain in the race to fill the CTM power vacuum when it inevitably opens up sometime in the near future. The first three years of his administration did not produce the record a contender for the top CTM position would want. Several factors went against him. While promoting economic development during the crisis was understandably difficult, Ramírez Gamero was far from distinguishing himself as a provider of creative solutions and new regional development plans. The governor, strongly identified with the PRI's labor sector, backed the wrong presidential candidate (del Mazo) in 1988. He also received poor marks in containing political conflict. As many commentators have noted, this is a key ingredient in political success in Mexico (Smith 1979; Grindle 1977).

are not privy to all the subtleties of specific agreements made and understandings reached between the CDP and various levels of the Mexican government, it remains reasonable to suggest that the improving relations with the governor have helped the CDP gain influence in local and state government and have increased the funding and political support forthcoming from the Salinas administration. This is *concertación social* in action.

On the federal level, the CDP leadership frequently makes favorable comments about Salinas. For example, Yáñez followed up his comments on improved relations between the CDP and the governor with the following observation: "With respect to the government of Carlos Salinas de Gortari, there exists a rather good relationship, one characterized by mutual respect. We have delivered various demands to the federal government, and we have received very favorable responses" (Yáñez 1991: 22).

Even more important than the rapprochement between the CDP and state and national governments has been the formation of a national political party separate from the PRD, important for both political outcomes and public perception. Creating and registering the new Labor Party (PT) has been an important element in the changing balance of electoral power, a change closely linked to PRONASOL. Much of the PT membership is urban popular movements from northern Mexico. Several campesino organizations and union factions were also among the member organizations who founded the party in December 1990.[13] Most member organizations are associated with the Mexican left faction known as the Mass Line, although there were some important exceptions, notably the CDP of Chihuahua.

The formation of the PT, followed two months later by legal authorization to participate in midterm elections in August 1991, produced a storm of commentary and criticism. The president of the PAN called the PT membership "political merchants," and Luis Javier Garrido charged that another "parastatal" party had been created. Garrido went so far as to accuse the Durango CDP of "actively collaborating with the PRI in fraud against the citizenry" (cited in Hernández Navarro 1991a: 21).

A number of factors fueled the criticism, skepticism, and outrage that accompanied the PT's registration process, proof to many that the PT member organizations had cut unsavory deals with the president. First, the

---

[13]Twenty-two organizations signed the petition for party registration, addressed to Fernando Gutiérrez Barrios, president of the Federal Election Commission, on December 11, 1991: CDP de Chihuahua; CDP de Coahuila; CDP de Durango; CDP de Fresnillo; CDP de La Laguna; CDP de Torreón; FPTyL de Nuevo León; Organización Campesina Popular Independiente de la Huasteca Veracruzana; Sociedad de Solidaridad Social Hijos de Emiliano Zapata (of Morelos); a CNTE faction headed by Teodoro Palomino Gutiérrez, called Alternativa Sindical (AS-CNTE); Frente Popular de Lucha de Zacatecas; Movimiento de Izquierda Revolucionaria de Guanajuato; Comités Populares del Valle de México; Uniones Unificadas de Vendedores Ambulantes de Toluca; Coordinadora Emiliano Zapata; UPVA 28 de Octubre (of Puebla); Comité Popular de Lucha Emiliano Zapata de Querétaro; Movimiento Vida Digna del Estado de México; Movimiento Campesino de San Luis Potosí; Movimiento Campesino de Guanajuato; Unión de Crédito de Zacatecas.

temporary registration, which allowed the PT to run candidates in the August election, was so expeditiously approved. Second, the PT purportedly failed to meet the letter of the Federal Electoral Code.[14] Third, of ten or so parties that applied for registration, only the PT was successful, along with re-registration of the PRT. Many parties soliciting registration in 1990, such as the Green Party and the party headed by PRI breakaway Rodolfo González, argued that only political favoritism could explain the rejection of their applications and the approval of the PT's. The fourth and most significant factor was that many PT members (including the most influential, such as the CDP) had been beneficiaries of PRONASOL programs and so had long been suspected of collaborating with the enemy. The PT is often referred to as the party of PRONASOL and the *"partido salinista."*

Many went so far as to characterize the party as created by Salinas himself, in the tradition of other state-sanctioned and affiliated parties such as the PARM, PPS, and PFCRN. According to this view, Salinas created the PT to split the PRD vote while simultaneously building support for himself and the regime.

Deliberations over the PT's formation exacerbated splits within the OIR-LM (and the National Coordinating Committee of the Urban Popular Movement, CONAMUP) which had been present since the 1989 *convenio* signings. When the decision was made to form the PT, a number of movements split off, adding their numbers to those ex-OIRistas who had already broken ranks to join the Cárdenas forces. For example, two important labor factions that had previously participated in OIR-LM (the UNAM and CNTE unions) refused to join with the PT. Many opposition forces went further, condemning the decision to form the PT.[15]

The PT failed to receive 1.5 percent of the national vote in the August 1991 midterm elections, garnering only 260,000 out of 24 million votes cast. This forced the PT to devote considerable time and resources to gain registration via the difficult path of holding state assemblies, something the PRD had been unable to accomplish.[16] The PT's ability to keep its registration is contingent on gaining 1.5 percent of the vote in future elections.

---

[14]Clause C of Point 3 of Article 33 of the new Código Federal de Instituciones y Procedimientos Electorales (COFIPE) stipulates that the successful candidate for registration must have been active for two years before soliciting registration. Commentators such as Ricardo Alemán claimed that while individual members of the PT surely had been in existence for more than two years, the PT as a party (and it was the party which was requesting registration) had not. For Alemán this was proof that the new code was not being respected (Alemán 1991).

[15]Hernández (1991a: 22) concludes that "the bulk of the militancy in the Federal District, the states of México, Veracruz, Guerrero, Morelos, Oaxaca, and Tabasco, and significant parts of La Laguna and Zacatecas view the national registration as an error."

[16]The PRD, after considerable debate, took over the Socialist Party's (PMS) registration rather than go through the arduous project of gaining its own registration via the holding of state conventions.

The initial decision to form the PT aimed in part to gain access to the large sums the state doles out to all registered political parties, and the additional funds made available by the Salinas administration. These resources were to advance the interests of member organizations and attract others to join. Anticipating winning elective offices, most often through proportional voting, PT representatives proposed using those offices likewise to advance themselves organizationally. While the PT is not likely to change the direction of national policy in most areas, it is a player in the Salinas administration's design and implementation of policies that affect the poor. The PT will probably continue to influence the administration of public works and grassroots development projects, particularly in areas where the party is strong. Should the PT falter, the CDP and other important member organizations will in all likelihood develop strategies to promote their respective organizations rather than submit their organizations to the PRD political project. The CDP's willingness to enter electoral or any other type of alliance or coalition with the PRD will continue to be a possibility. CDP decisions will be made in light of organizational empowerment, not according to the PRD's national strategic priorities. It is unlikely that the CDP would take political actions that jeopardized their favor with state reformers.

The CDP's decision to be the lead organization in the formation of the PT is consistent with the overriding logic of CDP actions, which traces back to conclusions reached in the 1970s regarding the advantages of combining negotiation and militancy in the pursuit of realistic goals. The fact that the PT lacks a coherent national program of governance is not particularly problematic and is far from inconsistent with the CDP mode of operation. The PT simply enhances member organizations' opportunities to provide services to the poor and empower themselves organizationally. While the PT failed to meet expectations in the 1991 midterm elections, of the 260,000 votes cast for the party, 36,000 went to the CDP-PT in the state of Durango. The CDP has continued to garner more votes with each succeeding election (6,000 votes in 1986; 12,000 in 1988; 18,000 in 1989; 36,000 in 1991). In the most recent elections (July 1992, described below) the CDP candidate for municipal president alone received 42,000 votes.

The position of Mass Line, and thus of the CDP, has always been that holding government positions or influencing policy outcomes are not goals in themselves but means to a greater end: power. The CDP is in constant pursuit of political, economic, and social power; within certain (but changing) limits, it will get it where and however it can. The CDP's efforts to enhance its power are made in the name of the Mexican poor, and more recently in the name of Durango's "citizenry." It claims to speak on behalf of those who are disadvantaged, oppressed, repressed, and marginalized by the existing system of political, economic, and social relationships. Its mission requires that practical considerations remain paramount. Because of practical, not doctrinal, considerations, the CDP is not and never has been an armed revolutionary movement. Similarly, it formed the PT and has participated in PRONASOL because practical considerations of organizational survival and the conditions of political power in Mexico made this the best course of action.

The PT should also be understood as one more step in the merging of electoral and social movement logics which have long divided the left in Mexico. The division between electoral activity and social movement activity remained quite clear-cut throughout the 1970s and into the early 1980s. Debate intensified during 1983 and 1984 over whether or not the steadfast resistance to electoral participation continued to be sound or whether it had outlived its usefulness.[17] One by one, movements entered into electoral races on the local and federal levels during the mid-1980s. The decisive year was 1988, when most popular movements, rural and urban, came out in support of the FDN and Cárdenas's presidential bid. In the wake of 1988—with much of the social left willing to participate in elections, if still wary of the costs (decreases in militancy, increased opportunities for co-optation, spreading scarce movement resources too thin as traditional movement concerns were augmented by the task of elections)—the question became what shape the new merger would take. The PT represents an important part of the answer. It enables movements to participate in elections on a platform that retains much of the old social left's language and priorities while also gaining the additional resources (and paying some of the costs) associated with electoral participation. The existing competition between the PT and the PRD for movement support, and the future relations between the two parties, will be an important element in the future of the Mexican left.

STATE-LEVEL ELECTIONS IN DURANGO, JULY 1992

The results of Durango's July 1992 statewide elections led political commentators to talk of a new balance of power in the state. While PRI candidate Maximiliano Silerio Esparza won the governor's race, almost half of the state legislature went to the opposition. Of twenty-five state deputies, thirteen are PRIístas and twelve are of the opposition: eight from the PAN, three from the CDP/PT, and one from the PRD. The opposition also won some important local races.

The CDP poured substantial resources into the campaign, concentrating on the candidacy of CDP leader "Gonzalo" Yáñez for municipal president in the capital city of Durango. The campaign and election results

---

[17]One of the most important instances of this debate took place within the National Coordinating Committee of the Urban Popular Movement (CONAMUP). On one side of the debate was the People's Revolutionary Movement (MRP) and movements closely affiliated to it, such as the Union of Popular Neighborhoods (UCP); on the other were movements tied to the OIR-LM, including the CDP. The former argued for electoral participation and ties with existing leftist political parties, while the OIR resisted such changes. For more details, see Haber 1992: chap. 3.

raise interesting questions about *concertación social* in the state of Durango. Yáñez's record in office will likewise provide interesting data concerning the political fortunes of popular movements willing and able to participate in *concertación*. Should momentum build toward a CDP challenge in the next governor's race, it would certainly test the next Mexican president's willingness to extend *concertación* to sponsoring new leadership that directly threatens the PRI's electoral power.

Yáñez won the three-way election with over 42,000 votes (the PRI candidate won 35,000; the PAN candidate, 33,000). How did the CDP win such an important office? A number of factors contributed to the result. First and most frequently cited was the amount spent on the campaign. Yáñez himself admitted spending 500 million pesos on the campaign (Reséndiz and Zamarripa 1992). Other estimates run even higher (author interviews), and it is generally agreed that CDP spending equaled or surpassed that of the PRI candidate.

Second, Yáñez is by most accounts an able campaigner. He ran a very effective populist campaign. He promised more effective administration of public resources. His language was inclusive, extending to the middle class. He made good use of the CDP's track record, now well established in Durango, of administering funds more honestly and effectively than competing parties. Thanks to PRONASOL, Yáñez was able to remind potential voters that the CDP has also garnered significant state resources.

PRONASOL funding—what passes to the CDP aboveboard, as well as cash transfers outside of official public accounting—was directly responsible for the CDP's ability to challenge traditional political contenders on the state level. The CDP has certainly gained political influence over the last decade. But it could not have won the municipal presidency in the state's capital without the political legitimacy and organizational empowerment born directly out of *concertación social* and PRONASOL.

Not unexpectedly, the election results were criticized. Charges were levied that the PRI's gubernatorial candidate instructed his followers to vote for the CDP candidate for municipal president, something Silerio has denied (Reséndiz and Zamarripa 1992). Also widely noted was the fact that CDP candidates for state deputyships received only 16,000 votes, in contrast to Yáñez's 42,000. While some cried fraud, a more likely explanation includes the factors discussed above: Yáñez is well known and popular in Durango, and he ran a brilliant and well-financed campaign. No other CDP candidate came close in terms of political talent or campaign monies.

Yáñez's campaign recalls the PRI in better days. He traveled from campaign stop to campaign stop handing out millions of pesos daily in support of highly visible and popular public works projects (church expansions, day care centers, health clinics, etc.). In each neighborhood, Yáñez pledged the CDP to work steadfastly on the demands put forward by each community. He told crowds that the CDP, win or lose, would continue to work toward meeting their demands. The seed money left behind and the CDP's growing credibility as an effective organization lured voters away from traditional politicians and parties (both the PRI and the PAN) as well as new parties (the PRD).

The CDP's effort to establish itself as a capable administrator of public works did not begin with the advent of PRONASOL. Nor has disillusionment with the PRI or the PAN been born overnight in Durango. PRONASOL funds are responsible, however, for the CDP's ability to extend into new areas, including working-class and middle-class neighborhoods previously dominated by the PRI or PAN. PRONASOL has also introduced a high-profile program in a region where traditional electoral powers have been unable to match the CDP's financial efficiency in implementing public works, a central concern for Durango voters.

CONCLUSION

How are we to assess the CDP's actions and their implications for Mexican politics? As suggested at the outset of this chapter, it is theoretically possible for PRONASOL to enhance President Salinas's legitimacy (and his reluctance to institutionalize democratic electoral reforms for fear of losing political control during economic transformation) while simultaneously contributing to democratization via alternative routes. The CDP's changing political behavior and political fortunes provide support for this theory.

In 1988–1989, the CDP undertook a series of actions favored by the Salinas team, who were then initiating programs to shore up the administration's image and further its definition of economic and political reform. Neoliberal economic reforms demanded fiscal conservancy, and this led to cuts in general subsidies in favor of programs targeted toward the poor and its representatives. This strategy serves the administration's goals of increasing political and economic efficiency, undermining dangerous opposition, and creating the perception of a strong and somewhat just government, able to implement radical economic reforms while maintaining political stability. Such programs, in Mexico and elsewhere, are not carried out only to benefit the poor. Political stability is a necessary, though perhaps not sufficient, condition for creating a prosperous investment environment. Salinas must project the image of political capacity and stability to the Mexican middle class, and to investment capital, both domestic and foreign.

The CDP and other popular movements following similar paths since 1988 have aided the Salinas project. In so doing, they have also contributed to their own organizational empowerment, and thus to a more pluralistic Mexico. I base this conclusion on my conviction that the CDP represents the interests of Durango's poorer citizens better than do the alternatives. Should Municipal President Yáñez succeed at building political relationships that channel significant discretionary funding to his administration, the CDP may go a long way toward demonstrating that it is a rational choice for the working and middle classes as well.

Advocates of popular movement involvement in PRONASOL see it as the type of antipoverty program for which the movements have long advocated. It transfers resources, however limited, to popular movement organizations best situated to deliver badly needed basic services. Few PRONASOL advocates within the popular movement sector would claim that the program is adequately funded. Nor would they deny that a large percentage of its funding is directed more for political reasons than to mitigate poverty. However, advocates argue, it is there and it is an improvement over the past. This is the criterion against which progress must be measured. While this relationship may contain elements of clientelism, through it the state is empowering popular movements that demand and exercise a more just distribution of resources, both political and economic. Popular movements such as the CDP would be the first to argue that they still lack the power and resources needed to meet the vast needs of the poor they represent. But again, it is more than was previously possible. This is an essential element of liberalization, an important development in Mexico's complex—and uncertain—path to democratization.

14

National Solidarity in the Northern Borderlands: Social Participation and Community Leadership

Oscar F. Contreras and *Vivienne Bennett*

INTRODUCTION

The National Solidarity Program represents a turning point in the Mexican government's social policy. Its breadth and vitality make it an unprecedented response to a prolonged economic crisis which in 1988 took on the dimensions of a profound political crisis and placed the continuity of the Mexican political system in jeopardy. PRONASOL's programmatic principles mark a significant change in the conceptualization of state management of social welfare.

President Salinas launched the National Solidarity Program during the first public event of his government in December 1988, while protests and street mobilizations still challenged the presidential election results. He framed it as aimed at the "productive improvement of popular welfare," one of his administration's four basic commitments. At that same December 1988 event, Salinas defined his central objective to be the eradication of extreme poverty in the country and an improved standard of living for the population, with a plan for social co-responsibility and participation (Salinas de Gortari 1988).[1]

The authors wish to thank Sergio Hernández for his contribution to an earlier version of this work, and Maritza Pérez and Martha Parada for their support in the preparation of the materials and manuscript. Translation by Aníbal Yáñez.

[1]Later the global objectives enunciated in the president's speech were grouped into three strategic areas: "Solidaridad para el Bienestar," which seeks to address problems related to health, education, food, supplies, housing, and urban services; "Solidaridad para la Producción," centered on building infrastructure for agriculture and livestock activities, providing direct support for peasants, and fostering agroindustry and microindustries; and "Solidaridad para el Desarrollo Regional," which includes infrastructure with a regional impact as well as integrated programs for specific groups and geographical zones (PRONASOL 1990b: 7).

Four years after that announcement, the Solidarity Program occupies a central place on the Mexican government's social agenda and in its political strategy. Economic stabilization and political negotiation are undoubtedly the arenas where Salinas has garnered his greatest successes, and in this context the program has consolidated its presence to the point of becoming the main link in a new social policy which seeks to reconcile the social costs of economic adjustment with the government's promise of equitable development (Dresser 1992b).

Some general data can give an idea of the program's importance. Resources channeled through Solidarity rose from 1.064 billion pesos in 1989 to 6.8 billion in 1992 (Consejo Consultivo del Programa Nacional de Solidaridad 1992). This figure represents less than 4 percent of the government's programmable spending[2] and 7.7 percent of its social spending. However, Solidarity's resources represent 17.6 percent of investment spending and 45 percent of investment in social development (Peón Escalante 1992). In other words, by 1992 nearly half of all public investment in social development was channeled through Solidarity.

Among the most salient features of the program, and perhaps those that distinguish it from previous government antipoverty programs, are its direct appeal to community participation and the beneficiaries' co-responsibility in promoting development. The main social agents in this plan for participation and co-responsibility are the Solidarity Committees created by the communities themselves.[3] According to official figures, a total of 25,354 Solidarity Committees were created throughout Mexico between 1989 and 1990, and 46,052 committees were created in 1991, for a total of 71,405 committees established in the first three years of the program's operation.

The growing amount of resources channeled through Solidarity, as well as the political consequences inherent to its operational plan, have been the subject of interminable controversy from the very inception of the program. One of the most heated points concerns the political character of the program and of the Solidarity Committees.

In this chapter we examine some implications of the organizational model promoted by Solidarity. First, we present data that allow us to determine the magnitude and explore the characteristics of social participation. Next we analyze the mechanisms for incorporating preexisting community leadership into the committee structure, and some implications of this for the committees themselves, their internal structure, and

---

[2]Programmable spending is total spending minus debt service minus revenue sharing. *Translator's note.*

[3]In the words of the program's national coordinator, the Solidarity Committees are the means by which "the community exercises direct democracy by electing its representatives, deciding which works and projects will be carried out, establishing each family's contributions and responsibility, controlling the quality of the work, and evaluating the results based on the resources which have been allocated and the goals which have been established" (C. Rojas 1991a).

their forms of decision making. Overall, the chapter documents the degree to which Solidarity's organizational model has penetrated the beneficiary communities, analyzes the differences among three northern border cities, and explores Solidarity's potential repercussions in the organizational fabric of the local communities.

The analysis focuses on three border cities: Tijuana and Mexicali in the state of Baja California, and Nuevo Laredo in the state of Tamaulipas. The data are from two surveys carried out in 1991, one with leaders of 199 Solidarity Committees and the other among beneficiaries of the Solidarity Program (see chapter appendix).

The Solidarity Program and Social Participation

Four years after its creation, it is clear that Solidarity is more than an emergency program to temper the social discontent generated by the crisis; it is a vast and ambitious strategy which operates simultaneously on various fronts. In the first place, it develops social programs intended to combat conditions of extreme poverty among peasant groups, indigenous peoples, and the urban poor (conditions largely inherited from the previous economic model and aggravated dramatically during the 1980s), as well as to soften the inequalities and social isolation caused by the transition to the new model, characterized by economic opening and privatization. Second, the program generates integrated regional development projects with broad coverage, in which infrastructure construction with a regional impact plays an important part. A third component of the program, just begun in 1992, consists of developing productive projects for the creation of permanent jobs. This represents a renewed emphasis of the program, a sort of "second stage" that aims to go beyond taking care of the urgent backlog in infrastructure and services.[4] Finally, and this is the point we hope to highlight, the program promotes the creation of structures for participation by the community (the Solidarity Committees), which entail principles of cooperation and social responsibility at all stages of the projects and activities that are carried out.

Taken as a whole, the program's four components are aimed at producing a qualitative change in the conception of social policy. On the one hand, the program seeks to raise the level of welfare of the population in the context of significantly diminished real public spending, first as a consequence of the crisis and later as part of the government strategy of reshaping the role of the state. On the other hand, the

---

[4]Carlos Rojas, national coordinator of the program, declared in an interview that, "The social program part—health, education, roads, urban development, regulation of land ownership—is the part that we already have in motion. . . . We need the second part. . . . The Solidarity Program will not be complete if we cannot construct an employment and income alternative among these same marginalized groups, indigenous peoples, people in the poorest neighborhoods, and peasants in the poorest areas. This is the principal goal of the Solidarity Program" (Reyes Heroles and Delgado 1991).

emphasis on community participation entails a plan for real social participation in defining priorities and implementing program projects.

Thus, from the government's viewpoint, Solidarity represents a key point on the agenda for modernizing the state, in the search for a new relationship between government and society. The (self-)criticism of state intervention and of the politics of redistribution entails a redefinition of the state's role, in terms of both the quantity and the quality of its regulatory functions. Salinas has defined this as the passage from "the proprietary state to the solidarity state."

A corollary of this re-posing of the state's role is one of Solidarity's explicit objectives: to promote the social welfare of the population living in poverty through their organized participation in government programs.

During an interview in late 1991, in answer to a question on the political utilization of PRONASOL, Carlos Rojas said:

> What is most important, and it is a political effect, is for us to be able to establish a different relationship between citizens and institutions. That we . . . not only seek or have justice as a goal, seek to bring social services to the communities . . . but to do it in another way. The program has a very important characteristic: we do not initiate any public action unless we first have an assembly where a Solidarity Committee is elected in a democratic way. . . . In some cases the committees themselves not only plan their program but also carry it out, administer the resources and then evaluate it. . . . This has enabled us to generate true genuine social oversight (in Reyes Heroles and Delgado 1991).

This government call for organized community participation has generated numerous interpretations regarding the character, the intensity, and the political repercussions of such participation. Regarding the significance of participation and its repercussions, we find four different positions in the literature.

The first interpretation maintains that Solidarity's emphasis on organization and co-responsible participation between society and government has allowed it to become the principal pathway to renewed forms of association in Mexican society, "attempting to gainfully and harmoniously integrate the different groups and movements that are arising today alongside older and more established ones." It is also argued that the program "is the motor for a democratic reform of the state and of federalism in general," which "has put society in motion from below," and that this mobilization "opens up a political-democratic space for a more productive and fruitful relationship between society and the state" (cf. González Tiburcio 1992; Martínez Nateras 1992b).

At the opposite extreme, a radical interpretation holds that the social organization promoted through the Solidarity Committees is part of a long-range plan spearheaded by Salinas and aimed at reformulating the bases of support of the Mexican political system in the context of structural adjustment. This would occur by displacing traditional leaderships and weakening corporatist organizations. According to this view, the committees are the foundation for a new structure of incorporation, organization, and control, upon which the government is attempting to reconstitute the social bases of the regime (Dresser 1991).

A third position, which is quite close to the previous one, argues that in addition to being part of a strategic neo-corporatist project, the organizational structures created through the Solidarity Committees are used by the government to deactivate or weaken autonomous and independent social organizations (Bartra 1992).

The fourth and last interpretation proposes focusing on participation in a limited sense, directly related to the content of the programs: "that of the intervention of the poor in the execution of concrete works for the betterment of their standard of living" (Provencio 1992). While not dismissing the possibility that these schemes may result in a new form of political manipulation, this view emphasizes the fact that the relationship between participation in the programs and the broader political process is not a direct one; rather, it manifests itself through creating and strengthening the basic associative ties that promote participation in a broad sense (Provencio 1992). From this point of view, as Hirschman has shown in another context, what should be noted is that collective participation in social welfare programs tends to produce a series of unplanned collateral effects (or "intangible benefits") of an interactive and organizational nature, besides the net benefits directly associated with the projects' goals. Participants get to know each other, discuss their problems, make plans for the future, etc. That is, they create new social networks and increase their organizational experience, which in turn becomes part of the community's stock of "social energy" (Hirschman 1986).[5]

SOLIDARITY ON THE BORDER: THE INTENSITY AND CHARACTER OF SOCIAL PARTICIPATION

One notable finding of the survey of beneficiaries in Tijuana, Mexicali, and Nuevo Laredo is the broad coverage achieved by PRONASOL in these cities. A total of 303,223 families were benefited, a figure that

[5]Other theories of collective movements, particularly those that place emphasis on action, have underlined the importance of "membership networks" as the premise for participation in collective actions, as well as the fact that collective action promotes the transfer of preexisting resources (organizational, political, cultural) to new objectives for transformation. Also, they emphasize the existence of certain prerequisites of leadership that are inherent in mobilization. See, for example, Melucci 1985; Obershall 1972.

includes 55 percent of households in Tijuana, 69 percent of those in Mexicali, and 100 percent of those in Nuevo Laredo. The urban infrastructure, school improvement, and electrification programs were most important. However, this coverage is not directly reflected in the community's level of participation. Due to a lack of precise information on the projects and how Solidarity works, a very low proportion of direct beneficiaries know that the improvements under way in their immediate surroundings (quarter, neighborhood, or block) are being carried out by Solidarity. While 92 percent of the population surveyed had heard of the program, only 25 percent knew that there were Solidarity projects in their neighborhood. Partly for this reason, and also because larger-scale works still follow traditional planning and execution mechanisms, community participation is relatively low, as shown in figure 14.1.

It is estimated that a total of 38,862 heads of benefited families in the three cities analyzed had some degree of real participation in the development of Solidarity's programs. Considering that 476 committees were registered in these same cities at the time of the survey, the social participation average comes to 81 participating people per committee.

On the other hand, the beneficiaries' perception of the program shows little understanding of its organizational and participatory contents. In general, their opinion continues to be based on an instrumental and assistance-oriented view of the role of government (figures 14.2 through 14.5).

An initial general overview of these data leads us to posit that there are three forms of participation that should be taken into account when considering social participation in Solidarity programs:

- Participation for purely instrumental reasons, in order to obtain government transfers channeled through the program. This is suggested by the data on the subjective perception of the program: for the most part the beneficiaries refer to Solidarity as a program of "government aid for the poor" or of public works and services provided by the government.

- Participation for political-instrumental reasons, when participation occurs through already existing community organizations that join Solidarity programs as a way to obtain additional political and material resources.

- Participation for political-social reasons, in cases where participation transcends the instrumental plane and results in a certain redefinition of the basic components of social action. Only in these cases are the conditions created for the development of a broad social transformation, one able to effectively influence the state-society relationship.

Thus, we can expect that the participation of organized communities by means of committees will show a wide range of variation—both

Figure 14.1

Beneficiary Population's Knowledge about and Participation in Solidarity

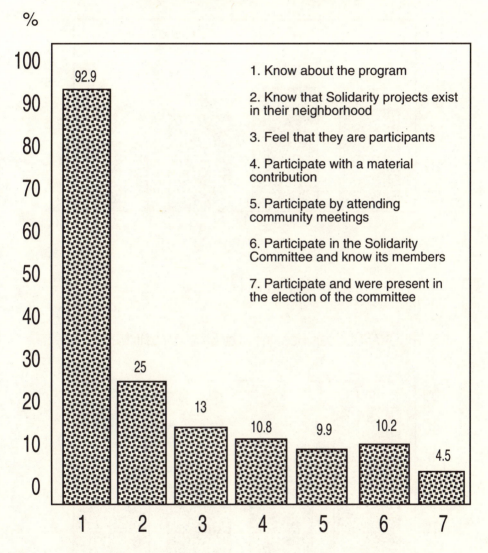

Source (figures 14.1-14.5): Depto. de Estudios Sociales, COLEF, Encuesta de Evaluación del Programa Nacional de Solidaridad, Tijuana, B.C., 1991.

Figure 14.2

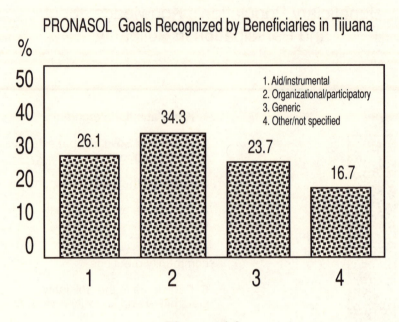

PRONASOL Goals Recognized by Beneficiaries in Tijuana

%

1. Aid/instrumental
2. Organizational/participatory
3. Generic
4. Other/not specified

26.1   34.3   23.7   16.7

1   2   3   4

Figure 14.3

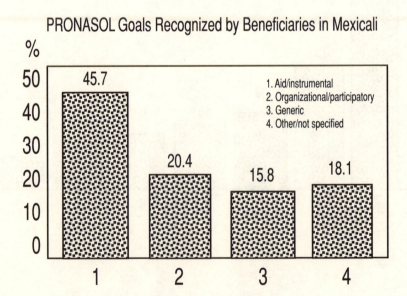

PRONASOL Goals Recognized by Beneficiaries in Mexicali

%

1. Aid/instrumental
2. Organizational/participatory
3. Generic
4. Other/not specified

45.7   20.4   15.8   18.1

1   2   3   4

Figure 14.4

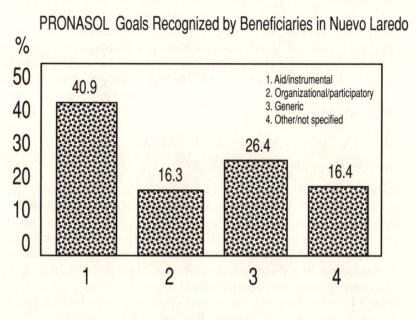

PRONASOL Goals Recognized by Beneficiaries in Nuevo Laredo

%

- 1. Aid/instrumental
- 2. Organizational/participatory
- 3. Generic
- 4. Other/not specified

40.9
16.3
26.4
16.4

1   2   3   4

Figure 14.5

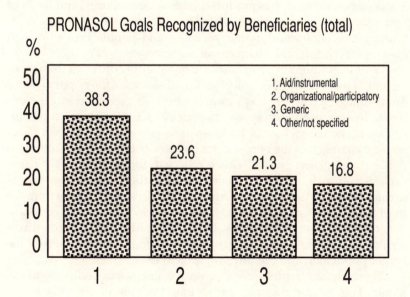

PRONASOL Goals Recognized by Beneficiaries (total)

%

- 1. Aid/instrumental
- 2. Organizational/participatory
- 3. Generic
- 4. Other/not specified

38.3
23.6
21.3
16.8

1   2   3   4

in intensity and extent and in the very character of participation—in a spectrum that goes from the instrumental to the societal. At the spectrum's lowest point, participation is limited to the minimum presence and contribution necessary to secure transfers; at its highest point it means the organizational and political transformation of the community. The information analyzed thus far does not permit us to precisely estimate this aspect. However, it does allow us to suggest that the potential associative-political effect of Solidarity programs works upon only a tenth of the population benefiting from these programs (columns 4–6 of figure 14.1).

OTHER ORGANIZATIONS AND LEADERS IN SOLIDARITY

THE SOCIAL AND POLITICAL CONTEXT

Tijuana, Mexicali, and Nuevo Laredo differ in terms of social and political structure. At the same time, they have commonalities stemming from being border cities: not only from their geographical proximity to the United States but above all from their intense economic and social interaction with that country. Throughout their history the three cities have experienced a significant development of commercial and service activities (Tijuana), agroindustry (Mexicali), and large- scale trade flows (Nuevo Laredo). Recently these three cities have been undergoing an important process of industrialization linked to the expansion of *maquiladora* activity.

This interaction, a feature which they share with the most important northern border cities, has produced rates of development and levels of well-being which are markedly above national averages. All three cities have open economies, dynamic societies, and populations with high geographic, social, and occupational mobility.

While conditions in these cities are qualitatively different from other regions of the country, they still place broad sectors of the population at a disadvantage, excluding them from the benefits generated by development. In this economic space characterized by rapid development, serious economic and social backwardness persists since the very economic dynamism of the border cities has produced persisting immigration and population growth. This is reflected, for example, in the cities' explosive growth, which has overwhelmed their capacity to supply urban land and housing, as well as public services of all types—from the most basic such as potable water, sewers, and electricity, to paved roads, street lighting, and public safety. Land ownership, housing, and urban services lag the most, and they are clearly tied to the social growth of the border population and the physical growth of the cities.

These characteristics have a corresponding social and political dynamic. Tijuana, for example, with a long tradition of collective action and protests and a very active and demanding civil society, has played a significant role in deciding the present political course of Baja California by providing the principal support for the election of an opposition state governor. The long and rich experience of Mexicali's popular organizations has generated an extensive network of organizations (both official and independent) focused on urban demands. In Nuevo Laredo, which has a political structure largely dominated by labor corporatism, the demands for participation by new social groups have begun to erode the bases of traditional domination embodied in the local union bureaucracy.

Within this heterogeneous picture, a feature the three cities share is that Solidarity occupies a central place in the local political scene. It has become a crucial point of reference toward which the various local political actors must take a position. Solidarity's presence represents a challenge in terms of representation and control, particularly for the social leaderships and political organizations linked to the urban movements.

For community leaders with clientelist ties (mostly, but not exclusively, those linked to the PRI), the new organizational proposal based on community participation and co-responsibility represents a threat to the clientelist type of relationship they had maintained with the government and political parties. This is because it questions the functionality of their political mediation and, therefore, their very reason to exist. However, the threat is no less serious for the independent organizations, as many of their traditional demands have begun to be channeled through the Solidarity programs.

ORGANIZATIONS AND LEADERSHIPS

A range of organized groups with different interests and capacities for collective action occupy a central place in a social-political project such as that promoted by Solidarity. In particular, squatters' or neighborhood organizations take on special importance since they proliferate in the cities' marginal areas and bring together the most demanding sectors of the urban population. Furthermore, in this milieu community leaders are usually the principal channel of political intermediation between group demands and government action.[6]

At this point it should be recalled that, according to procedures established by PRONASOL, Solidarity Committees are to be formed through a public call for a neighborhood assembly, in which participants discuss their community's priorities and democratically elect representatives. These representatives are responsible for managing and coordinating activities with Solidarity and with public agencies involved in the projects agreed upon with Solidarity's promoters.

---

[6]The emergence of urban popular movements in most Mexican cities can be dated to the beginning of the 1970s. The works of Ramírez Saiz (1986) and Bennett (1992a) analyze the development of these movements and the evolution of the relationship between urban popular movements and the state through the 1970s and 1980s.

There are various ways for Solidarity Committee leaderships to be formed. The first is that community members elect as representatives individuals who are already leaders of other organizations (neighborhood groups, parties, unions, etc.) and whose organizational work is recognized by the community. In some cases leaders are elected because of their individual capacities, and in others because voters identify them with their respective organization. The second possibility is that the neighborhood assembly may choose to replace traditional leaders with people not tied to organizations or groups that had previously represented the community. A third possibility is that the community may have very weak or nonexistent recognized leaders or organizations; in these cases, forming a Solidarity Committee entails creating a new structure without significant organizational antecedents.

These three possibilities have been outlined in figure 14.6 in order to explore their repercussions in the social fabric of the communities. Even though multiple combinations are possible, to simplify matters we only explore three outcomes. Thus, only those structures generated in communities where no previous organization existed, or generated on the basis of new leaders with no previous leadership experience, are considered to be new organizational structures. On the other hand, the restructuring of organizations and/or leaderships occurs when committees are formed by incorporating members from organizations that predate the committee. The inclusion of such leaders enriches the committee structure with the community's previous organizational experience. In both cases, whether it is a matter of new or incorporated leaderships, upon entering the committee, leaders must work within a structure with organizational rules and channels to transmit demands that are defined by the program's norms and based on a new network of alliances developed around Solidarity.

In this scheme, the impacts on the organizational fabric of local societies can be summarized in three types of outcomes: (1) The creation of new organizational structures when the program is implemented in weakly organized communities or those without well-defined leaderships. (2) The adaptation of preexisting organizations when they become involved in the program and adopt its norms; in these cases the extent of the organization's internal transformations depends upon its flexibility and the degree of control exercised by its leaders.[7] (3) The weakening of previous organizational structures and leaders who are displaced as intermediaries when new leaders are elected to represent the community's specific interests through the Solidarity Committee.

---

[7]However, what remains to be explored is the intensity of the adaptation that is experienced; one might expect different results in cases where, for example, local leaderships decide to take advantage of the program's benefits for instrumental reasons (using the program as a resource to increase their control and influence), in contrast to situations in which the program's norms become a part of an organization's regular practice (such as public discussions, direct elections, etc.).

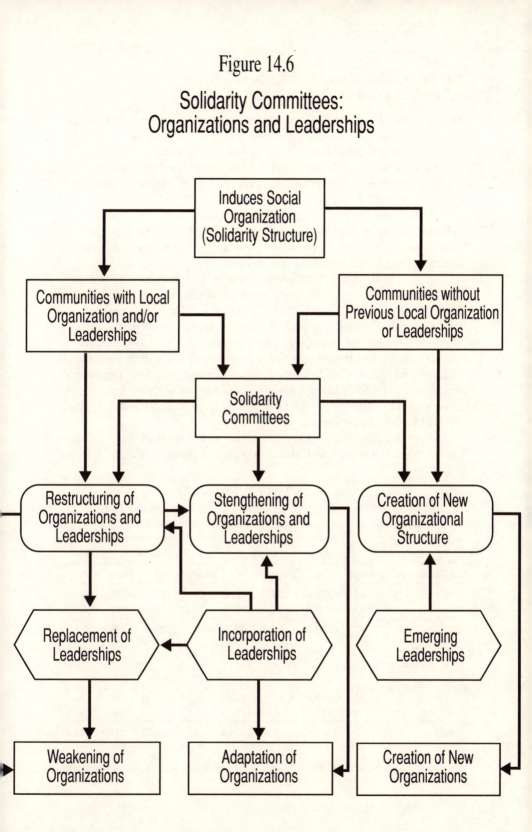

Figure 14.6

Solidarity Committees:
Organizations and Leaderships

Induces Social Organization (Solidarity Structure)

Communities with Local Organization and/or Leaderships

Communities without Previous Local Organization or Leaderships

Solidarity Committees

Restructuring of Organizations and Leaderships

Stengthening of Organizations and Leaderships

Creation of New Organizational Structure

Replacement of Leaderships

Incorporation of Leaderships

Emerging Leaderships

Weakening of Organizations

Adaptation of Organizations

Creation of New Organizations

The Organizational Experience of
Solidarity Committee Leadership

The creation of Solidarity Committees has strengthened the organizational structures of some communities. At the same time, new spaces for leadership and representation have opened up in others.

As shown in table 14.1, Solidarity's operations in Tijuana and Mexicali have been based mainly on preexisting community leaders and organizations (73.6 and 81.6 percent, respectively). In Nuevo Laredo, on the other hand, a high percentage of communities that now have Solidarity Committees had no previous organization or leaderships; here Solidarity's efforts have been aimed at creating new organizational structures (82.5 percent of the committees).

Tijuana and Mexicali show very similar proportions of Solidarity projects carried out with the support of previously existing community leaderships or organizations. This similarity may have two complementary explanations: on the one hand, popular sectors in both Tijuana and Mexicali have extensive organizational experience, which is lacking in Nuevo Laredo. On the other hand, internal conflicts within the official PRI party in Nuevo Laredo seem to have oriented Solidarity promoters' organizational efforts toward creating committees with no links to the most organized and influential sector in the local political structure, i.e., the CTM trade union bureaucracy.

Table 14.1 also shows that more than one-fourth of all Solidarity Committees have explicit links to a political party, and that a large

Table 14.1
Solidarity Committees That Arose from a Preexisting
Community Organization, and Party Affiliation, by City

Previous Organization	Tijuana Freq.	%	Mexicali Freq.	%	N. Laredo Freq.	%	Total Freq.	%
Yes	64	(73.6)	40	(81.6)	11	(17.5)	115	(57.8)
No	23	(26.4)	9	(18.4)	52	(82.5)	84	(42.2)
Total	87	(100.0)	49	(100.0)	63	(100.0)	199	(100.0)
Have Party Affiliation	33	(37.9)	14	(28.6)	6	(9.5)	53	(26.6)
Party Affiliation								
PRI	29	(87.9)	12	(85.7)	6	(100.0)	47	(90.4)
Other	4	(12.1)	2	(14.7)	–	–	6	(11.5)
Total	33	(100.0)	14	(100.0)	6	(100.0)	53	(100.0)

Source: COLEF, Departamento de Estudios Sociales, Encuesta de Evaluación del Programa Nacional de Solidaridad, Tijuana, Baja California, 1991.

majority of these are linked to the PRI (90.4 percent). While these data refer exclusively to committee leaders who stated explicitly that they had a party affiliation, statements gathered in the course of the research allow us to assume that there are many implicit links with party organizations; in this sense the PRI's presence within Solidarity Committees is even greater.

Table 14.2 shows two different patterns in the experience of the committee leaderships: in Tijuana and Mexicali, the majority of the committees were formed in communities (schools, neighborhoods, blocks) where some type of leadership already existed. This is true for 67.8 percent of committees in Tijuana and 77.6 percent in Mexicali. Furthermore, in both cases a significant percentage of previous leaders (66.1 percent in Tijuana, 63.2 percent in Mexicali) became leaders of Solidarity Committees.

In contrast, in Nuevo Laredo only 17.5 percent of the committees operate in communities with previous leaderships. Further, of this smaller percentage only 27.3 percent of prior leaders joined the committees.

As mentioned above, the fact that previous leaders do not join may reflect their replacement by new leaders. There is another explanation as well for their not joining: if there was more than one leader in the community but only one committee was formed, it was not possible to fully incorporate all previous leaders. Of the committee leaders interviewed, 80.8 percent stated that there was only one committee in their neighborhood. Overall, however, three times out of five, leaders with previous experience did join the Solidarity structure. The incorporation of prior leaders may be interpreted (following Hirschman 1986) as a way

TABLE 14.2

SOLIDARITY COMMITTEES THAT OPERATE IN COMMUNITIES WHERE COMMUNITY LEADERS ALREADY EXISTED, BY CITY

	Tijuana		Mexicali		N. Laredo		Total	
	Freq.	%	Freq.	%	Freq.	%	Freq.	%
Without previous leaders	28	(32.2)	11	(22.4)	52	(82.5)	91	(45.7)
With previous leaders	59	(67.8)	38	(77.6)	11	(17.5)	108	(54.3)
Total	87	(100.0)	49	(100.0)	63	(100.0)	199	(100.0)
Incorporated leaders	39	(66.1)	24	(63.2)	3	(27.3)	66	(61.1)
Nonincorporated leaders	20	(33.9)	14	(36.8)	8	(72.7)	42	(38.9)
Total	59	(100.0)	38	(100.0)	11	(100.0)	108	(100.0)

Source: COLEF, Departamento de Estudios Sociales, Encuesta de Evaluación del Programa Nacional de Solidaridad, Tijuana, Baja California, 1991.

for the community to use its stock of organizational experience to further the creation and functioning of new organizational structures, while their nonincorporation would be a squandering of this resource.

From another point of view, the nonincorporation of prior leaders could be a way to deactivate or weaken preexisting organizations (Dresser 1992b; Bartra 1992), to the degree that those leaders who are incorporated appropriate the channels for transmitting demands and become the social agents mediating between community and government.

The organizations that predominate as the source of leadership transfers in Mexico's northern border cities are trade unions, neighborhood or squatters' organizations, and political parties (table 14.3). In Mexicali and Nuevo Laredo, a large majority of the leaders were members of trade unions or political parties before and after joining Solidarity Committees. In Tijuana a significant number of leaders belonged to neighborhood organizations both before and after joining the committees. While in Mexicali only 12.3 percent of leaders belong to neighborhood organizations and in Nuevo Laredo only 14.3 percent, in Tijuana the figure is 31.0 percent. Out of 209 leaders who belonged to other social organizations before the Solidarity Committees were formed, 169 belonged to other social organizations after becoming committee leaders. Leaders who belonged to other social organizations in the past,

TABLE 14.3

LEADERS' MEMBERSHIP IN OTHER SOCIAL ORGANIZATIONS BEFORE
THE FORMATION OF THE SOLIDARITY COMMITTEE, BY CITY

	Tijuana		Mexicali		N. Laredo		Total	
	Freq.	%	Freq.	%	Freq.	%	Freq.	%
Type of Organization to Which You Belonged								
Trade union	19	(16.8)	22	(37.9)	13	(34.2)	54	(25.8)
Neighborhood organization	40	(35.4)	11	(19.0)	7	(18.4)	58	(27.8)
Political party	30	(26.5)	21	(36.2)	10	(26.3)	61	(29.2)
Other	24	(21.3)	4	(6.8)	8	(21.1)	36	(17.2)
Total	113	(100.0)	58	(100.0)	38	(100.0)	209	(100.0)
Type of Organization to Which You Belong								
Trade union	15	(17.9)	22	(38.6)	9	(32.1)	46	(27.2)
Neighborhood organization	26	(31.0)	7	(12.3)	4	(14.3)	37	(21.9)
Political party	25	(29.8)	25	(43.9)	10	(35.7)	60	(35.5)
Other	18	(21.4)	3	(5.3)	5	(17.8)	26	(15.4)
Total	84	(100.0)	57	(100.0)	28	(100.0)	169	(100.0)

Source: COLEF, Departamento de Estudios Sociales, Encuesta de Evaluación del Programa Nacional de Solidaridad, Tijuana, Baja California, 1991.

as well as those who currently belong, bring their organizational experience to the work of the committees.

It is important to note that most of the organizational experience presumably incorporated into the functioning of the committees comes from individuals whose previous experience was as leaders (32.1 percent) or as middle cadres (25.8 percent) of other social organizations (table 14.4). This implies that a majority of committee leaders have had concrete experience in taking responsibility for the effective functioning of a social organization. Whether as leaders or middle cadres of other organizations, they bring to the Solidarity Committees the learning and maturity that comes from previous leadership experience and not only experience as participants. Even after joining Solidarity Committees, leaders who maintain their affiliation with other social organizations do so mostly as leadership (27.5 percent) or middle cadres (20.7 percent). The case of Tijuana is noteworthy because of the high percentage of committee leaders who had (43.3 percent) and continue to have (42.5 percent) leadership posts in other social organizations.

SOLIDARITY COMMITTEES: STRUCTURE AND DECISION MAKING

Solidarity Committees vary in structure, from a minimal structure comprising a president, secretary, treasurer, and council members (*vocales*); to a minimal structure plus a project subcommittee; to a minimal structure plus other subcommittees. In Tijuana the structure of the committees is more diversified than in Mexicali and Nuevo Laredo (table 14.5);

TABLE 14.4
STATUS OF THE LEADERS IN THEIR ORIGINAL ORGANIZATION,
BEFORE AND AFTER JOINING THE SOLIDARITY COMMITTEE

	Tijuana		Mexicali		N. Laredo		Total	
	Freq.	%	Freq.	%	Freq.	%	Freq.	%
Before Joining the Committee								
Leader	48	(43.3)	10	(17.2)	9	(23.7)	67	(32.1)
Middle cadre	23	(20.7)	15	(25.9)	16	(42.1)	54	(25.8)
Member	40	(36.0)	33	(56.9)	13	(34.2)	86	(41.1)
Total	111	(100.0)	58	(100.0)	38	(100.0)	209	(100.0)
After Joining the Committee								
Leader	34	(42.5)	8	(14.3)	3	(10.7)	45	(27.5)
Middle cadre	10	(12.5)	14	(25.0)	10	(35.7)	34	(20.7)
Member	36	(45.0)	34	(60.7)	15	(53.6)	85	(51.8)
Total	80	(100.0)	56	(100.0)	28	(100.0)	164	(100.0)

Source: COLEF, Departamento de Estudios Sociales, Encuesta de Evaluación del Programa Nacional de Solidaridad, Tijuana, Baja California, 1991.

TABLE 14.5
SOLIDARITY COMMITTEE STRUCTURE, BY CITY

	Tijuana		Mexicali		N. Laredo		Total	
	Freq.	%	Freq.	%	Freq.	%	Freq.	%
Minimal structure	40	(46.5)	42	(87.5)	61	(96.8)	143	(72.6)
Minimal structure + project subcommittee	24	(27.9)	3	(6.3)	1	(1.6)	28	(14.2)
Minimal structure + other subcommittee	22	(25.6)	3	(6.3)	1	(1.6)	26	(13.2)
Total	86	(100.0)	48	(100.0)	63	(100.0)	197	(100.0)

Source: COLEF, Departamento de Estudios Sociales, Encuesta de Evaluación del Programa Nacional de Solidaridad, Tijuana, Baja California, 1991.

46.5 percent of Tijuana committees have a minimal organizational structure; 27.9 percent also include a project subcommittee; and 25.6 percent also comprise other subcommittees. Mexicali and Nuevo Laredo resemble one another in that the traditional (minimal) organizational structure predominates over other broader forms of organization.

Although the Solidarity Committees in Mexicali come for the most part out of preexisting community organizations (table 14.1) while most of the committees in Nuevo Laredo did not arise from previous community organizations, in both cities the same minimal or traditional formal structure predominates over other forms of organization. It is not surprising that a minimal organization structure predominates in communities without organizational experience (Nuevo Laredo). However, what is noteworthy is that this structure predominates in Mexicali, a city with a significant tradition of association and a strong urban popular movement, and where more than 80 percent of the Solidarity Committees arose in communities with previous organizational experience.

Since the committee leaders of Mexicali belong in their majority to unions and political parties (and not to neighborhood organizations) (table 14.3), we cannot dismiss the possibility that leaders reproduce the centralized organizational structure that prevails in those types of organizations, resulting in the predominance of a minimal traditional form of organization.

In Tijuana, however, Solidarity Committees present a broader array of organizational structures; just under half have the minimal structure. Following the reasoning applied to the cases of Mexicali and Nuevo Laredo, in Tijuana too it may be said that committee leaders' organizational experience influences the organizational structure that is adopted. Thus, in Tijuana greater experience with neighborhood organizations would be reflected in a greater diversity in committee structure.

On the other hand, some elements of the local political context may contribute to the differences found in the committees' organizational structures. In Mexicali and Nuevo Laredo, despite marked differences in terms of organizational tradition, the promotion of Solidarity has remained in the hands of municipal authorities from the PRI, individuals closely identified with the federal government and with PRONASOL itself. Those authorities have had a greater and more direct influence on the formation of Solidarity Committees, which would explain why there are few committees with a projects subcommittee or other subcommittees. In other words, there are few committees with substructures that control and supervise projects, or that can broaden the committees' prerogatives.[8]

In terms of where proposals for committee activities originate (table 14.6), most arise from assemblies (50.5 percent) and some from committee leaders (35.7 percent) and promoters (13.8 percent). In Tijuana and Nuevo Laredo more than half of the activities being carried out by the committees were initiated by the assembly, and approximately one-fourth were initiated by committee leaders. In Tijuana, the assemblies' high level of participation in initiating activities may denote the fact that most committees arose from preexisting community organizations (table 14.1), and that a high proportion of leaders are affiliated to neighborhood organizations (table 14.3).

TABLE 14.6

SOLIDARITY COMMITTEES: ORIGIN OF PROPOSALS FOR ACTIVITIES THAT ARE CURRENTLY BEING CARRIED OUT, BY CITY

	Tijuana		Mexicali		N. Laredo		Total	
	Freq.	%	Freq.	%	Freq.	%	Freq.	%
Leaders	23	(28.4)	28	(59.6)	16	(26.7)	67	(35.7)
Promoters	10	(12.4)	8	(17.0)	8	(13.3)	26	(13.8)
Assembly	48	(59.2)	11	(23.4)	36	(60.0)	95	(50.5)
Others	3	(3.6)	1	(2.1)	2	(3.2)	6	(3.1)
Total	81	(100.0)	47	(100.0)	60	(100.0)	188	(100.0)

Source: COLEF, Departamento de Estudios Sociales, Encuesta de Evaluación del Programa Nacional de Solidaridad, Tijuana, Baja California, 1991.

[8]In the case of a committee with a minimal structure, the committee itself is responsible for deciding on and requesting projects that are needed by the community. However, there is no one within the committee's structure who is formally responsible for the contracting, control, and supervision of projects. Often this means that PRONASOL itself carries out these functions. In a committee that also has a project subcommittee, the latter's mission is the control and supervision of projects, as well as the occasional contracting of smaller projects, although very often the project subcommittee is made up of only one person who has the post but not the ability to effectively control and supervise. The existence of a project subcommittee is not a guarantee of greater committee autonomy; but the absence of such a subcommittee does imply that the committee is less able to control the project.

However, most committees in Nuevo Laredo did not arise from preexisting community organizations (table 14.1), and the leaders scarcely participate in neighborhood organizations (table 14.3); nevertheless, most committee proposals originate in assemblies. This may indicate that not having a previous form of organization—and therefore no organizational scheme that can serve as a point of reference and be replicated—has favored community participation.

In Mexicali, in contrast, there is a marked tendency for leaders to initiate committee activities. While committees in Mexicali come for the most part from preexisting community organizations (table 14.1), Mexicali committees, like those in Tijuana, show a strong tendency to organize with a traditional minimal structure, as noted in table 14.5. Mexicali's low community participation in initiating proposals for committee activities is linked to the minimal structure of the committees themselves.

The committees' decision-making mechanisms (table 14.7) reinforce the tendency prefigured in the committees' structures and in the origin of proposals for their activities: leaderships in Tijuana and Nuevo Laredo are more open to community participation in defining committee activities, and this feature extends to participation in decision making. In the case of Mexicali, committee leaders have overwhelmingly formed minimal organizational structures; in most cases they determine their own activities, and they concentrate decision making to a similar degree. In sum, there is no clear relationship between initial organizational conditions and the style of leadership generated within committees. The relationship between having previous organizations in the community (table 14.1), leaders' membership in social organizations (table 14.3), committee structure (table 14.5), and decision making (tables 14.6 and 14.7) can only be explained by taking into account factors such as earlier independent organizational experiences and the strength of the PRI and of the corporatist unions in each city. Thus, the fact that the majority of committees in Tijuana and Mexicali came out of previous organizations can be explained by those cities' earlier organizational experiences. However, the PRI's greater influence on committees in Mexicali (a municipality ruled by the PRI) is a factor in their more traditional structure and more centralized leadership style. In contrast, committees in Tijuana (a municipality ruled by the PAN and one in which Solidarity faces strong competition from local community support programs) reflect greater diversity in their organizational structure and greater decentralization in decision making since the presence of civil society and of noncorporatist organizations is greater.

The structure of committees and the way they initiate activities and make decisions have an impact on leaders' recommendations for improving the committees' work. In Tijuana, where the participation of the assemblies in initiating proposals and making decisions is relatively high, leaders prioritized strengthening committee organization in order

TABLE 14.7

SOLIDARITY COMMITTEES: PRINCIPAL DECISION-MAKING MECHANISM,
BY CITY

	Tijuana		Mexicali		N. Laredo		Total	
	Freq.	%	Freq.	%	Freq.	%	Freq.	%
Promoters' recommendations	14	(16.7)	5	(10.2)	7	(11.3)	26	(13.3)
Assembly resolutions	50	(59.5)	19	(38.8)	37	(59.7)	106	(54.4)
Leader resolutions	17	(20.2)	25	(51.0)	17	(27.4)	59	(30.3)
Other	3	(3.6)	—	—	1	(1.6)	4	(2.0)
Total	84	(100.0)	49	(100.0)	62	(100.0)	195	(100.0)

Source: COLEF, Departamento de Estudios Sociales, Encuesta de Evaluación del Programa Nacional de Solidaridad, Tijuana, Baja California, 1991.

to improve their work, although they also emphasized increasing the support received from authorities (table 14.8). In Nuevo Laredo, even though a large majority of the committees are organized on the basis of a minimal structure, the assemblies' participation in proposals and decision making is also relatively high, and it is reflected in the leaders' recommendations to strengthen committee organization to improve their work. However, in Mexicali, where a minimal committee structure

TABLE 14.8

SOLIDARITY COMMITTEE LEADERS: RECOMMENDATIONS TO IMPROVE
THE WORK OF THE COMMITTEES, BY CITY

	Tijuana		Mexicali		N. Laredo		Total	
	Freq.	%	Freq.	%	Freq.	%	Freq.	%
Strengthen committee organization	42	(57.5)	7	(17.9)	44	(80.0)	93	(55.7)
Strengthen support from authorities	21	(32.9)	30	(76.9)	5	(9.0)	56	(33.5)
Coordination between committees	7	(9.5)	1	(2.6)	3	(5.5)	11	(6.6)
Leadership training	3	(4.1)	1	(2.6)	3	(5.5)	7	(4.2)
Total	73	(100.0)	39	(100.0)	55	(100.0)	167	(100.0)

Source: COLEF, Departamento de Estudios Sociales, Encuesta de Evaluación del Programa Nacional de Solidaridad, Tijuana, Baja California, 1991.

prevails and where most proposals and decisions come from the leaders, not the assemblies, leaders recommend strengthening the support from authorities in order to improve the work of the committees.

What is noteworthy in table 14.8 is that leaders focus on both the organization of the committees *and* their relationship with the authorities as ways to improve the committees' work. This double focus is striking since an important component of Solidarity is social co-responsibility and participation of the community and the state in eradicating extreme poverty.

CONCLUSIONS

In this chapter we have examined some impacts of the National Solidarity Program on social participation and organizational networks in three northern border cities. Three of the most important findings follow.

First, the data on social participation in the program yield paradoxical results. While the figures on families benefited by Solidarity projects and actions indicate very broad program coverage, direct popular participation in these projects and actions involves just over 13 percent of the beneficiaries. For a program that sets itself the task of involving the population in "all stages of projects and actions that are developed," the penetration of the plan for co-responsibility between society and the state seems to be relatively meager.[9]

This fact leads us to question the more radical interpretations of Solidarity's impact on Mexican society. Indeed, the assertion that Solidarity represents a renewal of society's forms of association and that it is the engine of democratic reform—as well as the assumption that it is the embryo of a new structure of political control, whose mission is to reformulate the bases of the political system—are both excessive. The evidence points to a degree of social participation that does not correspond to the premise of society's broad and co-responsible participation. The majority of those who benefit from the program do so through government welfare transfers or through conventional public works.

On the other hand, even among beneficiaries who actively participate in the program's normative framework (that is, the segment who are members of Solidarity Committees or who contribute in some way to projects and actions), participation does not automatically translate into organizational recruitment or ideological acceptance of Solidarity's programmatic principles. In this regard, we have shown that a good part of the participation can be explained as expressing an instrumental attitude

---

[9]The question arises whether, in fact, the active participation of 13 percent of beneficiaries of PRONASOL programs is a meager or a rich response. What percent of actual community participation does PRONASOL consider desirable? What percent would constitute a real shift in the level of active community participation? These questions merit further research.

toward the possibility of obtaining government works, services, and transfers (figures 14.1 through 14.5).

Second, and within the limits noted above, the political and associational impact of social participation through Solidarity Committees yields different results in the three municipalities. These differences relate closely to the local contexts in which the program operates.

In cities with a strong organizational tradition (Tijuana and Mexicali), committee leaders for the most part have some experience as leaders, middle cadres, or members of local organizations and groups. However, while in Tijuana most leaders have a background in neighborhood organizations, in Mexicali most leaders have previous experience in political parties and trade unions. In Nuevo Laredo most committee leaders lack previous organizational experience.

Not only do these differences reflect the characteristics of the social milieus in the three cities; they also express differences in program implementation which arise from the respective local political situations. In Mexicali the operation of Solidarity is based on a close identification between Solidarity officials, federal agencies, and municipal authorities from the PRI. This has enhanced the official party and federal government's capacity to promote the election of like-minded leaders as committees are formed. In Tijuana, in contrast, committee formation developed in the midst of tight political competition between PAN municipal authorities, on the one hand, and Solidarity officials and federal agencies on the other. This competition led the municipal government to create its own self- management program (with features very much like those of Solidarity). The result was that in practice local groups promoted their own leaders in a relatively independent way. Faced with the municipal government's work in the *colonias*, Solidarity promoters were pressured into issuing a very broad call to form committees and allowing greater autonomy for the neighborhood assemblies. The experience in Nuevo Laredo was entirely different; besides the weak tradition of local organization there, internal struggles within the PRI were decisive and led the modernizing sector of the party (with Solidarity's implicit support) to sidestep the influence of the CTM in Solidarity projects. This was reflected in the creation of committees that entail a new organizational structure and leaderships rather than an adaptation of previous ones.

Third, local political contexts influence the formation of Solidarity Committees and the selection of their leaders, and also have a significant impact on the type of actions the committees carry out. In a situation of greater local community autonomy, as in Tijuana, committees generate broader and more diversified organizational structures, grant greater decision-making power to neighborhood assemblies, and develop expectations of success that are based more on strengthening their own organization than on government support. Except for the diversity of organizational structures, committees that are formed with new leaderships follow a similar pattern. This is the case in Nuevo Laredo, where initiatives tend to arise from neighborhood organizations, assemblies participate to a significant degree in the main decisions, and organizational strengthening is emphasized.

In contrast, in the context of Mexicali, where committees were created without the pressure of intense political competition and where PRI-controlled federal agencies and organizations exerted a strong influence, the result is greater official control. This inhibits Solidarity's potential organizational impact. In this case, the committees generate centralized structures in which most initiatives for Solidarity projects come from the leadership, neighborhood assemblies participate only marginally in decision making, and leaders' expectations for their organization center on obtaining greater government support.

APPENDIX: METHODOLOGICAL NOTE

A. *Survey of Solidarity Committee Leaders*

A standardized questionnaire was designed for interviews with leaders of Solidarity Committees. A census of Solidarity Committees was taken (based on the promoting agencies' lists) and their leaders were interviewed, except in the case of the Escuela Digna program in Tijuana and Mexicali, which had a large number of projects and committees. A random sample based on the sample framework developed for the survey of beneficiaries was carried out in the case of the Escuela Digna committees. Under these conditions, the authors' conclusions refer to all Solidarity Committees in each city.

Interviews with Solidarity Committee Leaders

City	N	%
Tijuana	87	43.7
Mexicali	49	24.6
Nuevo Laredo	63	31.7
Total	199	100.0

B. *Survey of Program Beneficiaries*

A questionnaire was designed and a survey using probabilistic sampling techniques was carried out. For the purposes of this survey, the target population was households directly benefited by Solidarity projects. In order to define this universe, official lists of Solidarity projects were obtained from regional offices of Mexico's Ministry of Budget and Planning (SPP). Projects were grouped into three types of programs: Escuela Digna (type 1); urban infrastructure (type 2); and community works and services (type 3). The operational definition of "directly benefited household" for each type of program was as follows:

For type 1 programs, households with students enrolled in the school. For types 2 and 3, households located within a "zone of influence," defined according to the scale of the project under consideration and the feasibility of obtaining a random sample of that zone.

Thus, the conclusions refer to households benefited by Solidarity, according to type of project and by city. In terms of sample size, a calculation was made based on the central limit theorem, with a 90 percent level of confidence. The results of the calculation of sample size for each type of project are as follows:

Sample Size for the Social Interpretation Survey

Project	Tijuana		Mexicali		N. Laredo		Total	
	P	S	P	S	P	S	P	S
Type 1	146	82	139	135	80	76	365	293
Type 2	160	138	161	161	346	318	667	617
Type 3	176	152	174	174	74	74	424	400
Total	482	372	474	470	500	468	1456	1310

Note: P = projected; S = surveyed.

V

Comparative Perspectives

15

Mexico's Solidarity Program in Comparative Context: Demand-based Poverty Alleviation Programs in Latin America, Africa, and Eastern Europe

Carol Graham

When evaluating the record of Mexico's PRONASOL program, it is difficult to separate what may be justified criticisms of the political system or economic strategy from those of the actual design or content of the program. Like any poverty alleviation effort, PRONASOL is inherently limited by the political and economic context in which it takes place. Thus a realistic evaluation of the program's poverty alleviation effects or potential effects must recognize the contextual constraints in which it operates. PRONASOL is being implemented in a semi-authoritarian system which is in theory in the process of liberalizing, and in an economy recovering from a severe economic crisis caused by heavy external indebtedness and macroeconomic distortions.[1]

The author would like to acknowledge the support of the Inter-American Development Bank and the John D. and Catherine T. MacArthur Foundation for the research upon which this chapter is based.

[1] An underlying assumption of this chapter is that the alternative to making painful but necessary adjustments in Mexico, as in many other Latin American countries, would have resulted in more severe economic crises with worse implications for the poor, and that the resource constraints that those adjustments entailed required a new approach to protecting the poor. For a detailed description of the record of a government that prolonged the implementation of such adjustments by implementing a so-called "heterodox" economic strategy, see Graham 1992a. Data on the fate of the poorest sectors during that period are found in Instituto Cuanto 1991.

As in many other Latin American countries, the adjustment necessary to overcome the economic crisis of the early 1980s in Mexico
required difficult choices in the realm of public expenditures, with the
social sectors often suffering disproportionately—and mistakenly—in
the reduction in the size and scope of the state sector. While concern
about the social costs of those adjustments increased throughout the
continent in the 1980s, the resources available to address those costs did
not. By the late 1980s resource constraints, as well as changing political
views, had a major impact on social policy not only in Latin America but
also in Africa and Eastern Europe. The focus of government spending
shifted from development efforts that relied on large-scale infrastructure
projects and universal subsidies, to universal provision of only basic
health and education services and targeted interventions to help the
neediest groups.

While PRONASOL is distinguished by its national context, it also
shares several important characteristics with other programs implemented to alleviate poverty in the context of adjustment in Latin America
and Africa. Almost all the programs, PRONASOL included, have been
strongly influenced by the concept of incorporating the demands of
beneficiaries and their organizations into program design and content.
This concept was first introduced in Bolivia's Emergency Social Fund
(ESF); despite its potential drawbacks,[2] this idea has proven a powerful
tool for enhancing poverty alleviation and institutional development at
the local level. PRONASOL clearly grew out of Salinas's earlier thinking
and writing about development,[3] as well as previous government programs such as Manos de Obra and COPLAMAR, which relied on
community initiative in the form of manual labor and food supply.[4] Yet it
also draws from regional experience with demand-based social programs or social funds, the ESF in particular. The experience of all
programs, meanwhile, is strongly influenced by the political context in
which they are implemented. A review of experiences of poverty alleviation efforts during adjustment in Latin America, Africa, and Eastern
Europe should help determine which of PRONASOL's traits—both
positive and negative—are unique to the Mexican context and which are
more generic.

Three broad lessons emerge from the experiences of Chile, Bolivia,
Peru, Zambia, Senegal, and Poland, and provide a basis for the analysis
of the political economy of poverty alleviation programs such as PRO-
NASOL. The first lesson is that open political environments are more

---

[2]These are discussed in detail in the review of the various programs.

[3]Salinas's Ph.D. dissertation basically lays out the framework for the PRONASOL
program. For detail, see Grayson 1991.

[4]Dresser 1991: 15. Community labor and programs to encourage children to go to school
have been implemented in Mexico for decades, meanwhile, as noted by Knight, this
volume.

likely to result in a broad political base of support for economic reform and, therefore, a policy environment in which effective poverty reduction can take place. The second and related lesson is that open political systems are more likely to encourage the participation of diverse groups such as nongovernmental organizations (NGOs) and local institutions in their antipoverty strategies. This enhances their capacity to reach poor and marginalized groups, thereby giving those groups a stake in the ongoing process of economic reform. The final lesson is that strategies that rely on the participation of beneficiaries and the organizations that represent them have the longer-term effect of strengthening the capacity of these institutions, thereby giving previously marginalized groups a more effective political voice.

The details about PRONASOL's design, programs, scale, and record are well documented in the other chapters in this volume.[5] The objective of this chapter is to provide a comparative framework for the evaluation of PRONASOL, and to briefly touch on some of the contextual aspects which affect PRONASOL's performance in both poverty alleviation and institutional development.[6]

POVERTY ALLEVIATION DURING ADJUSTMENT:
SELECTED EXPERIENCES

BOLIVIA

Bolivia's Emergency Social Fund was the first of a kind, and attracted a great deal of national as well as international attention. Enthusiasts of the ESF cite its demand-based approach, its efficiency and transparency, and its rapid results. Critics question the program's position outside the public sector and its ability to provide permanent poverty alleviation or to target the poorest sectors. The program did not reach those most directly affected by adjustment—tin miners—and had a disproportionately low reach among the poorest two poverty deciles.[7] Yet the ESF administered U.S. $240 million in its four years of operation, and the

---

[5] Another very good detailed description of the PRONASOL program is Dresser 1991.

[6] The following section is primarily based on my ongoing research on the politics of protecting the poor during adjustment. I conducted field studies in six countries in three regions: Chile, Bolivia, Peru, Senegal, Zambia, and Poland. Results from the Latin American cases have been published in Graham 1991a, 1991b, and 1992b. The Africa case studies are in circulation as discussion papers in the Social Dimensions of Adjustment Unit at the World Bank (Graham n.d.1, n.d.3), and the Polish case is forthcoming in Graham n.d.2.

[7] The poorest regions benefited least from the ESF in terms of per capita expenditures: the wealthiest of five income areas received $23.97 per capita, while the poorest received $9.45. ESF workers represented 6.25 and 7.75 percent, respectively, of workers in income deciles 1 and 2, but 13.25, 21.5, and 15.3 percent, respectively, in deciles 3, 4, and 5. By regional standards, however, deciles 3, 4, and 5 in Bolivia are still considered quite poor. For detail, see Graham 1992b; Jorgensen et al. 1992.

projects that it created, which ranged from infrastructure such as health posts, schools, and low-income homes to services such as job creation and school lunch programs, benefited over one million poor, a substantial number in a population of just under seven million. Despite relatively weak targeting, the program had substantial impact on the political sustainability of economic reform and on poverty alleviation.

First, the ESF had a positive political impact by demonstrating that it could work in a transparent and nonpartisan manner—with local governments and NGOs of all political bents—in a country where aid programs were usually influenced by patronage politics. The ESF resulted in an unprecedented collaboration of efforts between NGOs—the groups with the closest ties to the poor—and the state. This allowed the ESF to reach the poor in remote communities who had rarely, if ever, seen the state follow through on promises. The ESF also enhanced local governments' capacity by providing them with funds independent of the central government. And due to its demand-based structure, the ESF could not be monopolized by any one political actor at election time: a diversity of actors, from the governing party to local governments and NGOs, could claim credit for ESF projects. As a result, there was no correlation between ESF funds and the outcomes of the 1989 presidential and 1987/89 municipal elections.[8]

The ESF provided the poor with a means to help themselves, thereby giving them a stake in the ongoing process of economic reform. By doing so, it contributed to support for the government among previously marginalized sectors—if not for the adjustment program per se—at a critical time, which enhanced the feasibility of economic reform. Even if the ESF had instead focused its efforts on those who were directly affected by the adjustment program—tin miners—it is unlikely that it could have eroded their entrenched opposition to the government's economic strategy. The rapid pace of adjustment, coupled with the crash of world tin prices, meanwhile, reduced the political power of the miners' traditionally influential confederation. This does not imply that those who are directly affected by adjustment do not merit compensation,[9] but that most efforts directed at those groups will have marginal impact on the political sustainability of adjustment. This suggests that pro-poor programs implemented during adjustment may create opportunities for building "pro-reform" coalitions among the poorest groups by enhancing their economic potential and political voice, which are also important elements of poverty reduction. The extent to which PRONASOL is able to reach previously marginalized groups, and to serve as an alternative to the PRI by providing a channel

---

[8]For detailed results by district, see Graham 1992b.

[9]Tin miners were granted relatively generous one-shot severance payments when they were laid off.

"through which popular groups can express their demands" (Dresser 1991: 26), will determine if the program can have similar effects on the economic potential and political voice of the poor.

SENEGAL AND ZAMBIA

The two Africa cases in the study, Senegal and Zambia, provide an interesting contrast in terms of the impact of political opening on sustaining adjustment, reaching the poor, and capacity building—or lack thereof. In Senegal, adjustment has progressed at a rather slow pace for over a decade, and the political system has remained a relatively stable—if limited—democracy. The first major attempt to compensate the losers from adjustment was the Délégation a l'Insertion a le Réinsertion et a l'Emploi (DIRE), set up in 1987. The DIRE, which was funded by USAID, the World Bank, and the government of Senegal, provided civil servants who had retired voluntarily (the *déflatés*) and university graduates who would previously have gotten jobs in the civil service (the *maîtrisards*) with credits of up to $50,000 to start their own businesses. Due to a lack of training and follow-up, and to the prevalence of clientelistic criteria in the disbursement of loans, the DIRE had a very poor record, both in terms of repayment and in terms of mortality of enterprises (32 percent). In addition, as the program's budget was administered through the public treasury, approximately $3 million were lost or "filtered" in the process. The beneficiaries were a relatively privileged group, and the projects funded included bookstores and travel agencies in central Dakar. In short, an enormous amount of resources for a country as poor as Senegal was squandered on relatively privileged groups.

This poor record resulted in the DIRE's gradual fading out. Despite the program's original high visibility, its effects on the political sustainability of adjustment were minimal: the program's image as dominated by clientelism and the governing party limited its impact among any groups except its direct beneficiaries. Meanwhile, the program did not have any impact on poverty alleviation.

After a wave of civil unrest in February 1988, the government made another attempt to address the social costs of adjustment and set up the Agetip program in conjunction with the World Bank. Agetip was influenced by the success of the ESF, and was also set up as an independent agency with a private-sector director, in sharp contrast to the DIRE. The Agetip responded to proposals from municipalities for labor-intensive infrastructure projects. In terms of efficiency and number of projects, the Agetip has been remarkably successful[10] and has even been cited as a model for the reform of the Senegalese private sector.

---

[10]From its inception in 1990 to the end of 1991, the program implemented over one hundred projects and created over 11,000 temporary jobs.

Yet the Agetip is also influenced by the political context in which it operates. There is no debate about reaching the poor and needy groups in Senegal, nor is there any kind of cooperative relationship between the government and the NGOs, which are the only organizations with extensive links to the poor. The Agetip does not use poverty criteria for allocating its projects. In addition, since the opposition boycotted the 1990 municipal elections, the only proposals that the Agetip is funding are those from the mayors of the governing party. While in some cases such proposals do have poverty reduction goals, such as the installation of sewage and water facilities, in others they may be pet projects of the mayor, such as renovating the town hotel. However, the agency does employ primarily unskilled youth.

Since the Agetip does not work with NGOs, it has very weak links to the poorest groups. There is a widespread popular perception that the Agetip is "of the system" or a tool of the governing party, and thus its impact on the political sustainability of adjustment—at least among those groups who are not of the governing party—has been limited. Its record on the poverty alleviation front is mixed: while it has provided a large number of temporary jobs and some sorely needed infrastructure in poor areas, the limited nature of beneficiary participation, and particularly of the organizations that are most closely linked to the poor, has restricted its potential in terms of both project sustainability and capacity building.

In Senegal, the goal of poverty reduction—and indeed even any debate on poverty—has been subordinate to the interests of politically vocal groups within or linked to the state sector. The slow pace of reform has given these groups much more opportunity to "protect" their privileged positions within the system. The limited nature of political participation, meanwhile, has resulted in a great deal of suspicion of government-sponsored initiatives, limiting the potential impact of the Agetip. This stands in sharp contrast to Bolivia's ESF, which, by working with a variety of political parties and NGOs, was able to create support for adjustment—or at least good will toward the government implementing adjustment—among the sectors of society that had traditionally been marginalized from state benefits. By concentrating its efforts on these sectors, the ESF had much more impact on poverty alleviation than it would have had by focusing on compensating the tin miners. PRO-NASOL's ability to reach beyond traditional PRI-controlled organizations is not yet fully clear. However, the extent to which the program has already come into conflict with authoritarian party bosses at the local level indicates that nontraditional actors have been able to benefit at least to some extent.[11]

---

[11] For detail on these relations, see Fox 1992; A. Craig 1992b.

Zambia provides a sharp contrast to Senegal. While adjustment in Zambia was postponed for years under the UNIP government and all state benefits were linked to party membership, the October 31, 1991, elections ushered in dramatic political change. Frederick Chiluba and the Movement for Multi-Party Democracy, which campaigned on a pro-adjustment platform, took over 75 percent of the vote. Upon taking office, the government began to implement a pro-free market economic strategy *and* made reaching the poorest and most vulnerable groups a public priority. Due to the dramatic nature of political change, the groups that had traditionally had privileged access to state resources saw their influence substantially reduced, allowing the government to focus its efforts on the poorest.

The pricing policy for maize meal is telling. The heavily subsidized price of maize—which consumed over 15 percent of government revenue—had been the political bête noire for the Kaunda government, and repeated attempts to raise the price resulted in food riots and even a coup attempt in 1990. A coupon system, which in theory was to provide cheaper maize to poor groups, had become a tool of the UNIP party, while many of the poor were marginalized from the system and had to pay three to four times the official price for maize on the black market. When the Chiluba government liberalized the price of maize in December 1991, keeping subsidies on roller meal—the coarse grind which only the poorest eat, there was no popular unrest. This was due in large part to the government's explaining the measures, and the need to allocate scarce resources for the most vulnerable groups, to the public. This differs notably from the Kaunda government, which usually announced measures overnight, and where entrenched interest groups with a stake in state subsidies had much more influence. The dramatic nature of political change in Zambia, as well as the pace of reform measures, undermined the influence of these groups, allowing for an increased focus on the poor.

The Micro-Projects Unit (MPU) in Zambia, which is funded by the World Bank and the European Community and run out of the government's National Development Planning Office, is a good example of a program that reaches the needy rather than the privileged; it is being expanded substantially under the Chiluba government. The MPU, also influenced by the ESF, responds to proposals from community organizations, mostly for renovation of existing infrastructure.[12] The program requires a 25 percent community contribution in cash or in labor. It has

---

[12]The proposals must go through local governments to prevent duplication and to ensure that they are in line with local government priorities. To prevent bureaucratic lag, however, the proposals are simultaneously sent directly to the MPU. Thus if a viable proposal seems to be unfairly held up or denied in the local government, the MPU is able to follow up on it.

been successful in revitalizing the self-help spirit in many communities and in reaching remote areas long neglected by the state.

By giving communities contact with and a stake in a government poverty alleviation program, the MPU enhances the political sustainability of economic reform, creating a basis of support among previously marginalized but numerically significant groups. In addition, the demand-based nature of the program inherently encourages such groups to exercise their political voice, something unprecedented in the Zambian context, where a one-party state dominated the system for several decades. The MPU's focus on community initiative and self-help and its providing the poor with an alternative to a monopoly party suggest the potential role PRONASOL could play in Mexico.

CHILE

A very different example and model for reaching the poor developed in Chile. Chile had an extensive social welfare structure prior to adjustment; the system was revamped and targeted to the poorest groups during the Pinochet years. While social spending per capita declined during the adjustment years, it actually increased for the poorest two deciles (see Graham 1991b). Yet many people at the margin lost access to what had been one of the most comprehensive social systems in Latin America. This was not necessarily a positive result, nor is it one that a government more responsive to electoral pressure would be able to implement. Yet it proved extremely effective in protecting the poorest sectors during severe economic crisis. The infant mortality rate, for example, not only continued to decline but accelerated its rate of decline and is one of the lowest on the continent, below those of Colombia, Argentina, and Mexico.

In conjunction with targeting social-sector spending, large-scale employment programs were implemented from 1975 to 1987. At the height of the economic crisis in 1982, with unemployment at almost 30 percent, these programs employed up to 13 percent of the work force. The programs paid one-fourth to one-half the minimum wage, providing a self-targeting mechanism, although many critics argue that the subsidy was far too low. Implementation at the beginning was a bit haphazard, and labor was often not used productively, tainting the image of the programs. With time, program design was improved, and the programs incorporated some private-sector hiring and training. Workers in the private sector-linked programs were often able to find permanent jobs with the same firms, a positive effect in terms of poverty alleviation. While the programs had several flaws—particularly the authoritarian manner in which they were implemented—even their harshest critics agree that their scale and duration had some impact on reducing the potential for social explosion at a time of unprecedented unemployment rates. It is unlikely that a demand-based program could attain the systematic coverage, scale, and speed in implementation that the Chilean programs did, particularly with the resources available relative to population size.[13]

The Pinochet regime's protection of the poorest—through a variety of programs—is an example worth noting. Chile's record vis-à-vis its neighbors in protecting basic health and welfare of the poor during a period of adjustment, and targeting and reaching the very poorest, is indeed remarkable. Yet according to other indicators, such as income distribution and per capita consumption, Chile fares less well. It is no coincidence that the government of President Aylwin made poverty reduction a major focus of its economic program. The new government also set up a demand-based social fund, the Fund for Solidarity and Social Investment (FOSIS), to complement the works of line ministries with outreach programs for the poorest communities and unskilled youth. The FOSIS seeks to correct a major flaw in the Pinochet government's approach: that it failed to incorporate any kind of beneficiary participation. The authoritarian government's top-down manner precluded the kind of participation from below which often enhances the sustainability of programs, and limited their positive political effects. Jobs were withdrawn from shantytowns that were active in political protests, for example. Finally, since targeting social welfare spending entails political as well as economic choices and the Pinochet regime was free of the constraints faced by most democratic regimes, its lessons on the political sustainability front are far less clear cut, as is the replicability of its targeting the poorest at the expense of middle sectors. Some aspects of the PRONASOL program, such as withholding the *tortivales* food program from forty-eight Mexico City neighborhoods where the opposition was particularly active (Dresser 1991: 15), unfortunately demonstrate similar authoritarian tendencies.

PERU

It is also extremely important to note that programs designed to protect or benefit the poor, if poorly implemented, can do more harm than good. They often alienate the potential beneficiaries, as the case of the Peruvian PAIT (Programa de Apoyo al Ingreso Temporal) demonstrates. The PAIT program was a public works employment program, modeled on Chile's programs, which was implemented in Lima's shantytowns by the 1985–90 APRA government. The program provided sorely needed income support as well as some socially useful infrastructure. Yet it was

---

[13]In 1987, the programs allocated 5 billion pesos or approximately U.S. $20 million in the government's total social spending budget of 274 billion pesos, and employed approximately 165,000 people. The ESF, meanwhile, had approximately $240 million for its four years of operations, and on average employed approximately 3,000, or 0.3 percent, of the economically active population.

implemented in an extremely top-down and partisan manner, with a great deal of clientelism in hiring as well as constant political manipulation of the workers. PAIT workers were often taken to political rallies to cheer for President García, for example. The program's budget was also manipulated, drastically increasing hiring prior to elections and then fading jobs out quietly afterward, which kept applicants in a constant state of uncertainty.[14] The perception that the program was used as a tool by the governing party ultimately undermined its public image. Most damaging, however, was the program's excessive centralism and top-down implementation, which resulted in its disrupting, duplicating, and undermining the efforts of local self-help groups, which are critical to the survival of the poor in Peru. Its effects ran directly counter to the capacity building that is integral to poverty reduction.

Whatever marginal effects the PAIT program had on poverty alleviation were temporary, while the disruption caused to local organizations often had permanent effects. The case of Peru demonstrates the importance of incorporating the participation of local groups in the programs that are designed to benefit them, as well as the damage that programs for the poor can cause if they are manipulated for partisan political purposes. The PRONASOL program, run by a political party with traits similar to the APRA in Peru, has repeatedly been accused of being a tool of the party. There is one major difference between the PAIT program and PRONASOL: the latter's demand-based structure allows for autonomous pressure from below on the program leadership. While this does not always prevent manipulation of the program, it does mean that the local power structure and the nature of grassroots organizations can be countervailing factors to government party control of the program.[15]

POLAND

A final experience that demonstrates the political constraints on reaching the poor and vulnerable is the case of Poland. In January 1990, soon after its inauguration, the first noncommunist government in Poland launched a dramatic, Bolivia-style stabilization and adjustment program. The program successfully stabilized hyperinflation. Yet political uncertainty soon stalled reform efforts, as several attempts failed to maintain a coherent government coalition in Parliament. Structural reforms, such as privatization of the financially unviable state industrial conglomerates, have been postponed, creating an unsustainable drain on the state budget. The longer reforms are postponed, the greater the anxiety about their potential social costs, increasing political opposition to the adjustment program despite the absence of any viable alternative

---

[14]For detail on enrollments and election results by district, see Graham 1991b.

[15]For detail on clientelism and local organizational structures in PRONASOL, see A. Craig 1992b.

proposals. The rapidly rising budget deficit makes it increasingly unviable for the government to maintain the current social welfare system. Even prior to the collapse of public finances, the system, which is based on universal free access to all benefits, was characterized by poor quality of services, unequal access, a growing system of "informal" payments for services, and a skewed incentive system. Among other negative effects, the incentive structure promotes premature retirement among pensioners in the social security system, and excessive usage of specialized care and emergency and hospital services in the health system, creating dramatic shortages. In combination, government insolvency and the need to provide protection for the poor and unemployed (whose numbers will increase in the future) dictate an immediate revamping of the social welfare system.

Proposals being considered in government circles for reform of the health and social security systems would guarantee basic health care and social security insurance for those who need them, while introducing private providers and choice of services for those who can afford them. This would alleviate the financial burden on the government and enhance service quality by introducing competition. Concurrently, government resources would be targeted at the provision of a safety net for the increasing numbers of poor and unemployed. Unemployment prior to 1990 in Poland was "hidden" by the maintenance of excess workers on government and industrial payrolls. Open unemployment is now at 12 percent, and in towns or regions that were dependent on insolvent state-owned enterprises it is as high as 30 percent. There is a clear need for programs that are more extensive than unemployment insurance for these regions. Chile-style public works or a social fund like the ESF would be ideal mechanisms to provide employment and infrastructure improvement, and give impetus to municipal government development. Unfortunately the political debate in Poland on the safety net lags far behind the proposals for reform, centering on emotional criticisms of government proposals rather than on any provision of realistic alternatives. This is a major impediment to progress of any kind.

At the popular level there is widespread ignorance—and anxiety— about future social welfare due to the incoherent debate and the government's past failure to communicate or explain the ongoing reform process to the public. Populist opposition movements have been quick to capitalize on this anxiety. By the summer of 1992, failure to adequately address the safety net issue and anxiety about the potential social costs of reform led to a series of industrial strikes which virtually paralyzed the government and forced it to make the safety net issue a priority. In September 1992 the government announced two social pacts—one on the future of state enterprises, and one on the future of the social safety net—that were to be negotiated with unions and the private sector. The government's new attempt to communicate its proposals to the public and to incorporate popular participation is a first step toward a realistic treatment of safety net and poverty issues in Poland.

Yet the delivery mechanisms for new forms of social assistance are severely underdeveloped. Elected local governments were only recently constituted, yet they have been given primary responsibility for the provision of benefits to the poor and unemployed. There are a host of unresolved issues about the nature of benefits, their financing, and who should be eligible, as well as their delivery. In the absence of progress, the appeal of both right- and left-wing strains of authoritarian populism is on the rise (Wnuk-Lipinski 1992), based on latent fears about social welfare. Failure to resolve the poverty and safety net issues threatens to derail the economic reform process and jeopardizes the democratic transition. In Poland there is a great deal of room for learning from Latin American experiences, PRONASOL included.

LESSONS FOR PRONASOL?

Several lessons emerge from the experiences of other countries. Programs such as PRONASOL can reduce poverty and have positive political effects on sustaining economic reform processes. Yet these effects hinge on the program operating in a transparent manner that incorporates the participation of the poor, thereby enhancing their economic potential *and* political voice. The ability to perform in such a manner on a large scale depends on available resources, institutional structure, and commitment from the highest levels to insulate the programs from partisan pressures, a commitment which is not fully clear in President Salinas's case. Programs must be implemented as an integral part of the macroeconomic reform program, so that successive governments have a stake in their successful implementation, and so that beneficiaries have a stake in the ongoing process of economic transformation. These conditions are not always readily available. To a certain extent, the amount of resources available and the political leadership in the case of Bolivia's ESF were unique. Even then, the ESF was not able to overcome the obstacle of reaching the poorest; indications are that PRONASOL has not been able to do so either (Moguel 1990). "The actual degree of accountability and antipoverty targeting of this revenue sharing depends largely on whether the democratic process was allowed to operate in a given locality. Even under democratically elected local governments, moreover, there is no guarantee that Solidarity funding will be clearly targeted to the poorest of the poor" (Fox 1992: 18–19). It may well be that in the Mexican case the authoritarian and clientelist nature of the party structure and some local governments serves as an additional constraint to the inherent difficulty that demand-based programs have in reaching the poorest of the poor.

There is no established link between democracy and reaching the poorest, however, since even in democracies the poor are usually poor with respect to political voice as well as to resources. Ironically, of the cases covered here, the Pinochet regime had the most success in targeting the poorest, precisely because it was free of the political constraints of having to answer to the more vocal middle sectors that a democratic regime would have (Graham 1991b). On the other hand, a broader view of poverty reduction, which includes the poor's participation in designing their own solutions as integral to the sustainability and long-term impact of any antipoverty effort, might place less value on the ability to target the poorest of the poor versus the program's ability to incorporate the participation of disadvantaged groups, even if they are not the poorest ones. Many projects, such as new schools or health posts, also have indirect positive effects for poorer groups who did not participate in their design. Finally, targeting can entail high costs in terms of time and resources.[16] In this light, PRONASOL's success or failure would hinge more on its ability to generate autonomous grassroots participation than on reaching the poorest among the poor. And while the maximum size of its projects ($17,000) has been criticized as being too small to have an impact, small-sized projects are a good means of reaching poorer groups through self-selection, as higher income groups are less likely to compete for small-scale projects.

The scale and diversity of PRONASOL and its programs, as in the case of the ESF, dictate some impact on politics and on poverty alleviation. The ESF channeled $240 million in four years in a total population of just under seven million, and its works benefited an estimated 1.2 million poor. Solidarity started with a budget of $680 million in 1989 and increased to a projected $2.3 billion for 1992.[17] If administrative and infrastructure costs were waived, the ESF would have spent approximately $50 per year on each of its 1.2 million beneficiaries.[18] By the same calculation, with its 1992 budget PRONASOL would have spent $135 on each of the seventeen million in extreme poverty in Mexico. This indicates that the program's *resource* impact is even greater than Bolivia's. PRONASOL's highly visible nature—such as its prominent appearance

---

[16]This raises a question which faces all policymakers attempting to reduce poverty: whether it is better to lift the largest possible number of people at the margin of the poverty line above it, using a straight head-count measure of poverty, or to focus efforts on improving the lot of the poorest, even if the number of people below the poverty line remains the same. (Amartya Sen made a major contribution to the measurement of poverty by combining the head-count ratio with the average income shortfall of the poor and the measure of inequality among them [Gini coefficient]. Sen's theory and its implications for antipoverty policy are discussed in Bourguignon and Fields 1990.)

[17]It is somewhat difficult to accurately quantify PRONASOL's budget, as some money may have been diverted from what would previously have been social-sector spending (Dresser 1991; Golden 1992a).

[18]Administrative costs were approximately 5 percent of the total in the case of the ESF.

in the president's 1992 annual address to the nation—also indicates that it is having an impact in political terms which is similar to or greater than that of Bolivia's ESF. Also like the ESF, the effects of PRONASOL's outreach to groups that had received little or no state attention in the past cannot be underestimated.

President Salinas's personal commitment to the program, meanwhile, may serve to enhance his personal power; but perhaps equally as important, it is a key factor guaranteeing that the program receives resource and administrative priority. His apparent desire to use the program as a showcase, meanwhile, probably limits the likelihood that it will become a tool of PRI party hacks. A potential drawback, however, is the increased concentration of power in the hands of the president.

Institutional autonomy is an issue in many countries with such programs. On the one hand, autonomy allows for rapid, transparent action which bypasses public-sector bureaucratic procedures (which are often costly and time-consuming), reducing administrative costs and directly channeling benefits to the poor. A case in point is the DIRE in Senegal, where $3 million was "lost" in the public-sector process. On the other hand, there is the issue of longevity of extra-institutional programs, as neither their budgets nor their operating procedures have any permanent guarantees. To the extent that such programs are considered short-term measures during periods of adjustment or recovery, then institutional autonomy is less of a concern. To the extent that they are considered longer-term complements to social-sector policies, then it is usually necessary to establish some sort of institutional links. Other programs have a hybrid nature: the Agetip in Senegal is a semipublic corporation which is managed like a private-sector firm. The successor to the ESF in Bolivia, the Social Investment Fund, remains a separate, autonomous agency which responds to the president but has new formalized links with the sectoral ministries. In Mexico, the establishment of SEDESOL as an umbrella institution for PRONASOL seems an attempt to provide the program with more formal links and to ensure its continuation after the departure of Salinas, although it is too soon to tell how successful this attempt will be.[19]

Political context also makes an enormous difference in the possibilities for redirecting resources to the poor. Dramatic political change, as in the case of Zambia, or swift implementation of stabilization and adjustment, as in the case of Bolivia, provides unique opportunities for doing so. Less open political systems and stalled economic reform, as in the case of Senegal, give entrenched interest groups greater opportunities to protect their positions. In the case of Mexico, economic

---

[19]Bulletin of the Instituto Nacional de Solidaridad, June 1992; and lecture by Marco Antonio Bernal Gutiérrez, president of the Instituto Nacional de Solidaridad, at Johns Hopkins University School of Advanced International Studies, Washington, D.C., October 15, 1992.

change has been less sudden than in either Bolivia or Zambia. Political opening, meanwhile, has been far less straightforward. "PRONASOL's political success over the long term will depend as well on political and administrative reforms *outside* PRONASOL. Political reform has not so far buttressed Pronasol's transformative role" (A. Craig 1992b).

In addition, PRONASOL's very origins—like those of many other such programs—can be traced to the political context. In the face of new mobilizing forces on the left, the PRI had the worst showing of its history in the 1988 elections, and President Salinas took power amidst widespread accusations of fraud. Senegal's Agetip originated in the context of major civil unrest protesting the social costs of adjustment in the aftermath of the February 1988 elections; Chile's employment programs were set up due to the Pinochet government's fear of popular unrest in the face of unprecedented unemployment rates; and the Polish government is finally acting on the safety net issue due to the political challenge posed by widespread strikes related to the social costs of economic reform. While Salinas did not fear massive social unrest, as some other governments did, he was painfully aware of how unpopular the cutting of social services by the de la Madrid government was, and that reversing the trend could have important effects on popular perceptions of government legitimacy. Recent electoral results seem to indicate that this is indeed the case.

Some critics of PRONASOL argue that it is a populist strategy with one difference: that it associates social welfare with economic liberalization. An example is Salinas's justification of the privatization of the state airline by arguing that the proceeds from the sale would be used to assist the poor; indeed they were used to provide electricity for 500,000 residents in Mexico's poorest regions. "By associating it with redistribution, Mexico's leaders are recasting a generally unpalatable privatization drive as prerequisite to gaining social justice for the country's lower income strata" (Dresser 1991: 16). Whether or not one agrees with the philosophy behind PRONASOL, it is difficult to consider it populist. It is a demand-based poverty alleviation program implemented in the context of recovery from severe economic crisis and adjustment. The program fits into a neoliberal conception of the state: getting the state out of the production realm and into the business of providing social services. Thus nothing could be more appropriate than using the proceeds from privatized industries to fund social services that are not part of the sectoral ministries' normal budgetary allocation. PRONASOL and the many programs of its kind are inextricably linked to the "neoliberal"—if it must be labeled as such—vision of a smaller and more efficient state. PRONASOL is an integral part of Salinas's strategy to legitimize his economic program; this hardly qualifies it as "populist."

In addition to political context, the *nature* of pro-poor programs is a factor in determining their political as well as antipoverty impacts.

Demand-based programs that require community contributions or participation are best suited to creating the sustainable kinds of projects that are key to poverty alleviation, particularly if they become self-sustaining community initiatives or enhance local institutional capacity. Yet centrally implemented public works schemes may be better suited for rapid, mass-scale impact to relieve the social costs of adjustment and for targeting the poorest groups.

PRONASOL is a demand-based program, yet it is being implemented on a scale at least as great as the mass-based public employment programs in Chile. The range and diversity of Solidarity's programs make it difficult to form a single judgment about it. "In sum, PRONASOL is so large, dynamic, complex, and variegated that many different, and even contradictory, claims about it can be true" (Bailey 1992a). There are, no doubt, some PRONASOL programs that are more successful than others, as well as some that are more prone to political manipulation. Yet the components of PRONASOL, at least in theory, are ideally suited to the role such programs are intended to play: on the one hand they complement the work of the sectoral ministries in providing basic health and education services with benefits such as scholarships and school lunches, or infrastructure such as new or repaired buildings. On the other, they strengthen and increase the capacity of local institutions to better deliver those services in the future.

PRONASOL—or any program of its kind—cannot be expected to substitute for basic service provision or to make structural changes in asset distribution or ownership structures. Neither can they make up for major adjustment-related trends in real wages or sectoral spending. At best they are useful complements to the activities of weak sectoral ministries and can, at the same time, provide short-term income or employment; they cannot substitute for long-run economic growth. Yet programs like PRONASOL *can* make revolutionary changes at the local institutional level by incorporating the participation of previously marginalized groups—such as NGOs or neighborhood organizations. This participation may take the form of cooperation with the state in the design or delivery of social services as well as in providing more effective channels for demand making.

Ultimately poverty alleviation initiatives cannot substitute for a broader central-level commitment to poverty alleviation and for functioning line ministries, nor can they operate effectively without a central-level commitment to allow participation of actors of all political bents. Without such commitments, the impact of such programs will be limited at best.

Herein lie the most important unanswered questions about PRONASOL. The president is committed to the program, but it is not clear whether it is for poverty alleviation or political reasons. If the program is allowed to function according to its design and lets all political actors participate, it will enhance local-level institutional development. If that is the case, then whether or not Salinas garners some political gain from the program is irrelevant in poverty alleviation and political development terms. Indeed, there are few countries in the world where one could expect the government *not* to capitalize on the political benefits of a successful social program. In the Mexican context, however, success hinges on Salinas's commitment to political liberalization and to allowing genuine party competition at the local and central levels.

Salinas seems willing to let the program undermine the position of local-level party bosses, as is evidenced by, for example, the constant conflicts between local party officials and PRONASOL Leadership Councils. Yet it is less evident how much independence he is willing to allow the local Solidarity Committees to develop if they sympathize with the opposition. It seems that anti-PRI but progovernment committees are welcome and even encouraged at times. It is less clear what the government or program's response is when committees or munici-palities ally with the opposition. The record to date seems mixed. "While PRONASOL was fairly constant in its efforts to bypass overly rigid party bosses and recalcitrant opposition mayors, it had a more mixed record with autonomous social organizations, recognizing some while bypassing others" (Fox 1992).

Results depend in part on the local political power structure and on the organizational diversity and sophistication at the community level (A. Craig 1992b). There are three general categories of results: "more of the same classical clientelism, which does often involve vote buying; 'modernized' semi-clientelism, defined as attempted but unenforceable vote buying; and pluralism, where resource allocation is not conditioned on political subordination" (Fox 1992: 34). The PRI has been able to influence PRONASOL; yet it has not been able to control it completely due largely to the built-in incorporation of grassroots participation.

One gauge of the program's openness to various political actors is whether or not the allocation of funds correlates with electoral objec-tives. In the case of the PAIT program in Peru, for example, the APRA party blatantly manipulated program enrollments for electoral reasons, dramatically increasing jobs offered in municipalities held by the oppo-sition. Yet the strategy had only partial success in attracting votes, as the partisan manipulation of the program was obvious to much of the public. In the case of Bolivia's ESF, while actors at all different levels— from the governing party's presidential candidate to opposition party mayors—tried to reap electoral benefit from completed or projected ESF projects, there was no correlation between numbers of ESF projects and electoral results (see Graham 1992b). This was because the ESF genu-inely allowed participation from a variety of organizations and political parties. Thus municipal authorities or NGOs of the political opposition could take as much credit for ESF projects as could the MNR government, even though the ESF was clearly affiliated with the governing party in the public vision, as is PRONASOL in Mexico.

There were clear attempts—which were ultimately successful—to use PRONASOL to change the PRI's status in provinces where the PRI fared badly in 1988, such as Michoacán, Nueva Laguna, and Morelos (Dresser 1991: 23), as well as attempts to hold back the *tortivale* program in Mexico City municipalities where the opposition was strong. Yet the success of the PRI in these provinces may have had as much to do with low inflation and renewed economic growth as with the PRONASOL program. The more democratic and open the PRONASOL program is, the less likely it will be able to directly influence elections. As mentioned previously, this is also affected by the political and autonomous organizational structures at the local level, which have varying degrees of capacity and independence. However, it should be no surprise if an effective program that introduces new democratic elements as well as socially useful infrastructure to areas that have rarely, if ever, received government attention, creates increased goodwill and support for the governing party.

CONCLUSION

To date, PRONASOL's record is mixed. There are clearly areas where the program is victim to traditional clientelistic structures, others where these structures have been overthrown, and then some where the clientelistic and pluralist structures coexist. At the grassroots level, PRONASOL seems to provide opportunities for leadership development and the basis for associational life, particularly among groups that were excluded in the past, such as women (A. Craig 1992b). At this level, the program gives impetus to existing autonomous organizations as well as to the traditional self-help spirit of many Mexican communities. The concurrent provision of socially useful infrastructure, meanwhile, is also a contribution to poverty alleviation.

"Ultimately the degree of representation and popular participation that PRONASOL offers will depend on Mexican leaders' resolve to promote genuine political democratization" (Dresser 1991: 37). In the same manner, PRONASOL's impact on poverty alleviation will inevitably be linked to a government commitment to making the program function efficiently and transparently *and* to the broader context for poverty alleviation within which the program takes place. Neither PRONASOL nor any other program of its kind can take the place of viable sectoral policies. Programs like PRONASOL are designed as important *complements* to mainstream services, which have institutional development as well as infrastructure and income-enhancing goals. In addition, they operate within a fixed economic parameter: their ability to make long-term contributions to poverty alleviation hinges on the renewal of growth after adjustment and therefore on sound macroeconomic management. Advocates of poverty alleviation strategies based on major structural changes, or on redistribution of ownership and assets, will be disappointed in programs like PRONASOL and the ESF.

Finally, without a government commitment to allow all political groups to participate, the programs will be bound to fail precisely in the arena where they have the most potential to make permanent contributions to poverty reduction: the development of institutional capacity. If the PRONASOL program is merely a tool for President Salinas's personal political machinery, as its harsher critics contend, then it will fail in the long term. If, rather, it is a genuine attempt to implement a demand-based poverty alleviation program—which has made some errors and at times fallen into the hands of political opportunists on the way—then it may have a great deal of potential.

Appendix

National Solidarity: A Summary of Program Elements

John Bailey and Jennifer Boone

Solidarity is an umbrella covering many program elements, and the reader of this volume can easily get lost in a blur of agencies, budgets, and indicators of various types. The purpose of the appendix is to summarize information in a quick-reference format about the origins, type, bureaucratic structure, financing, and target groups of the various elements. Also, we comment on the significance of the elements. We were unable to find a single source that provided information on all the elements in a comparative and complete format. Our approach was to rely mainly on information taken from *La Solidaridad en el desarrollo nacional* (April 1992), which was the most comprehensive document we could locate, and to supplement this with material from interviews and other documents.

To guide the reader through the chart, "Program Name" follows PRONASOL use and is given in Spanish to avoid additional confusion of different possible translations into English. "Established" can refer either to when the program was announced or when actual implementation began. We have used Solidarity's categories of "Type": Production, Social Welfare, Special, and Regional Development. The terms are reasonably self-evident, although they might not fit one's intuitive notions. For example, Escuela Digna deals with physical maintenance of school buildings, which might fit more logically as infrastructure than welfare.

"New" indicates that the element originates after 1989; "Regular" means that a preexisting program was incorporated into Solidarity with one or another degree of alteration. The change may be as minor as a relabeling, or it might be substantial, as in the cases of "Urbanización" and "Apoyo a Comunidades Indígenas." To indicate where we think an ongoing program was substantially changed we use "Regular+." By "Bureaucratic Mechanisms" we refer to the agencies and levels of government that implement the program; also, we indicate whether grassroots committees participate. "Finance" refers to which level(s) pay(s) the costs. By "Target Group" we mean the principal, intended beneficiaries.

"Coverage" is an effort to convey something about the magnitude of product. Coverage may be amounts of money spent, numbers of committees created, numbers of land titles conveyed, and the like. With a general audience in mind, we represent expenditures in U.S. dollars at the average exchange rate of the year of implementation. Many of the programs are co-financed by different levels of government (federal, state, and/or municipal), and some require contributions by beneficiaries, in either cash or kind. At least one program, Fondos Municipales, receives funds from the World Bank. We have not done a systematic effort of financial accounting; we simply report in the chart the amounts cited in public documents. Thus the reader should not assume that the sum of the various items for a given year equals the total expenditure for the overall program.

With regard to the "Comments" column, we hasten to emphasize that in no way do we suggest any evaluation of Solidarity as a whole or of any of its elements. "Comments" is a catchall of observations that occurred to us in making sense out of the various elements.

To reiterate, we offer this chart for the purpose of simplifying and clarifying what is known about a large, dynamic, and complex program. An apt, if foreign, metaphor might be of a grainy photograph taken in a drizzly twilight of a rugby scrum on a muddy field. A much clearer picture can be taken after the action stops on this particular match and the teams are reconstituted for the next season.

Overview of Program Elements

Program Name	Established	Type	New/Regular	Bureaucratic Mechanisms	Finance	Target Group-Coverage	Comments
Alimentación y Abasto	1989	Welfare	Regular	CONASUPO + DIF	Federal + state	1989: 23.7M,* created 527 stores, 20 milk dispensaries, 81 kitchens 1990: 17M – 1241 stores, 149 milk dispensaries, 332 kitchens 1991: 16.5M – 1066 stores, 272 milk dispensaries, 400 kitchens 1992: no figures yet available	Kitchens seem urban-oriented while stores seem primarily rural. Appears that milk dispensaries are targeted to urban areas due to transit difficulty of liquid milk to rural areas. A number of this program's components serve as additions to the existing *abasto* programs administered by CONASUPO, particularly the LICONSA program and Tiendas Campesinas.
Electrificación Rural y Urbana	1989	Welfare	Regular	CFE, CLFC, local communities, COPLADE	Federal + local communities	1989: 34.6M – 2097 projects (urban + rural) 1990: 59.1M – 2942 projects (urban + rural) 1991: 83.2M – 3070 urban projects + 1934 rural 1992: 103.9M – 961 urban + 2912 rural 1993: 89.9M – federal	Appears that COPLADE certifies technical feasibility of projects and checks on strength of local committees; CFE does installation.
Urbanización	1989	Welfare	Regular +	Unclear; SEDESOL + local governments	Federal + state + municipal	1989: 57.5M (36.8M federal + 20.7M state & local) 1990: 116.3M (71.1M federal + 41.8M state & local) 1991: 173M (90.5M federal + 82.5M other) 1992: 149.6M (federal)	Appears to be a more flexible program for urban infrastructure; funds used for paving streets, building parks, sidewalks, sports facilities, plazas. Also appears to include some potable water. Available to wealthier states.
Vivienda	1989	Infrastructure	Regular	PRONASOL + FONHAPO	Federal + state	1989: 12.2M – 50k homes 1990: 25.5M – 26k homes + 55k "actions" 1991: 46.4M (includes 48k in "actions") 1992: 18M (federal) 1883L 48.1M (federal)	Program tries to involve beneficiaries in projects of housing construction and maintenance. Will become more important in reorganization with SEDESOL.

Program Name	Established	Type	New/Regular	Bureaucratic Mechanisms	Finance	Target Group-Coverage	Comments
Regularización del Suelo Urbano	1989	Welfare	Regular	PRONASOL + CORETT	Federal + state	No budget figures 1989: 325k titles (federal + state) 1990: 450k titles (federal + state) 1991: 450k titles (205k federal & CORETT, 245k state) 1992: 450k titles	Seems to basically be a speedup of CORETT work coupled with better coordination with state agencies.
Infraestructura Carretera	1989	Regional Development	Regular	COPLADE	Federal + state + Programa Tripartita de Carreteras	1989: 171.4M (3702 kilometers new; 3366 repair, 33k maintenance) 1990: 222M (4038 new; 3681 repair; 38k maintenance) 1991: 428.4M (5527 new; 2063 repair; 30k maintenance) 1992: 308.7M (5894 new; 1575 repair; 30k maintenance) 1993: 256.7M (federal)	PRONASOL part appears to focus on rural feeder roads. Has a substantial budget.
Programa de Apoyo a Cafeticultores	1989	Productive/Welfare	New	PRONASOL (regional committees); INI; SARH; states	Federal + state	1989: 3.7M for 89 organizations 1990: 29.5M for 188k producers on 234k hectares 1991: 27.3M for 176k producers on 276k hectares 1992: 23.6M for 276k producers on 294k hectares	Support for small-scale coffee growers left unprotected by privatization of INMECAFE; support channeled through INI centers and support centers of INMECAFE; use revolving mechanisms where appropriate; projects aimed mostly at production.
Apoyo a Comunidades Indígenas	1989	Special	Regular +	PRONASOL + INI; operates through indigenous communities, CCI	Federal + local communities	1989: 13.7M 1990: 47.6M 1991: 81.8M 1992: 102.3M (federal) 1993: 120.3M (federal)	Seeks to promote local participation; seeks economically efficient projects; some projects have revolving fund feature; several federal agencies involved in culture-related programs. Complicated and administratively intensive.

Program Name	Established	Type	New/ Regular	Bureaucratic Mechanisms	Finance	Target Group-Coverage	Comments
Proyectos Productivos a) Apoyo a Productores Forestales	5/90	Productive	New	PRONASOL within framework of the Programa Nacional de Reforestación	Federal + social (probably co-ops)	p1990: 1.7M federal + 510K social (to 31 organizations in 16 states) 1991: 5.5M (3.8M federal, 1.7M social) (to 87 organizations in 21 states) 1992: 5.6M (federal)	Fits better with new SEDESOL structure than with SPP.
b) Pescadores ribereños y acuacultura	1989	Productive	Regular	PRONASOL		?	Some mention of Michoacán, Yucatán, Campeche & Veracruz.
c) Pequeña minería	1989	Productive	Regular	PRONASOL (regional committees)		?	Some mention of Durango, Tlaxcala, Zacatecas, Sonora, Jalisco.
d) Infraestructura de Apoyo Productivo	1989	Productive	New	PRONASOL	Federal	1989: 19.9M (develop. of irrigation works) 4.1M (develop. of dryland areas for cultivation) 1990–91: continued develop. of irrigation systems	Aim is to develop the agricultural infrastructure of campesinos through focus on irrigation. Increase cultivation of basic grains.
e) Convenios SARH-Solidaridad	1990	Productive	New	PRONASOL + SARH	Federal	1990: assisted 65 organized rural groups	Designed to assist in the cultivation of some crops, plants, trees; rehabilitate irrigation channels; build some basic agric. infrastruc.
f) Programa Solidaridad-BAN-MURAL	1991	Productive	New	PRONASOL + BANMURAL	Federal	1991: 1.6M (to 71 projects) 1992: 3.9M + 3.6M credit (78 projects)	Assistance to producers involved in areas of fishing and agric.; by 1992, extended to 2243 producers in 12 states.
Programa para Jornaleros Agrícolas	5/1990	Special	New	IMSS; INI; INEA; CONAFE; CONASUPO; FONHAPO; FONAVIR	Federal (probably earmarking of central budgets)	Migratory workers targeted	Aimed at migratory workers in northeast originally; later extended to other states; focuses on nutrition, housing, hygiene, potable water.

Program Name	Established	Type	New/Regular	Bureaucratic Mechanisms	Finance	Target Group-Coverage	Comments
Fondos Municipales de Solidaridad	1990	Regional Development	New	Consejos Municipales de Solidaridad + Comités de Solidaridad	Federal + state	1990: 128.2M for 1439 *municipios* in 19 states (19k projects) 1991: 170.8M 1992: 141.7M 1993: 208.6M (federal)	Main recipients seem to be Guerrero, México, Oaxaca, Jalisco, Zacatecas, Yucatán, Puebla. Emphasizes grassroots participation through neighborhood committees.
Fondos de Solidaridad para la Producción	1990	Productive	New	Municipal + Comités de Validación y Seguimiento	Federal + state	1990: 134.3M federal + 36.7M state = 171M total to benefit 648k farmers in 1350 *municipios* (61% of total *municipios*) and 13k ejidos in 27 states 1991: 166.4M federal + 38.5M state = 204.9M to benefit 667k farmers in 1444 *municipios* in 28 states 1992: 220.4M to benefit 715k farmers 1993: 128.4M (federal)	Aimed at farmers dropped from BAN-RURAL lending; later extended, to some degree, to farmers not covered by BANRURAL. Each farmer gets 300k. Goes to dryland districts (*agricultura temporalera*); supposed to supplement other programs. Revolving fund feature, with proceeds to benefit community-chosen projects. Emphasizes participation. Innovative.
Fondo Nacional de Apoyo a Empresas de Solidaridad	1991	Productive	New	PRONASOL + Municipal	Federal + state	1992: 116M federal + 409K = 116.4M 1993: 128.4M federal	The primary recipients of fund attention are to be poor campesinos with or without land, indigenous groups, and urban dwellers who live in poverty with no access to financial assistance from commercial banks. Primary objectives: promote projects and identify areas of develop.; help toward commercialization; develop. of appropriate tech. Rapid growth.
Mujeres en Solidaridad	1989	Special	Regular + (Iteration of PINMUDE)	Local: "Operative Group" State: Subcomité Técnico de Mujeres en Solidaridad (federal, state, and municipal reps + reps from social and private sectors)	Federal + state	1989: 5.7M (federal + state) in 738 projects; 431 welfare projects benefiting 10k women in 955 communities in 29 *municipios* in 29 states 1990: 10.5M (federal + state) in 887 production projects + 387 welfare projects benefiting 25k women in 1046 communities in 375 *municipios* in 32 states 1991: 12.3M for 627 productive + 467 welfare projects 1992: 15.7M for estimated 1244 projects 1993: 16M (federal)	Administratively complex; small in scale; problem of designing economically viable projects.

Program Name	Established	Type	New/Regular	Bureaucratic Mechanisms	Finance	Target Group-Coverage	Comments
Programa para una Ecología Productiva	1992	Productive	New	Community Solidarity Committees	?	1992: governments of México, Michoacán, Oaxaca, Chiapas execute actions to protect Monarch butterfly	Community organizes in Solidarity Committees to contribute to the adequate use of the soil, to the protection and conservation of flora, fauna, and air. Consistent with SEDESOL organization.
Programas Regionales a) Nueva Laguna	1989	Regional Development	New	Comité de Concertación	Federal + state + communities	1989: 9.5M 1990: 17M (7.1M from state & other sources; not clear whether the 17 number includes the 7.1) 1991: 29.4M (23.6M PRONASOL; 5.2M state; 646K communities; 323K credit)	Integral community development, with productive, welfare, and infrastructure investment.
b) Istmo de Tehuantepec	3/1990	Regional Development	?	Communities, local governments, regional reps	Federal + ?	Covers 64 *municipios*; some beneficiaries are those dropped from BANRURAL	Focus on region connecting Atlantic-Pacific traffic; urban infrastructure; agriculture + forestry; roads; fishing; industry and commerce.
c) Costa de Oaxaca	3/1990	Regional Development	New	?	Federal + ?	49 *municipios*	Community development in broad sense.
d) Oriente de Michoacán	2/1991	Regional Development	New	PRONASOL + COPLADEM	Federal (PRONASOL + regular agency spending) + state + communities	16 *municipios* – 1991: 646K for *zonas indígenas*, 18.1M for agriculture and infrastructure, 11.3M for *microempresas*	Goal is to help in shift from subsistence to market-oriented farming.
e) Tierra Caliente de Guerrero	?	Regional Development	New	?	Federal + ?	9 *municipios* – 1991: 32.3M authorized	Legalize land titles; advise farmer organizations; develop fishing.
f) Sur del Estado de México	5/1991	Regional Development	New	Solidarity Committees	Federal + state + municipal	Benefits 138k residents – 1991; 21M authorized	

Program Name	Established	Type	New/Regular	Bureaucratic Mechanisms	Finance	Target Group-Coverage	Comments
g) Centro y Carbonífera de Coahuila	9/1991	Regional Development	New	Comités de Desarrollo, COPLADE, Solidarity Committees	Federal	1991: 2.5M	Broad community development programs.
h) Costa de Michoacán	1/1992	Regional Development	New	Municipal + PRONASOL	Federal + state + municipal	1992: 25.9M (federal, state, and municipal); 968 planned regional actions between 1992–94	Focus on agriculture, industrial and commercial modernization, territorial integration, social development projects, urban and municipal modernization.
i) Meseta Purépecha de Michoacán	1/1992	Regional Development	New	Comité de Seguimiento y Evaluación	Federal + state + municipal	1992: 37.2M (state + municipal; no federal numbers)	Focus on agriculture, social infrastructure, public municipal functions.
j) Sierra Norte de Puebla	2/1992	Regional Development	New	State, Delegación de Programación y Presupuesto, Solidarity Committees, *municipios*, COPLADE	Federal + state + municipal	1992: 32.9M (federal + state)	Focus on social infrastructure, communications, general community development.
k) Costa de Chiapas	4/1992	Regional Development	New	3 levels of government + community groups	Federal	1992: 399.9K (federal)	Focus on agriculture, development in commerce and tourism, urban infrastructure, social programs.
Programa IMSS-Solidaridad	12/1988	Welfare	Regular	IMSS (18 states); state health agencies (14)	Federal + state	1988–91: claims to have helped in formation of 10420+ committees for health 1991: 267 medical units in 18 states 1992: 31 rural medical units	Follows on pattern of IMSS-COPLAMAR, which functioned to extend health care to poor areas.

Program Name	Established	Type	New/Regular	Bureaucratic Mechanisms	Finance	Target Group-Coverage	Comments
Programa de Solidaridad con SSA	12/1988	Welfare	Regular	SSA + local committees	Federal	1989: 122 new health centers and 24 hospitals; rehab of 601 health centers and 81 hospitals 1990: 180 new health centers and 26 hospitals; rehab of 458 health centers and 34 hospitals 1991: 144 new health centers and 28 hospitals; rehab of 239 health centers and 26 hospitals 1992: rehab and construction of 240 health centers and 16 new hospitals	Appears to be relabeled health care, with more local participation. 1990: mention of Guerrero, Nayarit, Nuevo León, Oaxaca, Tamaulipas. 1991: mention of Campeche, México, Michoacán, Tlaxcala.
Hospital Digno	1991	Welfare	Regular	SSA; IMSS; IMSS-PRONASOL; ISSSTE	Federal + state	1991: 37 committees in 30 hospitals in 16 states; budget of 11M (7.8M federal, 3.2M state) 1992: unspecified increase in resources to 100 hospitals in different states	SSA + local committees created to implement programs; nature and significance of program is unclear.
Infraestructura Educativa	1989	Welfare	Regular	CAPFCE	Federal	1989: 81.4M (14606 educational spaces) to benefit 800k students 1990: 105.1M (13801 educational spaces) to benefit 600k students 1991: 143.7M (20k educational spaces) to benefit 800k students 1992: 105.5M (22.5k educational spaces) 1993: 195.8M (federal)	This is basically relabeled school construction. 1990: mention of Oaxaca, Chiapas, Guerrero, Veracruz, Puebla. 1991: mention of Puebla, Michoacán, Chiapas, Veracruz, México.
Escuela Digna	1989	Welfare	Regular	CAPFCE; state; municipal; community committees	Federal + state + municipal + community committees	1990: federal = 37.1M; others = 25.2M 1991: federal = 62.7M; others = 43.6M 1992: federal = 66.1M	Significant: Program reaches all the states; in 1990 they claimed to treat 21k units, creating 21k committees. Also, program reaches schools that might fall into the cracks between federal and state systems.

Program Name	Established	Type	New/Regular	Bureaucratic Mechanisms	Finance	Target Group-Coverage	Comments
Niños en Solidaridad	10/1990	Welfare	New	CONASUPO-DICONSA; IMSS; SSA, ISSSTE; DIF; states; *municipios*; committees from Escuela Digna	Federal + state	1990: 65.6M 1991: 58M: 182k grants, 1.2m food baskets, 300k checkups 1992: 110.2M: 557k scholarships 1993: 205M (federal)	Innovative and administratively complex. Targets rural poor. Attempts to keep children in school and to treat general family problems by working through the children.
Apoyo a Servicio Social	1990	Welfare	Regular	COPLADE	Federal	1990: 35M in 115k grants 1991: 53.7M in 177k grants 1992: 53.5M in 188k grants 1993: 54.6M	Program supports students doing social service through assignment to PRONASOL-related projects. Each student receives 250k/month. Potentially important.
Agua Potable y Alcantarillado	1989	Welfare	Regular	CNA + SARH; PRONASOL; BANOBRAS; *municipios*; local committees	Federal + state + international + municipal	1989: 327.6M – 422 urban + 1152 rural (1197 potable water; 377 sewerage) 1990: 941.9M – 356 urban + 1623 rural (benefiting 2 million residents) 1991: 1,099.8M – 925 urban + 1985 rural (2253 potable water; 657 sewerage) 1992: 256.6M – 1000 urban + 2397 rural (2397 potable water; 787 sewerage)	This would appear to be the "big ticket" item and heart of PRONASOL. No significant committee structure or grassroots participation.

*Expenditures refer to authorized, not actual, outlays and are given in current U.S. dollars for 1989–92 at annual average exchange rates (as reported in *Latin American Weekly Report*, WR-92-50, 24 December 1992). Estimates for 1993 are estimated at exchange rate of 1 January 1993 (as reported in *The New York Times*). Budget sums are given in millions (M) or thousands (K) of U.S. dollars.

Source: La Solidaridad en el Desarrollo Nacional, Coordinación General del Programa Nacional de Solidaridad, April 1992.

Bibliography

Acevedo Pesquera, Luis. 1992. "En marcha la expansión del gasto público: quitan amarras a infraestructura y Pronasol," *El Financiero*, May 21.

Acosta, Carlos. 1992. "Ayer opositores de izquierda; hoy dirigen y ejecutan programas de Pronasol," *Proceso* 827 (September 7).

Aguilar Camín, Héctor. 1991. *La guerra de Galio*. Mexico: Cal y Arena.

Aguilar Villanueva, Luis F. 1991. "Solidaridad: tres puntos de vista." In *Solidaridad a debate*. Mexico: El Nacional.

Alemán, Ricardo. 1991. "Clase política," *La Jornada*, January 26.

Alvarado Mendoza, Arturo, ed. 1987. *Electoral Patterns and Perspectives in Mexico*. Monograph Series, no. 22. La Jolla: Center for U.S.-Mexican Studies, University of California, San Diego.

Americas Watch. 1990. *Human Rights in Mexico: A Policy of Impunity*. New York: Americas Watch.

———. 1991. "Unceasing Abuses: Human Rights in Mexico One Year after the Introduction of Reform." September.

Ames, Barry. 1987. *Political Survival: Politicians and Public Policy in Latin America*. Berkeley: University of California Press.

Amnesty International. 1986. *Mexico: Human Rights in Rural Areas*. Exchange of Documents with the Mexican Government on Human Rights Violations in Oaxaca and Chiapas. London: AI Publications.

Arellanes Caballero, Rafael. 1992. "Fidecafé, opción para el desarrollo integral de la caficultura," *El Nacional*, April 6.

Aziz Nassif, Alberto. 1992. "Las elecciones de la restauración en México. In *Las elecciones federales de 1991*, edited by A. Aziz Nassif and Jacqueline Peschard. Mexico: Miguel Angel Porrúa/UNAM.

Bailey, John. 1988. *Governing Mexico: The Statecraft of Crisis Management*. New York: St. Martin's Press.

———. 1992a. "Centralism and Political Change in Mexico: PRONASOL in Nuevo León, 1989–91." Paper presented at the workshop

"Mexico's National Solidarity Program: A Preliminary Assessment," University of California, San Diego, La Jolla, February.

———. 1992b. "Fiscal Recentralization in Mexico, 1979–91." Paper presented at the XVII International Congress of the Latin American Studies Association, Los Angeles, September.

———. n.d. "Fiscal Recentralization and Pragmatic Accommodation of Oppositions in Nuevo León." In *Opposition Government in Mexico: Past Experiences and Future Opportunities*, edited by Victoria Rodríguez and Peter Ward. Albuquerque: University of New Mexico Press, forthcoming 1994.

Ball, N. 1984. "Measuring Third World Security Expenditure: A Research Note," *World Development* 12:2:157–64.

Banco de México. 1992. *The Mexican Economy*. México: D.F.: Banco de México.

Barabás, Alicia, and Miguel Bartolomé, eds. 1986. *Etnicidad y pluralismo cultural: la dinámica étnica en Oaxaca*. Mexico: INAH.

Barre, Marie-Chantal. 1983. *Ideologías indigenistas y movimientos indios*. Mexico: Siglo Veintiuno.

Barry, Tom, ed. 1992. *Mexico: A Country Guide*. Albuquerque, N.M.: Inter-Hemispheric Education Resource Center.

Bartra, Armando. 1992. "Más sobre Pronasol." In *Desigualdad y democracia*, by A. Bartra et al. Mexico: El Nacional.

Bataillon, Claude. 1988. "Notas sobre el indigenismo mexicano." In *Indianidad, etnocidio, indigenismo en América Latina*. Mexico: Instituto Indigenista Interamericano/Centre d'Etudes Mexicaines et Centreamericaines.

Behrman, J., and S. Craig. 1987. "The Distribution of Public Services: An Exploration of Local Government Preferences," *American Economic Review* 77:37–49.

Beltrán, Ulises, and Santiago Portilla. 1986. "El proyecto de descentralización del gobierno mexicano (1983–1984)." In *Descentralización y democracia en México*, edited by Blanca Torres. Mexico: El Colegio de México.

Beltrán del Río, Pascal. 1990a. "Solidaridad, oxígeno para el PRI, en el rescate de votos, *Proceso* 718 (August 6).

———. 1990b. "El memorandum de Pichardo, prueba de que el Pronasol es para servir al PRI," *Proceso* 730 (October 29).

Bennett, Vivienne. 1992a. "The Evolution of Urban Popular Movements in Mexico between 1968 and 1988." In *The Making of Social Movements in Latin America: Identity, Strategy, and Democracy*, edited by Arturo Escobar and Sonia Alvarez. Boulder, Colo.: Westview.

———. 1992b. "The Origins of Mexican Urban Popular Movements: Political Thought and Clandestine Political Organizing of the 1960s and 1970s." Paper presented at the XVII International Congress of the

Latin American Studies Association, Los Angeles, California, September.

BID/PNUD (Banco Interamericano de Desarrollo/Programa de las Naciones Unidas para el Desarrollo). 1992. "Reforma social y pobreza." Washington, D.C.: BID/PNUD.

Blanco, José. 1992. "Solidaridad y política de masas," *La Jornada*, September 17.

Blanco Rivera, Rafael. 1991. "Oaxaca, 1980." Cuadernos de Demografía Indígena. Mexico: Dirección de Investigación y Promoción Cultural, INI.

Bonfil, Guillermo. 1990. *México profundo, una civilización negada*. Mexico: Grijalbo/CONACULT.

Bourguignon, Francois. 1989. "Optimal Poverty Reduction, Adjustment and Growth. An Applied Framework." Document de Travail No. 89–22. Paris: DELTA, October.

Bourguignon, Francois, and Gary S. Fields. 1990. "Poverty Measures and Anti-Poverty Policy." Document de Travail. Paris: DELTA, February.

Calder, Kent. 1988. *Crisis and Compensation: Public Policy and Political Stability in Japan, 1949–1986*. Princeton, N.J.: Princeton University Press.

Camou, Antonio. 1992. "Gobernabilidad y democracia: once tesis sobre la transición mexicana," *Nexos* 170 (February): 55–65.

Campbell, Tim, et al. 1991. "Mexico: Decentralization and Urban Management Urban Sector Study." Report No. 8924-ME. Washington, D.C.: World Bank.

Cantú, Fausto. 1976. *Aspectos jurídico-económicos de la cafeticultura en México*. Mexico: INMECAFE.

Cantú, Jesús. 1992. "Solidaridad, además de electorero, se manejó en Michoacán coercitivamente," *Proceso* 819 (July 13).

Canudas, Rocío Carmen. 1991. *La modernización económica en Durango*. Durango: Instituto de Ciencias Sociales, Universidad Juárez del Estado de Durango.

Cardosa, Rosa. 1991. "Baño propio." In *La voz común: testimonios de solidaridad*. Mexico: El Nacional.

Carrasco Licea, Rosalba, and Francisco Hernández Puente. 1992. "Más allá de Solidaridad," *La Jornada*, September 7.

Centeno, Miguel, and Sylvia Maxfield. 1992. "The Marriage of Finance and Order: Change in the Mexican Political Elite," *Journal of Latin American Studies* 24:1 (February).

CEPAL (Comisión Económica para América Latina y el Caribe). 1990. *Magnitud de la pobreza en América Latina en los años ochenta*. Santiago de Chile: CEPAL.

———. 1992. *Equidad y transformación productiva: un enfoque integrado*. LC/L668. Santiago de Chile: CEPAL.

Chávez, Elías. 1992. "Michoacán: cada voto del PRI costó 239,188 pesos; cada uno del PRD costó 6,916 pesos," *Proceso* 821 (July 27): 22–27.

Cobo, Rosario, and Lorena Paz Paredes. 1992. "El sistema de abasto campesino en la Costa Grande de Guerrero: los retos de la autonomía." In *Autonomía y nuevos sujetos sociales en el desarrollo rural*, edited by Julio Moguel, Carlota Botey, and Luis Hernández. Mexico: Siglo Veintiuno/CEHAM.

Collier, Ruth Berins. 1982. "Popular Sector Incorporation and Political Supremacy: Regime Evolution in Brazil and Mexico." In *Brazil and Mexico: Patterns in Late Development*, edited by Sylvia Ann Hewlett and Richard S. Weinert. Philadelphia, Penn.: Institute for the Study of Human Issues.

Collin, Laura, and Felix Báez Jorge. 1979. "La participación política y los grupos étnicos en Mexico," *Revista Mexicana de Ciencias Políticas y Sociales* 97 (July–September).

Comisión Nacional del Agua. 1992. *Situación actual del subsector agua potable, alcantarillado y saneamiento*. Mexico.

Concha Malo, Miguel. 1988. "Las violaciones a los derechos humanos individuales en México (período: 1971–1986)." In *Primer Informe sobre la Democracia: México 1988*, edited by Pablo González Casanova and Jorge Cadena Roa. Mexico: Siglo Veintiuno/UNAM.

Consejo Consultivo del Programa Nacional de Solidaridad. 1992. *El combate a la pobreza: lineamientos programáticos*. Mexico: El Nacional.

Consejo Consultivo del Programa Nacional de Solidaridad/API Consultores. 1992. "Combate a la pobreza: vertiente alimentaria." Unpublished document.

Consejo Consultivo del Sector Social para la Reestructuración del Inmecafé. 1991. "Financiamiento integral de la caficultura del sector social." Typescript.

Consejo Mexicano 500 Años de Resistencia India y Popular. 1991. "Declaración de Principios y Objetivos," *Cuadernos Agrarios* 2 (nueva época).

Contreras, Oscar. 1992. Presentation to the Panel "The Recuperation of One-Party Dominance in Mexico, 1988–92: The 'National Solidarity Strategy'," XVII International Congress of the Latin American Studies Association, Los Angeles, Calif., September 24.

Cook, Maria L. 1990. "Organizing Opposition in the Teachers' Movement in Oaxaca." In *Popular Movements and Political Change in Mexico*, edited by Joe Foweraker and Ann L. Craig. Boulder, Colo.: Lynne Rienner, in association with the Center for U.S.-Mexican Studies, University of California, San Diego.

Cordera Campos, Rolando. 1991a. "Necesidad política, ética, constitucional y económica de PRONASOL," *El Nacional*, September 10.

———. 1991b. "Solidaridad y su problemática." In *Solidaridad a debate*. Mexico: El Nacional.

————. 1991c. "Solidaridad y su problemática," Suplemento Político, *El Nacional*, September 5.

————. 1992. "Las parábolas del lobo neoliberal," *El Nacional*, March 21.

Córdoba, José. 1994. "Mexico." In *The Political Economy of Policy Reform*, edited by John Williamson. Washington, D.C.: Institute for International Economics, January.

Cornelius, Wayne A. 1975. *Politics and the Migrant Poor in Mexico City*. Stanford, Calif.: Stanford University Press.

Cornelius, Wayne A., Judith Gentleman, and Peter H. Smith, eds. 1989a. *Mexico's Alternative Political Futures*. Monograph Series, no. 30. La Jolla: Center for U.S.-Mexican Studies, University of California, San Diego.

Cornelius, Wayne A., Judith Gentleman, and Peter H. Smith. 1989b. "Overview: The Dynamics of Political Change in Mexico." In *Mexico's Alternative Political Futures*, edited by W.A. Cornelius et al. Monograph Series, no. 30. La Jolla: Center for U.S.-Mexican Studies, University of California, San Diego.

Correa, Guillermo. 1990. "EL PRONASOL, que nació como esperanza, ha generado corrupción y protestas," *Proceso* 727 (October 8).

Cortés, Fernando, and Rosa María Rubalcava. 1992. "Cambio estructural y concentración: un análisis de la distribución del ingreso familiar en México, 1984–1989." Paper presented at the conference "Social Effects of the Crisis," University of Texas at Austin, April 23–25.

Coulomb, René. 1989. "Rental Housing and the Dynamics of Urban Growth in Mexico City." In *Housing and Land in Urban Mexico*, edited by Alan Gilbert. Monograph Series, no. 31. La Jolla: Center for U.S.-Mexican Studies, University of California, San Diego.

Cox, G.W., M.D. McCubbins, and T. Sullivan. 1984. "Policy Choice as an Electoral Investment," *Social Choice and Welfare* 1:231–42.

Craig, Ann L. 1992a. "The National Solidarity Program in Mexico: The Politics of Autonomy, Concertation and Empowerment." Paper presented at the Latin American Center, St. Antony's College, Oxford, April 30.

————. 1992b. "Solidarity: Deconstructing Discourse and Practice in the Politics of Concertation." Paper presented to the workshop "Mexico's National Solidarity Program: A Preliminary Assessment," University of California, San Diego, La Jolla, February.

Craig, S. 1987. "The Deterrent of Police: An Examination of Locally Provided Public Service," *Journal of Urban Economics* 21:298–311.

Crespo, José Antonio. 1992. "El contexto político de las elecciones de 1991." In *Las elecciones federales de 1991*, edited by Alberto Aziz and Jacqueline Peschard. Mexico: CIIH, UNAM/Miguel Angel Porrúa.

Dirección de Desarrollo. 1991. "Programa de apoyo a productores de café. Fondos Regionales de Solidaridad para el Desarrollo de la Cafeticultura." Working Paper.

Dresser, Denise. 1991. *Neopopulist Solutions to Neoliberal Problems: Mexico's National Solidarity Program*. Current Issue Brief Series, no. 3. La Jolla: Center for U.S.-Mexican Studies, University of California, San Diego.

————. 1992a. "Embellishment, Empowerment, or Euthanasia of the PRI? Neoliberalism and Party Reform in Mexico." Paper presented at the seminar "The Politics of Economic Restructuring," Mexico City, June 15–16.

————. 1992b. "Pronasol: los dilemas de la gobernabilidad." Paper presented at the workshop "Mexico's National Solidarity Program: A Preliminary Assessment," Center for U.S.-Mexican Studies, University of California, San Diego, February 25.

————. 1992c. "Pronasol: los dilemas de la gobernabilidad," *El Cotidiano* 49 (July–August).

Drucker-Brown, Susan. 1985. "Introduction." In *Malinowski in Mexico: The Economics of a Mexican Market System*, by Bronislaw Malinowski and Julio de la Fuente. London: Routledge.

Eckstein, Susan. 1988. *The Poverty of Revolution: The State and the Urban Poor in Mexico*. 2d ed. Princeton, N.J.: Princeton University Press.

Ejea, Gabriela. 1992. "La resistencia cafetalera en Chiapas," *Unomasuno*, Supplement, March 23.

Ejea, Gabriela, and Luis Hernández. 1991. "Cafetaleros: la construcción de la autonomía," *Cuadernos Desarrollo de Base* 3.

Escuela Digna. 1992. "Memoria de evaluación." Mexico: Solidaridad para una Escuela Digna. Mimeo.

Fábregas Puig, Andrés. 1992. "Las culturas tradicionales en la modernidad." Paper presented at the "Seminario sobre Sociedad Urbana," Monterrey, Nuevo León, May.

Fernández, Jorge. 1991. "El PRI ante su propia transición," *Unomasuno*, November 7.

Fernández Santillán, José. 1991. "Aspectos ideológicos del PRONASOL." In *Solidaridad a debate*. Mexico: El Nacional.

Flores, Juan. 1991. "Proyectos de etnodesarrollo = los ricos más ricos y los pobres más pobres," *Etnias* 2:8 (January).

Flores de la Vega, Margarita, and Arturo León López. 1979. "La política del Inmecafé y la Sierra Mazateca (1973–1976)," *Comercio Exterior* 29:7 (July).

Foweraker, Joe, and Ann L. Craig, eds. 1990. *Popular Movements and Political Change in Mexico*. Boulder, Colo.: Lynne Rienner, in association with the Center for U.S.-Mexican Studies, University of California, San Diego.

Fox, Jonathan. 1992. "Targeting the Poorest: The Role of the National Indigenous Institute in Mexico's Solidarity Program." Paper presented at the workshop "Mexico's National Solidarity Program: A Preliminary Assessment," University of California, San Diego, La Jolla, February.

————. 1993. *The Politics of Food in Mexico: State Power and Social Mobilization*. Ithaca, N.Y.: Cornell University Press.

————. 1994. "The Difficult Transition from Clientelism to Citizenship: Lessons from Mexico," *World Politics* 46:2 (January).

————. n.d. "The Politics of Mexico's New Peasant Economy." In *The Politics of Economic Restructuring in Mexico*, edited by Maria Lorena Cook, Kevin Middlebrook, and Juan Molinar Horcasitas. U.S.-Mexico Contemporary Perspectives Series. La Jolla: Center for U.S.-Mexican Studies, University of California, San Diego, forthcoming 1994.

Fox, Jonathan, and Gustavo Gordillo. 1989. "Between State and Market: The Campesinos' Quest for Autonomy." In *Mexico's Alternative Political Futures*, edited by Wayne A. Cornelius, Judith Gentleman, and Peter H. Smith. Monograph Series, no. 30. La Jolla: Center for U.S.-Mexican Studies, University of California, San Diego.

Fox, Jonathan, and Julio Moguel. n.d. "Pluralism and Anti-Poverty Policy: Mexico's National Solidarity Program and Left Opposition Municipalities." In *Opposition Government in Mexico: Past Experiences and Future Opportunities*, edited by Victoria Rodríguez and Peter Ward. Albuquerque: University of New Mexico Press, forthcoming 1994.

Friedmann, Santiago, Nora Lustig, and Arianna Legovini. 1992. "Social Spending and Food Subsidies during Adjustment in Mexico." Paper prepared for the conference "Confronting the Challenge of Poverty and Inequality in Latin America," Brookings Institution, Washington, D.C., July.

Funes, Guillermo. 1991. "Informe del Director General." Mexico: IN-MECAFE. Typescript.

García Rocha, Adalberto, and Miguel Szekely Pardo. 1992. "Equidad del financiamiento de la educación pública en México." Mexico: Centro de Estudios Económicos, El Colegio de México. Mimeo.

Gershberg, Alec Ian, and Til Schuermann. 1992. "Welfare Considerations in the Provision of Public Services: Educational Expenditures and Outcomes in Mexico." Philadelphia: University of Pennsylvania. Mimeo.

Gibson, Edward. 1992. "Conservative Parties and Democratic Politics: Core Constituencies, Coalition-Building, and the Latin American Electoral Right." In *The Right and Democracy in Latin America*, edited by Douglas Chalmers, Maria do Carmo Campello de Souza, and Atilio Borón. New York: Praeger.

Gil Villegas, Francisco. 1986. "Descentralización y democracia: una perspectiva teórica." In *Descentralización y democracia en México*, edited by Blanca Torres. Mexico: El Colegio de México.

Gilbert, Alan, and Peter Ward. 1985. *Housing, the State and the Poor: Policy and Practice in Latin American Cities*. Cambridge: Cambridge University Press.

Gobierno Constitucional de los Estados Unidos Mexicanos y el Gobierno Constitucional del Estado de Durango. 1987. *Plan Estatal de Desarrollo, Durango 1987–1992.* Mexico.

Golden, Tim. 1992a. "Mexico's Leader Cautiously Backs Some Big Changes," *New York Times*, November 2.

———. 1992b. "Point of Attack for Mexico's Retooled Party Machine: The Leftist Stronghold," *New York Times*, July 12.

Gómez Leyva, Ciro. 1991. "Solidaridad gratuita en todas las pantallas," *Este País* 7 (October).

Gómez Tagle, Silvia. 1990. *Las estadísticas electorales de la reforma política.* Cuadernos del CES, no. 34. Mexico: El Colegio de México.

González, Alvaro, Teresa Valdivia, and Martha Rees. 1987. "Evaluación de los Programas Agrícolas del INI: Chiapas, Puebla y Oaxaca." Paper presented at the Society for Applied Anthropology, Oaxaca, April.

González de la Rocha, Mercedes, and Agustín Escobar Latapí, eds. 1991. *Social Responses to Mexico's Economic Crisis of the 1980s.* U.S.-Mexico Contemporary Perspectives Series, no. 1. La Jolla: Center for U.S.-Mexican Studies, University of California, San Diego.

González Navarro, Moisés. 1985. *La pobreza en México.* Mexico: El Colegio de México.

González Tiburcio, Enrique. 1991. "De lo cuantitativo a lo cualitativo. PRONASOL: hacia la nueva síntesis," *Cuaderno de Nexos* 40 (October).

———. 1992. "Seis tesis sobre el Programa Nacional de Solidaridad," *El Cotidiano* 8:49 (July–August): 3–13.

Graham, Carol. 1991a. "The APRA Government and the Urban Poor: The PAIT Programme in Lima's Pueblos Jóvenes," *Journal of Latin American Studies* 23:1 (February).

———. 1991b. "From Emergency Employment to Social Investment: Alleviating Poverty in Chile." Brookings Occasional Paper. Washington, D.C.: Brookings Institution, November.

———. 1991c. "Parties and Grass Roots Organization in Chile, Bolivia, and Peru: Poverty Alleviation and Democratic Consolidation." Paper presented at the XVI International Congress of the Latin American Studies Association, Washington, D.C., April 4–6.

———. 1992a. *Peru's APRA: Parties, Politics, and the Elusive Quest for Democracy.* Boulder, Colo.: Lynne Rienner.

———. 1992b. "The Politics of Protecting the Poor during Adjustment: Bolivia's Emergency Social Fund," *World Development* 20:9.

———. n.d.1. "The Politics of Adjustment and Poverty in Zambia: The Hour Has Come." Discussion Paper. New York: Social Dimensions of Adjustment Unit, World Bank, forthcoming 1994.

———. n.d.2. "The Politics of Safety Nets during Market Transitions: The Case of Poland." Discussion Paper. New York: Socialist Economies Reform Unit, World Bank, forthcoming 1994.

————. n.d.3. "The Vocal versus the Needy in Senegal: The Politics of Poverty during Adjustment." Discussion Paper. New York: Social Dimensions of Adjustment Unit, World Bank, forthcoming 1994.

Granados Chapa, Miguel Angel. 1992. "Plaza pública," *La Jornada*, May 9.

Grayson, George. 1991. "Mexico's New Politics: Building Sewers, Reaping Votes," *Commonweal*, October 25, pp. 612–14.

Grindle, Merilee. 1977. *Bureaucrats, Politicians, and Peasants in Mexico*. Berkeley: University of California Press.

————. 1986. *State and Countryside: Development Policy and Agrarian Politics in Latin America*. Baltimore, Md.: Johns Hopkins University Press.

Gruening, Ernest. 1928. *Mexico and Its Heritage*. London: Century.

Guerra, François-Xavier. 1985. *Le Méxique: De l'Ancien Régime à la Révolution*. 2 vols. Paris: L'Harmattan.

Guillén López, Tonatiuh. 1989. "The Social Bases of the PRI." In *Mexico's Alternative Political Futures*, edited by Wayne A. Cornelius, Judith Gentleman, and Peter H. Smith. Monograph Series, no. 30. La Jolla: Center for U.S.-Mexican Studies, University of California, San Diego.

Haber, Paul Lawrence. 1990. "Cárdenas, Salinas y los movimientos populares urbanos en México: el caso del Comité de Defensa Popular, General Francisco Villa de Durango." In *Movimientos sociales en México durante la década de los 80*, edited by Sergio Zermeño and Jesús Aurelio Cuevas. Mexico: Centro de Investigaciones Interdisciplinarias en Humanidades, UNAM.

————. 1992. "Collective Dissent in Mexico: The Politics of Contemporary Urban Popular Movements." Ph.D. dissertation, Columbia University.

————. n.d.1. "The Art and Implications of Political Restructuring in Mexico: The Case of Urban Popular Movements." In *The Politics of Economic Restructuring in Mexico*, edited by Maria Lorena Cook, Kevin J. Middlebrook, and Juan Molinar Horcasitas. La Jolla: Center for U.S.-Mexican Studies, University of California, San Diego, forthcoming 1994.

————. n.d.2. "Cárdenas, Salinas and Urban Popular Movements in Mexico." In *Crisis and Response in Mexico*, edited by Neil Harvey. New York: St. Martin's Press, forthcoming 1994.

Handy, Jim. 1988. "'The Most Precious Fruit of the Revolution': The Guatemalan Agrarian Reform, 1952–54," *Hispanic American Historical Review* 68:4:675–705.

Harvey, Neil. 1993. "The Limits of Concertation in Rural Mexico." In *Mexico: Dilemmas of Transition*, edited by N. Harvey. London: Institute of Latin American Studies, University of London.

Hellman, Judith Adler. 1992. "The Study of New Social Movements in Latin America and the Question of Autonomy." In *The Making of Social*

Movements in Latin America, edited by Arturo Escobar and Sonia Alvarez. Boulder, Colo.: Westview.

Heredia, Blanca. 1992. "Making Economic Reform Politically Viable: The Mexican Experience." Paper presented at the conference "Markets, Democracy, and Structural Adjustment in Latin America," CEDES, Buenos Aires, March.

Hernández, Crescencio. 1991. "Dudas, retos y nuevos enfoques." In *Solidaridad a debate*. Mexico: El Nacional.

Hernández Alvarez, Gonzalo. 1991. "Nuevos solidarios en la cabecera municipal de Ocosingo." In *La voz común: Testimonios de solidaridad*. Mexico: El Nacional.

Hernández Navarro, Luis. 1983. "Los retos de la CNTE," *Que sí, que no*, no. 2. Monthly supplement to the *Gaceta Popular de la Universidad Autónoma de Guerrero*, October 8.

———. 1991a. "El Partido del Trabajo: Realidades y perspectivas," *El Cotidiano* 40 (March–April).

———. 1991b. "Privatización y concertación social." In *La modernización del sector agropecuario*, edited by Cuauhtémoc González Pacheco. Mexico: Instituto de Investigaciones Económicas, UNAM.

Hernández Rodríguez, Rogelio. 1987. "Los hombres del Presidente de la Madrid," *Foro Internacional* 109 (July–September).

Hewitt de Alcántara, Cynthia. 1984. *Anthropological Perspectives on Rural Mexico*. London: Routledge and Kegan Paul.

Hinojosa, Oscar. 1992. "Sirve el Pronasol al gobierno como instrumento electoral y factor de legitimidad y estabilidad," *El Financiero*, June.

Hirales, Gustavo. 1992. "Movilidad social," *Cuaderno de Nexos* 52 (October).

Hirschman, Albert O. 1979. "The Turn to Authoritarianism in Latin America and the Search for Its Economic Determinants." In *The New Authoritarianism in Latin America*, edited by David Collier. Princeton, N.J.: Princeton University Press.

———. 1986. *El avance en colectividad. Experimentos populares en América Latina*. Mexico: Fondo de Cultura Económica.

INI (Instituto Nacional Indigenista). 1978. "Treinta años después, revisión crítica," *México Indígena*, número especial de aniversario, December.

———. 1990. *Programa Nacional de Desarrollo de los Pueblos Indígenas, 1991–1994*. Mexico: INI.

———. 1991. "Manual de Operación de los Fondos Regionales de Solidaridad para el Desarrollo de los Pueblos Indígenas." Mexico: INI, November. Unpublished.

———. 1993. *Manual de Operación de los Fondos Regionales de Solidaridad para el Desarrollo de los Pueblos Indígenas*. Mexico: SEDESOL.

INMECAFE (Instituto Mexicano del Café). 1974. *Manual del promotor*. Mexico: Gerencia de Organización de Productores, INMECAFE.

————. 1975. *Informe de labores*. Mexico: INMECAFE.

————. 1989a. "Bases para el cambio estructural del Instituto Mexicano del Café." Mexico: INMECAFE. Typescript.

————. 1989b. "Reestructuración del sector cafetalero mexicano." Mexico: INMECAFE. Mimeo.

Instituto Cuanto. 1991. *Ajuste y economía familiar: 1985–1990*. Lima: Cuanto.

Jorgensen, Steen, Margaret Grosh, and Mark Schacter. 1992. *Bolivia's Answer to Poverty, Economic Crisis, and Adjustment: The Emergency Social Fund*. Washington, D.C.: World Bank.

Joseph, Gilbert, and Daniel Nugent. n.d. *The Mexican Revolution, Hegemony and Popular Culture*. Forthcoming.

Juárez Quezada, Ma. Isabel. 1991. "Ma." In *La voz común: testimonios de solidaridad*. Mexico: El Nacional.

Kaufman, Robert R. 1990. "How Societies Change Developmental Models or Keep Them: Reflections on the Latin American Experience in the 1930s and the Postwar World." In *Manufacturing Miracles: Paths of Industrialization in Latin America and East Asia*, edited by Gary Gereffi and Donald Wyman. Princeton, N.J.: Princeton University Press, in association with the Center for U.S.-Mexican Studies, University of California, San Diego.

Kenyon, J.P., ed. 1969. *Halifax. Complete Works*. Harmondsworth: Penguin.

Klesner, Joseph. 1988. "Electoral Reform in an Authoritarian Regime: The Case of Mexico." Ph.D. dissertation, Massachusetts Institute of Technology.

————. n.d. "Realignment or Dealignment? Consequences of Economic Crisis and Economic Restructuring for the Mexican Party System." In *The Politics of Economic Restructuring*, edited by Maria Lorena Cook, Kevin Middlebrook, and Juan Molinar Horcasitas. La Jolla: Center for U.S. Mexican Studies, University of California, San Diego, forthcoming 1994.

Knight, Alan. 1990a. "Historical Continuities in Social Movements." In *Popular Movements and Political Change in Mexico*, edited by Joe Foweraker and Ann L. Craig. Boulder, Colo.: Lynne Rienner, in association with the Center for U.S.-Mexican Studies, University of California, San Diego.

————. 1990b. "Revolutionary Project, Recalcitrant People." In *The Revolutionary Process in Mexico. Essays in Political and Social Change*, edited by Jaime Rodríguez. Los Angeles: University of California, Los Angeles.

————. 1992. "The Peculiarities of Mexican History: Mexico Compared to Latin America, 1821–1992," *Journal of Latin American Studies* 24, quincentenary supplement, pp. 99–144.

La Jornada. 1991a. "El Pronasol atrae más sufragio que el mismo PRI en Chalco," *La Jornada*, August 18.

———. 1991b. "Warman: reciente, la visión de los indígenas como un grupo con futuro," October 12.

Lasswell, Harold. 1958. *Politics: Who Gets What, When, How*. New York: Meridian.

Levy, Daniel. 1979. *University and Government in Mexico: Autonomy in an Authoritarian System*. New York: Praeger.

———. 1989. "Mexico: Sustained Civilian Rule without Democracy." In *Democracy in Developing Countries: Latin America*, edited by Larry Diamond et al. Boulder, Colo.: Lynne Rienner.

Levy, Santiago. 1991. "Poverty Alleviation in Mexico." World Bank Working Paper Series, no. 679. Washington, D.C.: World Bank, May.

Limón, Miguel. 1988. "Análisis histórico del indigenismo." In *México, 75 Años de Revolución, Desarrollo Social I*. Mexico: Fondo de Cultura Económica.

Llanos Samaniego, Raúl. 1992. "Liberados durante la actual administración, 4 mil 120 indígenas," *La Jornada*, August 30.

Lomas, Emilio. 1991a. "La democracia ya no es de las cúpulas, afirma Salinas," *La Jornada*, September 13.

———. 1991b. "Salinas: nueva relación Estado-sociedad civil," *La Jornada*, September 15.

López Acuña, Daniel. 1980. *La salud desigual en México*. Mexico: Siglo Veintiuno.

Lozano Asencio, Fernando. 1993. *Bringing It Back Home: Remittances to Mexico from Migrant Workers in the United States*. Monograph Series, no. 37. La Jolla: Center for U.S.-Mexican Studies, University of California, San Diego.

Lustig, Nora. 1992. *Mexico. The Remaking of an Economy*. Washington, D.C.: Brookings Institution.

Macciocchi, Maria Antonietta. 1975. Gramsci y la revolución de occidente. Mexico: Siglo Veintiuno.

Mainwaring, Scott. 1990. "Presidentialism in Latin America," *Latin American Research Review* 25:1.

———. 1991. "Clientelism, Patrimonialism, and Economic Crisis: Brazil since 1979." Paper presented at the XVI International Congress of the Latin American Studies Association, Washington, D.C., April 4–7.

Malloy, James. 1985. "Statecraft and Social Security Policy and Crisis: A Comparison of Latin America and the United States." In *The Crisis of Social Security and Health Care: Latin American Experiences and Lessons*, edited by Carmelo Mesa-Lago. Latin American Monograph Series, no 9. Pittsburgh, Penn.: University of Pittsburgh.

Martínez Nateras, Arturo. 1991. "Solidaridad y gobernabilidad." In *Solidaridad a debate*. Mexico: El Nacional.

————. 1992a. "Programación regional, prioridad de la Secretaría de Desarrollo Social," *Excélsior*, May 19.

————. 1992b. "Solidaridad: cambio y permanencia. La programación, un caso," *El Cotidiano* 8:49 (July–August): 29–36.

Martínez Saldaña, Tomás. 1980. *El costo social de un éxito político: la política expansionista del Estado mexicano en el agro lagunero*. Chapingo: El Colegio de Postgraduados.

Maxfield, Sylvia. 1990. *Governing Capital: International Finance and Mexican Politics*. Ithaca, N.Y.: Cornell University Press.

Medina A., José Luis. 1992. "Políticas sociales: la experiencia mexicana en el contexto internacional." Mimeo.

Mejía Pineros, María Consuelo, and Sergio Sarmiento. 1987. *La lucha indígena: un reto a la ortodoxia*. Mexico: Siglo Veintiuno.

Melucci, Alberto. 1985. "The Symbolic Challenge of Contemporary Movements," *Social Research* 52:4 (Winter): 789–816.

Memorias del Seminario de Análisis para la Integración de una Política Nacional de la Caficultura. 1991. Jalapa, Veracruz.

Méndez, Luis, Miguel Angel Romero, and Augusto Bolívar. 1992. "Solidaridad se institucionaliza," *El Cotidiano* 8:49 (July–August).

Mesa-Lago, Carmelo. 1992. *Economic and Financial Aspects of Social Security in Latin America and the Caribbean: Tendencies, Problems and Alternatives for the Year 2000*. Human Resources Division Report No. IDP-095. Washington, D.C.: World Bank.

Meyer, Lorenzo. 1993. "Solidaridad para ganar votos," *Excélsior*, May 20.

Middlebrook, Kevin. 1986. "Political Liberalization in an Authoritarian Regime: The Case of Mexico." In *Transitions from Authoritarian Rule: Latin America*, edited by Guillermo O'Donnell et al. Baltimore, Md.: Johns Hopkins University Press.

Midgley, James. 1984. *Social Security, Inequality, and the Third World*, Chichester, Eng.: Wiley.

Migdal, Joel. 1988. *Strong Societies and Weak States: State-Society Relations and State Capabilities in the Third World*. Princeton, N.J.: Princeton University Press.

Moguel, Julio. 1987. *Los caminos de la izquierda*. Mexico: Juan Pablos.

————. 1990. "National Solidarity Program Fails to Help the Very Poor," *Voices of Mexico* 15 (October–December).

————. 1991. "Poder local y alternativas de desarrollo: la experiencia del movimiento urbano en una región del Norte de México." Paper prepared for the Inter-American Foundation, Washington, D.C.

Moguel, Julio, and Josefina Aranda. 1992. "La Coordinadora Estatal de Productores de Café de Oaxaca." In *Autonomía y nuevos sujetos sociales en el desarrollo rural*, edited by Julio Moguel, Carlota Botey, and Luis Hernández. Mexico: Siglo Veintiuno/CEHAM.

Molinar Horcasitas, Juan. 1991. *El tiempo de la legitimidad: elecciones, autoritarismo y democracia en México*. Mexico: Cal y Arena.

Molinar Horcasitas, Juan, and Jeffrey A. Weldon. 1991. "Elecciones de 1988 en México: crisis del autoritarismo," *Revista Mexicana de Sociología* 4.

Monahan, Jane. 1993. "Rebuilding Mexico's Small Towns," *Journal of Commerce*, July 27.

Montaño, Jorge. 1976. *Los pobres de la ciudad en los asentamientos espontáneos.* Mexico: Siglo Veintiuno.

Morales, Cesáreo. 1991. "Solidaridad: programa para una sociedad abierta." In *Solidaridad a debate*. Mexico: El Nacional.

Moyao M., Eliseo. 1991. "¿Hay un cambio de fondo en la política social del gobierno?," *Barrio Nuevo* 1:8:1–5.

Muñoz Izquierdo, Carlos, Manuel Ignacio Ulloa Herrero et al. 1992. *Educación y pobreza: resultados de un estudio patrocinado por el Consejo Consultivo del Programa Nacional de Solidaridad.* Mexico: Centro de Estudios Educativos.

Nachmad, Salomón. n.d. "Una experiencia indigenista: 20 años de lucha desde investigador hasta la carcel en defensa de los indios de México." Manuscript.

Nagengast, Carole, and Michael Kearney. 1990. "Mixtec Ethnicity: Social Identity, Political Consciousness and Political Activism," *Latin American Research Review* 25:2.

Nelson, Joan, et al. 1989. *Fragile Coalitions: The Politics of Economic Adjustment.* New Brunswick, N.J.: Transaction Books.

Obershall, Anthony. 1972. *Social Conflicts and Social Movements.* New York: Prentice Hall.

O'Connor, James. 1973. *The Fiscal Crisis of the State.* New York: St. Martin's Press.

O'Donnell, Guillermo, and Philippe Schmitter. 1986. *Transitions from Authoritarian Rule: Tentative Conclusions about Uncertain Democracies.* Baltimore, Md.: Johns Hopkins University Press.

Olson, Mancur. 1982. *The Rise and Decline of Nations.* New Haven, Conn.: Yale University Press.

Ortega Lomelín, Roberto. 1988. *El nuevo federalismo: la descentralización.* Mexico: Porrúa.

Palacios, Juan José. 1989. *La política regional en México, 1970–1982.* Guadalajara: Universidad de Guadalajara.

Peniche, Antonio. 1992. "El PRONASOL: algunas notas y reflexiones generales," *El Cotidiano* 49 (July–August).

Peón Escalante, Fernando. 1992. "Solidaridad en el marco de la política social," *El Cotidiano* 8:49 (July–August): 14–19.

Pérez, Matilde. 1991. "El ejido es un sistema equitativo y eficaz: INI," *La Jornada*, October 23.

Portilla, Santiago. 1993. "Programa Nacional de Solidaridad." Mexico City. Mimeo.

PRONASOL (Programa Nacional de Solidaridad). 1990a. "Propuesta para la Creación de Empresas de Solidaridad." Mexico, March 3. Mimeo.

————. 1990b. "Sumario." Mexico: Comité Técnico de Evaluación del Programa Nacional de Solidaridad. Manuscript.

————. 1991a. "La solidaridad en el desarrollo nacional." Mexico: Coordinación del Programa Nacional de Solidaridad, Secretaría de Programación y Presupuesto, September.

————. 1991b. *La voz común: testimonios de solidaridad*. Mexico: El Nacional.

————. 1991c. *Manual único de operación: Programa Nacional de Solidaridad*. Mexico: SPP.

————. 1992. *Guía para la operación de los Fondos Municipales de Solidaridad, ejercicio 1992*. Mexico: SPP, January.

————. 1993. "Manual Unico de Operación." Mexico: SEDESOL.

————. n.d. "El Programa Nacional de Solidaridad ante los problemas de la cafeticultura." Mexico. Typescript.

Provencio, Enrique. 1992. "La incierta relación entre desarrollo y democracia." In *Desigualdad y democracia*, by Armando Bartra et al. Mexico: El Nacional.

Przeworski, Adam. 1986. "Some Problems in the Study of the Transition to Democracy." In *Transitions from Authoritarian Rule: Comparative Perspectives*, edited by Guillermo O'Donnell, Philippe Schmitter, and Laurence Whitehead. Baltimore, Md.: Johns Hopkins University Press.

Ramírez, Carlos. 1992. "Indicador político," *El Financiero*, August 21.

Ramírez Saiz, Juan Manuel. 1986. *El movimiento urbano popular en México*. Mexico: Siglo Veintiuno.

Ramos, Ignacio. 1985. "Concertación social en DICONSA," *Sistema C* 36 (August).

Rascón, Marco, and Javier Hidalgo. 1992. "Los propietarios de Solidaridad y la irritación gubernamental," *La Jornada*, September 15.

Regalado Santillán, Jorge. 1986. "El movimiento popular independiente en Guadalajara." In *Perspectivas de los movimientos sociales en la región Centro-Occidente*, edited by Jaime Tamayo. Mexico: Línea.

Reséndiz, Jesús, and Roberto Zamarripa. 1992. "Durango formalizó nuevo equilibrio político; el PT estrenó alcaldía," *La Jornada*, September 10.

Reyes Heroles, Federico, and René Delgado. 1991. "Empleo e ingreso, reto del Pronasol. Entrevista con el Ing. Carlos Rojas," *Este País* 7 (October): 3–7.

Rico, Salvador. 1989. "Los indígenas, carne de *acarreo* de los partidos políticos: Warman," *Punto*, May 1.

Rodríguez, Victoria. 1993. "The Politics of Decentralization in Mexico: From Municipio Libre to Solidaridad," *Bulletin of Latin American Research* 12:2.

———. n.d. *Decentralization in Mexico: The Facade of Power*. Boulder, Colo.: Westview, forthcoming.

Rodríguez, Victoria, and Peter Ward. 1992. *Policymaking, Politics, and Urban Governance in Chihuahua: The Experience of Recent PANista Governments*. Mexican Policy Studies Report No. 3. Austin: LBJ School of Public Affairs, University of Texas at Austin.

———. 1993. "Disentangling the PRI from the Government in Mexico." Austin: LBJ School of Public Affairs, University of Texas at Austin. Manuscript.

Rojas, Carlos. 1991a. "Avances del Programa Nacional de Solidaridad," *Comercio Exterior* 41:5 (May): 443–46.

———. 1991b. "Solidaridad en México." In *Solidaridad a debate*, by Carlos Rojas et al. Mexico: El Nacional.

———. 1992a. "El Programa Nacional de Solidaridad en la práctica." Presentation at the "Seminario sobre Reforma del Estado," El Colegio de México, Mexico City, March 20.

———. 1992b. Interview with *El Nacional*, March 20.

———. 1993. "Las cuentas del gran profesor," *Excélsior*, May 24.

Rojas, Carlos, et al. 1991. *Solidaridad a Debate*. Mexico: El Nacional.

Rojas, Rosa. 1991a. "Se violan derechos humanos dentro del aparato judicial," *La Jornada*, August 10.

———. 1991b. "INI: hace falta un *ombudsman* para los derechos indígenas," *La Jornada*, August 11.

———. 1992a. "Ha distribuido el INI 280 mil millones en 115 fondos," *La Jornada*, August 22.

———. 1992b. "Indígenas de Chiapas piden se libere a 3 funcionarios del INI," *La Jornada*, March 21.

Rubiell, Jesús. 1992. "Conferencia para procuradores agrarios." Presentation at the Instituto Nacional de Solidaridad, Mexico City, June.

Rubin, Jeffrey W. 1990. "Popular Mobilization and the Myth of State Corporatism." In *Popular Movements and Political Change in Mexico*, edited by Joe Foweraker and Ann L. Craig. Boulder, Colo.: Lynne Rienner, in association with the Center for U.S.-Mexican Studies, University of California, San Diego.

———. n.d. "COCEI in Juchitán: Grassroots Radicalism and Regional History," *Journal of Latin American Studies*, forthcoming 1994.

Ruiz Hernández, Margarito Xib. 1993. "Todo indigenismo es lo mismo," *Ojarasca*, February.

Sabines, Jaime. 1991. "Presentación." In *La voz común: testimonios de solidaridad*. Mexico: El Nacional.

Salinas de Gortari, Carlos. 1978. "Political Participation, Public Investment, and System Support: A Study of Three Rural Communities in
Central Mexico." Ph.D. dissertation, Harvard University.
————. 1980. *Producción y participación en el campo*. Mexico: UNAM.
————. 1982. *Political Participation, Public Investment, and Support for the
System: A Comparative Study of Rural Communities in Mexico*. Research
Report Series, no. 35. La Jolla: Center for U.S.-Mexican Studies,
University of California, San Diego.
————. 1988. Speech announcing the establishment of the Comisión
Nacional de Programas de Solidaridad Social, Palacio Nacional, December 2. Manuscript.
————. 1990. "Second State of the Nation Report," November 1, 1990.
Mexico: Office of the Press Secretary to the President.
————. 1991. *Tercer Informe de Gobierno*. Mexico: Presidencia de la República.
————. 1993a. "Fifth State of the Nation Report," November 1, 1993.
Mexico: Office of the Press Secretary to the President.
————. 1993b. "Liberalismo social: responsabilidad comprometida Estado-sociedad," *Gaceta de Solidaridad*, vol. 3, número especial, June.
Sánchez, Héctor. 1991. "Aires de cambio en Juchitán." In *Solidaridad a
debate*. Mexico: El Nacional.
Sarmiento, Sergio. 1985. "El Consejo Nacional de Pueblos Indígenas y la
política indigenista," *Revista Mexicana de Sociología* 47:3 (July–
September).
————. 1991a. "Movimiento indio y modernización," *Cuadernos Agrarios*
2 (nueva época).
————. 1991b. "Solidarity Offers Hope for Votes," *El Financiero Internacional*, September 30.
Schmitter, Philippe C. 1992. *Neocorporativismo II: más allá y el mercado*.
Mexico: Alianza.
Schneider, Ben. 1988. "Partly for Sale: Privatization in Brazil and Mexico," *Journal of Interamerican Studies and World Affairs*, Winter.
Scott, James C. 1991. *Domination and the Arts of Resistance. Hidden
Transcripts*. New Haven, Conn.: Yale University Press.
SEDESOL (Secretaría de Desarrollo Social). 1992a. *Empresas de Solidaridad: lineamientos generales de operación*. Mexico: Instituto Nacional
de Solidaridad, September.
————. 1992b. *Fondos Municipales de Solidaridad: guía técnica*. Mexico:
Dirección General de Integración Sectorial.
————. 1992c. "Principales políticas y criterios para la operación del
programa de agua potable, alcantarillado y saneamiento en zonas
urbanas, 1993." Mexico. Mimeo.
————. 1993. *Solidarity in National Development: New Relations between
Society and Government*. Mexico: SEDESOL, March.

Sheahan, John. 1991. *Conflict and Change in Mexican Economic Strategy*. Monograph Series, no. 34. La Jolla: Center for U.S.-Mexican Studies, University of California, San Diego.

Sikkink, Kathryn. 1991. *Ideas and Institutions: Developmentalism in Brazil and Argentina*. Ithaca, N.Y.: Cornell University Press.

Smith, Peter. 1979. *Labyrinths of Power: Political Recruitment in Twentieth-Century Mexico*. Princeton, N.J.: Princeton University Press.

SPP (Secretaría de Programación y Presupuesto). 1988. *México: desarrollo regional y descentralización de la vida nacional*. Mexico: SPP.

Stavenhagen, Rodolfo, and Margarita Nolasco, eds. 1988. *Política cultural para un país multiétnico*. Mexico: Secretaría de Educación Pública.

Tamburi, G. 1985. "Social Security in Latin America: Trends and Outlook." In *The Crisis of Social Security and Health Care: Latin American Experiences and Lessons*, edited by Carmelo Mesa-Lago. Latin American Monograph Series, no. 9. Pittsburgh, Penn.: University of Pittsburgh.

Teichman, Judith. 1988. *Policymaking in Mexico: From Boom to Crisis*. Boston: Allen & Unwin.

Vera, Ramón. 1990. "Expulsados por el paraíso," *México Indígena* 7 (April).

Villa, Manuel. 1991. "El PRONASOL en la vida democrática de la nación." In *Solidaridad a debate*. Mexico: El Nacional.

Villarreal, René. 1993. *Liberalismo social y reforma del estado: México en la era del capitalismo posmoderno*. Mexico: Nacional Financiera/Fondo de Cultura Económica.

Vizcaíno, Rogelio. 1992. Interview in "Gente Solidaria," *El Nacional*, April.

Ward, Peter M. 1981. "Political Pressure for Urban Services: The Response of Two Mexico City Administrations," *Development and Change* 12:379–407.

———. 1986. *Welfare Politics in Mexico: Papering over the Cracks*. Boston, Mass.: Allen & Unwin.

———. 1989. "Government without Democracy in Mexico City: Defending the High Ground." In *Mexico's Alternative Political Futures*, edited by Wayne A. Cornelius, Judith Gentleman, and Peter H. Smith. Monograph Series, no. 30. La Jolla: Center for U.S.-Mexican Studies, University of California, San Diego.

———. 1990. *Mexico City: The Production and Reproduction of an Urban Environment*. Boston, Mass.: G.K. Hall and London: Belhaven.

———. 1992. "Los cambios en las políticas de bienestar social en la apertura política de México." Paper presented at the Encuentro Internacional "Sociedad Urbana," Monterrey, N.L., May 18–20.

Ward, Peter, Edith Jiménez, and Gareth Jones. 1993. "Residential Land Price Changes in Mexican Cities and the Affordability of Land for Lower-income Groups," *Urban Studies* 30:10.

Warman, Arturo. 1992. "Solidaridad y reforma del Estado." Mexico: Instituto Nacional de Solidaridad.

Warman, Arturo, et al. 1970. *De eso que llaman antropología mexicana.* Mexico: Nuestro Tiempo.

Waterbury, John. n.d. *Exposed to Innumerable Delusions: Public Enterprise and State Power in Egypt, India, Mexico and Turkey.* New York: Oxford University Press, forthcoming.

Whitecotton, Joseph. 1984. *The Zapotecs: Princes, Priests and Peasants.* Norman: University of Oklahoma Press.

Whitehead, Laurence. 1980. "From Bust to Boom: A Political Evaluation of the 1976–9 Stabilization Program," *World Development* 8:843–63.

Wilkie, James W. 1973. *The Mexican Revolution: Federal Expenditure and Social Change since 1910.* Berkeley: University of California Press.

Wnuk-Lipinski, Edmund. 1992. "Freedom or Equality: An Old Dilemma in a New Context." In *Social Policy, Social Justice, and Citizenship in Eastern Europe*, edited by Bob Deacon. Aldershoot: Avebury.

Yáñez, Alejandro González. 1991. "Reflexiones de Diputado Alejandro Yáñez," *Contacto Durango* 283 (February 3).

Zepeda, Mario. 1991. "El Pronasol, la política y la pobreza (tejiendo en el telar de Penélope)," *Memorias, CEMOS* 36 (October).

Acronyms

ACNR	Asociación Cívica Nacional Revolucionaria/National Revolutionary Civic Association
ANAMUP	Asociación Nacional del Movimiento Urbano Popular/National Association of the Urban Popular Movement
ANOCP	Asamblea Nacional de Obreros y Campesinos Popular/National Popular Assembly of Workers and Peasants
BANCOMEXT	Banco Nacional de Comercio Exterior/Foreign Trade Bank
BANOBRAS	Banco Nacional de Obras y Servicios Públicas/National Public Works Bank
BANRURAL	Banco Nacional de Crédito Rural/Rural Credit Bank
CAPFCE	Comité Administrador del Programa Federal de Construcción de Escuelas/Administrative Committee of the Federal School Building Program
CCI	Confederación Campesina Independiente/Independent Peasant Confederation
	Also
	Centros Coordinadores Indigenistas/*Indigenista* Coordinating Centers
CDP	Comité de Defensa Popular/Committee for Popular Defense
CDS	Convenio de Desarrollo Social/Social Development Agreement
CEPCO	Coordinadora Estatal de Productores del Café de Oaxaca/Oaxaca State Coffee Producers' Network

CEU	Consejo Estudiantil Universitario/Council of University Students
CFE	Comisión Federal de Electricidad/Federal Electricity Commission
CIOAC	Central Independiente de Obreros Agrícolas y Campesinos/Independent Confederation of Agricultural Workers and Peasants
CLFC	Compañía de Luz y Fuerza del Centro/Central Power and Light Company
CNA	Comisión Nacional del Agua/National Water Commission
CNAC	Comité Nacional de Auscultación y Coordinación/National Consultation and Coordinating Committee
CNC	Confederación Nacional Campesina/National Peasants' Confederation
CNOC	Coordinadora Nacional de Organizaciones Cafetaleras/National Coordinating Committee of Coffee-Producers' Organizations
CNOP	Confederación Nacional de Organizaciones Populares/National Confederation of Popular Organizations
CNPA	Coordinadora Nacional Plan de Ayala/National "Plan de Ayala" Coordinating Committee
CNTE	Coordinadora Nacional de Trabajadores de la Educación/National Coordinating Committee of Education Workers
COCEI	Coalición de Obreros, Campesinos y Estudiantes del Istmo/Coalition of Workers, Peasants, and Students of the Isthmus
COFIPE	Código Federal de Instituciones y Procedimientos Electorales/Federal Code for Institutions and Electoral Procedures
CONAMUP	Coordinadora Nacional del Movimiento Urbano Popular/National Coordinating Committee of the Urban Popular Movement
CONASUPO	Compañía Nacional de Subsistencias Populares/National Subsidized Staple Products Company
COPLADE	Comité de Planeación para el Desarrollo Estatal/Planning Committee for State Development
COPLAMAR	Coordinación General del Plan Nacional de Zonas Deprimidas y Grupos Marginados/Central Coordination of the National Plan of Economically Depressed Regions and Marginalized Groups

COPRODE	Coordinación de Proyectos de Desarrollo/Promotion Committee for Economic Development
CORETT	Comisión para la Regularización de la Tenencia de la Tierra/Commission for the Regularization of Land Tenure
COSINA	Coordinadora Sindical Nacional/National Union Coordinating Committee
CROM	Confederación Regional Obrera Mexicana/Mexican Regional Labor Confederation
CTM	Confederación de Trabajadores de México/Confederation of Mexican Workers
CUC	Convenio Unico de Coordinación/Single Coordinating Agreement
CUD	Convenio Unico de Desarrollo/Single Development Agreement
DICONSA	Distribuidora CONASUPO, S.A./Distributor CONASUPO
DIF	Desarrollo Integral de la Familia/Family Services Agency
FDN	Frente Democrático Nacional/National Democratic Front
FIDECAFE	Fideicomiso para el Café/Coffee Trust Fund
FNCR	Frente Nacional Contra la Represión/National Front Against Repression
FNDSCAC	Frente Nacional en Defensa del Salario y contra la Austeridad y la Carestía/National Front for the Defense of Salaries and in Opposition to Austerity and Shortages
FONAVIR	Fondo para la Vivienda Rural/Rural Housing Fund
FONHAPO	Fondo Nacional de Habitaciones Populares/National Popular Housing Fund
FOVISSSTE	Fondo de la Vivienda para los Trabajadores del Instituto de Seguridad y Servicios Sociales de los Trabajadores del Estado/State Employees' Housing Fund
FPI	Frente Popular Independiente/Independent Popular Front
FPTyL	Frente Popular Tierra y Libertad/"Land and Liberty" Popular Front
GCI	Grupo Comunista Internacional/International Communist Group
IMSS	Instituto Mexicano del Seguro Social/Mexican Social Security Institute

INAH	Instituto Nacional de Antropología e Historia/ National Institute of Anthropology and History
INDECO	Instituto Nacional para el Desarrollo de la Comunidad y de la Vivienda Popular/National Institute for Community Development and Housing
INEA	Instituto Nacional para la Educación de los Adultos/ National Institute for Adult Education
INFONAVIT	Instituto del Fondo Nacional de la Vivienda para los Trabajadores/National Fund for Workers' Housing
INI	Instituto Nacional Indigenista/National Indigenous Institute
INMECAFE	Instituto Mexicano del Café/Mexican Coffee Institute
ISSSTE	Instituto de Seguridad y Servicios Sociales de los Trabajadores del Estado/Social Security Institute for State Workers
LP	Línea Proletaria/Proletarian Line
MAP	Movimiento de Acción Popular/Popular Action Movement
MAUS	Movimiento de Acción y Unidad Socialista/Socialist Action and Unity Movement
MLN	Movimiento de Liberación Nacional/National Liberation Movement
MRP	Movimiento Revolucionario del Pueblo/People's Revolutionary Movement
NAFTA	North American Free Trade Agreement
OIR-LM	Organización de Izquierda Revolucionaria-Línea de Masas/Organization of the Revolutionary Left-Mass Line
ORPC	Organización Revolucionaria Punto Crítico/ Revolutionary Organization "Punto Crítico"
PAN	Partido Acción Nacional/National Action Party
PARM	Partido Auténtico de la Revolución Mexicana/ Authentic Party of the Mexican Revolution
PCDP	Partido del CDP/Party of the CDP
PCM	Partido Comunista Mexicano/Mexican Communist Party
PFCRN	Partido del Frente Cardenista de Reconstrucción Nacional/Party of the Cardenista Front for National Reconstruction
PIDER	Programa Integral para el Desarrollo Rural/Integral Program for Rural Development
PINMUDE	Programa para la Integración de la Mujer en el Desarrollo/Program to Involve Women in Development

PMS	Partido Mexicano Socialista/Mexican Socialist Party
PMT	Partido Mexicano de los Trabajadores/Mexican Workers' Party
PPM	Partido Popular Mexicano/Mexican People's Party
PPS	Partido Popular Socialista/Popular Socialist Party
PRD	Partido de la Revolución Democrática/Party of the Democratic Revolution
PRI	Partido Revolucionario Institucional/Institutional Revolutionary Party
PRONASOL	Programa Nacional de Solidaridad/National Solidarity Program
PRT	Partido Revolucionario de los Trabajadores/Trotskyist Revolutionary Workers' Party
PSR	Partido Socialista Revolucionario/Revolutionary Socialist Party
PST	Partido Socialista de los Trabajadores/Socialist Workers' Party
PSUM	Partido Socialista Unificado de México/United Mexican Socialist Party
PT	Partido de Trabajo/Labor Party
SAM	Sistema Alimentario Mexicano/Mexican Food System
SARH	Secretaría de Agricultura y Recursos Hidráulicos/ Ministry of Agriculture and Water Resources
SECOFI	Secretaría de Comercio y Fomento Industrial/ Ministry of Commerce and Industrial Development
SEDESOL	Secretaría de Desarrollo Social/Ministry of Social Development
SEDUE	Secretaría de Desarrollo Urbano y Ecología/Ministry of Ecology and Urban Development
SEP	Secretaría de Educación Pública/Ministry of Education
SHCP	Secretaría de Hacienda y Crédito Público/Ministry of the Treasury and Public Credit
SPP	Secretaría de Programación y Presupuesto/Ministry of Budget and Planning
SRA	Secretaría de la Reforma Agraria/Ministry of Agrarian Reform
SSA	Secretaría de Salubridad y Asistencia/Ministry of Health and Welfare
UCP	Unión de Colonias Populares/Union of Popular Neighborhoods
UEPC	Unidades Económicas de Producción y Comercialización/Economic Units for Production and Marketing

UNAM   Universidad Nacional Autónoma de México/National
                Autonomous University of Mexico
UNORCA   Unión Nacional de Organizaciones Regionales
                Campesinas/National Union of Regional Peasant
                Organizations

About the Contributors

John Bailey is Professor of Government at Georgetown University. His chapter in this volume draws on recent research on center-periphery relations within Mexico in the areas of fiscal policy and electoral politics.

Vivienne Bennett, a political scientist who received her doctorate in Latin American studies from the University of Texas at Austin, is a faculty member in the Department of Political Science at Sarah Lawrence College. Her research focuses on urban popular movements and on clandestine political organizing in Mexico during the 1960s and 1970s. She is the author of the forthcoming *The Politics of Water: Urban Protest, Gender and Power in Monterrey, Mexico*.

Jennifer Boone is a recent graduate of the School of Foreign Service at Georgetown University and was the 1993 recipient of the school's Rowe Citation for outstanding senior thesis in Latin American Studies.

Fernando Célis Callejas is a historian and member of the Comisión de Enlace de la Coordinadora Nacional de Organizaciones Cafetaleras (CNOC).

Oscar F. Contreras, a sociologist, completed his graduate work in the Department of Political and Social Sciences at Mexico's National Autonomous University (UNAM). He has been a researcher at UNAM and also at El Colegio de Sonora and El Colegio de la Frontera Norte (COLEF). He currently serves as COLEF's Academic General Secretary.

Wayne A. Cornelius is the Gildred Professor of U.S.-Mexican Relations and the Founding Director of the Center for U.S.-Mexican Studies at the University of California, San Diego. He is also Professor of Political Science at UCSD. He received his Ph.D. from Stanford University, and for eight years was a member of the Political Science faculty at the Massachusetts Institute of Technology. He has conducted field research in Mexico since 1962, and has published extensively on rural-to-urban migration in Mexico, Mexican labor migration to the United States, and the Mexican political system. Among his recent books are *Mexico's Alternative Political Futures* (co-editor, 1989), *Mexican Migration to the United States: Process, Consequences, and Policy Options* (co-editor, 1990), and *The Mexican Political System in Transition* (co-author, 1991).

Ann L. Craig is Associate Professor and director of undergraduate studies in the Department of Political Science at the University of California, San Diego. Beginning with an interest in agrarian reform and peasant movements, her research has expanded to include all popular movements and, most recently, government poverty programs that require organized community participation. Her previous publications include *The First Agraristas: An Oral History of an Agrarian Reform Movement in Mexico* (1983), *The Mexican Political System in Transition* (co-author, 1991), and *Popular Movements and Political Change in Mexico* (co-editor, 1990).

Denise Dresser is a Ph.D. candidate in the Politics Department of Princeton University, completing a dissertation on economic liberalization and political coalitions in Mexico. She also teaches at the Instituto Tecnológico Autónomo de México (ITAM) in Mexico City. She is the author of *Neopopulist Solutions to Neoliberal Problems: Mexico's National Solidarity Program* (1991).

Jonathan Fox is Associate Professor of Political Science at the Massachusetts Institute of Technology. He is author of *The Politics of Food in Mexico: State Power and Social Mobilization* (1993) and editor of *The Challenge of Rural Democratization: Perspectives from Latin America and the Philippines* (1990).

Alec Ian Gershberg is Assistant Professor of Urban Policy Analysis and Management at the Graduate School of Management and Urban Policy of the New School for Social Research, New York. He did his doctoral work in Regional Science at the University of Pennsylvania on fiscal decentralization, intergovernmental relations, and education finance with an application to Mexico.

Enrique González Tiburcio, an economist, received his graduate training at Mexico's National Autonomous University, where he later joined the faculty. He has held a number of high-ranking government posts and is currently Secretary of the Consultative Council of the National Solidarity Program and Director General of Research and Development in Mexico's Instituto Nacional de Solidaridad (National Solidarity Institute). He is the co-author of seven books and his articles have appeared in numerous academic journals.

Carol Graham is a Guest Scholar in the Foreign Policy Studies Program at the Brookings Institution and Adjunct Professor in the Department of Government at Georgetown University. She is the author of *Peru's APRA: Parties, Politics, and the Elusive Quest for Democracy* (1992) and several journal articles and book chapters on the political economy of Peru, Bolivia, and Chile. Her current project at Brookings on the politics of implementing safety nets during market transitions in Latin America, Africa, and Eastern Europe will be published as *Market Transitions and the Poor: Comparative Studies in Sustaining Reform*.

Paul Haber received his doctorate in Political Science from Columbia University and since 1991 has taught at the Department of Political Science, University of Montana. His publications focus on Mexican agrarian policy and the politics of urban popular movements. Most recently, he has embarked on a comparative analysis of poor people's movements in Mexico and the United States.

Luis Hernández Navarro, a social anthropologist, is a consultant to the Coordinadora Nacional de Organizaciones Cafetaleras (CNOC) and a researcher at the Centro de Estudios para el Cambio en el Campo Mexicano (CECCAM) in Mexico City. He has written widely on rural issues and social and peasant movements in Mexico. Among his recent publications are "Maiceros: de la guerra por los precios de desarrollo rural integral," in *Crisis y restructuración* (1992), and *Autonomía y nuevos sujetos sociales en el desarrollo rural* (co-editor, 1992).

Alan Knight received his doctorate from the University of Oxford and has taught at Essex University and the University of Texas at Austin, where he held the C.B. Smith Chair in Mexican Studies. His two-volume *The Mexican Revolution* (1986) won the Bolton and Beveridge prizes of the American Historical Association. He is currently Professor of the History of Latin America and Director of the Latin American Centre at Oxford University (St. Antony's College).

Nora Lustig is a Senior Fellow in the Foreign Policy Studies Program at the Brookings Institution. From 1975 to 1991, Lustig was Professor of Economics with El Colegio de México's Center of Economic Studies in Mexico City. Her research focuses on economic restructuring in Mexico, NAFTA, and income distribution and poverty in Latin America. Her recent publications include *Mexico: The Remaking of an Economy* (1992) and *North American Free Trade: Assessing the Impact* (co-editor, 1992).

Julio Moguel is a professor and researcher in the Economics Department of Mexico's National Autonomous University. He has written several books and articles on Mexican rural issues, on urban and rural popular organizations and movements, and on social problems more generally. His most recent publications are volumes 7–9 of the series *Historia de la* *cuestión agraria mexicana* (editor, 1989–91) and *Autonomía y nuevos sujetos sociales en el desarrollo rural* (1992), which he co-edited.

Juan Molinar Horcasitas holds a Master's degree from El Colegio de México and is currently a Ph.D. candidate in Political Science at the University of California, San Diego, as well as a researcher at El Colegio de México. His investigations focus on electoral behavior in Mexico, a subject covered in his most recently published book, *Los tiempos de la legitimidad: elecciones, autoritarismo y democracia en México* (1991).

Peter M. Ward received his Ph.D. in Latin American Geography from the University of Liverpool. He has held tenured teaching positions at University College London and the University of Cambridge. In 1991 he moved to the University of Texas at Austin, where he is Professor of Sociology and of Public Affairs in the Department of Sociology and the LBJ School of Public Affairs, respectively, and Director of the Mexican Center in the Institute of Latin American Studies. He has directed several major research projects on Mexico: on self-help housing and urban development; land markets and land valorization processes; and most recently on "opposition" (non-PRI) governments. Among his more recent books are: *Mexico City: The Production and Reproduction of an Urban Environment* (1990); and *Policy Making, Politics and Urban Governance in Chihuahua: The Experience of Recent Panista Governments* (co-author, 1992).

Jeffrey A. Weldon, a Ph.D. candidate in Political Science at the University of California, San Diego, focuses his research on elections and electoral reforms, past and present, in Mexico. Formerly a research assistant at the Center for U.S.-Mexican Studies, UCSD, he is now teaching at the Instituto Tecnológico Autónomo de México (ITAM) in Mexico City.